Tolerable Differences

Living with Deviance

Second Edition

Tolerable Differences

Living with Deviance

Second Edition

Robert A. Stebbins
Department of Sociology
University of Calgary

McGraw-Hill Ryerson Limited

Toronto New York Auckland Bogotá Caracas
Lisbon London Madrid Mexico Milan New Delhi
San Juan Singapore Sydney Tokyo

Tolerable Differences
Living with Deviance
Second Edition

ISBN: 0-07-552519-4

2 3 4 5 6 7 8 9 10 RRD 5 4 3 2 1 0 9 8 7

Printed and bound in the United States of America

Care has been taken to trace ownership of copyright material contained in this text. The publisher will gladly take any information that will enable them to rectify any reference or credit in subsequent editions.

Sponsoring Editor: Gord Muschett
Production Editor: Olga V. Domján
Developmental Editor: Norma Christensen
Production Co-ordinator: Nicla Dattolico
Cover Design: Dianna Little
Cover Photo: Ron Chapple/Masterfile
Background Photo: Laurie Graham
Typesetter: McGraphics Desktop Publishing
Typeface(s): Optima
Printer: R.R. Donnelley & Sons Company

Canadian Cataloguing in Publication Data

Stebbins, Robert A.,
Tolerable differences : living with deviance

2nd ed.
First ed. published under title: Deviance : tolerable differences.
Includes bibliographical references and index.
ISBN 0-07-552519-4

1. Deviant behaviour. I. Title. II. Title: Deviance : tolerable differences.

HM291.S72 1995 302.5'42 C95-931529-2

To Helen J. Breslauer

CONTENTS

PREFACE

This book sprang from the conception that the field of deviant behaviour is far broader than its most publicized component: crime. Crime, because it is thought of as especially harmful to society, or at least to an influential segment of it, has tended to receive more public, academic, and scientific attention than other areas of deviance. Most people find crime intolerable, an attitude that engenders attempts to control if not eliminate it. The societal response to crime has forced criminals into a special set of life circumstances where they have become the centre of attention for research and for teaching in criminology.

Less threatening and hence less publicized are the forms of deviance or difference that we presently tolerate. Whether they are instances of minor crime that we choose to overlook or non-criminal acts that fall outside the criminal law, these forms of deviance constitute significantly less serious violations of our moral norms than do the various intolerable crimes. Still, they are seen by most people as types of behaviour and/or thought too repugnant to adopt. The tolerable forms occupy a middle ground, both attitudinally and emotionally, between acceptable, normative practices and disdainful, criminal practices.

The title of the first edition of this book — *Deviance: Tolerable Differences* — reflected my allegiance to this middle ground. I should like to stress that I have not abandoned this allegiance, even though the title of the present edition, which represents a sizable revision and expansion of its predecessor, is intended to signal an important parallel stance. The forms of behaviour examined in Chapters 3 through 10 are considered deviant, albeit tolerably so, by substantial segments of the North American public. Sociologists,who have had a longstanding fascination with the causes and effects of the public's moral stance, have quite understandably dubbed their field of research "deviant behaviour". Yet such an appellation ignores an important minority point of view: the outlook of many deviants themselves on the aspects of their own behaviour stigmatized as deviant by the larger society. Very often, they hold that this behaviour is merely *different* rather than glaringly deviant, which is to say that they see nothing seriously or morally wrong with it. Thus, the title of this edition recognizes better than that of the first edition the outlook of the deviants themselves on their so-called deviant behaviour. By extension, the deviants' point of view has been made even more prominent in the revised and expanded edition than in the earlier one, with the intent of communicating a sense of their uncommon motives. But in the final analysis, I wrote this book for students, professors, and researchers in sociology and related fields. For this reason only, I will use the professional term "deviance" more often than the lay term "difference".

That tolerable deviance is less threatening and less publicized than crime should not be misunderstood as making it less interesting and less important as a social phenomenon. Certain forms of tolerable deviance, among them alcoholism, mental disorder, marijuana use, and prescription drug abuse, are regarded by some as social problems. And even if the society as a whole can live with these personal aberrations, they often adversely affect and sometimes even wreck individual lives. Some forms of tolerable deviance are important because they stand as tentative alternative solutions to the basic problems of human collective living. Nudism, homosexuality, group sex, pornography, religious deviance, and political deviance exemplify such solutions.

This book introduces readers to the social scientific research on selected forms of tolerable deviance. However, since its frame of reference is sociological, the research literature in the related fields of anthropology, psychiatry, psychology, and social welfare has been less systematically reviewed. From this background, I examined deviant sexual identities (transsexualism, transvestism), sexual practices (homosexuality, pornography, striptease, group sex), alcohol use, consumption of cannabis and prescription drugs, gambling, mental disorder, lifestyles (chronically homeless street people, nudism), and belief systems (religious, scientific, political). Chapters 1 and 2 provide the theoretical background for the substantive discussion of these forms of deviance in Chapters 3 through 10. Although the ideal way to read the eight substantive chapters is in the order presented, no serious distortion will result if that order is altered. Chapter 11 is designed to bring readers back to some of the broader issues connected with tolerance and thereby provide an overview of tolerable deviance as an aspect of human social life.

Robert A. Stebbins

ACKNOWLEDGMENTS

A number of people gave generously of their time to read portions of the manuscript of this edition and to suggest many helpful additions and revisions. Though they may not always identify with what is printed on these pages, the following have contributed mightily to the final product: Shawn Berry, Concordia University; John A. Casey, Grant MacEwan Community College; Thomas Fleming, University of Windsor; Colin Goff, University of Winnipeg; Gail Grant, University of Guelph; Wendy McLeod MacKnight, University of New Brunswick; Ken Morrison, Wilfrid Laurier University; Frank Pearce, Queen's University; Douglas Skoog, University of Winnipeg.

I have also benefitted enormously from a new set of consultants, among them Augustine Brannigan and Jan Dixon, and from the fine editorial work of Ms. O.V. Domján.

1

TOLERATING DEVIANCE

Deviance from or non-conformity with the norms of the group with an interest in morality is one of humanity's oldest concerns. Collective life is possible only when certain crucial rules of behaviour are observed by all or a large majority of the members of the community. These rules are an important part of the complicated, standardized solutions that evolve in response to the problems people encounter while living in proximity to one another. They are nothing less than strategies for personal and social survival (Martindale, 1962:39). Such solutions take years to develop and crystallize. They are seen by most community members, especially those who have the greatest power and interest in preserving the status quo, as indispensable to the quality of community life.

Standardized solutions to similar problems eventually coalesce into social institutions that, in turn, become the backbone of all societies and their constituent communities. Some of the problems solved in this fashion are basic to physical and social life; they deal with how to secure food and shelter, how to transform biological individuals into social persons, and how to make sure that members of the community conform to the rules considered necessary to its welfare. These are the institutions of the economy, polity, family, and education. Other problems and their solutions, though perhaps not quite so basic to human survival, are nevertheless very seriously regarded in many societies. They include the problems and solutions associated with engaging in sex, using power, dealing with the supernatural, exposing the human body, owning property, dealing with other people, using mind- and mood-altering substances, and pursuing leisure (when it is proper not to work, and what one does at this time). Here we find the aforementioned institutions, as well as those of religion, work, leisure, and culture (e.g., art, science, popular culture).

At bottom, many of these solutions are *arbitrary.* Objectively speaking, other strategies are possible. That different solutions to the same problems are often found in different societies, and occasionally in different communities within the same society, substantiates this observation. For example, Tripp (1987:64) writes that certain tribes of eastern Peruvian natives are predominantly homosexual. Heterosexual acts are undertaken only two or three times a year, and then in a hasty, perfunctory manner.

The possibility of adopting a different solution to a given problem is soon recognized by those in the community who are least committed to the prevailing solution. The next logical step for them is to seize the initiative and explore an option more compatible with their interests. Thus, there is always a sociological side to morality: exploration, or straying from the accepted ways of meeting a major institutional problem, is "deviance" or "wrong", while abiding by those ways is "conformity" or "right".

MORAL NORMS

One important aspect of behaviour called "deviant" is that it is a violation of the community's moral norms. **Moral norms** are the broad directives by which community members implement their institutionalized solutions to the problems significantly affecting their valued way of life. These directives serve as guidelines for behaviour. They indicate in a general way what the community expects of its members in a particular area of social life and what it considers rejections of those expectations.

From its institutional location in the community, a moral norm provides a standard of right and wrong behaviour for the members. It also constitutes a moral imperative. Conformity to the norm is no optional matter; its violation brings sanctions roughly equivalent to the threat it poses. Thus, if the violation becomes public knowledge, then the person responsible is likely to suffer an enduring stigma. Given this outlook on the behaviour ranging within the scope of moral norms, it is understandable that their violation and enforcement are emotional matters for those who consider them important. Indeed, these people see the very welfare of the community as hinging in significant measure on the existence and enforcement of the norms, although these two conditions vary with the level of threat that accompanies their violation.

Table 1.1 indicates that moral norms — those norms whose violation is considered deviant — are but a small proportion of all norms in the community. They are, however, the most seriously regarded, because their violation is most threatening... so much so that they are sometimes institutionalized as criminal law or as ultrasensitive mores or both, as incest, suicide, and cannibalism are in Canada. Less seriously regarded, although still a matter of legal albeit non-criminal concern, are the many civil ordinances and regulations whose violation brings the miscreant such sanctions as a fine or revocation of a licence. Of even

TABLE 1.1 SERIOUSNESS OF NORM VIOLATIONS

Threat Scale	Norms	Category of Violations
Great — Mild	Mores; Criminal Law; Other Moral Norms	Deviance
Marginal	Ordinances; Regulations	Not deviance (civil violations)
None	Customs; Folkways	Not deviance (non-conformity)

lesser seriousness is the rejection of a particular custom or folkway, exemplified by slurping one's soup at a formal dinner or sporting an outlandish hairdo. Civil violations, non-conformity with a custom or folkway, and eccentric behaviour are usually not considered deviant by society or science. As Guy Rocher (1969:49–50) notes, society accepts a certain amount of variance from its moral norms and its solutions to collective problems.

TOLERABLE VERSUS INTOLERABLE DEVIANCE

Despite the moral overtones of some acts, most members of the community tolerate their existence. **Tolerance** is an attitude or orientation that we hold toward certain activities or thoughts of others which differ substantially from our own (Stebbins, 1971). It is a relatively passive disposition, falling roughly midway between scorn or disdain toward an activity or thought pattern on the one hand, and embracement or acceptance of it on the other. Both scorn and embracement, in contrast to tolerance, are active approaches to the behaviour in question. When something is tolerated we accord it legitimacy, though perhaps grudgingly so. We see it as having a level of threat low enough to refrain from actively opposing it. As Flugel (1951:197) put it, one endures "with a certain fortitude and lack of fuss, without undue arousal or aggression or anxiety, self-pity, or complaint" the offensive activities of others. At the same time, we have little interest in actually adopting their behaviours or thought patterns as our own, or even accepting any of them as an alternative we might conceivably adopt in the future.

The presence of tolerance in our society gives **tolerable deviance** its special status. In the case of tolerable deviance, the welfare of the community is still believed to be preserved. But this outlook holds true just so long as such behaviour is enacted only by a small proportion of the members in a way that is only mildly threatening to the majority of the community.

Tolerable deviance stands in contrast to **intolerable deviance**, which greatly threatens the established order, causing the community to scorn it and therefore to try to eliminate it. Hagan (1991:11–12) has supplied us with three measures whereby we may empirically distinguish the mildly threatening tolerable deviance from the highly threatening intolerable variety. Intolerable deviance is likely to be accompanied by the following: considerable agreement about its wrongfulness; a harsh community reaction; and a judgment that it is especially harmful. With tolerable deviance there is a significantly lower level of agreement about its wrongfulness; a significantly more lenient community reaction; and a belief that only the deviant is harmed, and then not seriously. To paraphrase Edwin Schur (1984:183–184), tolerable deviance is "complainantless"; no-one feels harmed or threatened enough to lodge a formal complaint about the behaviour.

Many Canadians are ambivalent about one or more of the activities falling under the heading of tolerable deviance. They know they ought to refrain from engaging in them, yet they find it difficult to escape their magnetic pull. It is this type of deviance that Howard Becker (1963:26) had in mind when he observed that "it is much more likely that most people experience deviant impulses frequently. At least in fantasy, people are much more deviant than they appear."

Types of Tolerable Deviance

The relationship between tolerable and intolerable deviance is, however, more complicated than the preceding pages suggest. In this connection, we must note that tolerable deviance may be classed as criminal, non-criminal, or legitimate.

Criminal tolerable deviance, though actually illegal according to criminal law, is generally treated by the police and the wider community alike as if it were of minor importance when compared with mainstream intolerable deviance. That is, criminal tolerable deviance is seldom officially challenged. There are several reasons for this response. The laws in question may be vague; examples are those pertaining to the production and sale of pornography. Or the laws may be difficult to enforce, as they are in the case of group sex or cheating at gambling. And some laws have, for the present at least, a low police priority. Those dealing with disorderliness, marijuana consumption, and recreational use of prescription drugs are three examples. In short, those who tolerate a form of deviance fail to see it as inherently evil. Rather, it is *mala prohibita*, wrong chiefly because our moral norms (formal and informal) say it is. And even then, "when the law forbids acts which the public considers inoffensive, we are indignant with the law, not with the act it punishes" (Durkheim, 1951:372).

Non-criminal tolerable deviance lies outside the jurisdiction of the law. In Canada, there are presently no laws prohibiting adultery (so long as the morals of minor children are not endangered), homosexuality (when done in private between two consenting adults), and striptease work (when done within the legal limits of undress). Nudism, as practised in private resorts, is not illegal, nor are heavy drinking and non-public drunkenness. The Criminal Code of Canada defines as illegal only certain forms of gambling, while saying nothing about others. Lastly, transsexualism and transvestism are omitted from the Criminal Code, although they are treated as deviant in the larger community.

Turning to **legitimate tolerable deviance**, it is important to note that it is actually guaranteed by law. Canadians have the legal right to think as they wish. It follows that they may hold religious and political beliefs that deviate significantly from those of the majority in the community. They may also embrace beliefs about the supernatural, even rejecting scientific explanations of psychological and physical reality. Certain minor forms of mental disorder are also tolerable and quite within the law. Serious or mild, mental disorder is a guaranteed right, so long as it amounts to no more than a "warped" set of beliefs by the standards of the general public. Neuroses, as opposed to psychoses, which are classified as intolerable deviance, include such reactions as neurotic anxiety, partial personality impairment, phobias, and obsessive-compulsive acts.

The relationship between tolerable and intolerable deviance is portrayed in Table 1.2. Note the overlap in the criminal deviance–criminal laws cell.

TABLE 1.2 TOLERABLE AND INTOLERABLE DEVIANCE

Threat Scale	Norms	Criminal Deviance	Non-criminal Deviance	Legitimate Deviance
Great	Mores	ID	ID	—
|	Criminal laws	ID/TD	—	—
|	Other moral			
Mild	norms	—	TD	TD

ID = Intolerable deviance
TD = Tolerable deviance
— = Logically impossible cross-classification

Of course, much more of a case must be made for the classification of a type of deviance as tolerable or intolerable than has been made so far. This is done in Chapters 3 through 10, for the types of deviance covered in the book. In the meantime, it should be understood that the types of tolerable and intolerable deviance in a community at a particular time in history reflect the current values of those who are collectively powerful enough to shape its legislative, enforcement, and judicial practices and to influence public opinion. In other words, their definition of threat is the one by which some forms of deviance are officially treated as intolerable, while other forms are unofficially treated as tolerable. Those groups who lack such power may look askance at some of these generally tolerated forms of deviance. Kent (1990) points out, for instance, that members of the countercult movement see religious cultism not as legitimate tolerable deviance, as the influential majority does, but rather as illegitimate intolerable deviance that should be controlled by criminal law.

The foregoing three types of tolerable deviance constitute an incomplete list. Knowledge of the public's image of certain forms of behaviour is still too limited to allow their classification as tolerable deviance or as civil violation, eccentricity, or non-conformity. The production and sale of pornography have been labelled as deviant, but what about its consumption? Is it deviant too? Prostitution is deviant, perhaps intolerably so. But what about the male patron; how deviant is he?

Finally, because the distribution of power changes, the list is also likely to change. Some forms of intolerable deviance may gradually become tolerable, as is evident to a greater or lesser extent in the case of abortion, homosexuality, heroin addiction, and obscenity and pornography (Winick, 1991). Meanwhile, tolerable forms may drift toward intolerability. The latter transformation is happening today with respect to smoking (Markle and Troyer, 1979), elite or corporate deviance (Simon and Eitzen, 1990: Ch. 1), and physical violence against women (Silverman, 1988). (In the fourth edition of its *Diagnostic and Statistical Manual of Mental Disorders,* the American Psychiatric Association identifies the addictive use of tobacco as a type of mental disorder.) Finally, if the countercult movement succeeds, our definition of cultistic behaviour will change accordingly.

Intolerable Deviance

Intolerable deviance is behaviour in violation of powerful criminal and non-criminal moral norms. It is behaviour that is *mala in se,* inherently evil or wrong according to natural law in accordance with universal standards. Its core forms are illegal — what Glaser (1974:60) calls "crimes of predation". These behaviours include theft, burglary, murder, forgery, rape, assault, embezzlement, and confidence games and other types of fraud. Forms of intolerable deviance which are non-criminal include suicide, alcoholism, drug addiction, compulsive gambling, and severe mental disorder (e.g., psychosis). We see them as bizarre mental aberrations or severe, destructive addictions. They violate the moral precept that we should be in control of our thoughts, behaviour, and emotions. Clearly, some forms of deviance are tolerable when carried out at a certain level, for example, heavy drinking or habitual gambling, but grow intolerable when they develop into addictions.

Despite the inherent, universal wrongness of intolerable deviance, the world seems to be full of people who want to perpetrate it. Thus, contrary to common sense, the moral rules referring to this category of deviance are not made to be broken; at least, that is not the intention when they are enacted. Rather, moral rules, once made, will be broken; the very act of making them presupposes the existence of people who are prepared to break them. There is no need to make a rule if no-one seems likely to violate it.

Hinging the case for tolerable deviance on the violation of certain moral norms, as we have done here, logically forces us to exclude from consideration in this book certain categories of stigmatized people whose rejection rests on non-moral grounds. One such category subsumes those with bodily abnormalities. Although stigmatized because of their affliction, the deaf, blind, physically handicapped, and mentally handicapped have violated no community moral standard in being born or accidentally forced into this class of humankind (Haber and Smith, 1971:95; Bynder and New, 1976).[1] They are not strictly speaking deviants, but rather physical and mental aberrations living in a society where their kind of differentness is disvalued (Goffman, 1963:4). Other groups stigmatized on non-moral grounds include certain racial and ethnic minorities and, in some circles, women and the aged.

By the same token, we shall not treat exceptional people as deviant (Stebbins, 1980), even though a handful of analyses exist which do precisely that (e.g., Huryn, 1990; Coakley and Hughes, 1991). Exceptional people are remarkable for their success, artistry, intelligence, or athletic ability. Oftentimes, they are objects of wonder or models to follow, rather than despicable contraveners of the community's moral principles. Their so-called "positive deviance", Sagarin (1990) and Goode (1991) correctly point out, constitutes an oxymoron.

JUSTIFICATIONS FOR TOLERABLE DEVIANCE

The main condition distinguishing tolerable deviance from intolerable deviance is the presence or absence of tolerance: the former is passively endured, the latter actively scorned. These reactions constitute the perception of the dominant majority (or the powerful minority) within the community of the threatening extra-institutional behaviour taking place within it. However, they often do not comprise the perception of the deviants themselves. Many who engage in tolerable deviance argue that their values and activities are merely different, and they readily offer views of and reasons for doing what the community regards as wayward behaviour. The deviants' views and reasons are considered here as the three *justifications* for tolerable deviance: as leisure, as work, and as adjustment. Some forms of deviance are justified predominantly in one of these ways; others require two or all three justifications. Finally, as noted earlier, these justifications are often used to challenge the label of deviance itself, which is at bottom a derisive community judgment. In general, the deviants' position is that their behaviour carries no real threat; it causes no significant harm to the community or to themselves.

Tolerable Deviance as Leisure

Tolerable deviance is seen by many of those who pursue it as something interesting or fun to do in one's non-working time. We can find the same qualities in tolerable deviance as in more conventional pastimes: it is the antithesis of work as an economic function; it carries a minimum of involuntary role obligations; it contains the psychological perception of freedom; and it has a pleasant expectation and recollection (Kaplan, 1978:22). There are undoubtedly times when certain forms of intolerable deviance are engaged in as recreation; for instance, the pre-addiction stage of drug use, the youthful rolling of drunks, or the vandalism of juveniles (e.g., Katz, 1988; Sato, 1991). But for most who practise intolerable deviance, it is either a full- or part-time livelihood (Letkemann, 1973; Ritzer and Walczak, 1986: Ch. 13) or an expression of some uncontrollable mental or physiological condition. It is anything but leisure.

The idea that leisure can occasionally be deviant is nothing new, at least on the common sense level. It was early in the eighteenth century that Isaac Watts wrote his famous line, "For Satan finds some mischief still for idle hands to do." Sixty years later, Samuel Johnson proclaimed: "I am a great friend to public amusement, for they keep people from vice." But we now live in the late twentieth century, in a post-industrial society where the orientation toward leisure is dramatically different. In the industrial society preceding it, of which Watts and Johnson were an early part, leisure was used for the recuperation or regeneration of workers between periods of labour. Too much leisure was itself considered a deviant practice — to say nothing of the possibility it held for the perpetration of unsavory deeds. At the time, work was regarded as the central life activity. John Kelly (1990:89) describes how these views are changing:

> For many, employment will continue to be instrumental. These people will work under conditions of constraint for enough security and financial resources to develop their life style. Insofar as that life style emphasizes freedom, expression, the love of family and friends, and a communion with the environment — the values of a humanistic leisure ethic — then work may be less rather than more central for many people.

Leisure *per se* is no longer deviant, but the possibility of engaging in deviant leisure remains. Why, then, do some people spend their free time at deviant activities, while others spend it at conventional pursuits? One answer to this question has already been given: there are those who wish to explore particular alternatives to the institutionalized ways of the community. Another answer centres on the observation that it is exciting to go against the grain of society. In other words, stress seeking, whether in leisure or in work, can be enjoyable so long as the possibility of failure is manageable, so long as one can largely control the outcome of the stressful activity (cf. Klausner, 1968:vi; Czikszentmihalyi, 1990:49-53). Tolerable deviance is stress-seeking behaviour, since it carries only mild sanctions and only a slight chance of being caught in the act.

A third answer to the question of why some people engage in deviance while at leisure relates to the first: many tolerable deviants see nothing seriously wrong with their aberrant behaviour. They maintain that their behaviour is not despicably deviant, but merely a "different" way that is equally reasonable for solving basic collective problems. Hence, society should be tolerant, if not accepting, of their differentness. In effect, the deviants argue that the dominant solutions to their problems should be revamped because they fail to take their needs and values into account. In connection with these problems, deviance is the most satisfactory means these people have of expressing certain interests or fulfilling their particular human potential in a post-industrial society, where these goals are met at least as much in leisure as at work.

Deviant leisure has as its main justification, or one of its main justifications, the pursuit of pleasure. It is never solely or principally motivated by pecuniary ends, as are many of the aforementioned crimes of predation. This is not to argue, however, that in committing such crimes, as in other forms of work, the element of fun is wholly absent. Moreover, we shall see shortly that there are forms of tolerable deviance that are not justified as leisure. The occupation of striptease — a form of tolerable deviance — exemplifies well those activities where the monetary return is clearly more important to the practitioner than the meagre enjoyment derived from them (Ronai and Ellis, 1989). In another example, when such activities as gambling, drinking, and drug consumption become compulsive or addictive, their pleasure vanishes; they cease to be leisure. Finally, there are forms of deviance, notably eccentric behaviour and transsexualism, that are serious attempts to cope with a personal adjustment problem. They fall outside the work–leisure dimension altogether.

Forms of Deviant Leisure On the whole, however, leisure as a main motive fuels the pursuit of many of the known forms of tolerable deviance in present-day Canadian society. Modern sexual expression, for instance, according to some experts, is used these days for recreation at least as much as for procreation (Giddens, 1992; Neulinger, 1993). In Bryant's (1990:821) words:

> By the late 1960s and the 1970s the so-called "sexual revolution" had blossomed across America with sexual liberation for almost everyone. The prevailing sentiment was "If it feels good, do it." Premarital sexual activity was extremely widespread, even among younger adolescents. Married couples sought advice from books and sexual experts for new directions in their sexual life. According to some polls and surveys, extramarital sexual activity became relatively common. Both young unmarried adults and divorced persons often sought a hedonistic lifestyle in the "swinging singles" culture, and sexual variations and behavior hitherto thought scandalous, degenerate, perverted, or even unimaginable were incorporated into the sexual inventory of American culture and the sexual repertoire of many Americans.

But Bryant goes on to note that the excesses of the revolution may now be diminishing. Chapters 3 and 4 discuss aberrant, pleasurable solutions to the problem of sexual expression under such headings as homosexuality, group sex, pornography, and heterosexual transvestism.

The next example to consider involves the mind- and mood-altering drugs. Their use is nearly universal, with all but a few societies throughout recorded history having some sort of contact with them (Commission of Inquiry into the Non-Medical Use of Drugs, 1970:14). As a means of enjoyment, they have recently become prominent in the Western world. Szasz (1974) points out that, whatever the society or its historical period, drug use tends eventually to come under some kind of control, which in terms of the present discussion may be understood as an institutionalized solution to a major community problem. Chapter 5 deals with alcohol use, while Chapter 6 concentrates on the deviant consumption of marijuana and prescription drugs. These stigmatized practices have become tolerable alternatives in North America, subject to the kinds of controls mentioned by Szasz.

Gambling (Chapter 7) and nudism (Chapter 9) represent direct and deviant challenges to the Canadian institution of leisure. According to this institution, it is still morally improper to wager for pleasure, especially excessively; to reject gainful employment all or most of the time; and to engage in various semi-public activities in the nude, particularly in mixed company. In the latter case, there has been a recent shift in emphasis to relaxation and sociability from one of physical health. In North America before 1950 (and in contemporary Europe), nudism was justified as an alternative to prevailing health practices, with the curative rays of the sun and exercise in the buff being regarded as highly beneficial (Clapham and Constable, 1982). The modern nudist outlook is set out in Viewpoint 1.1.

Lastly, our political, religious, and scientific institutions have inadvertently encouraged their own sets of heretics. While there are often important non-leisure reasons for joining, say, the Communist Party, the Unification Church, or a coven of witches, their role in providing leisure is equally strong. When people intentionally join such collectivities, that action is voluntary. Bosserman and Gagan (1972:113) note that voluntary action is a special brand of leisure. These writers have also noted an increase in deviant behaviour patterns and groups in the voluntary sphere as an expression of dissatisfaction with today's established religious and political systems (Bosserman and Gagan, 1972:121–122). The same thing is happening in the area of science. The occult is the renegade movement that has emerged in response to the perceived inadequacies of science (sometimes mixed with those of religion). As Ben-Yehuda (1985:75–77) points out, the willful joining of occult groups and adoption of their ideas occur among members of the community who lose faith in its scientific institutions. These ideas are discussed in detail in Chapter 10.

VIEWPOINT 1.1

THE PLEASURES OF NUDISM

Is nude recreation bad? Inherently lewd? A small minority say it is. In 1983, however, 72 percent of a representative sample of the U.S. population told the Gallup Poll that people who enjoy nude sunbathing should be able to do so, at a beach accepted for the purpose. Moreover, nearly 15 percent told the pollsters that they themselves had joined a mixed group of men and women in order to skinnydip or sunbathe in the nude.

Skinnydipping in mixed company is becoming increasingly common. It's thought to be free, natural, and rational — gloriously sensuous, not particularly sexy.

This still begs a question for many who approve: Where to find the beaches? The answer's at hand in the *World Guide to Nude Beaches & Recreation*, whose text and gorgeous photos — almost 200, mostly large, many in full color — introduce you to the lifestyle and the beaches. Hawaii, Greece, Texas, Thailand, Rhode Island, Jamaica, Illinois, Québec, Oregon, California, France, Virginia, and a host of other locations, near and far, offer you the scenes for your nude recreation.

Come! Enjoy the delight of innocence as an adult. Bring the family to the nude beaches and resorts of the modern world.

Source: Based on the promotional brochure *World Guide to Nude Beaches & Recreation.* Published by The Naturist Society. By permission.

Tolerable Deviance as Work

From the standpoint of the deviants themselves, most forms of tolerable deviance are justified as leisure; most forms of intolerable deviance, as work. Nevertheless, as noted earlier, a leisure orientation is evident in certain forms of crime, while a work orientation is evident in certain forms of tolerable deviance. Work is a goal-oriented activity leading to a personally desired accomplishment. It is also a disciplined activity, being carried out by means of persistent effort for the purpose of achieving the intended goal. In modern societies, one goal — sometimes the only goal — of work is to receive payment for it, possibly together with certain fringe benefits.

Work, by this definition, runs the entire scale of respectability from practising law or medicine to picking pockets or embezzling money to make a living. The living made by these various means may be full-time or part-time. It may offer a career of long or short duration, and may be skilled or unskilled. It may be acceptable, tolerable, or intolerable.

Tolerable deviance as work can be analyzed in some of the same ways in which sociologists analyze conventional occupations. For example, we can explore the nature and extent of the skills needed to be a moderately competent worker, as opposed to those needed to be an outstanding success, in a deviant occupation. To the extent that deviants of a certain kind are differentiated by their work skills, the prestige associated with these differences is worthy of scientific attention. As in other occupations, there are recruitment patterns and typical careers to be charted in connection with deviant work. Finally, we can study the socialization and commitment processes that lead to involvement in such work, and how these processes diverge from their counterparts in conventional employment.

Tolerable deviance as leisure can, of course, be analyzed from the same perspectives. Still, most people have to work at a job of some sort, whereas engaging in leisure is a matter of choice. The pressure to find work, in conjunction with the fact that some people have few acceptable alternatives open to them, pushes them into deviant occupations. From the standpoint of wages, hours, excitement, and perhaps even respectability, such work is their best alternative.

Deviant leisure is distinguished from deviant work because the former is generally unskilled. Indeed, it is often downright hedonistic (e.g., sexual deviance, drug use, heavy drinking). By contrast, most tolerably deviant work involves a certain level of skill, although it is not ordinarily highly skilled. Consider the examples of such work covered in subsequent chapters. The best visual pornography requires some acting ability, in addition to photographic and cinematic know-how (Chapter 4). Strippers (also discussed in Chapter 4) develop their dancing technique and an ability to sexually arouse their audiences. Female impersonators (Chapter 3) specialize in campy homosexual humour requiring a talent for comical singing, dancing, and speaking onstage. The skills of the fortuneteller are chiefly social. They include impression management and an acquired ability to "case" each client (Chapter 10).

The homeless are the main exception to the rule that deviant work involves a modicum of skill. Barred from regular employment for a number of reasons (examined in Chapter 9), they sustain their bodies, but seldom their souls, with panhandling, day labour, and, in the United States, the sale of plasma (Snow and Anderson, 1993: Ch. 4). Although the public stereotypically explains the deviant working lifestyle of the homeless with reference to sloth, it is deviant, in reality, because the homeless are chronically unemployed and penniless in a society where the vast majority of people can avoid these two conditions.

In short, tolerably deviant work provides a living or at least contributes significantly to one. Whether it amounts to a partial or a complete livelihood, it is seen as indispensable. But there are leisure participants who make a certain amount of money at their pursuits, notably certain kinds of amateurs, hobbyists, and career volunteers (Stebbins, 1992). Thus, deviant leisure cannot be distinguished from deviant work on the basis of remuneration alone; the remuneration must be of such an amount as to be indispensable. This is not true even for those racetrack gamblers and casino players (Chapter 7) who try to live by wagering, for their goals are doomed by the system of odds against which they play. Nevertheless, as Viewpoint 1.2 illustrates, gamblers meet with inducements to seek easy money at the betting table.

The evidence to date suggests that tolerable deviance as work is motivated principally by extrinsic goals: money, excitement, attractive working hours, and the relative freedom of self-employment. Love for the work itself — an attitude often found in the professional, managerial, and entrepreneural occupations — is largely absent. There is little doubt that this is true for stripping and pornography production (Ronai and Ellis, 1989; Douglas and Waksler, 1982:181). Tatro's (1974:294–298) observations of the fortunetelling scene suggest that a similar outlook prevails there. Only stage-based female impersonators appear to find intrinsic satisfaction in their jobs (Newton, 1972). But, for most of the tolerable deviants who try to make a living of some kind from their activities, there is little or no sense of leisure to be found.

Tolerable Deviance as Adjustment

When we adjust to something in life, we achieve a harmonious mental and behavioural balance between our personal needs and goals and the demands made on us by other people and society. This is ordinarily a long-term process taking several years. While most, if not all, tolerable deviance can be seen as a form of adjustment, we are able to identify and justify much of it as leisure or work or both. But we are left with a residual category of deviant adjustment for which there is no explicit term in our culture. Residual adjustments, which are known in sociology as **residual rule breaking** (Scheff, 1984:38), are sometimes lumped by professionals and the general public under the heading of mental illness or **mental disorder**.

Keep in mind, however, that we are also examining the deviants' views here. Science and the public may have found suitable categories and labels for these

VIEWPOINT 1.2

MAKING MONEY AT GAMBLING

This new bingo is hard work, if you are going to play seriously. Go to the community halls for relaxation and conviviality. Go to the bingo barns for heavy-duty intense playing. Why not the casinos or races instead? "I don't know the rules there," explained one tastefully dressed woman. "You don't need to know anything to play bingo."

When the bonanza ($1800 and change) is won by a grey-haired, sweater-clad man with a slight limp, one woman exclaims, "He won the bonanza last week, too." Another asks, "How can he do that? How can he win two weeks in a row?" The woman shrugs, "I dunno. It just happens sometimes." A third adds, "Remember two weeks ago? There was a man at that other bingo — in one day he won a car, and then the $5000 big one!" She growls, "And he had the nerve to say he didn't need the car because he already had two Cadillacs!"

At another table, a twentyish woman jabs her finger on her card, complaining loudly to a young man in tight stonewashed denim, "See that sucker? I need that sucker for the bonanza."

So, ultimately, no matter how many cards are strewn before you with careful calculations and handicapping, luck is the final arbitrator.

Debbie Serpentini, 31, a bingo regular, recalls a spectacular winning streak during July which has since disappeared. She won $400 on a Friday night at Airways, then won $35 at a late-night bingo the same evening. She next won a bonanza at Airways ($1000 split between two people), then the following Monday picked up $240 in two separate bingos. Within the week, she won another $280, then went to a midnight bingo at King's and halved the $2300 jackpot. Two weeks later, she won two separate $400 pots. "They say if you're on a streak, you should keep going until it stops," she says. And her streak stopped. So convincingly, in fact, that she now says she has cut back to one bingo outing a week with a friend. She arrives at half time to save money, and sometimes stays for the late-night bingo, spending an average of $30 an evening.

Serpentini says two friends who bingoed together did so well last year that they opened a joint account and went to Hawaii on their winnings. In the past year, however, they have not won and have given up bingo.

Despite her lack of winnings in the past two months, Serpentini concedes, "It's like an obsession. You think you're wasting time. You come home and you stink (from the smoke). But I really enjoy it and get excited about the money. I've won big and I know what it's like."

Which is probably what drives most people on, from the bankrupt couple who haunt the Ogden bingo in an attempt to get back on their feet, to those who hope to stave off bills with a bonanza. "Nowadays, it's an easy way to make money," says one bingo veteran. "You could come out at the end of the evening with one, two thousand bucks. I'm willing to spend fifteen or twenty to get a chance at that payoff."

Source: L. Kupecek, "Bingo goes High-Tech," *Herald Sunday Magazine,* 1988, December 11:22. By permission.

leftover forms of deviance. But for the individual deviant, they are a special way of achieving mental and behavioural balance in everyday life. From the deviants' perspective, residual rule breaking or mental illness is first and foremost a long-term adjustment.

Residual rule breaking or mental disorder, justified as personal adjustment, is sometimes found in tolerably deviant work and leisure. For instance, women who work as strippers may have the personality disorder known as exhibitionism. Some habitual drug users may be existential neurotics who believe that life is meaningless, that there are no values worth pursuing. And those who believe in the occult may turn to psychic healers, such as Norma Cowie (Viewpoint 1.3), to help them with their deviant adjustment. In other words, some tolerable deviants justify their actions as some combination of adjustment, work, and leisure.

Adjustive deviance, whether work, leisure, or pure adjustment, covers the entire scale of threat. Although the classification scheme of the American Psychiatric Association (*Diagnostic and Statistical Manual of Mental Disorders, IV,* 1994) is no longer this simple, most lay people recognize differences in the seriousness of mental disorders. Less serious and hence more tolerable as deviance are the neuroses and the somatoform disorders (e.g., hypochondriasis) and psychoactive substance-induced disorders (e.g., hallucinations, *delirium tremens*). At the serious, intolerable end of the scale we find the various mood, paranoid, and organic disorders (including senility and Alzheimer's disease), among others. Indeed, there are more disorders, both tolerable and intolerable, than this book can cover.

One factor separating tolerable adjustive deviance from its intolerable cousin is the family and community reaction to the unusual behaviour of the deviant person. Gallagher (1987:304–305) says that families of adjustive deviants first try to ignore the deviants' questionable thoughts and actions. There are several reasons for this "blind-eye" approach. One is that many families prefer to put up with behaviour that is only mildly threatening, rather than face the ignominy of community gossip about deviance at home or the difficulty of dealing with a

VIEWPOINT 1.3

A DEVIANT SOLUTION TO A DEVIANT ADJUSTMENT

Reading tarot cards may conjure up images of fortunetellers draped in flowing sequined robes, mumbling magic incantations.

But the cloak of mysticism that shrouded tarot cards for thousands of years is being shed. Today, tarot is being used by all types of people who want to enhance their day-to-day lives.

"Tarot cards are more of a form of self-development than a fortune-telling device these days," said Norma Cowie, who was in Calgary this month to conduct a tarot lecture and workshop.

People are using tarot to become aware of what's happening in all aspects of their lives, ranging from financial concerns to affairs of the heart, says Cowie, a psychic consultant, lecturer, and author who lives in White Rock, B.C.

Cowie's clientele are not just superstitious people, looking to have evil curses removed, or fortune-hunting fanatics, seeking the lucky numbers in next week's 6/49 lottery draw.

Rather, they're entrepreneurs or electricians. Lawyers or locksmiths. Doctors or drafters.

"I've done tarot consultations for all kinds of people," Cowie says. "Most of my customers just want to enhance their lives, understand their lives and deal with relationship or work problems."

"People are becoming more aware of the potential they have to create within their own minds," she says. "Rather than waiting for somebody out there to do things for them, they're willing to realize they can effectively change their lives through what they do."

"I've found that tarot will help people find out anything that they want. I don't know anything it can't help with, if you're objective enough when reading the cards."

Source: Monica Zurowski, "Tarot Sheds Mystic Cloak as Self-Development Tool," *Calgary Herald,* 1986, Saturday, November 29: H11. By permission.

relative who resists treatment. At the community level, Bittner (1967) found that the police are inclined to take action (become intolerant) only when there exist suicidal or homicidal tendencies, odd public behaviour such as nudity or alarming postures, indications of violence, or disruptiveness in public places. In general, if the behaviour can be handled in the course of the normal routine of the family or community, it is likely to be considered tolerable deviance, and the police will not become involved.

Further, the conception of tolerable deviance as adjustment brings to the fore the notion that deviance, whatever its level of threat to the community, may be voluntary or involuntary. Both the work and the leisure justifications for deviance rest on the assumption that people have alternatives to deviance. Nevertheless, some of them *choose* deviance, because they see it as the best way of coping with a certain problem in life. Of course, the number of alternatives is always limited. Education, sex, age, residence, period of history, and many other factors narrow every person's list of options in all forms of work and leisure, whether deviant or not.

By way of illustration, consider the 60-year-old pensioner who has lost his left hand in an industrial accident and is now no longer employable at any form of labour. Even in a time of history plagued by high unemployment, the handicapped elderly have alternatives, albeit rather unattractive ones: they may try to live cheaply in a skid-row "flop" where their meagre pension cheque stretches far enough to allow an occasional semi-nutritious meal and a local movie. Or they may try to live in a small room where the rent consumes nearly all the money needed for food and drink.

Tolerable deviance as adjustment, since it is involuntary, offers the individual no alternatives. People with neurotic, personality, and sexual disorders have not chosen these states of mind, which develop over the months and years quite against their desire to avoid them, the results of a combination of past experiences and interpretations of those experiences. To be sure, the lesbian finds pleasure in her liaisons with other women. In a sense, she is engaging in tolerable deviance as a form of leisure. But past experiences and possibly other factors combine to allow little real choice in the present between homosexuality and heterosexuality. Short of renouncing sex altogether, a choice is largely absent. Thus, it is arguable whether such deviance can be viewed as a form of leisure at all. More accurately, it is an adjustment, which the deviant has come to depend on and, in some instances, even to enjoy. In the eyes of the community, he or she is tolerably deviant.

CONTROLLING TOLERABLE DEVIANCE

The control of tolerable deviance can be viewed from three perspectives: the deviant's, the community's, and that of the close associates of the deviant. The deviant is quite inclined to minimize the moral implications of his or her actions. In later chapters, we shall see that a common defence for the leisure or work form of deviance is that it is a matter of personal choice that causes no significant harm to anyone, especially the deviant person. Indeed, the deviance is seen as benefitting that person in some way. The deviant may even view the conforming majority as out of step with the times or, at the very least, unenlightened.

Those for whom deviance is an adjustment have, as mentioned, significantly less choice. In fact, these deviants may recognize that they are suffering from their deviant practices. People with phobias or sporadic cases of anxiety, for example, would prefer to be rid of these mental afflictions. Still, they appear to hold the view that no-one else is victimized in any important way by their adjustment. Other adjustive deviants, moreover, find a degree of pleasure in their activities. Voyeurs, exhibitionists, and hypersexed individuals, for instance, often try to continue their behaviour and, when necessary, justify it as a harmless difference, as mere variance.

Since tolerable deviants are either unable or unwilling to control their behaviour, control — if there is to be any — must come from elsewhere. To the extent that the community tolerates deviant acts, its members generally avoid formally sanctioning them. Formal sanctions, such as imprisonment and fines, are usually meted out in connection with violations of the Criminal Code. Tolerable deviance, if controlled at all, is controlled with informal sanctions, notably ridicule, gossip, ostracism, and scolding. Here, the pressure to conform, consistent with the threat level of tolerable deviance, is relatively slight. For the community is inclined to mount little opposition against such behaviour as long as it remains within bounds — as long as it involves an unthreateningly low number of individuals (as defined by the community) and no-one, especially those with the power to change laws and enforcement practices, is harmed.

The close associates of deviants adopt one of two perspectives: the deviance is seen either as a *fait accompli* or as "something wrong". Deviance as a *fait accompli* is on the order of a revelation. Suddenly it becomes known that a friend, relative, workmate, or neighbour is a homosexual, marijuana user, mate swapper, religious cultist, or whatever. At least this is what people in the neighbourhood, at work, or around the family are saying. Though the evidence for the accusation may be flimsy, and prudent associates will be inclined to seek further substantiation of it, the news that the person in question is deviant is abrupt.

From a control standpoint, there appear, at this point, to be two courses of action open to the associates of the tolerable deviant. Assuming that they accept the revelation as true, that their friend or relative is deviant, the associates may express their disapproval by scolding, ridiculing, or ostracizing him or her. Or they may tolerate the individual, even though his or her behaviour is repugnant to them. When associates ostracize a tolerably deviant friend or relative, the larger community still tolerates that person. The members of the community can maintain their distance from the deviant individual, while close associates cannot. That is, associates who remain close (fail to ostracize) acquire a "courtesy stigma" (Goffman, 1963:30) from the deviant which comes from being linked to that person in the eyes of the general community.

When deviance is perceived as something wrong, close associates are vaguely aware of trouble. Emerson and Messinger (1977) point out that when associates get a hint that a friend or relative is involved, becoming involved, or apt to become involved in some kind of deviance, one or more remedies are likely to be tried. Associates often move from one remedy to another in search of a solution. As the search continues, the nature of what is wrong tends to become clearer. That is, the processes of searching for a remedy and seeking clarification of the trouble take place over time — from several months to several years. The social control of tolerable deviance can have a history. This history is composed, in part, of the negotiations that take place between the actually or potentially deviant person and those searching for a remedy to the trouble he or she is creating. They negotiate such matters as whether the behaviour in question is really occurring and whether it is deviant. A psychiatrist, counsellor, social worker, or other third party may contribute to the negotiations. There may be victims or witnesses whose views influence the selection of a remedy or the perceived nature of the problem.

The outcome of all this may be a relatively clear case of tolerable deviance. Or it may be a standoff in which some associates and third parties believe the behaviour is deviant, while others do not. But only in the case of tolerable deviance are indecision and ambiguity likely. The violation of mores and criminal laws is more obviously wrong and intolerable, although demonstrating in court that a violation took place is sometimes difficult.

TOLERABLE DEVIANCE AND SELF-HELP

Since many types of tolerable deviants are actually or effectively within the law, they can publicly organize into associations and small communities: into **self-help groups**. Such groups are composed of members sharing a common condition, situation, heritage, symptom, or experience. They are largely self-governing, self-regulating, and self-supporting; emphasize self-reliance; and generally offer a face-to-face or phone-to-phone fellowship network that is accessible without charge (Lieberman, Borman, and Associates, 1979:2). Romeder (1990:33) adds that self-help groups may promote personal change, social change, or both.

Katz and Bender (1990:27) have identified five types of self-help groups. The first category is comprised of groups that are primarily therapeutic. Examples include mental health organizations such as Recovery, Inc., addiction organizations such as Smokers Anonymous and Overeaters Anonymous, groups devoted to stress reduction such as the Widowed and Family Bereavement Association, and those assisting with life transitions (e.g., divorce and retiree groups).

Other self-help groups are founded on certain principles of advocacy or action; they hope to change existing institutions, policies, services, and the like. Some, such as Mothers against Drunk Driving (MADD) are centred on a single problem. Others, such as the Gray Panthers, speak for a certain age group or for a particular ethnic or minority group.

Still other groups strive to create patterns of living which offer alternatives to our present-day institutions. Individual growth and fulfillment, although sometimes achieved in the process, are not primary goals. In this category we find gay liberation groups and rural and urban residential communes.

The fourth type subsumes the outcasts who are trying to save themselves from further mental or physical decline. Gamblers Anonymous, Alcoholics Anonymous, and the battered women's shelters fall into this category.

Lastly, a number of self-help groups fall into two or more of the first four categories. They include ex-prisoner associations, social-therapeutic organizations such as Parents without Partners and Families Anonymous, and certain economic organizations (e.g., food banks, self-help housing groups, and consumer/producer cooperatives).

All these groups have in common the characteristic of being operated by their members: in this case, deviants. Much of the time, this is done in opposition to traditional approaches to the deviance taken by professional practitioners, approaches that the deviants consider ineffective. On occasion, however, self-help groups of deviants may coordinate their efforts with those of professionals, as happens frequently in Alcoholics Anonymous. Even here, however, the professionals must go beyond their own disciplines (Lieberman, Borman, and Associates, 1979:5) to meet the deviants on their own terms. At other times, the possibility of professional help is irrelevant, for the deviants have no interest in reforming themselves. Rather, they intend only to promote or facilitate their way of life.

Self-help groups are included in this opening statement on tolerable deviance because they are exceptionally prevalent in this sphere of life, when compared with the spheres of conventional life and intolerable deviance. Self-help groups are either formal organizations or small communities. Thus, they are visible, legal entities, which criminals can safely join only when seeking to reinstate themselves in the upperworld (e.g., the Seventh Step Society for ex-offenders and Synanon for former drug users). Self-help groups exist in the non-deviant world too. Examples are women's consciousness-raising groups and groups formed to help people lose weight.

But, on the whole, deviants are more likely than non-deviants to be interested in changing existing institutions and in promoting alternatives to certain established ways of life. And deviants obviously have the greater interest in saving themselves from further mental and physical decline and in finding therapy for a psychological problem. As the remaining chapters in this book indicate, some sort of self-help network of organizations or communities plays an important role in the social organization of most forms of tolerable deviance.

SUMMARY

Deviance is made possible by the fact that humankind establishes arbitrary solutions to the basic problems of collective living. These solutions are implemented by sets of norms, of which the most important are moral, but which are nonetheless violated by those who believe they have a better, albeit deviant, solution to one of the basic problems. Some violations of moral norms are more threatening than others. Tolerable deviance is possible because some moral norms proscribe behaviour that is only mildly threatening.

Such behaviour falls into the three categories of criminal, non-criminal, and legitimate tolerable deviance. The first of these overlaps with criminal intolerable deviance because of legal ambiguities, enforcement difficulties, and low enforcement priorities. The list of forms of tolerable deviance that can be compiled for a community reflects the time in history at which it is compiled, the patterns of influence and power there, the adequacy of scientific knowledge about the forms, and the factors separating tolerable deviance from intolerable forms and from violations of ordinances and folkways.

The community view is joined by the views that the deviants themselves have of their behaviours and thoughts. The deviants justify their behaviour in three main ways. First, much tolerable deviance is seen as leisure, as something interesting or fun to do in one's non-working time. It is not pursued solely or principally for monetary ends, unlike many crimes of predation. Second, some forms of tolerable deviance are seen as work, as a disciplined, goal-oriented activity leading to a personally desired accomplishment. Tolerable deviance is rarely justified in both leisure and work terms. Rather, most tolerably deviant work is sought chiefly for its extrinsic benefits of money, excitement, attractive working hours, and relative freedom of self-employment. Finally, there are forms of tolerable deviance that are primarily an aberrant form of adjustment to a situation or problem in life. We adjust by achieving a harmonious mental and behavioural balance between our personal needs and goals and the demands made on us by other people and society. Deviant adjustments which cannot be classified as work or leisure are forms of residual rule-breaking.

The control of tolerable deviance is largely in the hands of the community and the close associates of individual deviants. The deviants themselves are inclined to minimize the moral implications of their actions by arguing that they are merely different and of no harm to anyone. The community is most likely to respond with informal sanctions, such as ridicule or ostracism. The deviants' associates must deal either with these acts as behaviour not worth opposing or with the emerging idea that something is wrong. Meanwhile, the deviants are apt to be busy promoting their own interests in self-help organizations and communities.

NOTES

1 There are some who reject the position taken here that people who are exceptional or who suffer with mental or physical abnormalities are not, for those reasons, deviant. See, for example, Kelly (1993), Becker (1978), and Clinard (1992).

SUGGESTED READING

Budziszewski, J. *True Tolerance: Liberalism and the Necessity of Judgment.* New Brunswick, NJ: Transaction, 1992. A critique of twentieth-century liberalism, in which tolerance is "falsely understood as ethical neutrality". True tolerance is rooted in such sentiments as humility, mercy, charity, and respect.

Ferrar, Jane W. "The Dimensions of Tolerance," *Pacific Sociological Review,* 1976:63–81. A general discussion of the concept of tolerance and its three major components: extent of approval and disapproval, extent of permission and prohibition, and origins of beliefs about the tolerated object.

Jones, Edward E., Amerigo Farina, Albert H. Hastorf, Hazel Markus, Dale T. Miller, and Robert A. Scott. *Social Stigma: The Psychology of Marked Relationships.* New York: W.H. Freeman, 1984. A set of studies of various stigmatized categories, from the disabled and disfigured to the deviant.

Sagarin, Edward. *Odd Man In.* Chicago: Quadrangle, 1969. The author discusses several self-help societies developed and run by various groups of deviants in the United States.

Schur, Edwin M. and Hugo Adam Bedau. *Victimless Crimes.* Englewood Cliffs, NJ: Prentice-Hall, 1974. A sociologist and a philosopher debate the question of whether crimes that harm only the deviant and no-one else should be abolished as unlawful acts.

REFERENCES

Becker, George. *The Mad Genius Controversy: A Study in the Sociology of Deviance.* Beverly Hills, CA: Sage Publications, 1978.

Becker, Howard S. *Outsiders.* New York: The Free Press, 1963.

Ben-Yehuda, Nachman. *Deviance and Moral Boundaries.* Chicago: University of Chicago Press, 1985.

Bittner, Egon. "Police Discretion in Apprehending the Mentally Ill," *Social Problems,* 1967, 14:278–292.

Bosserman, Phillip and Richard Gagan. "Leisure Behavior and Voluntary Action." In *Voluntary Action Research,* edited by David H. Smith, Richard D. Reddy, and Burt R. Baldwin, pp. 109–126. Lexington, MA: D.C. Heath, 1972.

Bryant, Clifton D. (ed.) *Deviant Behavior: Readings in the Sociology of Norm Violations.* New York: Hemisphere, 1990.

Bynder, Herbert and Peter K.M. New. "Time for a Change: From Micro- to Macro-Sociological Concepts in Disability Research," *Journal of Health and Social Behavior,* 1976, 17:45–52.

Clapham, Adam and Robin Constable. *As Nature Intended: A Pictorial History of the Nudists.* London: Heinemann/Quixote, 1982.

Clinard, Marshall B. *Sociology of Deviant Behavior.* (8th ed.) New York: Holt, Rinehart & Winston, 1992.

Coakley, Jay and Robert Hughes. "Positive Deviance among Athletes: Implications of Overconformity to the Sport Ethic," *Sociology of Sport Journal,* 1991, 8:307–325.

Commission of Inquiry into the Non-Medical Use of Drugs. *Interim Report.* Ottawa: Queen's Printer, 1970.

Czikszentmihalyi, Mihaly. *Flow: The Psychology of Optimal Experience.* New York: Harper & Row, 1990.

Douglas, Jack D. and Frances C. Waksler. *The Sociology of Deviance.* Boston: Little Brown, 1982.

Durkheim, Emile. *Suicide.* New York: The Free Press, 1951.

Emerson, Robert M. and Sheldon L. Messinger. "The Micro-Politics of Trouble," *Social Problems,* 1977, 25:121–134.

Flugel, J.C. "Tolerance." In *Psychoanalysis and Culture,* edited by G.B. Wilbur and W. Muensterberger, pp. 196–217. New York: International Universities Press, 1951.

Gallagher, Bernard J., III. *The Sociology of Mental Illness.* (2nd ed.) Englewood Cliffs, NJ: Prentice-Hall, 1987.

Giddens, Anthony. *The Transformation of Intimacy: Sexuality, Love and Eroticism in Modern Societies.* Stanford, CA: Stanford University Press, 1992.

Glaser, Daniel. "The Classification of Offenses and Offenders." In *Handbook of Criminology,* edited by Daniel Glaser, pp. 45–84. Chicago: Rand McNally, 1974.

Goffman, Erving. *Stigma: Notes on the Management of Spoiled Identity.* Englewood Cliffs, NJ: Prentice-Hall, 1963.

Haber, Lawrence D. and Richard T. Smith. "Disability and Deviance," *American Sociological Review,* 1971, 36:87–97.

Hagan, John. *The Disreputable Pleasures: Crime and Deviance in Canada.* (3rd ed.) Toronto: McGraw-Hill Ryerson, 1991.

Huryn, Jean S. "Giftedness as Deviance: A Test of Interaction Theories." In *Deviant Behavior: Readings in the Sociology of Norm Violation,* edited by Clifton D. Bryant, pp. 166–176. New York: Hemisphere, 1990.

Kaplan, Max. *Leisure: Perspectives on Education and Policy.* Washington, DC: National Education Association, 1978.

Katz, Alfred and Eugene I. Bender. *Helping One Another: Self-Help Groups in a Changing World.* Oakland, CA: Third Party Publishing, 1990.

Katz, Jack. *Seductions of Crime: Moral and Sensual Attractions of Doing Evil.* New York: Basic Books, 1988.

Kelly, Delos H. (ed.) *Deviant Behaviour.* (4th ed.) New York: St. Martin's Press, 1993.

Kelly, John R. *Leisure.* (2nd ed.) Englewood Cliffs, NJ: Prentice-Hall, 1990.

Kent, Stephen A. "Deviance, Labelling and Normative Strategies in the Canadian New Religious/Countercult Debate," *Canadian Journal of Sociology,* 1990, 15:393–416.

Klausner, Samuel Z. (ed.) *Why Man Takes Chances.* Garden City, NY: Doubleday, 1968.

Lieberman, Morton A., Leonard D. Borman, and Associates. *Self-Help Groups for Coping with Crises.* San Francisco: Jossey-Bass, 1979.

Letkemann, Peter. *Crime as Work.* Englewood Cliffs, NJ: Prentice-Hall, 1973.

Markle, Gerald E. and Ronald J. Troyer. "Smoke Gets in Your Eyes: Cigarette Smoking As Deviant Behavior," *Social Problems,* 1979, 26:611–625.

Martindale, Don. *Social Life and Cultural Change.* New York: D. Van Nostrand, 1962.

Neulinger, John. "Sex and Leisure, or Sex as Leisure," *Leisure Information Quarterly,* 1993, 19, 1:6–7.

Newton, Esther. *Mother Camp: Female Impersonators in America.* Englewood Cliffs, NJ: Prentice-Hall, 1972.

Ritzer, George and David Walczak. *Working: Conflict and Change.* Englewood Cliffs, NJ: Prentice-Hall, 1986.

Rocher, Guy. *Introduction à la Sociologie Générale.* LaSalle, PQ: Editions Hurtubise HMH, 1969.

Romeder, Jean-Marie. *The Self-Help Way: Mutual Aid and Health.* Ottawa: Canadian Council on Social Development, 1990.

Ronai, Carol R. and Carolyn Ellis. "Turn-Ons for Money: Interactional Strategies of the Table Dancer," *Journal of Contemporary Ethnography,* 1989, 18:271–298.

Sagarin, Edward. "Positive Deviance: An Oxymoron." In *Deviant Behavior: Readings in the Sociology of Norm Violation,* edited by Clifton D. Bryant, pp. 98–111. New York: Hemisphere, 1990.

Sato, Ikuya. *Kamikaze Biker: Parody and Anomy in Affluent Japan.* Chicago: University of Chicago Press, 1991.

Scheff, Thomas J. *Being Mentally Ill: A Sociological Theory.* (2nd ed.) New York: Aldine, 1984.

Schur, Edwin M. *Labeling Women Deviant.* New York: Random House, 1984.

Silverman, Robert A. "Interpersonal Criminal Violence." In *Deviance: Conformity and Control in Canadian Society,* edited by Vincent F. Sacco, pp. 152–184. Scarborough, ON: Prentice-Hall Canada, 1988.

Simon, David R. and D. Stanley Eitzen. *Elite Deviance.* (3rd ed.) Boston: Allyn and Bacon, 1990.

Snow, David A. and Leon Anderson. *Down on Their Luck: A Study of Homeless Street People.* Berkeley, CA: University of California Press, 1993.

Stebbins, Robert A. "The Nature and Development of Tolerance." Paper presented at the Annual Meeting of the American Sociological Association, Denver, 1971.

________ "Tolerable Deviance." Paper presented at the Annual Meeting of the Canadian Sociology and Anthropology Association, Montréal, 1980.

________ *Amateurs, Professionals, and Serious Leisure.* Montréal and Kingston: McGill-Queen's University Press, 1992.

Szasz, Thomas. *Ceremonial Chemistry.* Garden City, NY: Doubleday, 1974.

Tatro, Charlotte R. "Cross My Palm with Silver: Fortunetelling as an Occupational Way of Life." In *Deviant Behavior,* edited by Clifton D. Bryant, pp. 286–299. Chicago: Rand McNally, 1974.

Tripp, C.A. *The Homosexual Matrix.* (2nd ed.) New York: Meridian, 1987.

Winick, Charles. "A Paradigm to Clarify the Life Cycle of Changing Attitudes Toward Deviant Behavior." In *Perspectives on Deviance: Dominance, Degradation and Denigration,* edited by Robert J. Kelly and Donal E.J. MacNamara, pp. 1–14. Cincinnati, OH: Anderson, 1991.

2

EXPLANATIONS OF TOLERABLE DEVIANCE

Discussion of the idea of tolerance in the deviance literature is rare indeed. Today, it is confined chiefly to speculative passages in which a handful of writers have pondered its applicability to moral transgressions. We shall review some of these speculations in Chapter 11. Meanwhile, using tolerance as the starting point to explain deviance, as was done in Chapter 1, has, so far as I know, never been attempted.[1] When we search for direct references to tolerance, then, it is clear that the various sociological theories of deviance mostly ignore it. Yet some of these theories bear indirectly on the concept. Their relationship to tolerance and tolerable deviance is discussed throughout the book, in Chapters 3 through 10.

Accordingly, the goal of this chapter is not to review the many theories of crime and deviance, but to review only those theories and parts of theories that pertain in some way to tolerable deviance. While it is true that they never refer directly to tolerable deviance as such, they still help to explain its emergence, persistence, decline, and place in the larger society. But not all theories of deviance are constructed to do even this limited amount of explanatory work in the sphere of tolerable deviance. For instance, control theory, which centres on the patterns and effects of social control mechanisms, deals mainly with the formal expressions of the control process. As noted in the preceding chapter, however, social control, to the extent that it occurs at all in tolerable deviance, is overwhelmingly informal. Likewise, while the conflict perspective is treated in some detail in this chapter, its Marxian wing is omitted because it best explains property offences and certain other kinds of intolerable deviance. Marxian sociology is anchored in interclass relationships, whereas tolerable deviance focuses on interests which span class boundaries and have little or nothing to do with material possessions. (Chronic homelessness is an exception.) Finally, there are theories that have or once had currency in criminology, which are not covered here because they, too, centre on certain forms of intolerable deviance. Theories of criminal personality and criminogenic areas of cities (the ecology of crime) are examples.

In this book, and particularly in this chapter, we shall be concerned with the following theoretical approaches: anomie-strain, labelling, value-conflict, functionalism, and medicalization.

ANOMIE-STRAIN THEORY

Although not even indirectly related to tolerable deviance, anomie theory laid the foundation for theories bearing more directly on the subject. The theory got its start in the pioneering work of Emile Durkheim, who coined the French term *anomie* to explain one common form of suicide. Anomie is usually translated into English as "normlessness". Unfortunately, this translation is woefully inadequate and therefore an impediment to understanding the sociological uses of the word. For this reason, we shall use as our definition in this book a direct translation from the French: **anomie** is the absence of social and legal organization (Stebbins, 1992:469). An anomic society is hardly normless. As the following paragraphs demonstrate, it is in the course of reorganization, where old norms no longer apply and new norms are emerging. Durkheim (1951) saw this social condition as conducive to suicide.

Durkheim demonstrated that economic crises engender suicides in a population. Yet the suicides are not the result of poverty. Rather, the crises disturb the equilibrium of the social order, a process that unfolds in the following manner. Each person, says Durkheim, has certain insatiable desires for such things as sex, money, and material goods. If these desires are allowed free rein, they result in the torment of continually unfulfilled goals. To achieve peace of mind, people must restrain their endless striving. Only society is powerful enough to impose this constraint, because people will accept only an authority which is stronger than themselves and which they can respect. Durkheim states that society must assign reasonable limits to the striving, however, so that each person has something toward which to work. As for money and material goods, he sees them in relation to social class: each class assigns limits appropriate to the tastes and income of its members. Thus, people find that the social class context within which they are raised and pursue their adult work roles shapes their values. It also gives them a sense of what they may normally expect as a reward for the average effort at work. But, occasionally, the society in which they live is disturbed by an economic recession or depression which automatically drops each person to a lower social status, where he or she must now entertain less lofty goals. Such a situation demands greater self-control, since ordinary norms are no longer applicable.

The society of these people is now in the process of reorganization; the old rules are inappropriate to the new economic situation. A societal state of anomie prevails. This condition is worsened by the heightened desire unleashed by the collapse of societal regulation. It is in such circumstances, among others, that Durkheim was able to demonstrate the rise in the rate of suicide. Anomic suicide is a common individual reaction to a society in the throes of anomie.

Merton's Theory

Robert K. Merton (1957) continued Durkheim's line of thought. He noted that **strain** sometimes develops between the cultural structure and the social structure of a society. That is, there is a discrepancy between the norms and goals of the society (part of its culture) and the capacities of many of its members to reach those goals. Though he believed his theory applied to other culturally accepted goals as well, Merton (1957:181) limited his analysis to the pursuit of success goals of a materialistic nature. This orientation was particularly characteristic of American society, according to Merton. Although he never clarified what he meant by the "social structure" or "capacity" or "institutionalized means" by which these goals are reached, it is evident that he was referring chiefly to occupational roles.

Both Merton and Durkheim recognized that a disturbance in the equilibrium of society — in its social and legal organization — can lead to deviance. Both believed the disturbance to stem from the pursuit of goals lying beyond personal economic means. For people affected in this manner, society is anomic.

Merton suggested that people adapt to anomie in one of five "modes". An adaptation is deviant when it is expressed in behaviour that departs from cultural goals or institutional means of reaching those goals, or both. Table 2.1 depicts the five modes of adaptation identified by Merton and their relationship as deviance or conformity to the goals and means. The first mode, **conformity**, plays a negligible role in the theory. It is not deviance. It is most prevalent when the society is stable, when there is little or no anomie.

As the strain between cultural structure and social structure increases — as anomie increases — additional (deviant) adaptations are made by some members of the community. That is, most people continue to conform in these circumstances, but the number grows of those who do not. **Innovation** is the deviant adaptation springing from the acceptance of cultural goals and the rejection of institutionalized means of attaining them. People are most likely to make innovations in a society where, as in Canada, success goals are ideally open to all members, but in actuality are restricted or even completely closed to some of them. The incentives for success are provided by the established values of the culture. Yet certain barriers are present — such as educational requirements, monetary resources, and family background — which block achievement. In this situation, says Merton, pressure increases for the use of illegitimate means. This mode of adaptation, when implemented in response to monetary goals, typically

TABLE 2.1 A TYPOLOGY OF MODES OF INDIVIDUAL ADAPTATION

Modes of Adaptation	Cultural Goals	Institutionalized Means
I. Conformity	+	+
II. Innovation	+	–
III. Ritualism	–	+
IV. Retreatism	–	–
V. Rebellion	±	±

\+ = Acceptance
– = Rejection
± = Rejection followed by acceptance of new goals and means

Source: Adapted from R.K. Merton. *Social Theory and Social Structure.* (Rev. ed.) Glencoe, IL: The Free Press, 1957), p. 140.

manifests itself as crime or vice, particularly among those in the manual labour and lower white-collar occupations.

When an individual scales down or even abandons a culturally approved goal, but continues to abide almost compulsively by the means of attaining it, he or she has employed **ritualism** as an adaptation to anomie. By diluting achievement goals to manageable size, this person gains security, inasmuch as high ambitions invite possible frustration and failure. The rule-bound bureaucrat was the principal example used by Merton. Merton observed that this mode of adaptation is most likely to occur in lower-middle-class settings where conformity is a strong motive and where social climbing is less likely to be successful than in other parts of the middle class.

Merton believed that **retreatism**, the mode of adaptation in which both cultural goals and their means of attainment are rejected, is probably the least common of the five modes. Some of the behaviour of psychotics, pariahs, tramps, chronic drunkards, and drug addicts can be interpreted as retreatist. Originally, both the goals and the means were internalized, but these individuals found the way to them blocked. Internalization prevents the active innovation of illegitimate means or goals. Instead of innovating, the individual simply abandons the legitimate means and goals and retreats in a deviant manner. Although such deviants may have contact with others who share their proclivities, Merton held that this adaptation is essentially private. One noteworthy, albeit generally nondeviant, variation of retreatism is found in apathy, indifference, cynicism, and disenchantment.

The final mode of adaptation, **rebellion**, consists of the rejection of the established goals and means of the society for those of a new social system. Where the rebellion is small and concentrated among those with little power, subgroups may form which, though isolated from the rest of the community, develop into an integrated society in its own right, for instance, a religious commune. On the other hand, a rebellion involving a substantial number of the members of a society can culminate in a full-scale revolution. The final result in this case is modification of the established cultural and social structures.

Opportunity Theory

Richard A. Cloward (1959) extended Merton's theory by adding several propositions about the illegitimate opportunities open to those seeking a deviant adaptation to anomie. Cloward recognized that there are variations in the availability of illegitimate means, just as Merton had observed variations in legitimate means. The availability of illegitimate means is controlled by the same criteria that control the availability of conventional means. Both types of means are limited and both are differentially open to people in the society according to their positions in the social structure.

Cloward is more specific in his definition of "means" than Merton. For him, the term implies two things:

> First, that there are appropriate environments for the acquisition of the values and skills associated with the performance of a particular role; and second, that the individual has opportunities to discharge the role once he has been prepared. The term, therefore, subsumes both *learning structures* and *opportunity structures* (Cloward, 1959:168).

The availability of illegitimate means is well-illustrated in the process of becoming a marijuana user (Becker, 1963). The neophyte must first learn from experienced users how to smoke the drug and how to interpret as euphoric and desirable the sensations that result. He or she must somehow find or meet experienced users who can provide such instruction as well as the opportunity (place, material) to implement it.

Or consider another example pertaining to tolerable deviance. Block and Bernard (1988) found in their study of the waste oil industry that some refiners of the product were illegally supplementing it with various toxic chemicals, chemicals they publicly promised to dispose of. When used as fuel, the "refined" oil polluted the neighbourhoods in which the users were located. Opportunity theory suggests that, after an oil shortage shrank legitimate business opportunities for the companies involved, the availability of toxic chemical additives provided an attractive, if illegitimate, opportunity for turning a profit.

According to Cloward, some people encounter learning and opportunity structures that lead to deviance, whereas others do not. This contingency is partly explained by Sutherland's **theory of differential association**[2] (Sutherland and Cressey, 1978:80–82). The theory, which centres on crime, consists of nine propositions:

1. People learn how to engage in crime.
2. This learning comes about through interaction with others who have already learned criminal ways.
3. The learning occurs in small, face-to-face groups.

4 What is learned is criminal technique (e.g., how to open a safe), as well as motives, attitudes, and rationalizations.
5 Among criminals, one important learned attitude is a disregard for the community's legal code.
6 One acquires this attitude by differentially associating with those who hold it and failing to associate with those who do not.
7 Differential associations with criminals and non-criminals vary in frequency, duration, priority, and intensity.
8 Learning criminal behaviour through differential association rests on the same principles as learning any other kind of behaviour.
9 Criminal behaviour is a response to the same popular needs and values as non-criminal behaviour. For instance, one man steals to acquire money for a new suit of clothes, while another works as a carpenter to reach the same goal. Consequently, tying popular needs and values to crime fails to explain it.

Sutherland's theory adds scientific weight to the popular idea that people become deviant by hanging out with the "wrong crowd", with whom they come to identify and from whom they learn deviant ways.

Anomie-strain theory offers a causal explanation of deviance, particularly of intolerable deviance. Its focus is chiefly on the antecedents leading to the initial act or acts of deviance. Thanks to Cloward's addition of the principle of differential association, the theory now helps explain a variety of forms of deviance at the interactive level as well as at the structural-cultural level, the area of concern of Durkheim and Merton. We shall see in subsequent chapters that this explanation can be extended to some forms of tolerable deviance.

LABELLING THEORY

Anomie-strain theory dominated the study of crime and deviance from the early 1950s to the mid-1960s. Nevertheless, other perspectives also existed at the time, among them **labelling theory**. Labelling got its start in the late 1930s in a short statement by Frank Tannenbaum (1938), 11 years prior to Merton's initial publication of his generalized theory of anomie. Tannenbaum observed that the acts of juvenile delinquents are seen as evil in the wider community. This image eventually spreads to the delinquents themselves; they, too, are seen as evil. As the community comes to define delinquents as evil, juvenile delinquents' definitions of themselves change accordingly. The result is a sort of self-fulfilling prophecy:

> The process of making the criminal, therefore, is a process of tagging, defining, identifying, segregating, describing, emphasizing, making conscious and self-conscious; it becomes a way of stimulating, suggesting, emphasizing, and evoking the very traits that are complained of (Tannenbaum, 1938:19–20).

The study of deviance had to wait 13 years for a more complete statement on the process. At that time, Edwin Lemert (1951) published his **theory of sociopathic**

behaviour; later, he published elaborations (Lemert, 1972). Although the complete theory is considerably more detailed and complex, the following summary communicates its essentials:

> People and groups are differentiated in various ways, some of which are deviant and which bring them penalties, rejection, and segregation. Penalties, rejection, and segregation are aspects of a community, or societal reaction against the deviance. This reaction affects the initial process of differentiation by sometimes increasing and other times decreasing the tendency to deviate. Accordingly, deviance can be studied from both a collective perspective (society, community) and an individual perspective. (Paraphrased from Lemert, 1951:22)

Three important aspects of the theory receive a great deal of elaboration. The first, the process of **differentiation**, refers to the fact that people differ or deviate from average characteristics of the populations in which they are found and in which they interact. For instance, we have just seen that people differentially associate with other people who are deviant. People are also differentially disposed toward certain interests and activities; examples are the mathematician who engages in computer fraud, and the athlete who specializes in back-alley muggings.

The second aspect of Lemert's theory is the **societal reaction**, which refers to both the expressive reactions of others (moral indignation) toward deviance and the action directed toward its control. Of course, the reaction depends on the deviant individual or class of individuals being sufficiently visible to react toward.

Individuation is the third aspect of the theory. It refers to the manifestation of the causes of deviance in the individual deviant, as well as to how he or she comes to terms with the deviance.

Individuation

The process of individuation has become the core of modern labelling theory. Individuation can be best understood by looking at the events and processes associated with **primary deviation** and **secondary deviation**. The former refers to deviant behaviour that is normalized by the deviant person. The deviance remains primary or symptomatic and situational as long as it is rationalized or otherwise dealt with as part of a socially acceptable role (Lemert, 1972). This may occur through normalization, where the deviance is perceived by the individual as a normal variation or merely a minor problem of everyday living. Or it may be done in a way that does not seriously impede the basic accommodation deviants make to getting along with other people.

Secondary deviation refers to the responses people make to problems created by the societal reaction to their deviance. These problems are those generated by social control mechanisms, punishment, stigmatization, segregation, and the like. They are of exceptional importance to the individual in that they alter his or her personality and lifestyle. The secondary deviant is a person whose life and identity are organized around the facts of deviance.

Lemert (1951:77) expresses the relationship between primary and secondary deviation in the following way:

> The sequence of interaction leading to secondary deviation is roughly as follows: (1) primary deviation; (2) social penalties; (3) further primary deviation; (4) stronger penalties and rejections; (5) further deviation, perhaps with hostilities and resentment beginning to focus upon those doing the penalizing; (6) crisis reached in the tolerance quotient, expressed in formal action by the community stigmatizing the deviant; (7) strengthening of the deviant conduct as a reaction to the stigmatizing and penalties; (8) ultimate acceptance of deviant social status and efforts at adjustment on the basis of the associated role.

Stigmatization is an especially important part of the process of individuation. Goffman (1963:3) defines **stigma** as "an attribute that is deeply discrediting"; the word means "black mark" in Greek. As we have seen, such an attribute is not necessarily deviant; being physically handicapped, for example, is not a violation of moral norms. Deviant or not, a stigma is a source of shame and dishonour, according to a particular set of values, although it may be regarded neutrally or with respect according to another set. For instance, people might stigmatize a person who belongs to a religious cult, while the same person is praised by fellow group members for his or her faithful adherence to its sacred principles.

The process of individuation is illustrated in Viewpoint 2.1, which shows that it can, with little difficulty, be incorporated into the idea of deviant career.

The Deviant Career

Howard Becker (1963) pioneered the application of the concept of career to deviant behaviour. A **career**, whether in deviance or in an occupation, is the passage of the typical person through recognized stages in one or more related identities. A career is further comprised of the adjustments to and interpretations of the contingencies and turning points encountered at each stage.

Objectively, it is the initial act of deviance that launches a deviant career. However, career turning points, including this one, depend upon the actor's recognition and interpretation of them before they can be seen by that actor as part of a career. This usually occurs retrospectively, after the actor has spent a certain amount of time in the identity with which the career is associated. Thus, upon reflection, the first remembered act of homosexuality, the first interest in communist literature, or the first drag on a marijuana cigarette constitutes the inception of the person's deviant career. From a more objective point of view, the given act may or may not be the initial instance of deviance. It, like subsequent acts of primary deviation which may or may not follow, results from many factors — social, cultural, psychological, and physiological — and their various combinations. Of course, any discussion of deviance should not overlook the possibility of false accusation of deviant behaviour, which itself can also, under certain circumstances, lead to a deviant career.

VIEWPOINT 2.1

INDIVIDUATION IN THE DEVIANT CAREER OF A GAMBLER: LARRY'S STORY, AS WRITTEN BY "LARRY"

Larry's grandmother told him about the racetrack when, as a curious 10-year-old, he asked what was on the other side of the big grandstand at the fairgrounds. "What's in there has ruined many a good man," Granny declared. Without further explanation, she marched Larry and his younger brother off to the ferris wheel.

It didn't take long for Larry to satisfy his curiosity. Within a couple of years he was making regular trips to that place that had "ruined many a good man". But as time went by and the small bets turned into bigger ones, he started collecting his paper route money mid-week to satisfy his gambling needs.

Thirty years later, those patterns established as a teenager continued. Bigger lies to cover his whereabouts, bad cheques, lost relationships, lost family, lost self-worth. There were countless attempts to stop. Endless promises to loved ones and friends to give up the addictive lifestyle that brought only pain and misery to Larry and everyone around him.

There were periods of going straight, times when he really thought he could put his life in order, only to go spinning out of control whenever he reached the comfort zone. Complacency and his past were his biggest enemies. Thoughts of past actions reminded him that he did not deserve the recovery he was experiencing. Such thoughts often triggered a return to gambling. He was comfortable there. No-one condemned him. He could escape his past and his daily responsibilities. But each time he returned to gambling, he returned with a renewed fervour, betting more, losing more. Taking a faster track to insanity, prison, or death.

After more than 30 years of proving to himself that he could not win, that no win would ever be great enough and that the losses would always outnumber the wins, Larry decided to take one more shot at living a clean, normal life. He couldn't pin his choice down to one thing. Perhaps it was the need to console his still loving, forgiving spouse; to show that he still loved his children; that he could heed the advice of an understanding parole officer to explore all avenues of recovery.

Most importantly, he concluded, he had to do it for himself. He had to forgive himself, make amends to those he had harmed and start living his life one day at a time. At first it seemed like a huge mountain to climb. But with the help of his Higher Power and the support of friends who understood his sickness, Larry's life gradually began to turn around. There was no quick fix, no magic pill. It would be a life-long dedication to staying clean and developing a better way of life. He had to accept there would be those who would never forgive him and his past behaviour, that not everyone would like him. But he found peace knowing that he was making an honest attempt at arresting his addiction and... that he had asked for and received God's forgiveness.

Source: Alberta Council of Problem Gambling, *Newsletter*, 1994, Summer: 6.

Becker (1963:23) suggested three types of deviants who can be distinguished at this career point by one or a few deviant acts.[3] There are **secret deviants** whose behaviour is not known save by themselves and perhaps a few others. **Falsely accused deviants** believe in their own innocence — whether or not this attitude is in fact valid. They are "known" deviants in the sense that they have been apprehended for or suspected of deviant behaviour. Finally, there are the **pure deviants**, who are also known deviants, since they have behaved in an aberrant way, know it, and have been apprehended for or suspected of such activity by the larger community.

Residual Deviance

Any discussion of adjustive tolerable deviance cannot proceed without reference to Thomas J. Scheff's (1984) **theory of residual rule breaking**, which is an extension of labelling theory. Residual rule breaking is deviance for which society has no explicit label. The theory is intended as a sociological complement to psychiatric and psychological approaches to mental disorder.

According to Scheff, residual rule breaking springs from a range of stressful sources, which may be organic or psychological. It also stems from wilful acts of innovation (in the Mertonian sense) or defiance. Residual rule breaking is common; its unrecorded rate is much higher than official rates of mental disorder. This is so because most deviance of this kind is essentially primary; it is treated as a momentary occurrence of no great importance.

The practice of labelling residual rule breaking is rooted in our stereotypes of the mentally disordered. Scheff says we learn these stereotypes early in childhood, along with such labels as "nuts", "crazy", and "loony". The stereotypes are constantly reaffirmed in our social relations with both normal people and the mentally disordered.

Once a person is labelled as mentally disordered in harmony with our stereotypes of residual rule breaking, he or she is expected to act accordingly. That is, society believes that the mentally disordered should act like the kind of people they are, which includes acting in the stereotypical ways of residual rule breaking (Scheff, 1984:66). Despite the exhortations of others to rehabilitate themselves, residually labelled deviants are typically ostracized, ridiculed, and discriminated against when they attempt to resume a conventional role. Thus, they themselves usually have no choice but to accept the label of "crazy", if they are going to associate with those in the community who know of their mental condition.

* * * * * * * * * *

Labelling theory complements anomie theory to the extent that the former focuses on the deviant career and the processes and conditions that commit a person to many years of deviance. The labelling approach offers less insight into why deviants start their careers than into why they continue or fail to continue beyond the initial acts of deviance. Despite Lemert's early interests in the macrosociological processes of differentiation, culture conflict, and social organization, labelling theory has developed into a predominantly social-psychological explanation of continued deviance. Still, some of the best-known propositions in labelling theory have to do with the macrosociological conditions that lead to the establishment of moral norms, the violation of which makes deviance possible in the first place. This part of the theory, which is concerned with moral enterprise, is treated here as part of the value-conflict theory of deviance.

VALUE-CONFLICT THEORY

Wallace and Wolf (1991:76–77) have listed three assumptions underlying conflict theory. First, people have interests that often conflict with those of other people in the same society. Second, some people are able to gain more power than others, and use it to pursue their own interests. Hence, there is always inequality. Third, special interests and the use of power to achieve those interests are justified with a loose system of ideas and values — an **ideology**.

Allen Liska (1987:177–180) has reviewed the three main conflict perspectives in criminology and the broader study of deviance: culture conflict, pluralistic conflict, and radical criminology. Only the first two apply to tolerable deviance. The cultural perspective developed around the many different subcultural groupings in modern society; the pluralistic perspective emerged as an explanation for the clash of special interest groups. Together, they tell us, for example, that ethnic, neighbourhood, and other status groupings occasionally support values which conflict with the dominant values of the society. That is, there are conflicting interests, and they are extremely varied. Some are intolerably deviant, some are tolerably deviant, and some are merely instances of non-conformity.

What is called deviant and what escapes this label are the important outcomes of the struggle among groups to establish (i.e., institutionalize) their special interests as dominant, as *the* acceptable way of thinking and acting in the society. The presence of moral norms in general and criminal laws in particular is proof of the success of one party in such struggles and the failure of the others (now the deviants). Punishment and informal controls such as gossip and ridicule are among the means available to those who have succeeded in enforcing their norms and maintaining the ascendancy of their interests in this conflict. A sense of the conflict with respect to pornography, an issue that is far from settled in Canada, is presented in Viewpoint 2.2.

Value-conflict theory also helps explain how deviant groups and deviant segments of society come to have interests and values which are out of step with those of the majority. In the value-conflict perspective, deviant interests and values are seen as part of a shared tradition learned in face-to-face interaction with others in the group. Both interests and values are important to the members. For this reason, they tend to endure. Value-conflict theory overlaps with anomie-strain theory to the extent that both emphasize differential association and differential identification as key processes leading to membership in deviant groups. Such groups also teach new members how to justify their unusual interests and how to pursue them with minimal resistance from those who oppose them. In short, people learn from others how to be deviant and how to enact a deviant role.

Moral Entrepreneurs

Howard Becker's (1963) thoughts on the moral entrepreneur, although often associated with the labelling approach, actually fit better with value-conflict theory.[4] Groups of rule-makers, rule-enforcers, and ordinary, non-deviant members of the community join hands in the role of moral entrepreneur. Such people, be they crusading individuals or change-oriented organizations, create moral

VIEWPOINT 2.2

PORNOGRAPHY, PRO AND CON

PRO

The supply of arguments for the badness of sexual explicitness goes on and on, but the foregoing are common and representative. And they are all worthless. The fact is that all the standard arguments against pornography in itself are logical fallacies of one kind or another. That such patent rationalizations have been convincing to so many is a testament to the power of socialization, once again. It is very, very difficult even to recognize the real sources of, much less to consciously overcome, the beliefs one has been indoctrinated with and the feelings one has been conditioned to have; they seem so natural, so obviously right. But the price humanity has always had to pay for such blindness is a terrible one. Summoning the will to be honest in this regard is not only the moral thing but the only intelligent thing to do, for the sake of the welfare of all — as we shall continue to see.

Source: F.M. Christensen. *Pornography: The Other Side.* New York: Praeger, 1990, p. 39.

CON

From our discussion of the definition of obscenity, and the moral conservative normative theory that is implied by this definition, we may describe the components of this theory as follows: (a) to many people, explicit, public portrayals of sex are disgusting and offensive; (b) displays of sex are arousing, and this arousal, outside of monogamous relationships, may undermine these relationships; (c) by overemphasizing sexual gratification and sexual permissiveness, pornography can cause its consumers to behave in ways that undermine other traditional moral judgments about women and sex; (d) ultimately, society in general, and specific societal structures such as the family, may decay once these traditional judgments about women and sex are undermined. The socio-legal formulation of this theory, the obscenity law, limits public display of pornographic materials when two conditions are met: if the materials are found to appeal to a "prurient interest" in sex, and if they are presented in a way that is "patently offensive."

Source: D. Linz and N. Malamuth. *Pornography.* Newbury Park, CA: Sage Publications, 1993, p. 16.

norms on their own initiative and subsequently enforce them against those who disapprove of the new rules and deviate from them. Chapter 1 opened with a discussion of moral entrepreneurs, those who try to establish their interpretations of what is deviant and why (i.e., their ideology) as part of one or more of their society's social institutions.

The prototype of the rule creator, says Becker, is the "crusading reformer" whose dissatisfaction with existing rules is acute. This person campaigns for changes in the moral norms (e.g., to add new laws or procedures, to rescind old laws or procedures) or for changes in attitudes; in both cases, in order to produce what he or she considers proper behaviour. Canadian society is replete with past and present crusades. Groups and individuals have tried to eliminate drug abuse, discourage the overuse of alcohol, reduce the availability of pornography, and stop the exploitation of women in the workplace. Organizations have been formed to stress the need for mental health and for protection against break-and-entry.

Entrepreneurs also enforce the new norms which, once established, can be applied to those who misbehave. When the new norms are legislated laws, the enforcers (police, security personnel) are provided with jobs and justifications for them. Since the enforcers usually want to keep their jobs, they are eager to demonstrate that enforcement is being properly carried out. Yet they also realize that there are more infractions than they can possibly prevent and guard against, and so they must establish priorities. Moreover, as Becker (1963:161) has noted,

> [w]hether a person who commits a deviant act is in fact labeled a deviant depends on many things extraneous to his actual behavior: whether the enforcement official feels that at this time he must make some show of doing his job in order to justify his position, whether the misbehaver shows proper deference to the enforcer, whether the "fix" has been put in, and where the kind of act he has committed stands on the enforcer's list of priorities.

It is no accident, then, that the least influential members of society (i.e., the poor, powerless ethnic groups) are often disproportionately caught in the web of social control and labelled deviant. In other words, deviance is created by society. For moral entrepreneurs the infraction of moral norms constitutes deviance. They also apply these norms to particular people, thereby labelling them as deviants of some sort. As Becker (1963:9) further points out: "The deviant is one to whom that label has successfully been applied; deviant behavior is behavior that people so label." Lest this statement seem restrictive, it should be added that secret deviants are deviant, too. They have simply not been discovered and publicly labelled as such.

Ian Taylor (1982:131) argues that labelling theory and the moral enterprise part of value-conflict theory suffer from a romantic view of human nature; namely, that the legal repression of the threatening behaviour of others is the product of misinformed, sometimes mean people who are simply too powerful. Such people, according to the romantic labelling thesis, should be more tolerant of behaviour that is, in reality, largely harmless. Taylor and other radical conflict theorists hold that entrenched interests and the use of power to ensure their ascendancy are inherent, immutable aspects of modern societies. Telling people to be more tolerant is naive, since powerful people have little to gain and potentially much to lose by being tolerant. These conflict theorists believe that only a force more powerful than the entrenched interests can bring about change; in other words, that the less powerful deviants must at the very least organize to change the oppressive norms and bring social institutions in line with their interests. Taylor's observations demonstrate that moral entrepreneurship, whether conceived of naively or radically, falls outside the scope of tolerable deviance. Moral entrepreneurs can hardly be said to indulge the behaviour they scorn.

FUNCTIONALISM

What is the import of the existence of deviance and of changes in its meaning for the society as a whole? The theories examined so far have not considered this as a central question. Only functionalism has been systematically concerned with the consequences of deviance for the social system known as society.

Deviance as Dysfunctional

Talcott Parsons (1951:250) defines deviance as "the tendency on the part of one or more... actors to behave in such a way as to disturb the equilibrium of the interactive process." According to Parsons, deviance is dysfunctional; it results in an unwanted change in the balanced state of the social system. A new balance may be achieved, or the old balance restored, by the counteracting forces of social control acting on the deviants within the system.

Clearly, this view of deviance — as an inimical, dysfunctional force which undermines the equilibrium of society — fits poorly with the idea that deviance can be tolerable behaviour. Therefore, in keeping with the aim of this chapter, which is to discuss only those theories of deviance that bear on tolerance, little more will be said about the dysfunctional approach.

Deviance as Functional

In contrast to Parsons, some observers believe that deviance can have functional consequences for the social system, for society. When the functional and dysfunctional perspectives are combined, a mixed picture emerges about the overall harm or benefit society experiences as a result of the rejection of its moral norms. To the extent that people are aware of the functional side of deviance, they are likely to tolerate it.

One of the early thinkers to note the functionality of deviance, particularly crime, was Karl Marx (1956:158–159), who pointed out that crime renders a "service" by arousing moral and aesthetic sentiments in the public. Further, it interrupts the monotony and security of middle-class life. Finally, it begets a range of productive occupations designed to deal with crime, including those of locksmith, policeman, jailer, lawyer, and the professor who lectures and writes textbooks on the subject. According to Marx (1956:159), the criminal is "one of those natural 'equilibrating forces' which establishes a just balance".

More recently, Polsky (1985:183–200) has argued that the consumption of pornography and the patronage of prostitutes provide sexual gratification for those males unable to find legitimate release. In this context, deviance is said to be a "safety valve". Erikson (1966: Ch. 1) conjectures that, in limited amounts, deviance can contribute to the stability of social life. For example, prisons have a poor record of changing their inmates from deviant to respectable citizens. This failure agrees with the common sense view that such people as murderers and thieves are inherently bad and hence unlikely to change significantly. In short, our failure to reform imprisoned deviants is functional to the extent that it prevents a threat to collective beliefs about those deviants.

Erikson also notes that public labelling, punishment, and degradation, as in pillorying and flogging, dramatically demonstrate the points at which moral norms can be said to be violated. Furthermore, floggings, hangings, ordeals, and the like have had and still have entertainment value. They are community events, with those who follow them feeling that justice is being done to the enemies of the local way of life. Today's newspaper and magazine stories about rape, theft, and violence seem to serve the same function as yesterday's public executions and tortures.

A recent study of the intolerable side of crime in the United States shows how complicated the functionalist argument can become in modern societies. Liska and Warner (1991) empirically demonstrated the validity of their model: The routine activities and opportunity theories of crime suggest that life in contemporary society, especially in connection with work, disperses daily activities away from the home. With fewer people at home, the opportunity to commit crimes there increases. But the rise in crime generates fear which, in turn, prompts people to execute their routine activities at home as much as possible. The result is a decrease in the opportunity for criminal acts in the home, and a concomitant drop in the crime rate. According to the model, then, crime is both functional and dysfunctional.

That deviance may have both favourable and unfavourable consequences for the community in which it is enacted poses logical problems for functional theory. Can a form of deviance be both functional and dysfunctional? By whose definition is it functional and dysfunctional? To date, no solution to these problems has been proposed. Consequently, functional theorists have been unable to move beyond the level of describing the functional and dysfunctional aspects of particular forms of deviance and the impressionistic observation that modern societies generally survive (maintain equilibrium) both despite *and* because of the moderate amounts of deviance within.

MEDICALIZATION

Peter Conrad (1992:209) offers this definition of **medicalization**: "[It is] a process by which nonmedical problems become defined and treated as medical problems, usually in terms of illnesses or disorders." The definition indicates that moral entrepreneurs describe certain problems in medical terms, adopt a medical framework to understand them, or use a medical intervention to "treat" them. They may or may not be physicians, and physicians may or may not become involved with medicalization. That is, medicalization is not necessarily an expression of the desire of those in the medical profession to expand its boundaries.

During the latter half of the twentieth century, a wide range of phenomena have been medicalized, only some of them deviant. Of interest to the field of tolerable deviance is the medicalization of alcoholism, homosexuality, transsexualism, drug addiction, mental disorder, compulsive gambling, and aberrant sexual behaviour. Many sociologists see medicalization in these areas as a subtle form of social control. Conrad and Schneider (1992:8) explain that "the greatest social control power comes from having the authority to define certain behaviours, persons, and things," and to implement the definition against the wishes of certain groups.

Conrad (1992:216) identifies four types of medical social control. **Medical ideology** imposes a medical model of thought and practice on the problem under consideration. Through **medical collaboration**, physicians intervene in the problem by selecting eligible "patients", representing medical institutions, and supplying medical information. Control by means of **medical technology** involves drugs, surgery, and genetic or other types of screening. The fourth type of control is **medical surveillance**, which has been extensively explored by Michel Foucault (1977). He observed that, when physicians view particular conditions and behaviours from a medical perspective, they tend to claim all related activities as falling within their professional jurisdiction.

Medicalized social control brings with it a number of consequences, some of them undesirable. The moral stance on the problem taken by moral entrepreneurs tends to dominate. Furthermore, they assert their expertise, whatever its validity in this area. The medical approach centres on the individual, while underplaying if not ignoring the social and political background of a given problem. Moreover, there is frequently a dislocation of responsibility for dealing with the medicalized problem, from the person to a set of impersonal bodily and psychological forces — just as in the case of physical disease. Finally, powerful medical technologies may be brought to bear on problematic persons. Concrete examples of these consequences are examined in Chapters 3 through 10 for several forms of tolerable deviance.

Medicalization of a problem or behaviour occurs by degrees. That is, there may be competing explanations and forms of control of the problem or behaviour. For example, drug addiction, some forms of aberrant sexual behaviour (e.g., stripping), and (especially earlier in history) homosexuality are also legal concerns. Moreover, as Roman and Blum (1991) have noted, the vagueness of the concept of disease — especially when applied to non-medical problems — undermines the authoritativeness of medicalization.

Why are some forms of tolerable deviance subject to medicalization? After all, if they are truly tolerable, no control is needed. Yet one of the positive consequences of medicalization in this sphere may be that, by masking their moral import, medicalization has helped make tolerable some previously intolerable forms of deviance. This result is achieved in part because medicalization substantially reduces the stigma associated with a behaviour. Later chapters demonstrate how this happened with regard to transsexualism, alcoholism, and compulsive gambling.

SUMMARY

According to Durkheim, anomie is the state of society in which the norms that guide thought and behaviour have become significantly weakened or have disappeared altogether. It arises when the society is disturbed by an economic recession or depression. This condition automatically drops each person to a lower social status in which the old rules that limit monetary and material striving no longer apply. The status change engenders the societal state of anomie and a consequent increase in the rate of suicide.

Working in a similar vein, Merton noted that there are times when a discrepancy exists between the norms and goals of the society and the capacities of some of its members to reach those goals. This situation is also a form of anomie. People adapt to it according to one of five modes, four of which are deviant. Innovation is the adaptation resting on acceptance of cultural goals and rejection of institutionalized means of attaining them. When an individual downplays a culturally approved goal but continues to abide almost compulsively by the means of attaining that goal, he or she has adapted to anomie through ritualism. Retreatism is the mode of adaptation where both cultural goals and their means of attainment are rejected. Rebellion refers to the rejection of the established goals and means of the society and the substitution of new goals and means. The presence of certain illegitimate opportunities pursued through differential association with like-minded deviants facilitates the adaptation process.

The labelling perspective holds that people and groups are differentiated in various ways, some of which are deviant and carry penalties, rejection, and segregation. At the level of the individual deviant, the result is that life becomes involved with a deviant career of long or short duration. Such careers ordinarily commence at the level of primary deviation, where deviance is treated as an unproblematic variation in everyday life. Public labelling for some sort of deviance moves the individual from the state of secret deviant to that of pure or falsely accused deviant. Public labelling and the societal reaction that follows are two career contingencies which commonly signal the onset of secondary deviation, the tendency to organize one's everyday life around the pursuit of and the problems associated with deviance. Here, individuation reaches its fullest expression; here, stigma is felt at its greatest intensity. Scheff's theory of residual rule breaking is an extension of labelling theory. Residual rule breaking is that deviance for which society has no explicit label other than the general category of mental disorder.

Value-conflict theory centres on the conflicts of interest that separate groups and segments of society from one another. Some groups and segments have enough power to function as moral entrepreneurs, to protect their interests by institutionalizing and enforcing moral norms forbidding the expression of opposing interests. Uses of power of this sort are justified by an ideology. Deviant interests are learned in differential association and differential identification with other people whose interests are similar. Deviant groups nurture these interests and encourage their pursuit, against the dominant ethic of the society.

Functionalism helps explain why society survives the moderate levels of deviant behaviour that occur. Parsons observed that dysfunctional deviance actually commences in the interaction of a small number of people, but ends up disturbing the equilibrium of the larger social system, the society itself. But deviance may also be functional, providing interest and entertainment for some members of the society, as well as a range of occupations. Certain forms are seen as a safety valve for less-than-perfect institutional arrangements. Some modern urban crime has been demonstrated to be both functional and dysfunctional.

Medicalization is a process whereby non-medical problems become defined and treated as medical. Several forms of tolerable deviance have been medicalized in the twentieth century. Medicalization of deviance is, at bottom, a means of social control, which comes in four types: ideology, collaboration, technology, and surveillance. Medicalization of a problem or behaviour occurs in degrees. That is, there may be competing explanations and forms of control of the problem or behaviour.

The four theories reviewed in this chapter bear on tolerable deviance, each in its own way. The following chapters examine the importance of each perspective for the forms of deviance covered there.

NOTES

1 To the author's knowledge, the only substantial treatment of tolerance and deviance was written by Van Vechten (1940), over 45 years ago.
2 Sutherland first published this theory in 1939.
3 Becker actually discusses types of deviant behaviour rather than types of deviants, as we have done here.
4 A similar classification of the moral enterprise thesis is made by Taylor (1982) and Meier (1982).

SUGGESTED READING

Adler, Freda and William S. Laufer. *The Legacy of Anomie Theory, Advances in Criminological Theory,* Vol. 6. New Brunswick, NJ: Transaction, 1994. Assesses the theory's continuing usefulness, explains the relevance of Merton's concept of goals/means disparity, and compares anomie theory with control theory.

Conrad, Peter and Joseph W. Schneider. *Deviance and Medicalization: From Badness to Sickness.* (Expanded ed.) Philadelphia: Temple University Press, 1992. An explanation of the medicalization approach, with chapters on mental illness, alcoholism, opiate addiction, homosexuality, and the medicalization of delinquency, hyperactivity, and child abuse.

Jenness, Valerie. *Making It Work: The Prostitutes' Rights Movement in Perspective.* New York: Aldine de Gruyter, 1993. An analysis of the politics of the prostitutes' rights movement, with empirical emphasis on the organization known as COYOTE (Call Off Your Old Tired Ethics).

Liska, Allen E. *Perspectives on Deviance.* (2nd ed.) Englewood Cliffs, NJ: Prentice-Hall, 1987. An examination and critique of the major theories of deviance.

Traub, Stuart H. and Craig B. Little (eds.) *Theories of Deviance.* (4th ed.) Itasca, IL: F.E. Peacock, 1994. A collection of representative journal articles and book chapters written from the perspectives of the various theories of deviance.

Wolf, Daniel R. *The Rebels: A Brotherhood of Outlaw Bikers.* Toronto: University of Toronto Press, 1991. An extensive ethnography of an Edmonton motorcycle club.

REFERENCES

Becker, Howard S. *Outsiders.* New York: The Free Press, 1963.

Block, Alan and Thomas Bernard. "Crime in the Waste Oil Industry," *Deviant Behavior,* 1988, 9:113–129.

Cloward, Richard A. "Illegitimate Means, Anomie, and Deviant Behavior," *American Sociological Review,* 1959, 24:164–176.

Conrad Peter. "Medicalization and Social Control." In *Annual Review of Sociology,* Vol. 18, edited by Judith Blake and John Hagen, pp. 209–232. Palo Alto, CA: Annual Reviews, 1992.

__________ and Joseph W. Schneider. *Deviance and Medicalization: From Badness to Sickness.* (Expanded ed.) Philadelphia: Temple University Press, 1992.

Durkheim, Emile. *Suicide.* (Translated by John A. Spaulding) New York: The Free Press, 1951.

Erickson, Kai T. *Wayward Puritans.* New York: John Wiley & Sons, 1966.

Foucault, Michel. *Discipline and Punish.* New York: Random House, 1977.

Goffman, Erving. *Stigma: Notes on the Management of Spoiled Identity.* Englewood Cliffs, NJ: Prentice-Hall, 1963.

Lemert, Edwin M. *Social Pathology.* New York: McGraw-Hill, 1951.

__________ *Human Deviance, Social Problems, and Social Control.* (2nd ed.) Englewood Cliffs, NJ: Prentice-Hall, 1972.

Liska, Allen E. *Perspectives on Deviance.* (2nd ed.) Englewood Cliffs, NJ: Prentice-Hall, 1987.

__________ and Barbara D. Warner. "Functions of Crime: A Paradoxal Process," *American Journal of Sociology,* 1991, 96:1441–1463.

Marx, Karl. *Selected Writings in Sociology and Social Philosophy.* (Translated by T.B. Bottomore) New York: McGraw-Hill, 1956.

Merton, Robert K. *Social Theory and Social Structure.* (Rev. ed.) New York: The Free Press, 1957.

Parsons, Talcott. *The Social System.* New York: The Free Press, 1951.

Polsky, Ned. *Hustlers, Beats, and Others.* Chicago: University of Chicago Press, 1985.

Roman, Paul and T. Blum. "The Medicalized Conception of Alcohol Related Problems: Some Social Sources and Some Social Consequences of Murkiness and Confusion." In *Society, Culture, and Drinking Patterns Reexamined,* edited by David Pittman and Helen White, pp. 753–774. New Brunswick, NJ: Rutgers University Press, 1991.

Scheff, Thomas J. *Being Mentally Ill: A Sociological Theory.* (2nd ed.) New York: Aldine, 1984.

Stebbins, Robert A. "Deviance." In *Encyclopedia of Sociology,* Vol. 1, edited by Edgar F. Borgatta and Marie L. Borgatta, pp. 468–476. New York: Macmillan, 1992.

Sutherland, Edwin H. and David R. Cressey. *Principles of Criminology.* (10th ed.) Philadelphia: Lippincott, 1978.

Tannenbaum, Frank. *Crime and the Community.* New York: Columbia University Press, 1938.

Taylor, Ian. "Moral Enterprises, Moral Panic, and Law-and-Order Campaigns." In *The Sociology of Deviance,* edited by M. Michael Rosenberg, Robert A.

Stebbins, and Allan Turowetz, pp. 123–149. New York: St. Martin's Press, 1982.
Van Vechten, C. "The Tolerance Quotient as a Device for Defining Certain Social Concepts," *American Journal of Sociology*, 1940, 46:35–42.
Wallace, Ruth A. and Alison Wolf. *Contemporary Sociological Theory*. (3rd ed.) Englewood Cliffs, NJ: Prentice-Hall, 1991.

3

DEVIANT SEXUAL IDENTITIES

The 1994 *Diagnostic and Statistical Manual of Mental Disorders* of the American Psychiatric Association (DSM-IV) classifies sexually abnormal behaviour into four categories under the main heading of "Sexual and Gender Identity Disorders". One category comprises the **sexual dysfunctions**, which involve disturbances in sexual desire, arousal, orgasm, and the like. The **paraphilias** "are characterized by recurrent, intense sexual urges, fantasies, or behaviors that involve unusual objects, activities, or situations and cause chronically significant distress or impairment in social, occupational, or other important areas of functioning" (American Psychiatric Association, 1994:463). They include voyeurism (watching others in sexually stimulating activities), transvestic fetishism, sexual sadism (inflicting pain), sexual masochism (receiving pain), zoophilia (sex with animals), necrophilia (sex with corpses), frotteurism (rubbing against others), partialism (exclusive focus on one part of body), and telephone scatologia (obscene phone calls). The **gender identity disorders** "are characterized by strong and persistent cross gender identification accompanied by persistent discomfort with one's assigned sex" (American Psychiatric Association, 1994:463). Transsexualism is the chief example. The fourth category, **sexual disorders not otherwise specified**, is a residual class, and is of little concern to our discussion.[1]

With the exception of homosexuality, psychiatrists regard all sexual abnormalities as both sexual disorders and mental diseases. Sociologists see them as forms of deviance (and not always as mental disorders). To their list of deviant forms of sexual behaviour, sociologists add such practices as homosexuality, prostitution, striptease work, group and extramarital sex, and pornography production and consumption. In other words, the sociology of deviant sex identities and practices is more encompassing than the pathology of sexual abnormality.

There are still other forms of sexual variation that fall outside both psychiatry and deviance. For instance, Canadians appear to accept, though by no means always practise, such variations as fellatio, cunnilingus, masturbation, anal intercourse, and genital apposition (rubbing the genitals together, clothed or unclothed). Further, premarital sex in itself is rarely treated as deviant. Today it is less likely to be seen as a transgression of community morals than as a variation in personal standards held for particular relationships — especially by younger age groups (Bibby and Posterski, 1992).

This chapter, oriented as it is to the sociology of deviant sex identities, covers transsexualism and transvestism as complete or partial adjustments. Accordingly, they may be seen as psychological abnormalities as well as forms of deviance.

TRANSSEXUALISM

To avoid confusion, here we shall refer to a woman who desires to become a man as a *female transsexual* (she) and to one who has achieved this by surgical means as a *constructed man* (he). Conversely, we shall speak of as a *male transsexual* (he) a man who desires to become a woman, and of a man who succeeds as a *constructed woman* (she). This is a language of convenience. The literature on the subject simply refers to all the aforementioned categories as transsexuals. Increasingly these days, transsexuals are viewed medically as suffering from **gender dysphoria**, "a sense of awkwardness or discomfort in the anatomically congruent gender role and the desire to possess the body of the opposite sex, together with the negative affect associated with these ideas, namely, anxiety and reactive depression" (Steiner, Blanchard, and Zucker, 1985:5–6). Technically, however, the term is not limited to transsexuals, for transvestites and effeminate male and masculine female homosexuals suffer gender dysphoria as well.

Lothstein (1983: Ch. 2) provides a short history of early thought on transsexualism. The history rests on anecdotes, literary plots, and some scientific research. It displays a certain confusion (in the minds of the writers of these sources) between transvestism when it appears as a deviant expression of heterosexuality, and transsexualism as a crisis in sexual identity. We shall see later in our discussion of the transsexual's career why this confusion is possible.

Since the last half of the nineteenth century, transsexuals have been regarded as mentally disordered. Early in this period, they usually took their lives or ended their days in asylums in a deranged state which was no doubt caused as much by their identity problems in everyday life as by their drive to become bona fide members of the opposite sex. It is claimed, although the source is suspect, that a German woman had surgery in the 1880s to help change her into a man. More solid evidence holds that, by the early 1930s, the surgical techniques for transsexual change to either sex were known and occasionally used, albeit secretly (Money and Tucker, 1975:32). Most histories of transsexualism, however, trace the first scientifically sophisticated instance of sex reassignment surgery (SRS) to the celebrated transformation of George Jorgensen into Christine Jorgensen in 1952 in Denmark.

The publicity surrounding the Jorgensen case brought a flood of demands for SRS from around the world. A new era of medical surgery and psychological counselling had begun. Sex change operations are now conducted at the Clarke Institute of Psychiatry in Toronto and in at least four hospitals in the United States. Such surgery is also undertaken in Europe. Between 1975, the year SRS was first done at the Clarke Institute, and 1986, 700 patients were treated, of whom 148 were changed to the opposite sex (*The Globe and Mail*, 1986:D5). Nevertheless, according to Simon (1992:1770), many of the medical centres that once offered SRS and its supportive counselling have now abandoned these programs. The results were said to be too mixed to justify their continuation.

The Nature of Transsexualism

Transsexuals are born with normal, clearly identifiable genitalia. Babies with obvious genital defects are given corrective surgery as soon as possible. What, then, causes transsexualism? There are many theories, some of them suggesting that it is inherited, others claiming that it is learned as part of early childhood socialization. The latter are now the most widely accepted explanations of the disorder (Docter, 1988:66). They have coalesced into what is known as the gender dysphoria theory of transsexualism. The theory dates to the seminal work of physicians Harry Benjamin, whose ideas were summarized in *The Transsexual Phenomenon* (1966), and John Money (see, for example, Money and Ehrhardt, 1972). In brief, the gender dysphoria theory holds that, although biological factors may serve as underlying forces in the development of gender dysphoria, the incongruent gender role and identity which constitute the dysphoria itself are learned in the course of childhood socialization.

Two of the chief proponents of transsexualism as a learned phenomenon are John Money and Patricia Tucker (1975), who believe that the direction of a person's sex identity is set during the prenatal stage of fetal development and "locked tight" in the first 18 months of life. Many sociologists, however, would disagree with the implication that no significant change in sex role identity can occur after the first 18 months. Risman (1982), for example, offers the hypothesis that cross-gender behaviour may lead to the label of deviant which, in turn, is incorporated into the self-concept, promoting still further cross-gender deviance.

Whatever the age at which they learn their sexual orientation, many — though not all — transsexuals somehow learn the stereotyped role of the sex opposite their biological sex (cf. Eichler, 1987). They learn it so well that they are willing to undergo many years of expensive and often painful counselling, hormonal treatment, and surgery to bring body identity in line with sexual outlook. On the basis of clinic records at the Clarke Institute, the ratio of post-operative male transsexuals to female transsexuals in Canada is about equal today (*The Globe and Mail*, 1986:D5).

Clinicians suggest that some transsexuals were inadvertently encouraged to learn the role of the opposite sex when they were rejected during childhood by their parent of the opposite sex. In other cases, one or both parents wanted a child of the sex opposite to the sex of the child that was born. The parents tried to correct nature's "mistake" by treating a little girl as a little boy, or *vice versa*.

Some transsexuals learn the stereotypical role of the opposite sex to an extreme. Using a masculinity-femininity scale, Kando (1973: Ch. 2) found that constructed women scored significantly higher on the femininity scale than ordinary women did. Moreover, the constructed women scored significantly lower on the masculinity scale than either ordinary men or ordinary women. Kando (1973:24–27) also found that transsexuals of both sexes suffer sex-role strain, which they solve in good part by sex-change surgery. But Anne Bolin (1988: Ch. 8) found that her sample of constructed women were as diverse as the genetic females they were attempting to imitate. She (1988:107) went on to note:

> [H]yper-femininity... may be an artifact of the medical-mental health caretaker system and particular gender identity clinics where transsexuals are intensively involved in programs designed to turn them into women.... The medical and psychiatric communities reinforce sex-role stereotypes.

Kando (1973: Ch. 3) identified four types of constructed women. Of the four, the **housewife** passes most easily for an ordinary female, thanks to successful surgery. Youth at the time of the operation is apparently a factor in its success. It also allows this type more time to adjust to her new sex role than is available to older constructed women. In fact, the operation is so successful that these constructed women are able to entertain the goals of getting married, adopting children, and settling in to a respectable, middle-class lifestyle away from the transsexual community. The housewife can play the highly valued (for the large majority of male transsexuals) traditional sex role of wife and homemaker. Nevertheless, the available pool of mates for constructed females may be limited. Some of Kando's interviewees of the housewife type had married ex-criminals.

Transsexuals of the **show business** type find a career in the nightclub circuit of strippers and dancers, occasionally even promoting themselves as transsexuals. They may also supplement earnings from this work with those from prostitution. Thus, although these constructed women also seek the lifestyle and marital role of housewife, they are willing to exploit their new sex status for quick financial return. Several respondents of the show business type in Kando's sample were as young and attractive as the housewives. There were, however, retained aspects of their former maleness, such as a low voice or prominent Adam's apple. None of Kando's show business respondents was married.

The **aspiring housewife** has goals similar to the preceding two types. In her case, however, SRS has been less successful. Certain visible male characteristics linger, frustrating her efforts to marry and leave the transsexual community.

A small proportion of Kando's sample rejected the traditional female gender role, opting instead for that of **career woman**. They sought careers in science, writing, and business. The career woman has little taste for the traditional division of labour between the sexes, including the expectation that she play a support role to an aspiring male.

No typology has been developed for constructed male transsexuals. A summary of the literature by Sorensen and Hertoft (1980) suggests that sex-role strain is a problem at pre- and post-operative stages for these patients, and that they hope to solve the problem through surgery. For example, Sorensen and Hertoft note that the adopted male sex role is seen and enacted in stereotypical ways, that is, as a traditional male sex role. Constructed men have been found to be domineering toward women, whom they view as occupying traditional female roles. Even sex relations are conducted within this frame of reference, whether or not the sex-change operation has occurred. Constructed men also have a protective attitude toward their mothers and other women.

The Male Transsexual Career

Driscoll (1977) has described the five stages in one common deviant career of the male to constructed woman transsexual. The first is **effeminate childhood**, which runs from infancy to the tenth or twelfth year. It is a time of many tense experiences. In some cases, the boy's parents insist on treating him as a boy, against his own increasingly strong desire to be seen and treated as a girl. In others, his parents wanted a girl, got a biological boy at birth, then attempted to deny the fact by dressing him and treating him as a girl. Either way, the fiction between his emotional and biological sex becomes difficult to maintain once he enters school. It becomes even more difficult to maintain when he starts high school, where the distinction between the sexes grows sharper. Gym classes, for example, require students to be separated by sex. The practice accentuates the differences between the male transsexual with his effeminacy and female interests, and the other boys with their growing masculinity and male interests.

Transsexualism is tolerated more today than ever before, but only after the aforementioned circumstances have come to light (Matto, 1975:255). In general, during childhood and adolescence, the male transsexual is defined as a sissy. Consequently, he is teased, ostracized, and beaten up by his classmates. His public harassment, biological sex, and divergent sex identity spawn extensive personal confusion and anxiety, together with a strong drive to put an end to the tension. Even so, some male transsexuals may try, toward the end of adolescence, to solve their problems by becoming "true men", sometimes by joining the military (Matto, 1975:256). But this attempt seldom works.

In their search for relief from the situation, many male transsexuals move into the **homosexual** stage. Like many ordinary males, young male transsexuals experiment with homosexual activities without any sense of being homosexual. This "fooling around" turns out to be pleasurable for some of them, however, and leads them to the gay scene. Becoming part of this scene sometimes helps reduce the earlier tension and anxiety (Driscoll, 1977:175). It is at about this time that the transsexual leaves his home and perhaps his community. Behind him now are the conflicts with parents, schoolmates, and possibly even the police (conflicts over cross dressing and homosexuality). Whereas the young man's parents treated him as a girl when he was a child, as he grew into adolescence they expected him to act like a man, an expectation the transsexual was unable to meet.

Even in the gay scene, feminine tendencies are typically evident among male transsexuals who pass through this stage. They wear their hair long in a feminine coiffure. They prefer the female role in homosexual relations. While in the gay scene, they learn to use makeup. They may also engage in male prostitution.

The **transvestite** stage follows. Of course, the male transsexual has cross dressed periodically since childhood. Established transvestites in the gay scene now serve as models for him, leading him into secondary deviation by way of the conclusion that routine cross dressing and effeminate behaviour are the answer to his problems. But being a true woman with a man's body is no easy task. The transsexual is no longer merely playing at the female role; he is trying to enact it. He must learn the many subtle mannerisms that constitute femininity as he sees it. He must learn how to dress convincingly as an adult female. Most difficult, he must somehow disguise his male physical characteristics. It is for the latter reason that some transsexuals, such as Rose, turn to female hormones:

> It's a question of being honest with yourself and growing to maturity. One of the tragic things about so many drag queens is that they began taking hormones when they were still teenagers, before they had any understanding of the consequences. Their minds have never matured beyond that of a fifteen year old. It took me many traumatic years to make up my mind that that was what I wanted to be. It happened about five years ago when I had been working at the Tote for some time. I just felt it wasn't the life for me and in the end I was very ill. And I thought: "It is because I'm lying to myself. I mustn't do that." So I found out about hormones and decided I would see if this way worked better. Gradually, as you take the hormones your mind starts to work in a different way. When you are saturated with female hormones and the male hormones are held back, you even go through the menstrual cycle, emotionally. That was a thing that took me ages to get adjusted to. Hormones work like a drug: if you don't have enough, you start withdrawals, if you have too much, you have hormone poisoning. You only feel right if you have the right amount of injection. I had been on hormones once before and went off them. It's shattering experience. I would never go back now. Never, I like living this way. Once it used to be a giggle, like fooling the world. If you passed people without heads turning, then you would think you were a success. Long ago that went; now I just live an ordinary life. Nobody seems to take any notice at all (*Drag Show,* 1977:26–27).

This is one point at which the male transsexual may come into contact with the law. Many countries, including Canada, have no legislation that explicitly forbids cross dressing and transsexualism. Impersonation of the other sex or any other general category of humanity is not illegal in Canada, although it is proscribed in some American states (Bolin, 1988:180). Nevertheless, it is possible in Canada, as in many other countries, to arrest cross dressers under statutes pertaining to disorderly conduct or offences against public decency (Hoenig, 1977: 165–166).

Transsexuals under medical treatment may be given certificates stating that cross dressing is part of their "disorder"; cross dressing is not being done to defraud someone or achieve a sexual thrill. The former occurs, for example, when a male homosexual impersonates a woman with the intent of securing sexual relations with a heterosexual male. However, the police are under no legal obligation to refrain from arrest when such a certificate is produced.

According to Driscoll (1977:180), the transvestite stage is short-lived, usually no more than eight months. Either during this stage or before it, the male transsexual hears about the sex-change operation. To be a true woman, one must be freed of identifying male characteristics, especially male genitals and facial hair.

Some of these men, albeit a minority, therefore move to the **transsexual** stage of their careers. Keep in mind that this is a special use of the term. Elsewhere in this chapter and among gender dysphoric people themselves, "transsexual" is also used to refer to those who are in the pre-operative transvestite stage. If there was once a homosexual love for other men in the transsexual stage, it is now reinterpreted as a heterosexual love for them. What is required is the surgery and accompanying treatment to make such love truly possible. At this point, male homosexuals come to be regarded as inferior to, or at least different from, transsexuals. This sentiment is reciprocated by the gays, who define these transsexuals as "flaming queens" who deny their masculinity.

The operation and its accompanying treatment are difficult experiences. Before, during, and after his operation, the patient is attended to by a team of psychiatrists, surgeons, endocrinologists, psychologists, lawyers, clergy, social workers, and possibly others. Several years prior to the operation, he starts receiving the female hormones estrogen and progesterone, which suppress male physiological characteristics while developing and maintaining their female counterparts. This treatment may itself be preceded by lengthy counselling intended to ascertain that the person is truly transsexual and prepared to undergo the transformation which lies ahead.

In the operation, the skills of a urologist, gynecologist, and plastic surgeon are combined in the removal of the man's penis and testicles and their replacement with an artificial vagina. If he is lucky, he will be able to engage in sexual intercourse and experience orgasm, the latter made possible by the ingenious use of penile skin. Meanwhile he may decide to have his breasts enlarged by means of inserted implants and further estrogen therapy. Additional operations may be necessary to effect a proper female appearance, such as reshaping the chin, eyes, and limbs. The Adam's apple may have to be reduced in size. And complications requiring further surgery sometimes develop from the modification of the breasts and genitals.

Driscoll (1977:183–184) and Bolin (1988) indicate that other constructed women sometimes play an important role in helping the newly constructed woman. For instance, if she is interested in being feminine, they may show her how the masculine appearance of her legs can be softened by wearing two pairs of dark nylon stockings, or how she can wear long sleeves with ruffles at the cuff to minimize the apparent size of her hands. Even though the ultimate goals of many constructed women are marriage, domesticity, and middle-class respectability, association with other transsexuals, defined as deviant by society, may be a necessary step in reaching those goals.

The transition to marriage, domesticity, and respectability constitutes the **feminine** stage of the male transsexual career. As noted earlier, only some of those who undergo SRS reach these goals, and then only with certain limitations (e.g., inability to have children, need to continue hormonal treatment). Thus, some constructed women may be unhappy with the outcome of the sex-change operation (Raymond, 1979:35). Perhaps they are the ones who enter show business; the ones who Kando (1973:67) says find their marginal roles more acceptable than the tension, anxiety, and stigma of their pre-operation days.

Bolin (1988:180) describes the significance of the turning point provided by SRS:

> Perhaps the inability to experience sex and intimacy as women compared with the other limitations cited is only a fraction of transsexuals' total life experience as females, but this fraction is substantial to those denied access. Surgery provides closure to the liminality of their transition [to constructed women]. The greater their adjustment to their roles as women, the more glaringly does their [male] genitalia become a symbol of discontinuity. Surgery is the mechanism for transsexuals' integration into society. It is their opportunity for humanness and normalcy. Surgery is the final phase of their rebirth as women.

Post-operative adjustment to the surgery does not, however, free the constructed woman of all indicators of deviance. For example, the need to keep secret from almost everyone information about her former self practically eliminates the possibility of a career in politics or an occupation requiring an extensive security check (Bolin, 1988:182). And Ebaugh (1988:158) reports that, in every instance, at least one family member rejected the constructed men and women in her sample.

The need for some constructed women to keep in touch with others like themselves is met, in part, through self-help organizations such as *Transsexuelles Québec* in Montréal and the Renaissance Education Association and the International Foundation for Gender Education (IFGE) in the United States. These groups provide support and information for transsexuals at both the pre-operative and the post-operative stages. They also try to promote tolerance and understanding of this kind of deviance. The IFGE, founded in 1978, consists of some 200 regional groups. It not only holds an annual convention but also publishes a quarterly called the *TV/TS Tapestry Journal*. Post-operative transsexuals must remain informed about the physical risks that may result from the change procedures, including hypertension, phlebitis, stroke, and blood clots. Another function of the self-help organizations, then, is to disseminate information about these risks.

Such are the stages of one transsexual career. Not all constructed female transsexuals have histories of effeminacy or strive for a feminine outcome to their sex-change odyssey (Green, 1974:29). Mixtures of old and new habits, desires, and drives produce a complicated sexual identity in many transsexuals, both pre- and post-operative. More will be said about this in the conclusion to this chapter.

VIEWPOINT 3.1

THE TRANSSEXUAL'S PLIGHT: A VERY GRIMM TALE, by E. Sopp

Once upon a time, a very long time ago, there was a little log hut hidden deep in the heart of a forest. People very seldom passed that way and those who did seldom looked in at the window. It seemed to have few inhabitants and was of interest only to a few adventurous men who ventured sporadically into the woods.

As time went by, men changed their way of living. A new mechanical, industrial and scientific age was born. The towns became cities, the cities spread into the forest and eventually surrounded the hut with its small window. The hut-dwellers had multiplied and needed a bigger house which, in turn, required more windows. The inhabitants of the surrounding city found that they now had more windows through which they could observe the tenants. At the same time, the inhabitants of the house, looking out of the windows, became envious of the life that seemed to be enjoyed by people living on the outside. They wanted to come out into the open, but when they did so, they found that the city-dwellers did not want them. They were *different.*

Certain wise men from a temple in the city that was dedicated to the Goddess of Learning, brought their telescopes, their stethoscopes and their microscopes and proceeded to sound out the house and its inhabitants. If one of these ventured out of the house he was promptly escorted to a house of inquisition known as a clinic, popped into a specimen bottle, labelled, dissected and put under a microscope.

The wise men scratched their bald pates (for which reason some of the less respectful citizens called them *eggheads*) and wondered what name they could give to this house. In 1949 a learned man named Cauldwell, who was steeped in an old world tradition of Dog Latin, suggested calling it "Psychopathia Transsexualis". The other citizens thought that this was a bit of a mouthful, and shortened it to "Transsexualism". The people who lived in the house did not like this at all.

By this time, the little forest hut had grown out of all proportion and was becoming a veritable mansion. Like England during the nineteenth century, the citizens of Erehwyreve (pronounced Ere-we-leeve) levied a window tax. (Geographical note: Erehwyreve's twin city, Erehwon, lies just across the river Styx. The citizens of Erehwyreve have a ploblem plonouncing the letter 'r'.) Many of the tenants in Transsexualism could not afford to pay the tax; others preferred to live in the darkness. They dared to venture out only at night in the hope that they might share a bed with some warm, needy person — blankets were in short supply in their house and many of them had to sleep on the floor. Besides, they could always hope to gain enough money for to-morrow's breakfast, even if they did eat it in the afternoon.

At length the situation became unbearable. People inside the house wanted to get out. Certain people on the outside, who liked to be seen in shiny white armour (it was really quite rusty on the inside) did not like that. They talked to the city fathers who were dazzled by the shiny white armour (being a little old and rusty themselves, they did not realize that some joints needed oil). The city fathers spoke to their own knights in blue (they were all officers), who promptly apprehended the more adventurous "transsexuals" (the name by which the inhabitants of the house were now known) and took them to an unheated house (hence called "The Cooler"), known locally as the "Don". This name derived from the worshippers at the temple of Learning who recalled that, in their student days, they had been disciplined by "dons".

The citizens of Erehwyreve now became alarmed. The Don was overcrowded and the building of more coolers would raise their taxes. The tenants at Transsexualism had paid no window tax and the wise men had become so numerous that they could not look through the few small windows. There was only one thing for it: they must knock a few holes in the wall from outside and enlarge some of the existing windows. So that they can direct others to what they consider to be the right window, they have given their windows names: psychology, biology, sociology and a host of others.

One of the largest windows is named psychoanalysis, and at the top of a ladder looking through this window into the house of transsexualism is a man named Leslie Martin Lothstein. Through the window, which needs cleaning and is seldom open, he is looking into a room which is occupied by some unusual people. They are undoubtedly human, although the wearers of the creaky white armour do not treat them as such, but, while supposedly girls, they are behaving like boys. While looking through his sometimes cloudy window of psychoanalysis, Dr. Lothstein has written about these people in his book *Female to Male Transsexualism: Historical, Clinical and Theoretical Issues.*

Source: Gender Review, 1985, Summer, 3:3–4.

The Female Transsexual Career

Rather less systematic research has been done on female transsexuals than on male transsexuals, even though the ratio of women to men undergoing sex changes has been dropping at the Clarke Institute. Earlier, it was estimated that one biological female to eight biological males applied for SRS; today, the ratio is two to three (Steiner, Blanchard, and Zucker, 1985:2).

Most of what is known about female transsexuals comes from clinical records and must therefore be treated as hypothetical. It is from just such a background that psychiatrist Robert Stoller (1974: Ch. 18) concluded that female transsexualism differs in significant ways from its male counterpart. As previously mentioned, both types engage in stereotyped modelling of the role of the opposite sex. Thus there is, in effect, a **masculine childhood** stage during which the little girl becomes increasingly boylike in behaviour and interests, cross dressing, preferring boys' toys, and seeking boys as playmates. This transformation, however, is likely to be interpreted as merely tomboyish and provoke much less family and community concern than the opposite process in boys.

Stoller (1974:226–227) believes female transsexualism gets its start in the following conditions:

1. An infant who does not strike the parents at birth or later as beautiful, graceful, or "feminine" (whatever that would be to the parents of a newborn).
2. An infant who is not cuddly when held but who habitually pushes away, even if a good feeder.
3. A feminine mother who at the birth of this daughter and at times later in childhood is removed in affect from her child, most often by overt, severe emotional illness, usually depression.
4. A masculine father, who is nonetheless not present psychologically in at least two crucial areas:
   (a) He does not support his wife in her depression.
   (b) He does not encourage this daughter's femininity in the ways fathers of feminine daughters do.
5. Given these factors, the little girl is shot into the breach that her father abandoned the role of succoring husband; the motive that propels the drive toward masculinity seems to be the family's manufacturing out of this daughter a substitute male (a husband) to assuage (treat) mother's depression. This is done by constant encouragement of masculinity by both parents. Simultaneously, the child on her own is inventing a role — the masculine father-substitute — to mitigate her own terrible loneliness, produced by having a mother whom she cannot reach and who does not reach out to her. Soon the process becomes self-perpetuating.

Using 80 cases, Pauly (1974:520–521) proposes a similar chronology, which he calls "the process of gender identification". This process is probably complete by seven or eight years of age. By age 20, the individual has permanently passed into the male role. The operation, the transsexual feels, is all that is needed to complete the desired identity change.

Upon reaching maturity, Stoller believes, the female transsexual disappears into the general population of men, albeit as one who passes for male. That is, this type of transsexual goes directly to the **transvestite** stage. The homosexuality stage through which male transsexuals go is, as far as clinicians know, not part of the female transsexual's career. The latter idealizes feminine traits, much as if she were viewing the ideal woman through male eyes. The female transsexual's ideal woman is heterosexual, a woman who likes men. For that woman to be attracted to the female transsexual, the transsexual (who hopes she is seen as a man) must also be seen as having heterosexual interests. Such an orientation hardly fits with lesbian stereotypes.

Since some female transsexuals elect SRS, they too enter the **transsexual** stage. Like their male counterparts, some females begin with hormonal treatment, possibly preceded by counselling. Androgen is used to stop menstruation, stimulate growth of body hair, lower the voice somewhat, and partially reduce breast size. In addition, androgen sometimes creates a more masculine look to the muscles and overall body structure. Testosterone helps enlarge the clitoris.

There are several steps to female transsexual surgery, some of which the patient may refuse. Cost is a consideration here. Most patients request mastectomy and hysterectomy. Most have their ovaries removed as well. In all this, the vagina is left intact. Since the artificial penis can be of no sexual use (it has no orgasmic or procreative potential) and is imperfect, some constructed men decline this aspect of the transformation. Those who go through with it may receive a penis fashioned out of skin from the abdomen. Their vaginal canal may be closed, with urination redirected through the new penis. But since this procedure sometimes causes complications, many surgeons prefer to construct an artificial penis and leave the vaginal canal open. In this arrangement, urination takes place below the new penis. To simulate an erection, stiffening material is inserted through a channel in the penis.

All transsexuals worry that they may find themselves in situations beyond their control, in which they have to expose their genital area. Hospitals and restrooms are two such problematic situations. Thus, there is considerable motivation to be reconstructed to the point where they appear as normal as possible (Raymond, 1979:39).

In theory, the post-operative stage for surgically changed males and females depends on the success of the transsexual transition. In practice, however, this conclusion has so far been difficult to demonstrate. Docter (1988:68) says of the follow-up studies on sex reassignment that they are "so incomplete and methodologically flawed that few broad conclusions are warranted.... There seems never to have been an adequate commitment to reassignment follow-up research."

Not surprisingly, then, what little evidence exists on the post-operative stage for female transsexuals is mixed. Lothstein (1983:197–301) has noted that recent studies indicate that surgery has done little to improve their social and psychological condition. After studying six constructed men who left his clinic, he found they feared that they might be unable to satisfy their female partners. They also worried that the partners might react unfavourably to their new penis, and that it might fall off. The inability to have babies was also a problem. Lingering female characteristics, such as small stature and nipple sensitivity, caused further anxiety. Yet Hoenig and his colleagues (1973) concluded that the constructed man is, on the whole, less exhibitionistic, more stable emotionally, and better integrated socially than the constructed woman. Kando's (1973) findings also support this interpretation to some extent.

TRANSVESTISM

Before we move into our discussion of transvestism, a short methodological note is in order. There is no sociological research on this subject in Canada, and only a limited amount in the United States. To answer the inevitable question of how applicable the American research is to the Canadian transvestite scene, the organizer of the Canada-Wide TV and TS Contact Club and editor of its publication, *TV Guys,* was asked to read this section of the text. Her conclusion was that the American research reported here describes the Canadian transvestite scene as well.

Cross dressing is a broader term than transvestism. **Cross dressing** refers simply to wearing the clothing of the opposite sex. The Biblical proscription against it is clear:

> The woman shall not wear that which pertaineth unto a man, neither shall a man put on a woman's garment; for all that do so are an abomination unto the Lord thy God (Deuteronomy 22:5).

Notwithstanding the Bible, not all cross dressing is or has been considered deviant. For instance, in an act known as the "drag show", homosexual men impersonate women to produce a form of entertainment chiefly for other homosexual men, but generally for anyone who is willing to watch (Tewksbury, 1994). Other people (of both sexes) cross dress with the hope of disguising their motives. Spies are an example. So are the male homosexuals mentioned in the following chapter who appear as females in an attempt to lure unsuspecting males into homosexual liaisons. Finally, cross dressing was permitted in Europe as early as the Middle Ages, as long as it occurred in theatre or during festivals or carnivals (Bullough and Bullough, 1993:61–66). Hanna (1988:57–58) examines its presence in dance historically and cross-culturally.

Transvestism is the term used for cross dressing that is done as an adjustment to an inner need or compulsion. In transvestism, cross dressing becomes an important part of the person's routine existence and is accompanied by an attempt to enact the corresponding sex-role behaviour. The transsexual at the transvestite stage is one type of transvestite. A second is the effeminate homosexual, or "drag queen", who adopts female habits of dress, speech, and behaviour. The drag queen — a relative rarity in homosexual circles — is nonetheless a genuine homosexual; he is not on the way to a transsexual career. But it is the third type of transvestite who is the subject of the remainder of this section. This person is variously known as the fetishistic, femmiphilic, or heterosexual transvestite.

Heterosexual transvestism is predominantly a male practice, whose causes are still in doubt. It is a deviant means to sexual excitement and the expression of a hidden second (feminine) self. Steiner (1985:357) believes that it begins covertly at around 10 to 12 years of age and is usually accompanied by sexual arousal and masturbation in front of a mirror. Transvestism may continue into or start up during early or middle adulthood. Some transvestites marry, and eventually some wives become aware of their spouses' special interest because sexual gratification with them can be achieved only when the transvestites wear one or more items of feminine apparel. Other married transvestites conceal their cross dressing, though they, too, experience a sexual thrill from their deviance. They further enjoy the temporary change in identity and the opportunity to express feminine personality traits (Knox, 1984:399). Indeed, cross dressing may lose some of its fetishistic or sexual arousal potential over the years, but it may continue for these latter reasons.

Feinbloom (1976:20) notes that some transvestites wear just a few items of feminine clothing, whereas others dress entirely as females, including the use of makeup and wigs. Most dress only in private settings, although a minority venture (fully cross dressed) into certain public places. Some transvestites attend clandestine gatherings with others (sometimes as members of a transvestite club) where most or all of those present are sartorially transformed.

The Transvestite Career

Buckner (1971) traces the transvestite career through five indistinct stages. The first lasts from approximately the ages of 5 to 14. During this stage, the young boy learns to associate particular items of female clothing with sexual arousal. Toward the end of the period, this association may lead to masturbation. These early developments, however, are not necessarily sexual. The boy may act out roles that he will never adopt in later life, such as those of mother. Or his mother may encourage certain feminine activities or mannerisms through which her son comes to develop a partially feminine self-conception. Whatever the impetus, cross dressing becomes a way of expressing some inner drive or state of mind.

The second stage commences when the adolescent transvestite realizes that he may be unable to perform male roles satisfactorily. Buckner's research revealed several possible reasons for this condition. Perhaps the individual is a perfectionist in his relationship with others. Perhaps he has an exaggerated idea of male role requirement, gained, for example, from men's magazines. Perhaps he is too physically weak to fulfill adequately certain male roles that are important in adolescence. Sports roles might be problematic for this reason. The situation may produce a fear of failure at those roles, a fear that may encompass the adolescent's perception of his ability to perform sexually as a male. Whether as cause or as effect, these factors may also be accompanied by a comparatively low sex drive.

The third stage occurs when the transvestite realizes that homosexuality is not to his liking. A general attraction to femininity and a sexual attraction to women are two reasons for this orientation. A third is that he may have become aware of the community's rejection of homosexuals. Finally, he may simply never have had the opportunity to explore homosexual behaviour. The one arrangement that is both satisfying and unthreatening is the fetishistic use of certain articles of female apparel (e.g., bra, panties) for sexual release through masturbation. Heterosexual in orientation, it keeps the transvestite clear of risky involvements with both women and other men. According to anomie theory, the arrangement is a kind of innovation of means for reaching an acceptable cultural goal, namely, heterosexual sex expression.

The fourth stage of the transvestite career "involves this elaboration of masturbation fantasies into the development of a feminine self" (Buckner, 1971:90). This is the stage during which the young man crosses the line between primary and secondary deviation. He begins to develop and enact a transvestite role, which may include taking a female name for that role, employing certain feminine gestures, wearing certain female garments, and using facial makeup. The role is usually enacted only in select circumstances, public or private. These personality changes take place during middle and late adolescence, and usually occur with little shaping from other sources. Association with other transvestites, their magazines, and their organizations is generally unavailable to the young transvestite; he discovers them later, if at all.

The final stage unfolds between the ages of 18 and 20, possibly later. At this time the individual comes to grips with and learns how to manage satisfactorily the dual masculine and feminine personality he has developed over the preceding years. Buckner (1971:92) explains how this is accomplished:

> Once the transvestite discovers that he has, in a sense, both male and female within himself, he can play out many of the culturally prescribed heterosexual patterns internally. He can, for example, give himself gifts of shoes and nightgowns. He can also provide many of the male-female complementarity expectations all by himself. After a hard day at the office he doesn't need to come home to a nurturant wife; he becomes a nurturant wife. Furthermore he has an undemanding gratification scheme. His feminine self is highly predictable, something like playing chess with himself, which fits in well with his fear of failure or his passivity. "Connie [a transvestite's femme name] isn't bossy, she isn't demanding, she doesn't fly into jealous rages. She exists only for me, and she knows I'm her lord and master. I like it that way," a transvestite writes about himself. He can also cathect the female role by dressing and acting it out, and have sexuality by masturbation at the same time, without the inconvenience of dealing with a real woman who might provide him with a failure or with some disconfirmation of his masculine identity.

Nevertheless, some transvestites do marry. They do so in the belief that, since their transvestism is heterosexual in orientation, marriage can provide a respectable sexual outlet which will help them quit their deviance. But the marriage eventually loses its capacity to sexually gratify some transvestites, who are then tempted to return to their old ways.

Studies by Buckner (1971), Feinbloom (1976), and Docter (1988: Ch. 7) indicate that all but a small percentage of transvestites' wives disapprove of their husbands' cross dressing. The wives' solutions to the problem vary. The solutions chosen are certainly major turning points in the transvestite's deviant career.

One common solution is divorce (Talamini, 1982:35). Another is insistence that the husband see a counsellor. Some wives may tolerate cross dressing, but only after it is diagnosed as an incurable or a difficult-to-cure "disease". Other wives, who are usually highly dependent on their partners, stoically tolerate their interests or oppose them minimally. A few wives accept the transvestite's argument that his questionable behaviour is necessary for him to achieve adequate self-fulfillment and personal integration.

Buckner (1971:94) observes that the situation has aspects of a romantic triangle, with the husband's other personality being the equivalent of a mistress. Just as he would give to an actual mistress, he wants to express his feminine self. And since he can find social and sexual satisfaction with his other self, he need not rely solely on his wife and marriage for these benefits.

In a small number of cases where the wife is genuinely accepting of the transvestite, different motives enter the picture. She may have lesbian tendencies. Perhaps she likes to please her husband even at his deviant extreme. Feinbloom (1976:108) reports that some of the wives she interviewed said their husbands could discuss the fine details of fashion, style, and other female interests in which the typical male is poorly versed. Because of their husbands' attraction to things female and feminine, these women occasionally received special gifts. It should be added, too, that some relationships prosper from a mutual effort to solve a difficult problem.

Over 20 years after Buckner published his five-stage model of the career of the male transvestite, Vern and Bonnie Bullough (1993:332) concluded that "two decades of research have added significantly to the data base, but the outlines of this pattern after the first cross-dressing episode seem valid at least for some male transvestites." In their "updated scenario" of Buckner's model, the Bulloughs (1993:333) add a preliminary step in becoming a transvestite: the presence of a genetic predisposition and a set of physiological factors that combine to create a boy who is less active and aggressive than his peers. They also note that the boy's mother may be the dominant figure in the family, and that the family and the local community may strongly stigmatize homosexuality (part of Buckner's first stage).

The Transvestite Lifestyle

Both Talamini (1982: Ch. 4) and Woodhouse (1989:23–35) have examined the organizational world of the transvestite, which basically functions at two levels: national and local. In the United States, where Talamini conducted his study, many transvestites are members of one of the 27 local groups comprising the Society for the Second Self (SSS). The organization's mission is to encourage members to have happy lives as cross dressers and to accept their special desire.

The SSS publishes a quarterly magazine, *Femme Mirror,* and a newsletter, and also operates a communications network. As noted earlier, the United States is also the home of the International Foundation for Gender Education, which is guided by much the same goals as the SSS, publishes a quarterly entitled *TV/TS Tapestry Journal,* and holds an annual convention. In England, Woodhouse made contact with a similar group, the Transvestite/Transsexual Support Group (TV/TS), whose local clubs are found throughout the country. Its mission is much the same as that of its American counterparts, and it publishes a monthly called *Glad Rag.*

Transvestites, or "TVs" as they call themselves, meet in the local clubs and chapters of their organizations for the purposes of sociable conversation, the discussion of mutual problems and interests, and the display of their feminine selves. According to the Fall 1994 issue of *TV/TS Tapestry Journal,* Canada has 11 such clubs, serving both transsexuals and transvestites, in or near Montréal, Ottawa, Toronto, Calgary, Edmonton, Kamloops, and Vancouver. The "transgendered" in Canada can participate further in their subculture through two periodicals: *The Canadian Cross-Dresser* and *Notes from the Underground,* published in Toronto and Ottawa, respectively.

Both Feinbloom (1976:71–77) and Woodhouse (1989:23–35) have conducted fieldwork on the routine meetings of the local groups, which exist primarily for the purpose of display. Members typically meet in a rented club room or inner-city apartment, where they cross dress for each other, examine samples of feminine apparel and cosmetics, and take pictures of one another dressed as women. At the meetings, there are refreshments, soft music, several wall mirrors, various magazines (fashion and pornographic), sex-oriented books, and a notice board filled with announcements. In a typical evening, between 5 and 20 TVs are present, most of whom either arrive dressed in women's clothes or change into them on the premises. Conversation centres chiefly on sports, work, jokes, and transvestite subjects. There is also a certain amount of picture taking and viewing. It is expected that all will refrain from overt displays of sex, such as masturbation.

To quote John Money (1974), transvestites have "two names, two wardrobes, two personalities". Transvestism is largely a private phenomenon. The survey conducted by Prince and Butler (1972) of 1300 subscribers to *Transvestia* revealed that half the sample kept their transvestism entirely secret. Only 10 to 13 percent ventured out in public — that is, outside their club's meeting room — dressed as a woman.

There is good reason for most transvestites to be reluctant to appear cross dressed in public. They are in approximately the same legal situation as transsexuals: many countries, including Canada, have no laws explicitly prohibiting cross dressing, but public order laws have been used against transvestites on occasion (Brierly, 1979:145). In short, transvestites have clearly wound up on the losing side of the value-conflict struggle over acceptable forms of sexual expression in our society. Arrests are possible because the transvestite may be more feminine in fantasy than in reality; male features and actions and uncustomary use of female apparel and makeup may arouse suspicion on the part of passersby and the police that this is no woman (Brierley, 1979:154–155).

Despite this societal reaction to their deviance, transvestites continue to justify their behaviour as both leisure and adjustment. Only 1 percent of the Prince and Butler sample wanted to rid themselves of their orientation, while 72 percent wanted to improve their ability to cross dress. Like the other sexual deviants we have discussed, transvestites prefer to remain as they are and convince society of their point of view. The appeal of transvestism to its devotees is evident in Viewpoint 3.2.

In connection with these matters, there is the feminist concern, forcefully raised by Raymond (1979), Eichler (1987), and Devor (1989) about any practice that encourages traditional sex-role stereotypes in a patriarchal society. They hold, for instance, that the modern male-to-female SRS can be interpreted as "female castration". It is another contemporary method of keeping women in their place, analogous to the nineteenth century use of hysterectomies to control unwanted pregnancies in "promiscuous" women. From the perspective of value-conflict theory, then, sex-change operations can be seen as serving male interests, particularly those of the medical establishment. Although SRS affects only a very few members of our society, it does keep a very small number "properly oriented" to the traditional female role. At bottom, traditional gender roles, both male and female, are arbitrary, socially constructed phenomena. The process by which they arise is explored at length by Foucault (1978) in his analysis of eighteenth and nineteenth century sexuality.

The relationship between transvestism and sex identity is more complicated than that between transsexualism and sex identity. Four motives for transvestism have been identified in this chapter: to play the drag queen role in homosexuality, to entrap heterosexual males in homosexual liaisons, to explore the world of femininity as a stage in a transsexual career, and to achieve sexual gratification and self-expression by wearing clothing of the other sex. It is evident, however, that transvestites sometimes redefine their reasons for cross dressing and may not understand fully why cross dressing is satisfying. For instance, subtle indeed is the redefinition of sex identity for the drag queen transvestite, who concludes that he really prefers other men because he is fundamentally a woman rather than because he is a homosexual man. We might legitimately ask whether the heterosexual transvestite is not really a psychological female.

As we move to the next chapter, on deviant sexual practices, it is useful to note that homosexuals and transsexuals regard themselves as being different from each other, with the latter being particularly concerned about the distinction. In fact, transsexuals are clearly not homosexual, even though male transsexuals pass through a homosexual stage. To use the words of C.A. Tripp (1987:26):

> It can be argued that while transsexuals are seldom homosexual, they are so uninterested in sexual activity and tend to be so focused-in on matters of role and of gender-identity that they really do not fit either heterosexual or homosexual descriptions.

VIEWPOINT 3.2

DIANA'S FIRST PUBLIC APPEARANCE

After about two years of practice in the techniques of femininity, I felt I was ready for the world. But is the world ready for Diana? After arrangements with another TV friend who agreed to be my male escort for the evening, I began the transformation into a sexy girl in her late twenties planning to have a few drinks and a few dances at a local and quiet club.

Upon my completion of an expert make-up and dressing ritual, I left on the arm of my boyfriend escort.

There were butterflies in my panties when we entered the moody and dimly lit lounge but the rush I felt was unlike anything you can imagine, unless of course you've experienced your first night out too. After a few drinks I was relaxed and felt very fem. I enjoyed the attention that my shapely legs were getting from the boys. A solo guitarist was entertaining that night and a few couples were dancing.

After a while I had the urge to use the ladies' room and excused myself from the table. My escort headed off to the men's at the same time. I was all alone in the powder room when I noticed that the music had stopped. No big deal. It was just break time. So what do girls do when the music stops? They collect all their friends and head for the washroom, right? Well before you could say "drag," the bathroom was filled with girls, fixing hair, touching up lip gloss, and making tinkle sounds in the stalls. I was so worried that someone would talk to me.

My voice is not female so in a panic I exited the room and decided to wait in the corridor for my date's exit from the men's room.

Well, no date to be seen anywhere. An old lady is heading towards the girls' room and stops to ask me if it's crowded with ladies. Well, in my best female voice, I respond and she smiles and disappears into the washroom. Whew!

After an eternity, my date appears and poor Diana is thoroughly shook up. We decide to leave. Now, for female experience Number 1. Have you ever walked across a polished hardwood dance floor in 4-inch spike heels? The first time is an unforgettable feat. Don't think about it or you'll surely fall down.

Safely outside now, I giggle uncontrollably. I loved every second of it. That was five years ago. Now I take every opportunity to go out en femme that my life allows. I love being a transvestite!

Source: TV Guys, 2, 3:6–7.

Moreover, post-operative transsexuals do not always take on the sexual orientation corresponding to their new genitalia. Research evidence suggests that a large majority do so, however, with the result that their orientation is heterosexual (Blanchard, 1985:382–390; Bullough and Bullough, 1993:265–266). But a minority become, or remain, homosexual or bisexual, while some become asexual. The psychology and sociology of sex change are perhaps even more complicated than its physiology and anatomy.

CONCLUSIONS

This chapter has covered two forms of adjustive deviance centred on sexual identity. Clearly, sex-role deviance reaches its extreme expression in transsexualism as *total* sex-identity rejection. Many transsexuals imitate and emulate as best they can the thoughts and actions of the opposite sex. Their imitation and emulation are, however, of common sense thought and action as stereotypically interpreted by the individual. Indeed, as Billings and Urban (1982) point out, it is the common sense stereotype which patients use to convince physicians that they are transsexuals, and which physicians use to evaluate the sex-role claims of their patients.

As we have just seen, the extremes of transsexualism, especially when carried through to SRS, have raised a number of questions. Billings and Urban (1982) hold that physicians, in their eagerness to do "interesting" medicine, have been far too indiscriminate in whom they operate on. The medical profession itself has admitted that people who were not demonstrably transsexual, such as psychotics, masochists, and homosexuals, have been sexually transformed. Billings and Urban also question the true value to the patient of the sex-change procedures. After all, they produce a less-than-perfect conversion to the desired sexual identity. Yet after reviewing the follow-up studies of sex reassignment surgery, Docter (1988:69) has expressed cautious optimism: "Very little is factually known about the social or psychological effects of sexual reassignment, although it seems well-established from many reports that most individuals indicate they are happier and more comfortable in the cross-gender role."

NOTES

1 DSM-III was criticized by Kirk and Kutchins (1992) for its weak diagnostic reliability, a problem that also plagued the first and second editions. Whether the problem has been significantly ameliorated in the fourth edition remains to be seen. Meanwhile, it is important to remember that the estimates of the prevalence of particular mental disorders made in the present book are based on diagnostic criteria set out in the first three editions, and so must be accepted with caution.

SUGGESTED READING

Bolin, Anne. *In Search of Eve: Transsexual Rites of Passage*. New York: Bergin & Garvey, 1988. Bolin, an anthropologist, reports on her field research on the symbolic death and rebirth of sexual identities among a group of transsexuals.

Bullough, Vern L. and Bonnie Bullough, *Cross Dressing, Sex, and Gender*. Philadelphia: University of Pennsylvania Press, 1993. A comprehensive review of research and writing on cross dressing in history and modern times and across cultures. The Bulloughs specialize in sex and gender studies.

Gosselin, Chris and Glenn Wilson. *Sexual Variations: Fetishism, Sado-masochism and Transvestism*. London: Faber & Faber, 1980. A study of the personality and sexual fantasies and behaviour of members of fetishistic, sadomasochistic, transvestite, and transsexual clubs in Britain.

Raymond, Janet G. *The Transsexual Empire*. Boston: Beacon Press, 1979. A feminist view of the traditional medical treatment of transsexuals, particularly constructed women.

Talamini, John T. *Boys Will Be Girls: The Hidden World of the Heterosexual Male Transvestite*. Washington, DC: University Press of America, 1982. An empirical study of the lifestyle and social organization of transvestites. The book also examines the historical and cross-cultural aspects of transvestism, as well as the developments of androgyny and second self.

Woodhouse, Annie. *Fantastic Women: Sex, Gender, and Transvestism.* New Brunswick, NJ: Rutgers University Press, 1989. A sociological field study of the costs and rewards of cross dressing in a sample of men living in London, England.

REFERENCES

American Psychiatric Association. *Diagnostic and Statistical Manual of Mental Disorders.* (4th ed.) Washington, DC, 1994.

Benjamin, Harry. *The Transsexual Phenomenon.* New York: Julian Press, 1966.

Bibby, Reginald W. and Donald C. Posterski. *Teen Trends: A Nation in Motion.* Toronto: Stoddart, 1992.

Billings, Dwight B. and Thomas Urban. "The Socio-Medical Construction of Transsexualism," *Social Problems,* 1982, 29:266–282.

Blanchard, Ray. "Gender Dysphoria and Gender Reorientation." In *Gender Dysphoria: Development, Research, Management,* edited by Betty W. Steiner, pp. 365–392. New York: Plenum, 1985.

Bolin, Anne. *In Search of Eve: Transsexual Rites of Passage.* New York: Bergin & Garvey, 1988.

Brierley, Harry. *Transvestism: A Handbook with Case Studies for Psychologists, Psychiatrists, and Counsellors.* Oxford: Pergamon Press, 1979.

Brown, Ian. "Altered States," *The Globe and Mail,* 1986, Saturday, November 15: D5.

Buckner, H. Taylor. *Deviance, Reality, and Change.* New York: Random House, 1971.

Bullough, Vern L. and Bonnie Bullough. *Cross Dressing, Sex, and Gender.* Philadelphia: University of Pennsylvania Press, 1993.

Devor, Holly. *Gender Blending: Confronting the Limits of Duality.* Bloomington, IN: Indiana University Press, 1987.

Docter, Richard F. *Transvestites and Transsexuals: Toward a Theory of Cross-Gender Behavior.* New York: Plenum, 1988.

Drag Show. Woollahra, New South Wales, Australia: Currency Press, 1977.

Driscoll, James P. "Transsexuals." In *Deviant Life-Styles,* edited by James M. Henslin, pp. 167–190. New Brunswick, NJ: Transaction Books, 1977.

Ebaugh, Helen R.F. *Becoming and EX: The Process of Role Exit.* Chicago: University of Chicago Press, 1988.

Eichler, Margrit. "Sex Change Operations: The Last Bulwark of the Double Standard." In *Gender Roles: Doing What Comes Naturally?,* edited by E.D. Salamon and B.W. Robinson, pp. 69–78. Toronto: Methuen, 1987.

Feinbloom, Deborah H. *Transvestites and Transsexuals.* New York: Delacourte Press/Seymour Lawrence, 1976.

Foucault, Michel. *The History of Sexuality.* (Translated by Robert Hurley) New York: Pantheon Books, 1978.

Green, Richard. *Sexual Identity Conflict in Children and Adults.* New York: Basic Books, 1974.

Hanna, Judith L. *Dance, Sex, and Gender.* Chicago: University of Chicago Press, 1988.

Hoenig, J. "The Management of Transsexualism." In *Sexual Behaviour in Canada,* edited by Benjamin Schlesinger, pp. 162–170. Toronto: University of Toronto Press, 1977.

Hoeing, J. et al. "Epidemiological Aspects of Transsexualism," *Psychiatria Clinica,* 1973, 6:65–80.

Kando, Thomas. *Sex Change: The Achievement of Gender Identity Among Feminized Transsexuals.* Springfield, IL: Charles C. Thomas, 1973.

Kirk, Stuart A. and Herb Kutchins. *The Selling of the DSM: The Rhetoric of Science in Psychiatry.* New York: Aldine de Gruyter, 1992.

Knox, David. *Human Sexuality.* St. Paul, MN: West Publishing Co., 1984.

Lothstein, Leslie Martin. *Female-to-Male Transsexualism.* London: Routledge and Kegan Paul, 1983.

Matto, Michele S. "The Transsexual in Society." In *Deviance* (2nd ed.), edited by Simon Dinitz, Russell C. Dynes, and Alfred C. Clarke, pp. 248–258. New York: Oxford University Press, 1975.

Money, John. "Two Names, Two Wardrobes, Two Personalities," *Journal of Homosexuality,* 1974, 1:56–70.

_________ and Anke A. Ehrhardt. *Man and Woman, Boy and Girl.* Baltimore, MD: Johns Hopkins University Press, 1972.

_________ and Patricia Tucker. *Sexual Signatures: On Being a Man or a Woman.* Boston: Little Brown, 1975.

Pauly, Ira B. "Female Transsexualism: Part II," *Archives of Sexual Behavior,* 1974, 3:509–526.

Prince, V. and P.M. Butler. "Survey of 504 Cases of Transvestism," *Psychological Reports,* 1972, 31:903–917.

Raymond, Janice G. *The Transsexual Empire.* Boston: Beacon Press, 1979.

Risman, Barbara J. "The (Mis)acquisition of Gender Identity Among Transsexuals," *Qualitative Sociology,* 1982, 5:312–325.

Simon, William. "Sexual Orientation." In *Encyclopedia of Sociology,* Vol. 4, edited by Edgar F. Borgatta and Marie L. Borgatta, pp. 1762–1772. New York: Macmillan, 1992.

Sorensen, T. and P. Hertoft. "Transsexualism as a Nosological Unity in Men and Women," *Acta Psychiatrica Scandinavica,* 1980, 61:135–151.

Steiner, Betty W., Ray Blanchard, and Kenneth J. Zucker. "Introduction." In *Gender Dysphoria: Development, Research, Management,* edited by Betty W. Steiner, pp. 1–10, New York: Plenum, 1985.

Stoller, Robert J. *Sex and Gender,* Vol. 11: *The Transsexual Experiment.* New York: Jason Aronson, 1974.

Talamini, John T. *Boys Will Be Girls: The Hidden World of the Heterosexual Male Transvestite.* Washington, DC: University Press of America, 1982.

Tewksbury, Richard. "Gender Construction and the Female Impersonator: The Process of Transforming He to She," *Deviant Behavior,* 1994, 15:27–44.

Tripp, C.A. *The Homosexual Matrix.* (2nd ed.) New York: Meridian, 1987.

Woodhouse, Annie. *Fantastic Women: Sex, Gender, and Transvestism.* New Brunswick, NJ: Rutgers University Press, 1989.

4

DEVIANT SEXUAL PRACTICES

The preceding chapter focused predominantly on deviant sexual identities. Transsexualism and transvestism, when they are not clearly engaged in for heterosexual gratification, constitute two major examples of social deviance with reference to sexual category. This chapter extends the discussion by examining some of the prominent deviant sexual practices or patterns of behaviour found in our society. We turn first to homosexuality. Next, we consider as deviant the watching of sex: the consumption of pornography and striptease shows. The chapter ends with a look at group and extramarital sex.

HOMOSEXUALITY

Our moral norms on sexuality are part of the Judeo-Christian heritage that underlies contemporary Canadian society. Ancient Judaism had a most practical outlook on sexuality: its sole purpose was reproduction. That is, male ejaculation for purposes other than propagation, such as masturbation, homosexual or heterosexual fellatio, or anal intercourse, was clearly forbidden. These "abnormal" acts were seen as wasteful (of the male seed), unclean, against God's will, and enjoyable where enjoyment was inappropriate.

DeLamater (1981:264) points out that the Christian tradition further condemns non-reproductive, or recreational, sexuality on the grounds that it threatens the stability of the family. Incest, adultery, homosexuality, and prostitution are threatening to the extent that they discourage legitimate marital unions or compromise the intimacy of existing unions. In short, sexuality, by traditional Judeo-

Christian standards, is acceptable only when conducted for reproductive purposes with one's spouse when conception is physiologically possible. It follows that intercourse is also to be avoided during menstruation and pregnancy and after menopause.

Curiously, the early Christian writers inveighed almost exclusively against male sexual deviance. Mention of female sexual deviance, including lesbianism, was rare indeed. In fact, if the early church authorities wrote about lesbianism at all, it was usually to deny that it existed (Boswell, 1980:158).

Clearly, then, religion, the family, and, today, the media are the institutions that control sexuality in Canadian society.[1] It is also clear that the proscription of non-reproductive sex has now faded into oblivion. Masturbation and coition during pregnancy and menopause are no longer deviant, except in special circumstances (e.g., masturbation by married men). Such acts as heterosexual fellatio and anal intercourse exist today in a sort of moral twilight zone of private acceptance, practised by some and scorned by others. Male homosexuality, though tolerated more today than previously, is still on the public's list of deviant forms of behaviour.

Lesbianism, it appears, has suffered a fate opposite that of male homosexuality. It has moved from its non-problematic status in Biblical times to its present-day moderately threatening status as a form of tolerable deviance. What happened? Those who study women from a feminist perspective offer a plausible answer to this question: lesbians are considered deviant because "lesbianism threatens heterosexual males with the possibility that they will be rendered sexually superfluous" (Schur, 1984:118). That is, there is a male-generated belief in societies such as Canada that women seek each other primarily for sexual satisfaction, which they prefer to the satisfaction they receive from men. This belief, however, is at best a partial truth. We shall see later that there is evidence that sexuality is only one of the several reasons for lesbianism, and a minor one at that.

Legal and Social Status

The legal status of homosexuality is comparatively clear-cut in Canada. Present Canadian law follows the recommendations of Britain's Wolfenden Committee (Committee on Homosexual Offences and Prostitution, 1957), which declared that the law should stay out of the private lives of individuals and refrain from enforcing any particular pattern of behaviour. In 1968, sexual activities conducted in private between husband and wife or two consenting adults aged 21 or over were excepted from the Criminal Code of Canada. According to Goode (1994:237), 28 American states have taken a similar route. Despite a National Institute of Mental Health task force report (Livingood, 1972) which agreed with the Wolfenden Committee, homosexual acts between willing partners are still illegal in nearly half of all American states.

Freedom from legal constraints does not mean, however, that homosexuals escape the public view that their sexual orientation is deviant. For example, Rayside and Bowler (1988:649) observed that

> over the course of a generation, a major shift towards a more liberal position on the principle of equality rights for lesbians and gay men has been evident. Strong moral disapproval of homosexuality persists, however, as do fears rooted in traditional stereotypes which characterize homosexuals as deviant or sick, and threatening to children.

On a parallel note, 81 percent of a sample drawn by the *Gallup Report* (1991) believed that homosexuals are more accepted today than 25 years ago, an increase of 1 percent from 1988. In Canada, gay men and lesbians are now officially welcome in the military (Bindman, 1992) and, in 1990, the United Church reaffirmed its recognition of the right of all men and women, regardless or sexual orientation, to apply for the ministry (*Calgary Herald*, 1990). But older Canadians living in small communities and having a strong religious commitment have been more likely to see both male and female homosexuality as wrong than younger, less religious Canadians in larger communities. As for lesbians, while they, too, confront a hostile society (Martin and Lyon, 1972:28; Herek, 1993), Brooks (1981) found in her survey of lesbians in the United States that they regard being female (not deviant) as more problematic than being lesbian (deviant).

Male homosexuality is not always stigmatized to the same degree in other societies as it is in Canada. Ford and Beach (1951:130) studied 76 folk societies of which 49, or 64 percent, had male homosexual patterns which were considered acceptable at some time in the life cycle for certain members of the societies. Homosexuality may be a phase through which men are expected to pass. Or it may be normal behaviour for those in a particular role, such as priest or shaman, or for those in a certain social class, such as the upper classes in ancient Greece and Rome (see Greenberg, 1988: Ch. 2 and 3).

It is evident that in Canada and many other societies widespread male homosexuality is considered deviant and stigmatized because it is seen as dysfunctional: procreation and hence the perpetuation of a society can only take place through heterosexual intercourse (unless artificial insemination were to become an acceptable alternative). As mentioned earlier, both male and female homosexuality is dysfunctional for the family institution to the extent that it discourages marital unions or challenges the functioning of those already established. The dysfunctional status of homosexuality helps explain its deviant status. Its functionality is examined shortly.

Homosexuality is also deviant because the men and women who practise it have found themselves on the losing side of the value conflict over whose sex norms will prevail. In Western societies, however, this value conflict is different for males and females. There is a growing literature (Schur, 1984:118–132) suggesting that the lesbian's lifestyle is, in significant part, an attempt to escape male control and the traditional female role. Brooks (1981:31), for example, found that only 14 percent of the lesbians whom she surveyed defined sexual intercourse as unattractive, whereas 55 percent said they were displeased with male dominance and another 26 percent were unhappy with women's traditional role expectations. In Hedblom's (1975) sample, 48 percent had achieved orgasm with a man.

On the other hand, the male homosexual in the modern industrial society is often in conflict with that society only in the domain of sexual practices. He is sexually attracted to other men, often many other men, and tends to be promiscuous in his search for sex partners. By contrast, a lesbian seeks an enduring relationship with another woman (Rothblum, 1989:7). Sexual relations are only one benefit, sometimes not even an especially important benefit, sought in the relationship (Tripp, 1987:144n).

Male Homosexual Lifestyles

There is a wide variety of male homosexuals, as well as of situations in which they pursue sexual relations. Our discussion of homosexuals and their situations will be organized around the concept of lifestyle. Within each lifestyle there exists a particular homosexual role filled by men with interests and personalities consonant with it. Further, we are concerned with men who routinely engage in certain homosexual activities. Some of these men identify themselves as homosexual; others deny that they are homosexuals. However they see themselves, they are much more than mere dabblers or experimenters in deviant sex (MacIntosh, 1981). Moreover, they all must live with the possibility of discovery and stigma for a kind of behaviour they know the public disvalues. Five lifestyles and types of homosexuals are covered here. Four have been identified and described by Humphreys (1975:111–129) in a study conducted in the United States.

Homosexuals who are known in the gay world as **trade** are usually family men, married or divorced, with children. Most of them work at semiskilled occupations; most have normal masculine looks and mannerisms. In Humphreys' sample, their average age was 38.

For trade, conjugal sex relations are rare, which is one reason for seeking the impersonal sex available in homosexual "tearooms" (an in-group term of unknown origins) (Humphreys, 1975:2). Tearooms are public restrooms in parks, department stores, and air and bus terminals, and similar places where male homosexuals know that other men are available for fleeting, on-the-spot, sexual activity. Impersonal sex of all sorts has the advantage of being less involving, less risky socially, than heterosexual love affairs. It is less lonely than masturbation and cheaper, for men of modest income, than patronizing a male prostitute. The deviant lifestyle of trade is therefore highly secretive, filled with worries about accidental discovery by friends or acquaintances and apprehension by the police, who raid the tearooms from time to time. Today there is the additional worry about AIDS. The homosexual activities of trade are limited to their encounters in tearooms and to occasional liaisons with male prostitutes.

Ambisexuals are also family men, though they tend to have fewer children. They are somewhat older than trade, with an average age of 43 in Humphreys' sample. They are also of a higher socioeconomic status. That is, they are likely to have a college degree and hold an executive position or own a business. With more or less independent employment, they find it possible to hire personnel who share their interests, sexual and otherwise. Moreover, they typically have good sexual relationships with their wives. Thus, the ambisexual is bisexual in orientation, and seeks additional sexual pleasure in the tearooms. Stealth adds to the enjoyment of the illicit encounter. As a successful, self-assured upper-middle-class man in the community, he believes he can handle the problems that may arise from unwanted exposure of his homosexuality. The ambisexual's homosexuality may even be functional for him and his family: "It is possible that the sexual activity in his favourite tearoom may actually be functional for the maintenance of his marital stability" (Humphreys, 1975:122).

Closet queens are the third type of male homosexual. They are usually single and employed in a clerical, sales, or minor white-collar position. Most have completed high school only, although some in Humphreys' sample had a couple of years of university education as well. They are generally lonely men with few friends, none of whom is homosexual. Their average age in the sample was 35.

Of the types discussed here, the closet queen worries most about being caught and labelled homosexual. Nevertheless, he takes the risk that goes with patronizing tearooms and with "cruising", soliciting liaisons with older teenagers and young adult males whom he encounters on the streets. Those males who are not homosexual reject the advances of the closet queen. Others are prostitutes who sell their services to "queers", usually of the trade and closet queen types.

The category of **male prostitute** was not discussed by Humphreys. Ginsburg's (1977) summary of studies of male prostitutes indicates that they typically deny being homosexual, at least during this stage of their deviant career.[2] Still, these men become sexually excited enough to maintain an erection and ejaculate when fellatio is performed by another male. Ginsburg reports that such reactions have led analysts to conclude that male prostitutes are actually homosexual. Field studies undertaken by Visano (1987:145) and Luckenbill (1985:139) confirm this conclusion.

Most male prostitutes meet their clients on the street and engage in sex in a client's car or apartment, or in a hotel room. One study, however, suggests that there are also houses of male prostitution, which operate much like heterosexual brothels (Pittman, 1977). Edna Salamon (1989) has described a British homosexual escort agency. Wherever they perform their services, male prostitutes appear to justify them as both work and leisure.

Gays comprise the fourth category identified by Humphreys (1975). According to his study, gays are usually unmarried, young (average age of 24 in the sample), and more involved in a pervasive homosexual lifestyle than all the preceding types. The gays studied by Humphreys were college students or college graduates. It is from the gay–lesbian scene (discussed below) that gays learn of the tearooms and other places in the city for participating in impersonal sex. The typical gay is employed as an artist or beautician or in some other occupation where his sexual interests are unlikely to cause alarm.

Most of the gay's friends and social contacts are connected with the homosexual scene. Unlike the other categories of homosexuals, he eventually develops an interest in personal sex, which is part of an enduring, often lengthy, relationship.

Impersonal encounters in such places as tearooms become infrequent, chosen only when nothing else is available.

The Gay–Lesbian Scene The gay–lesbian scene is composed of a variety of distinctive establishments, services, and behavioural patterns whose extent depends on the local level of tolerance and the size of the city in which the scene is located. In Canada, this scene is most extensively developed in Toronto, the centre of homosexual activity in the country. For practising male homosexuals in Toronto, there are bars, baths, tearooms, restaurants, bookstores, churches, and residences that are patronized largely or exclusively by gays (see Kinsman, 1987:14ff).

In addition, there is a diversity of organizations, some 400 in Canada according to the most recently available list, which was published in the September 1985 issue of *The Body Politic* (a now defunct Toronto-based, nationally circulated monthly that promoted homosexual liberation). Some serve gays, some serve lesbians, some serve both. There are groups that book speakers, organize homosexuals for athletic pursuits, promote research into the history and problems of homosexuals, and run lending libraries of books and magazines. Several organizations offer counselling for special categories of homosexuals, including alcoholics, the handicapped, and those with AIDS, as well as for parents, spouses, and children of homosexuals. There are legal aid societies for homosexuals. Gay professionals have organized in Vancouver, Toronto, and Montréal. Last but not least are the political pressure groups, which lobby local, provincial, and federal governments for fairer laws for and treatment of homosexuals.

The gay–lesbian scene also contains many local events, among them dances, picnics, rallies, camping trips, ocean cruises (Jahr, 1978), theatre productions, and potluck suppers. And, according to the September 1985 issue of *The Body Politic*, 28 periodicals link members of the homosexual scene in towns and cities across the country. These publications carry articles on the campaign for homosexual liberation, lists and dates of events, reviews of books and films, and accounts of the treatment of homosexuals by straights, all interlaced with commercial advertisements aimed at gay clientele.

For the gay, opportunities to meet other gays for one-night stands possibly leading to an enduring relationship are paramount. Hence, certain bars, beaches, baths, hotels, street corners, movie theatres, and sections of municipal parks become known as places for such encounters and an important aspect of every local gay scene. In larger cities, these places may be differentiated by the type, race, ethnicity, and social class of homosexuals who frequent them. If sexual satisfaction is unavailable here, the gay can always turn to the tearooms.

Female Homosexual Lifestyles

The most recent evidence on lesbians indicates that they are now much less inclined to see themselves as homosexuals of a particular type than they previously were. Ettore's (1980) comprehensive study of lesbians in England suggests that many of them are taking pride in their capacity to relate sexually to each other in ways that are neither traditionally masculine nor traditionally feminine. The distinctions of **butch** — a lesbian who dresses and behaves according to masculine appearance norms — and **femme** — one who dresses and behaves according to feminine appearance norms — are now found chiefly among middle-aged women (Lewis, 1979; Auger, 1990:27). The younger lesbians described by Ettore are likely to be what the New York activist group the Radicalesbians call a **woman-identified-woman** (Faraday, 1981:128).

The woman-identified-woman is defined broadly in terms of her entire female gender identity, rather than narrowly in terms of her sexuality, as many heterosexual men and even some heterosexual women tend to do when talking about lesbians. Barbara Ponse (1984:28) lists three components of lesbianism that may be said to correspond to the woman-identified-woman type:

1 Some lesbians are attracted to another woman in particular or other women in general on a physical basis or an emotional basis or both.
2 Some dislike or have no interest in men at a time in life such as early adulthood when these attitudes are considered deviant by the heterosexual community.
3 Some reject the stereotyped woman's role.

It is important to note that some woman-identified-women *cannot* be described by point 2 above. Others, however, can be described by all three.

The practices of cruising and impersonal sex and the meeting places where they are conducted hold little interest for lesbians. The lesbians studied by Saghir and Robins (1973) said they had never engaged in sex in a public place. While the gay–lesbian scene includes lesbian bars and coffeehouses, they are rarely used for arranging one-night stands. Rather, their clientele finds friendly conversation there. When there is a search, it is for intimacy with another woman, only part of which is sexual. In such places, then, one woman may meet another woman to whom she eventually becomes romantically attracted. She may subsequently establish an enduring relationship with her in a common residence based on shared interests, tastes, and personal and sexual attraction. A more recent summary of research, carried out by Rothblum (1989:7–8), demonstrates that this description of the lesbian lifestyle still holds true.

Lesbians are active at the organizational level of the gay–lesbian scene in matters pertaining to their special interests and problems. In large cities, one is likely to find various counselling groups for lesbians in general, and for lesbians who are victims of incest or are mothers in particular. Sometimes lesbians join with gays in religious, ethnic, educational, and political activist groups to fight for legal and attitudinal changes that benefit all homosexuals. At other times they carry on their fight alone, as in the case of the different national and Ottawa-based organizations discussed by Carmen Paquette (1990).

Possibly the most vibrant part of the lesbian side of the gay–lesbian scene is that organized around the principles of lesbian–feminism. Wolf's (1979) study of the lesbian–feminist community in the San Francisco area demonstrates the extent to which homosexuality can become a way of life for women, just as it can for men. Wolf found numerous organizations for lesbian women. Newspapers, magazines, and books written by and for lesbians were readily available. A monthly newsletter facilitated communication throughout the community. A subculture of music, art, literature, and film helped members support one another with meetings, informal gatherings, and telephone conversations.

One of the principles of lesbian–feminism was briefly mentioned earlier in this chapter: women can find a significant level of warmth, equality, understanding, and affection among themselves that they cannot find in the heterosexual world (see Viewpoint 4.1). Lesbian–feminists say that they seek these qualities within a framework of sexuality suitable to the nature of women and within an identity of themselves as women. It is no wonder, then, that men and women in the gay–lesbian scene tend to go their separate ways, except when it is advantageous to join together to fight homosexual oppression from society at large or to pass as heterosexual. In this regard, Barry Adam (1987:92) describes the differences in orientation that have been driving the gay and lesbian movements since the early 1970s:

> Men took for granted many of the social conditions that made it possible for them to be gay. But lesbians needed to address fundamental problems facing all women — such as equal opportunity in employment and violence against women — in order to have sufficient independence to become lesbians.

In short, analyses of the homosexual scene and its members must proceed from both a male and a female perspective. With this in mind, we turn now to homosexual careers.

The Male Homosexual Career

Risman and Schwartz (1988) note that the etiology of homosexuality continues to dominate intellectual thought in the social and behavioural sciences which, today, follows two distinct models: **essentialist** and **constructionist**. The first holds that each person has, as part of the core of his or her personality, a true, essential, sexual self. This self, which some see as innate and others see as established in early childhood, is immutable. The essentialists argue that people *are* homosexual or heterosexual. The constructionists, by contrast, hold that people *do* things defined by society as homosexual or heterosexual. According to this view, people choose partners of the same or the opposite sex on the basis of the social opportunities and systems of meaning available to them.

Risman and Schwartz (1988:128–130) have found that the empirical support for the essentialist model is extremely thin. Tripp (1987:ix, Ch. 5) says that the theories comprising it portray homosexuality as a kind of blocked or damaged heterosexuality. Since they concentrate on the negative, theories of this sort are bound to fail. Rather, as Tripp observes, the very term "sexual attraction" implies that sexual choice involves positive motives, "real or imagined benefits a person

VIEWPOINT 4.1

AFFECTION IN A LESBIAN RELATIONSHIP

Susan and Lori care a great deal about each other and they have a good life together. Their one major source of contention is that Lori constantly pushes for "more romance" in the relationship. She asks to be touched, held, kissed, and courted, incessantly. At first, Susan was tolerant of these demands. She, too, felt the need for a lot of physical contact and time spent expressing affection. But now, three years later, she has become impatient with the intensity of Lori's demands on her.

If Susan forgets to kiss Lori when she comes home, Lori pouts for hours. If Susan does not tell Lori she loves her before they go to sleep at night, Lori lies awake and eventually wakes Susan to ask her if there is anything wrong. When they sit together watching television Lori wants to be held. If Susan moves away from her, she looks hurt and worried.

Periodically, Susan has had enough of this, and she tries to talk to Lori about it. These conversations do not work very well. Susan says, "Lori, you know I love you. I wouldn't be here with you if I didn't love you. You are so easily hurt by things I don't even know I'm doing."

Lori answers, "I don't think it's too much to ask to have a little affection from your own lover."

Susan says, "A little affection? You are a bottomless pit. No matter what I do it isn't enough."

Lori says, "That's not true. If you would just loosen up this relationship would be more fun. Don't you believe in romance?"

"Sure I believe in romance, but I also believe in reading and washing dishes and seeing friends and talking on the telephone and cooking and driving the car. Life is not just about sweet talk and holding hands and kissing and hugging. We're not a couple of moon-eyed teenagers."

"You are really cold."

"No, I'm not. I'm just not a full-time smoocher like you. I'm a regular grown-up with lots of different interests."

"Oh, and I suppose I'm not."

"Of course you are, but your main interest seems to be playing lovebirds. Enough already."

Lori begins to pout. "I guess it's obvious. You don't love me as much as I love you."

Susan erupts, "I love you. You, the person. I do not love the bottomless pit."

Lori is now angry, hurt, and frightened.

Susan is frustrated and resentful.

They have this conversation many times. It is the theater of their relationship.

Source: B. Berzon. *Permanent Partners: Building Gay and Lesbian Relationships that Last.* New York: Penguin, 1990, pp. 71–72.

hopes to gain by a sexual conquest, by 'possessing' the partner" (Tripp, 1987:74). In the language of Chapter 1, the sexual aspects of homosexuality constitute, among other things, an adjustment, which is achieved by developing a special (i.e., deviant) sexual value system.

Tripp says that, just as in the case of heterosexuality, there are many ways in which homosexuality may take root. Indeed, the broad pattern seems to be the same in both orientations. Through ego modelling after older males and females, younger males and females become attracted to certain qualities (e.g., mannerisms, accomplishments, characteristics, personality traits) exemplified in these models. Over the years, a unique heterosexual or homosexual value system emerges in each of us that predisposes us toward members of the opposite sex or the same sex who possess the valued qualities.

Further, some of these qualities eventually become eroticized. Tripp holds that the eroticized attributes are sought, in part, because they complement what those who seek them want for themselves inasmuch as they lack them. Essentially, the sought-after rewards of homosexual and heterosexual complementation are identical: the symbolic possession of those attributes of a partner which, when added to one's own, achieve the illusion of completeness (Tripp, 1987:93). For instance, the heterosexual male comes to value sexually the female shape and touch, while the homosexual male perhaps comes to value sexually male masculinity and aggressiveness.

One's sexual orientation usually develops during childhood and early adolescence, though change is always possible. This orientation includes one's sexual value system. Plummer (1981:72) notes that individuals are initially quite unaware of their orientation. Key sexual experiences in adolescence and early adulthood, however, may eventually come to be consciously defined as rewarding, in significant part because they facilitate the aforementioned complementation. Hence, they are worth seeking again. When these experiences are with members of the same sex, homosexuality may have been initiated.

In a study of 50 male homosexuals in Britain, Scholfield (1965) learned that a large majority of the sample had had sex with another male by the time they had reached adulthood. But a same-sex orientation and an interest in seeking more same-sex experiences do not necessarily mean that one identifies oneself, either publicly or privately, as homosexual. For instance, male homosexuals may reject the homosexual identity because they do not see themselves as fitting the stereotype held by heterosexuals (e.g., lisp, limp wrist, feminine gestures). Late adolescents do recognize, however, that sex with another male is not the norm and therefore try to conceal such sexual attractions as well as any other evidence of a same-sex orientation.

Meanwhile, homosexual contacts are sought and homosexual activities engaged in. Attempts to avoid discovery and stigma during this period of life may move a man from the primary to the secondary phase of deviance. To the extent that his everyday life is spent seeking contacts, avoiding police harassment, concealing these activities from "straight" friends and relatives, and possibly trying to keep up the appearance of heterosexuality, homosexuality becomes an all-consuming concern.

As secondary deviation sets in, it becomes increasingly difficult for the homosexual to deny to himself his different sexual orientation. Perhaps recognition is forced by arrest or police interrogation, or by the suspicions of heterosexual friends and relatives. Sometimes recognition comes with the discovery of the gay–lesbian scene, into which the newly arrived gay finds himself fitting well, to his surprise. To the extent that he participates in the scene, there is pressure from other gays to acknowledge his homosexuality publicly.

Such public acknowledgement is the main turning point in the male homosexual career. Referred to as **coming out**, it is a process of change in one's self-identity which occurs in three interrelated stages (Plummer, 1981:101): seeing oneself as a homosexual, identifying oneself to other gays as homosexual, and learning from other gays the justifications for homosexuality. According to Dank (1974:181), in the second stage of coming out the homosexual learns to regard his sexual orientation as legitimate, rather than as a matter for shame or concern. Dank's research suggests that the average age for coming out is 21. About 35 percent of his sample came out between the ages 15 and 19, about 31 percent between 20 and 24, and about 22 percent at age 25 or beyond.

In short, a person's homosexuality is a variable condition. It can be covert at some point, because the wider community disapproves of homosexual behaviour. It can subsequently become overt to a degree when the man leaves the "closet" and announces his sexual orientation. Nevertheless, many homosexuals never come out, perhaps because, as we have seen, they also have a heterosexual orientation and are often married, perhaps happily so. Coming out is not a career turning point faced by all homosexuals.

Recently, coming out has become an unexpected — and unintended — turning point for some prominent closet homosexuals. In these cases, coming out occurred through the practice of "outing", the public disclosure of the homosexuality of certain leading males in society. Viewpoint 4.2 further describes outing and the reasons used to justify it.

The gay scene into which some male homosexuals come out is largely for young people. The middle-aged homosexual finds the lifestyle there considerably less appealing than do his younger friends. Still, there is no evidence that older homosexual men are any more anxious or lonely than the habitués of the gay scene (Weinberg and Williams, 1975:310; Greene, 1994:14). They do engage less often in sex, but the same is true for heterosexual men of the same age. For older homosexual men, this pattern may be explained, in part, by the fact that sexual partners are not as easy to find outside the gay scene.

That one man engages in homosexual activities while identifying himself as heterosexual and another does the same things while identifying himself as gay poses severe problems for determining the prevalence of male homosexuality in a society. Kinsey and his associates (1948) estimated that at least 37 percent of the white male population in the United States had at least one homosexual experience between adolescence and old age. They found that 4 percent of American men were exclusively homosexual throughout their lives. The most recent estimates on the incidence of homosexuality in the Western world show that it is considerably lower than the 1948 study by Kinsey et al. suggested.[3] New surveys indicate that between 2 and 3 percent of men engage in homosexual acts and about 1 percent do so exclusively (Laumann et al., 1994:297; *Society*, 1993). Most studies have found that female homosexuality occurs at about half the male rate. The Kinsey team believed that the level of male homosexuality had been stable for many decades, a conclusion that appears to be as valid today as it was in 1948.

The Lesbian Career

Tripp's explanation of the origin of sexual orientation holds equally true for lesbians. They eroticize particular attributes of female role models of the same

VIEWPOINT 4.2

OUTING

SAN FRANCISCO — Gabriel Rotello knows his words are inflammatory, but he offers no apologies.

He's not a militant conservative warring against the alleged scourge of homosexuality. On the contrary: He's a militant gay, editor of the New York-based *Outweek*, one of the most influential homosexual publications on the continent.

His magazine is in the vanguard of a controversial "crusade" aimed at dragging prominent people — be they movie stars, industrialists or politicians — out of the closet and revealing them as homosexuals.

Rotello says the aim is to reduce prejudice against homosexuals by ending a news-media conspiracy that treats the gay life as "a dark, evil secret that needs to be covered up."

But the controversy over "outing" — the word coined to describe a process of publicizing the names of alleged homosexuals who hide their sexual preference — is causing painful soul-searching within the gay community.

In San Francisco, home of one of the largest gay populations in the world, critics denounce outing as a gross invasion of privacy. They also warn that supporters of the practice are entering into a distasteful alliance with mainstream sensationalist tabloids such as *The National Enquirer.*

"This is going to split the community if it goes on," warns Ray Chalker, publisher of the *San Francisco Sentinel*, a gay newspaper.

An opposing view comes from California gay militant Arthur Evans, who wants an annual "national outing day" when names of the famous who are secretly gay will be announced to the public.

Over the past year, gay activists have used a variety of channels — AIDS rallies, public speeches and gay newspapers — to reveal the names of alleged homosexuals.

But on March 18, the controversy boiled over when *Outweek* published a cover story detailing the alleged secret homosexual life of millionaire tycoon Malcolm Forbes, who had died a month previously.

That article appears to have opened the floodgates of accusation and innuendo.

Mass-market tabloids like *The National Enquirer* seized on the Forbes allegations and repeated them in their own pages.

Now it appears open season is being declared on Hollywood celebrities.

Several gay newspapers, including San Francisco's *Bay Area Reporter*, have carried stories alleging that Richard Chamberlain is homosexual, and have said the actor acknowledged his preferences in an interview with a French publication. The same story was picked up by *The National Enquirer.*

The allegations have been condemned by the actor's publicist, who says the interview with the French magazine never took place. She calls the publicity "absolutely hideous... infuriating, painful and shocking."

More recently, the *Enquirer* made similar allegations about John Travolta and Chastity Bono — and again there have been denials.

Outing has two main purposes. One is to expose the private lives of successful prominent homosexuals — for example entertainers and movie stars — to provide ordinary homosexuals with "role models" and to help them realize they shouldn't be ashamed of their lifestyle.

The other purpose is to punish politicians and other public figures who are allegedly closet homosexuals and don't support popular homosexual causes.

For several months Oregon Senator Mark Hatfield has been the target of an outing campaign because of an allegedly anti-gay voting record. Hatfield, a father of four, has labelled as "outrageous" gay claims that he is secretly homosexual.

Defenders of outing say the term also can apply to exposés in non-gay publications.

They cite the recent *New York Daily News* cover story in which Angela Bowie, ex-wife of David Bowie, alleges that she once caught her husband in bed with Mick Jagger. That, by their definition, constitutes an outing.

The controversy, which only a few months ago was largely confined to the gay community, has since become a mainstream issue.

Source: Jamie Portman, "Gay Outing," *Calgary Herald*, 1990, Sunday, May 20: C6. By permission of Jamie Portman, Southam News.

age or older, to form a lesbian value-system. Women, even more than men, drift, rather than intentionally move, into the sexual aspect of homosexuality. Norms about women rooming together, touching one another, and even being exclusively in one another's company are much looser than such norms are for men. Until they reach the stage of actual sexual contact, many women have little or no idea that they are behaving in a deviant manner, if in fact they are.

Hedblom (1975) reports that some sort of same-sex sexual contact ordinarily precedes a lesbian's entry into the gay–lesbian scene. Such contact usually occurs during the early or middle adolescent years and is seldom defined as homosexuality. With emancipation from her home and parents, the lesbian can explore deviant lifestyles, including those available in the homosexual community. Here, however, she must face up to her lesbian interests.

Exactly how the second and third components of lesbianism listed by Barbara Ponse fit with the development of lesbian sexuality is, at present, unclear. Perhaps an adolescent sexual interest in other women is combined with and partly motivated by a dislike of men or by a rejection of the traditional female role. Or these two components may become important only after the woman has left her family and entered the adult world of work and leisure. Or her sexual interests may eventually bring her in touch with the lesbian scene, where she accepts the other two components. Brooks' (1981) findings demonstrate the complexity of the interrelationship of the three components.

Whether it occurs before or after a woman enters the lesbian scene, self-acknowledgment as a lesbian is gradual. In the typical case, the transformation of identity becomes complete only with genital contact, which is most likely to happen during a later stage of an affectionate relationship (Cronin, 1974). Such contact may not lead to orgasm, however, nor is orgasm always sought. Stroking, hugging, and fondling may be just as desirable.

Self-acknowledgment as a lesbian is equivalent as a turning point to coming out for gays. Pressure from other lesbians may encourage a woman to come out in the gay–lesbian scene and, ultimately, even to the world at large. But a truly public declaration appears likely only if the woman in question is an activist in women's issues. In general, the motivation to make such a declaration is lower among lesbians than among male homosexuals, since life is less complicated by the practice of secret homosexuality for the former than for the latter. Lesbianism is often "socially invisible", enabling lesbian women to pass as heterosexual with an ease unknown to gays (Richardson, 1981:122).

The AIDS Crisis

AIDS (acquired immunodeficiency syndrome) was first diagnosed in 1981, and its cause, HIV (human immunodeficiency virus), was isolated in 1983. AIDS is transmitted through the exchange of bodily fluids (e.g., blood, semen). Although the virus may take as long as ten years to incubate, and drugs now exist to prolong the victim's life, death from AIDS is certain. While both males and females are susceptible to the disease, its rate among gay males is alarmingly high. Research indicates, for instance, that an estimated 48 to 70 percent of gays living in San Francisco have been exposed to the virus (Risman and Schwartz, 1988:139). Still, Goode (1994:269) cites evidence that the number of new AIDS cases among male homosexuals has now begun to drop, although the total number for the population as a whole is predicted to rise in the coming years.

The male propensity for casual sex has been a main factor in the extraordinary spread of the disease among gay men. The decline in the rate of new cases can be attributed in part to a move toward less promiscuity and safer sex practices (Goode, 1994:272). Nonetheless, as of 1991, homosexual contact was the principal means by which the disease was transmitted, with 56 percent; 27 percent of all cases were caused by intravenous injection; and approximately 9 percent resulted from heterosexual contact (often between a woman and a male who was bisexual or who injected drugs). The remaining 8 percent of cases were traced to miscellaneous sources (Garrett, 1992).

If, in response to the fear of acquiring AIDS, more gay males seek out monogamous relationships, then we can expect some fundamental changes in the nature of gay communities. But it is anyone's guess what these changes will be.

WATCHING SEX

Until perhaps 20 years ago, watching sex was generally regarded (mostly by men) as an acceptable adult male leisure activity. Looking at sexual acts in pornographic magazines and films and looking at sexually exciting actions and poses in striptease shows and girlie magazines caused little moral alarm. The only people considered deviant were the women who posed or acted in these productions. A double standard to be sure, and one not unlike that found in prostitution.[4]

Today, "listening to sex" could be added to the list of activities above, since pornographic telephone services are now widely available throughout Europe and North America (Livesay, 1994). Given the lack of research data on this innovation, however, our discussion will be confined to watching sex.

While the aforementioned double standard has by no means disappeared, the feminist movement has been instrumental in redefining, especially in middle- and upper-class circles, the watching of sex as deviant in its own right. A trend toward the liberalization of sex-oriented media which began in the 1950s (Winick, 1984:712) may have reached its conclusion. What lies at the root of feminists' perception that watching sex is deviant is the **objectification** of the women watched. Schur (1984:30–31) describes this process:

> Categorical evaluation implies treating people as objects. Others respond to the devalued persons in terms of their membership in the stigma-laden category. Individual qualities and actions become a secondary consideration. The stigmatized person is reacted to primarily as "an instance" of the category. At the extreme, he or she is viewed as having no other noteworthy status or identity. When that point is reached a

> person becomes — in the eyes of others, for all practical purposes — *nothing* but "a delinquent," "a cripple," "a homosexual," "a black," "a woman." The indefinite article "a" underlies the depersonalized nature of such a response. Members of the devalued category are treated as being virtually indistinguishable from, and in many respects substitutable for, one another.

Sexual objectification narrows the viewer's image of *a particular* woman to the sexually related aspects of that woman. In the eyes of the male viewer, she is a "piece of ass", an acquisition to be used for personal fulfillment without intimacy or commitment.

Feminists argue that the objectification of strippers and pornographic models and actresses — degrading as it is for these women — has further ramifications beyond them. That is, objectifying women in such productions encourages the men who watch or look at them to objectify all women, even their wives and girlfriends, with whom they are on intimate terms. Therefore, those who watch sex are deviant, along with those whose sex is watched.

Why deviant? Because, as feminists see it, and, it appears, as a growing number of other women and men see it, the sexual objectification of women violates an important moral norm: that other people should not be humiliated or degraded for personal gain. The violation threatens the welfare of the community.

It must be kept in mind, however, that this is one position taken on an extremely complex subject — the effects of pornographic productions — which is most difficult to study scientifically. It should also be remembered that there is no conclusive or even close to conclusive evidence that pornography (in which striptease is included here) has the consequences feminists claim: that it causes its consumers to alter their sexual practices or encourages them to hurt others (McKay and Dolff, 1985). Conversely, there is no conclusive evidence that their claims are wrong (Special Committee on Pornography and Prostitution, 1985:99). We shall amplify this discussion in the section on pornography.

The foregoing does not argue that a man who watches the sexually stimulating actions of his wife or girlfriend is deviant. Unless this man had learned to objectify all women, he may enjoy what he sees precisely because the actions observed are done by or with a woman he loves and respects, a person whom he treats as a unique individual, not as a member of a category. Nor should the watching of sex, as described here, be confused with voyeurism (see DSM-IV). Though considered deviant in some circles, the watching of sex is not pathological. It is considered pathological only when it and other activities such as window peeping become the preferred sexual activity, or an activity undertaken at considerable risk to the voyeur.

STRIPTEASE

In the preceding section, the case was made for treating males who watch impersonal sex as deviant. But there is only a scattered sociological literature on the men who do this watching, and they are rarely, if ever, defined as deviant within it. Hence, this section presents an unavoidably one-sided view of the occupation of stripping in which deviance is justified as work.

Such work has changed greatly in its nature and extent. In the days of the Victory Burlesk Theatre in Toronto, the dancers were required to wear "pasties" over their nipples and a G-string over their genitals (Fulford, 1970). In the Canada of the 1990s, women appear on stage or on tables (Ronai and Ellis, 1989), sometimes completely nude, to perform erotic dances and actions. Their acts are likely to be considered more exotic than the "bumps and grinds" of their burlesque counterparts three and four decades ago.

Today's strippers can also be hired from an entertainment agency or from the nightclub where they work to perform at private parties or for special occasions, such as the delivery of birthday messages. Recently, municipal nude beauty contests have sprung up, held in local auditoriums, not at nudist resorts. Moreover, male strippers who provide entertainment for female viewers are becoming more common.

The Female Stripper's Career

Most occupational careers have five stages: beginning, development, establishment, maintenance, and decline.[5] Skipper and McCaghy (1971) note that some sort of personal crisis typically marks the **beginning** of a stripper's career. The crisis is in one way or another financial. At the outset, these women need money, but lack the educational background and other formal qualifications needed to land well-paying, respectable jobs. The average level of education in Marilyn Salutin's (1971) sample of Canadian strippers was between Grades 7 and 8. The strippers she interviewed, like those interviewed in the United States by Skipper and McCaghy, had left home at an early age. (See also Ronai and Ellis, 1989:295–296.)

Skipper and McCaghy's study revealed that most aspiring strippers initially knew little about stripping as an activity or as a line of work. They had, however, worked in jobs that required some sort of display of their bodies: dancing, singing, or waitressing, for example. Through their interaction with male customers, they gradually became aware of their physical appeal. Eventually, someone — a friend, employer, or entertainment agent — suggested that striptease work would be more lucrative than their present job. Given their need for money, limited employment opportunities, recognition of their own sex appeal, and ease with being on display, stripping became a reasonable alternative livelihood (Thompson and Harred, 1992:299).

The **development** stage commences once the woman acquires an interest in stripping, usually at the time she acquires her first job. It lasts until she comes to define stripping as a form of work worth pursuing full-time. During this stage, she learns and polishes a few skills, gains experience using them, and absorbs the occupational lore of the striptease scene.

This lore consists, in part, of the techniques of stripping in an entertaining, sexually exciting way, of being able to produce a sense of "counterfeit intimacy" (Boles and Garbin, 1977). It also includes being able to avoid trouble with the audience. Yet the stripper's act must be good enough to encourage customers to purchase drinks or even a table dance (Ronai and Ellis, 1989). There is also a backstage component in the lore of stripping. The neophyte must learn how to interact with management, other strippers, and members of the band. For instance, strippers are expected to be tolerant of the sexual status (homosexual, heterosexual) of the other performers.

The developing stripper must learn the ideology surrounding her chosen occupation (Skipper and McCaghy, 1971; Salutin, 1971). Thus, she comes to see stripping as a legitimate form of entertainment with roots in the burlesque wing of show business. She also learns to see her act as a service that includes the provision of sexual release for some of the men who watch it; strippers are aware of the open masturbation taking place in the audience. Some strippers further believe that they provide instruction to the few women in attendance on how to act and appear seductive.

When the woman begins to define stripping as a full-time occupation, she enters the **establishment** stage of her deviant career. One way to become established is to advance from house performer to touring girl to headliner. The last of these is a national star whose night club acts are featured events publicized by advertisements on the premises and in local newspapers (Miller, 1978). Achieving headliner status is accompanied by more money and recognition than are available earlier in the stripping career, although it rarely brings more community respect. In the wider community, the star stripper is simply more infamous than her house and touring counterparts. She is, however, also more skilled and experienced than they are. The touring girl falls between the house girl and the headliner in terms of both recognition and wages. Touring girls, as the title implies, have significantly less community identification than house girls, since they work only a few weeks at a particular club before moving on to another city.

During the establishment stage, strippers routinize their work. Skipper and McCaghy (1971:287) point out that it is especially monotonous for the house and touring girls:

> Many acts, aside from those of the headliner or star feature, are simply exercises in divesting to the legal minimum with the emotion of a robot. What many of the girls lack in talent, they refuse to make up in enthusiasm. Among most headliners and others with talent and/or enthusiasm, the performances may be considerably embellished, but the outcome is never in question: what authorities will allow is displayed with aplomb. The product is sex with varying degrees of icing and, notwithstanding claims of humanitarian service, undressing before a roomful of men is a routine job.

Viewpoint 4.3 presents the stripper's perspective on the work.

Offstage, the established stripper meets with additional problems. Through their experiences onstage, many develop a hatred for men (even though some are married). This sentiment helps push them toward lesbianism (Salutin, 1971; McCaghy and Skipper, 1971). Others, probably with no greater fondness for men, supplement their earnings with prostitution. Skipper and McCaghy (1971) found little evidence of drug use among their sample. And only sporadically did

VIEWPOINT 4.3

WORKING LIFE: THE STRIPPER'S VIEW

The sultry gyrations, bedroom eyes and exposed skin may exude an invitation of sex to customers, but it might surprise some men to learn that the women who sport stage names like Delicious Debbie, Fantasia, and Shelly Sin are thinking about something quite different.

"I have this routine," giggles Charlene. "It's a move I can do where I get down on my knees and bend backwards" — she demonstrates by arching her back and flings her arms backward over her head — "so I can see my watch. Then I know how much more time I have to dance."

Rose uses a different technique to pass the time. "It may look like I'm lip-synching the words to the song," she reveals. "But I'm actually singing things to keep me smiling." She starts to hum in demonstration: "You're all a bunch of dick heads, and I don't want to be here..."

"Beige," La-Ree submits in reply, with an evil grin. "I always think beige. You know, that joke that asks what's the difference between a wife, a hooker and a girlfriend? A hooker says 'Are you done yet?' A girlfriend says, 'Are you done already?' And a wife says, 'Beige. I think we should paint the ceiling beige'."

She throws her head back and laughs uproariously.

The dancers like the city bars best, because they offer a more controlled environment and nicer hotel rooms.... [But] trouble is frequent on the job, whether it be over-amorous bar patrons, fleabag motels that provide baseball bats for security, or contracts that mysteriously dissolve if the club manager doesn't like the stripper's looks. Every dancer has a horror story to relate. Charlene examines her bed linen for human hair when she arrives for a job — several hotels she's been in make the bed, but don't change the sheets between customers.

Source: Lisa Church, "Life in the Skin Game," *Herald Sunday Magazine*, 1990, June 3:11–12. By permission.

the women pose for pornographic pictures or act in adult films. Salutin, however, found excessive drug use among the strippers she studied.

The stripper reaches the peak of her career during the **maintenance** stage. Depending on ability and work opportunities, this stage may unfold for her at the house, touring, or headliner level. Her main goal during maintenance is to maximize occupational opportunities. Reaching this goal will never be easier, for the stripper is now at the peak of her experience and physical attractiveness.

Some leave stripping at this point. Although no systematic data are available, it appears that a small proportion leave through marriage, which frees them of requiring financial support. A few of these unions are with "straight" men from the day world (Boles and Garbin, 1977). But most strippers, if they marry at all, do so within show business circles, not infrequently to men who eventually become their managers. When one works by night and sleeps by day, opportunities for meeting "day people" are clearly limited.

Despite the tedium and stigma of their work, most strippers cling to their line of employment. Eventually, they enter the **decline** stage of their careers. Marriage to an agent who values his wife's income is often a reason to continue stripping. But there are other factors as well. One is the lack of equally lucrative alternatives, deviant or otherwise.

Perhaps leaving the occupation is resisted as much for reasons of personal vanity as any other. Few men and women in our society like to think of themselves as losing their youthful vigour and appearance. After having made a living for several years on these very qualities, strippers are especially reluctant to signal their decline by quitting work.

Thus, as Salutin (1971) observed, when strippers discover that "they are no longer very persuasive sexually," they often turn to alcohol. They appear onstage drunk, which undoubtedly detracts still further from their acts. Moreover, they find that they must "spread" more (show more of their genital area) to retain their audience appeal. Increasingly, they become the butt of the emcee's dirty jokes. The conditions of being drunk, lewd, and a laughingstock interact to make the stripper's years of decline particularly painful. Yet many persist, with no contingency plans for the future. Eventually, no-one will hire them.

The evidence Skipper and McCaghy (1971) provided a quarter-century ago to the effect that stripping has a negative public image appears valid today. Some strippers, concerned about their reputation and that of their occupation, are trying to change public opinion by performing tasteful acts, avoiding prostitution and lesbianism, and even engaging in community projects, one of which is the annual strip marathon held in Montréal just before Christmas. Proceeds from the event go to the Montréal Children's Hospital. An unsavory community reputation has no doubt contributed to the exploitation of strippers by agents and management. In response, some of these women formed the Canadian Association of Burlesque Entertainers (CABE), Local 1689 (Toronto), of the Canadian Labour Congress. Operating at the edge of the laws pertaining to nudity (and sometimes beyond) places strippers under constant siege from the moral entrepreneurs in the larger society who are offended by their performances. Unfortunately, the failure of strippers themselves to support CABE led to its demise (Cooke, 1987:96).

Male Strippers

The 1980s saw the emergence of a new wrinkle in the world of striptease: males stripping for females. (Males stripping for males is a much older occupation; see Tewksbury, 1993.) Studies by Dressel and Petersen (1982), Petersen and Dressel (1982), and Clark (1985) describe the appeal for some women of nightclubs that feature male strippers performing in a relaxed atmosphere where patrons can have a drink and be entertained free from the unsolicited attentions of male strangers. Men are either permanently barred from these clubs, or temporarily barred until after the show. This form of entertainment is sometimes promoted as "equal time for the ladies".

In the male strip show, the men dance, acting and clothing themselves in stereotypically masculine ways. Most jurisdictions prohibit total nudity, as well as any kind of physical intimacy beyond kissing and hugging. Dressel and Petersen (1982) and Clark (1985) found that the vast majority of male strippers are in the occupation for the easy money it provides, particularly the generous tips admiring patrons insert in their G-strings. Some of them also enjoy the role of entertainer and the enhanced possibility of meeting women. Sporadic male heterosexual prostitution mediated by such allurements as gifts, money, and housing may result from these encounters.

Sexually, stripping is no more exciting for male strippers than for their female counterparts. For both, striptease very quickly becomes a routine job. Likewise, the men "often feel that the female patrons objectify and exploit them" (Petersen and Dressel, 1982:201–202) when abusing them verbally and sometimes even physically. One important difference separating the two types of ecdysiasts, however, is the degree of entrapment in their work. The men choose stripping, a form of employment that they consider both temporary and supplementary. The women, as we have seen, are far more often forced by economic circumstances to strip as a main and continuing livelihood.

PORNOGRAPHY

Part of the *social* problem of pornography in modern society lies in the fact that there is no definition of pornography which is at once valid and legally usable. Were such a definition available today, the production and consumption of this material might be treated legally and scientifically as a form of intolerable deviance, as a form of crime. Lack of a clear definition is one of the reasons — though not the only reason — why pornography is, in effect, tolerable deviance.

While there are laws that define pornography production, distribution, and sales as illegal, they are so vague as to lead to capricious and discriminatory enforcement. Parker (1987:85) describes the problem:

> No definition will work unless we can be assured that the arbiters of obscenity — whether they be police, customs officials, or members of the judiciary — are as impartial as a set of scales, as wise as Solomon, and as efficient as a computer. We cannot have this assurance. Police may not reflect "good" or *avant garde* taste; judges may be old and reactionary; and customs officials may be too cautious.

At present, section 163 of the Criminal Code of Canada defines as obscene any publication "the dominant characteristics of which are the undue exploitation of sex, or of sex and any one or more of the following subjects, namely, crime, horror, cruelty, and violence".

After reviewing the extensive literature on the question, Fischer and Barak (1991:66) have identified three types of pornography:

1. Violent pornography: Sexually explicit material that depicts and endorses the utility and normativeness of sexual violence
2. Degrading pornography: Sexually explicit material that degrades, debases, and dehumanizes people, generally women, although it lacks explicit depictions of aggression
3. Erotica: Sexually explicit material that presents non-violent, non-degrading, and consensual sexual activity

The lines separating the three are sometimes blurred, since, for example, the categories fail to consider the arousal- and affect-producing qualities of erotic stimuli.

The report of the Special Committee on Pornography and Prostitution (1985: 57–58) prepared for the Government of Canada equated the first two types with obscenity and thereby excluded erotica from its study of pornography. Gloria Steinem (1980:37) said of erotica:

> It is any depiction of lovemaking involving a mutually pleasurable, sexual expression between people who have enough power to be there by positive choice. It may or may not strike a sensitive memory in the viewer, or be creative enough to make the unknown seem real; but it doesn't require us to identify with a conqueror or a victim. It is truly sensuous, and may give us a contagion of pleasure.

The critical distinction is that pornography is intended to *cause* sexual excitement, whereas erotica is intended to *express* such excitement. All of this exemplifies well the labelling aspect of deviance in our society. What is considered erotic, sexually explicit, or violently and degradingly pornographic depends on the interpretation made by the consumer of the material.

Both erotica and pornography are available in a variety of forms, including films, drawings, sculptures, stories, photography, and performances.[6] Film and photographs are modern inventions, and so is the pornography so vividly portrayed through these media. But pornography through drawings, stories, sculptures, and possibly even live performances is as old as humankind. Moreover, in all ages its production and consumption have primarily been of interest to males (Yaffé and Nelson, 1982:2). Needless to say, the questions of what is pornographic, what is erotic, and what is neither have troubled all cultures, because the social acceptability of watching sex is always tied to local customs and beliefs.

The Effects of Pornography

Much of the social scientific research on pornography has centred on the question of its effects on its consumers. The amount of such research has increased in recent years, partly because pornography is changing. The changes are seen by many women and some men as exceeding the boundaries of tolerable deviance in our society.

The liberalization of sexual attitudes in the late 1960s and early 1970s affected the majority of the public, who redefined the photographs in such magazines as *Playboy* as unthreatening. *Penthouse* and *Hustler* were considered more questionable during this period. But the pornography of the 1980s and 1990s is often noticeably more violent and degrading to women than that of the 1970s (Fisher and Barak, 1991:66). Further, one source holds that the availability of pornographic materials in Canada, as in many other countries, increased dramatically during the previous 15 years, both in amount and in variety of outlet (Special Committee on Pornography and Prostitution, 1985:89).

Keeping in mind the observation made earlier — that there is still no solid scientific evidence about the broad effects of pornography — various claims nevertheless continue to be made. Linz and Malamuth (1993:7–12) identify three positions from which these claims are presently being made. The conservative-moralist/normative position holds that presentations of sex are harmful because they violate certain religious rules of behaviour and the supreme authority of God. According to this position, people have a right to protection from the disorder and moral disintegration that can result when individual members of society pursue their own sexual interests. The libertarian/liberal position emphasizes the individual and the belief that he or she should have free access to a full range of information and be allowed to make rational choices about sexual behaviour based on the information. The social responsibility/feminist position recognizes that the flow of ideas is often controlled by powerful people. In the case of pornography, control lies in the hands of men, who use it to maintain male dominance and female subordination.

Linz and Malamuth (1993:61) note that reviews of the research on the effects of pornography tend to reach conclusions consistent with one of these three positions because of the ideological allegiances of the reviewers themselves: e.g., conservative-moralist (Zillman and Bryant, 1988); liberal (Brannigan and Goldenberg, 1987); feminist (Russell, 1988). Thus, claims such as the ones we are about to examine can be said either to have scientific support or not, depending on the position from which they are made.

We have already reviewed the feminist claim, which is that pornography objectifies women, resulting in their humiliation and degradation. Another claim, for which there is no convincing evidence, is Ned Polsky's (1985) functionalistic "safety-valve" effect of pornography. The hypothesis rests on the proposition that pornography helps maintain sexual order in society. For instance, it provides an alternative outlet, through masturbation, for adolescent and adult males whose sex drive cannot be satisfied in socially acceptable ways. Pornography may also serve as a sort of sex-instruction manual, inasmuch as it provides, in its hard-core versions, vivid written and/or visual depictions of sex acts. Third, pornography has been used historically as well as in the present to stimulate sexual activity in people who, for whatever reason, are in need of such stimulation. Knox (1984:328) briefly describes the use in sexual dysfunction therapy of what he refers to as erotic films.

Lyman and Scott (1975) identify still another hypothetical effect of pornography through its role in the **adventure**. In adventures, people disconnect themselves from the routine of everyday life to assume temporarily new identities or different lifestyles, or to attempt untested capacities. In the framework of this book, adventures can be justified as either leisure or adjustment or both. In the case of pornography consumption, the adventure is imaginary (Lyman and Scott, 1975:156):

> Pornography is a catalyst to sexual imagination, and, in turn, to the mental states appropriate to masturbation. It may also stimulate other forms of sexual activity or be enjoyed for its own intrinsic qualities. Perusing pornography provides one with both a literary experience and an aphrodisiac, a combination not otherwise likely. For those who are foreclosed from sexual variety, inhibited by fears of exposure, or shamed by the possibility of humiliation before others who are more capably erotic, pornography provides a sexual outlet and a sure adventure. In the erotic exploits of storied heroes

and victims, a reader can forge a vicarious self and, in the continuing availability of the literature, realize that secret self again without moving from his easy chair.

Pornography as Work

Historically, making pornography has been a tolerably deviant form of work in our society which, as mentioned earlier, may be growing intolerable to the extent that the arguments of feminists and conservative moralists are being accepted by both sexes. To my knowledge, there are no empirical studies of the sociology of pornographic production as a livelihood and occupational career. Those who work in the field include producers, editors, photographers, cinematographers, script writers, story writers, lighting specialists, and models, actors, and actresses.

Steven Ziplow (1977:41–44), himself a former producer of and actor in pornographic films, says three types of people enter this area of film making: those out for a thrill, those who hope to enhance their legitimate acting career, and those who work in another part of the "sex industry". Ziplow believes that nearly twice as many men as women seek jobs in pornographic film. "There seems to be less of a stigma for male actors to appear in porno films," he explains.

Most pornographic actors and actresses seem to start this kind of acting because of the money it pays, which is reputed to be more than they could earn as neophytes in legitimate theatre. Some pornographic performers, however, seek the work for exhibitionistic reasons. And some seek it because they believe they will become "porno stars" or will acquire the acting experience needed to break into legitimate theatre. But, according to Ziplow, few people make much money through pornographic acting and even fewer reach stardom. Although the present evidence is, at best, incomplete, it suggests that, at the writing and acting level of pornography, production work very quickly becomes routine. It soon becomes a mediocre way of making money, just as stripteasing becomes for the stripper (Douglas and Waksler, 1982:181; Bond and Hill, 1974).

According to Sproat (1974), writing pornography is a deadening experience. He was required to turn out 40 pages of acceptable material daily on such varied themes as pedophilia and bestiality. His manuscripts belonged to the company that hired him. He was never given an opportunity to check the many editorial changes made to them, and saw his work only in final form, as a cheap pornographic paperback.

Pornography as Leisure

Not much more is known sociologically about the pornography consumer than about the producer. What knowledge there is centres on those who frequent "adult" bookstores, cinemas, and video stores. Lindquist and Cane (1979) found that the patrons of adult bookstores were usually white, middle-class men with relatively high-status jobs and more than a high school education. In their sample, 61 percent were married; nearly all were living with their wives. Lindquist and

Cane noted that similar studies describe a comparable status profile for this type of pornography consumer (see also Stein, 1990: Ch. 7). In addition to selling pornographic books and magazines, some of these establishments offer videos in private booths and, less often, live strippers and simulated sex acts on small stages surrounded by private cubicles. Inside the stores, patrons seldom talk to each other and talk only minimally to the clerk (Tewksbury, 1990; Potter, 1989).

According to studies carried out by Slade (1971), Sundholm (1973), and Donnelly (1981), male patrons of pornography theatres typically arrive alone, with a female companion, or in small groups. When alone they try to sit at a distance from others. Except for the occasional homosexual encounter, males occupy alone the booths equipped with coin-operated film machines. The darkness of the theatres and the privacy of the film machine booths permit, if not encourage, masturbation. Sex, whatever its type, is ordinarily a private act in our culture. Watching pornography in public theatres and film booths is no different in this regard. Distance from others in the theatres and partitions in the booths provide this privacy. As in the case of the bookstores, patrons tend to be white, middle-class males, although the occasional woman may accompany a man to the theatres.

The norm of civil inattention (Goffman, 1963; McKinstry, 1974; Stein, 1990:115) — the expectation that we show no overt interest in what others are doing — is met in the pornography bookstores and theatres. The practice coincides with the private nature of sex. It also squares with the view that adult male masturbation, even in these settings, is deviant. Knox (1984:159) reports that most males are used to masturbating alone wherever they are, and being discovered in the act is embarrassing. Hesslund (1976) found that most wives regard masturbation by adult males, especially their husbands, as unnatural, repulsive, and wrong. Finally, Davidson (1984:122) concludes from his review of the relevant literature that some people still believe that masturbation by either sex is not only an immoral act but also a cause of such conditions as insanity, damnation, impotence, and frigidity.

Implications

From the lofty standpoint of sociological deviance theory, pornography is a fine exemplar of the several perspectives presented in Chapter 2. Both producers and consumers run the risk of acquiring deviant labels that could tarnish their reputations and undermine their efforts to achieve success in the respectable world. Still, some pornographic actors, actresses, and models hope that employment in this sphere will further their opportunities in legitimate acting and modelling. For them, blue movies and photographs merely constitute an early stage in what they hope will be a largely conventional career.

Pornography as deviance has also been viewed as functional. Masturbation is seen as a safety valve and pornography itself is seen as a kind of instruction manual. Feminists and conservative moralists, however, would certainly argue that pornography is dysfunctional. For them, and, it appears, a growing number

VIEWPOINT 4.4

HOME-GROWN PORN

America's dirtiest home videos continue to be the fastest-growing segment of North America's $2 billion adult-video market, in an age where everything from natural disasters to alleged police brutality is captured on camera. Dozens of ordinary folks are loading up their camcorders to preserve their sexual exploits, and share them with the world.

The videos are raw, amateurish and sometimes unintentionally slapstick silly — Moe Howard meets Marilyn Chambers, if you will — and that's just the way the customers like 'em.

"It's pure fantasy — the perfect breasts, the perfect legs, the perfect body parts for both male and female. They are like athletes in professional baseball or football — whereas the amateurs are more like sandlot," said Gary Aptaker, president of Homegrown Video Inc., one of the United States' largest distributors of amateur adult video.

"The amateurs are not actors or actresses. For the most part, these are people in relationships, and that comes through in the video," he said. "They can be attractive people, but they don't look like the porn stars — and people like that."

Of the more than 400 million adult videos rented last year, 25–30 percent were made by ordinary folks who genuinely seem to enjoy making love in front of a video camera.

This is the age where 18 percent of U.S. households have camcorders, and shows like *America's Funniest Home Videos* are boffo TV. If we're willing to watch week after week of brides flopping face first into their wedding cakes or cherubic-faced tots inevitably whacking Daddy in the cojones with a plastic bat, why wouldn't we watch those same fumbling, bumbling slobs doin' the nasty?

For a $1 or $2 rental fee, we can all peep into the bedrooms of our neighbours legally, in the comfort of [our] homes. We can laugh. We can scream. We can rewind.

"These are everyday people in all walks of life. The common denominator we find is that there is a part of the personality of the individuals that is exhibitionist in nature," Aptaker said.

"I just got a letter from a submitter of videos who says it's a turn-on for him and his wife to know other people are watching them make love."

And it's a turn-on for some people to watch adult videos featuring folks who look so average, so much like us. No-one is going to mistake these people for the anatomically impossible Jeff Stryker or that D-cup darling Delores Del Rio, who go through the motions like well-oiled humanoids.... "The appeal is somebody can go to a supermarket any day of the week and see people there that look like the people in these movies," Aptaker said. "It's the reality. It's not staged."

Homegrown has about 450 volumes of amateur adult videos. The company's rules are fairly strict. All participants must sign releases and present a photo identification proving they are 21 years old. The company will not accept videos involving violence or animals, and has worked with California district attorneys to help nab child pornographers. Most companies pay about $15 per minute, depending on the technical quality of the tape.

Source: Renee Graham, "Smile — You're on very Candid Camera," *Calgary Herald*, 1993, Sunday, April 18: B2.

of men and women who would not usually identify themselves as feminists or moralists, pornography humiliates and degrades half our population.

It is within this climate of contradictions — of the functions and dysfunctions of pornography — that the Special Committee on Pornography and Prostitution (1985:264–272) proposed its three-tier system of legal controls of this material. If adopted by government, the first and most serious tier would attempt to control, with severe penalties, visual representations of people under the age of 18 participating in conduct that depicts, encourages, or condones sexual abuse and bodily harm to the participants. The second tier would encompass the same material, but would allow for arguments that it may have educational, scientific, or artistic merit. The third tier, which would not generally be accompanied by criminal sanctions, would consist of visual pornographic material excluding children, violence, or sexual abuse (i.e., erotica). Using this tier system as background, the Special Committee (1985:276–281) published a recommended revision of the sections of the Criminal Code of Canada pertaining to pornography. In the meantime, the conflict in Canada between those who favour pornography and those who oppose it has, according to one criminologist (Deschamps, 1985:6), led to police ambivalence with regard to the tendency to control it. The result is a level of *de facto* tolerance.

GROUP AND EXTRAMARITAL SEX

Swinging, adultery, and group sex all have in common the act of sexual relations with someone other than one's own spouse or steady sexual partner. **Swinging** and **group sex** are synonymous to the extent that mates are exchanged during a session of sexual promiscuity involving three or more men and women in the same or separate rooms. Swinging usually involves the exchange of spouses or partners, whereas group sex may involve those who have no steady relationship with one another. **Adultery** is the infidelity of one partner or spouse in a relationship.

Adultery itself is not illegal in Canada. It is, however, illegal to participate in adultery or other "sexual immorality" in a way that endangers the morals of a child in his or her own home. Explicit sexual activity with someone other than the child's parent in full view of the child is an example of such an act. Nonetheless, the same legal exceptions mentioned in the previous chapter for homosexuals apply to heterosexuals: sexual activities conducted in private between two consenting adults aged 21 or older, whether married or not, are outside the jurisdiction of the law. But swinging and group sex, because they involve at least *three* people, are legally considered acts of "gross indecency". However the law reads, Bibby's (1982) survey indicates that 79 percent of Canadians disapprove of extramarital sex, a proportion which has not changed significantly since 1975. American opinion on the matter is nearly identical — 78 percent of a sample drawn in 1989 (Wood, 1990:603).

The Social World of the Swinger

Although swinging undoubtedly has older roots, public knowledge of the practice in North America is usually traced to a scattered set of magazine articles published in the 1950s in the United States and to the "wife swapping" of the 1940s and 1950s as it was practised in clandestine "key clubs" (Leslie and Korman, 1989:443). The publicity, together with the liberalization of sexual attitudes in the early 1960s, helps account for Bartell's (1971:5) observation that there was a significant surge in swinging among Americans in 1963 and 1964. In Canada, The Key, a swingers' organization that claimed to be the oldest of its kind in the country, was established in 1967. It is now defunct. When journalist Carey French interviewed the president of the Toronto spouse-swapping club, Club Eros, in 1988, he estimated that as many as 4000 couples swing in that city alone. He also said that, at the time, similar clubs existed in Montréal, Edmonton, Calgary, and Vancouver. From surveys done in the United States, it is estimated that 2 to 3 percent of the population swing regularly; between 4 and 5 percent have tried it (DeLamater, 1981:282).

Bartell's (1971:130–197) study of Americans revealed four types of swinging: closed, open, threesomes, and large parties. **Closed swinging** refers to two couples exchanging partners. The two new pairs then go off to separate rooms for their sexual activity, returning at an appointed time later in the evening. In **open swinging** a similar exchange occurs. During at least part of the evening, however, sex is conducted in the same room, perhaps on the same bed, in pairs or in a four-way involvement.

In **three-way swinging** (group sex), a third person who is satisfactory to the other two is brought into the sexual activity. Bartell's (1971:146) research indicates that the third person is very likely to be a woman. When the threesome includes two men, one or both are sexually stimulated by watching the other perform with the woman. In the two women–one man arrangement, lesbian activity often contributes to the man's sexual excitement.

Large parties amount to a sort of modern orgy, where several men and women, single or married, engage in sex with several different partners, often in the same room. Considerable female homosexuality has been observed at these affairs as a means of satisfaction for the women and of excitement for the men. There is scant male homosexuality in any form of swinging. Although some women are pressured into performing at least passive homosexuality, the evidence indicates that many female swingers enjoy it as an alternative to heterosexuality (Symonds, 1971; Dixon, 1984).

Making Contact

Direct or indirect contact is made through four sources: books, periodicals, clubs, and bars. Books such as Gay Talese's *Thy Neighbor's Wife* (1980) and Myers and Liggett's *Adultery and Other Private Matters* (1975) describe swinging in particular and sometimes sexual liberation in general. They promote swinging by arguing its benefits and encouraging readers to seek direct contact by reading the personal advertisements in a swingers' periodical or the swingers' columns in a sexual liberation publication. Such magazines and tabloids are available at newsstands, variety stores, adult bookstores, and similar outlets in most North American cities.

The following are characteristic of the personal advertisements that appear in the swingers' literature:

> L7052: Swinging couple with lots of experience. She petite, 34, 5′3", 110 lbs. He 38, 5′8", 160 lbs. Both professionals. Love house and pool parties. Free to entertain or travel. Newcomers welcome. Oakville, Ont.
>
> L7053: Attractive, fun-loving couple, early 50s, very clean, gentle, discreet and warm. We enjoy dining, travel and same-room swinging. Wish to meet attractive couples, white or Oriental. No S/M or B/D. Absolute discretion. Single ladies most welcome. Can travel & entertain. Please, phone or write. Montreal–Kingston–Toronto.
>
> L7055: Happily married generous couple. He 36, 5′9"; she 33, 5′7", pretty. Would like to meet single or married females for threesomes. Very submissive feminine transsexual (*sic*) welcome. Open-minded in trying out most fantasies. Age, race unimportant. Can entertain but will travel if requested in Alberta, B.C., Saskatchewan. Cleanliness and discretion expected and assured. Reply with phone and photo for fast action. Calgary, Alta.

Such abbreviations as S/M and B/D are part of the in-group language of swinging. They refer, respectively, to the sadomasochistic and bondage and discipline forms of sexuality. Invitations such as those above are sometimes accompanied by a nude photograph of the wife or, more rarely, of the husband, or of both. Those interested in a particular notice can contact the person or couple by letter through the office of the publisher of the publication.

There are also swingers' clubs. Some of these amount to little more than membership on a mailing list to receive a swingers' or sexual liberation periodical. Others publish a newsletter and hold dances, dinners, and swingers' parties. Some clubs arrange occasional get-togethers at a nearby retreat. Lifestyle Tours (California) offers tours for swingers lasting from seven to ten days to such places as Japan and Mazatlan. *Mystique West* is published by another organization with the same name for swingers in western Canada and the United States. Club Confidential provides services for a Canadian–American clientele. And at least one travelling club is operating in Canada (see Viewpoint 4.5).

For the more promiscuous and adventuresome who want to swing regularly, many North American cities hold one or more bars that cater partly or exclusively to the swinging community. According to Thio (1988:260), swingers appear to be more aggressive than either gays or singles in making contact in bars catering to their interests. The typical swinging couple surveys the crowd until they spot an attractive pair, then moves quickly to determine whether the two people are interested in swinging with them. If the answer is "no", the first couple repeats the process with another pair.

"Party houses" serve a similar purpose to bars, offering regular weekend swingers' get-togethers, usually at a private home. In the American swingers' literature, they are described as having a hot tub, slow dance music, adult films, and private and public rooms, as well as food and drink. Since only telephone numbers appear in the advertisements, the hosts are able to screen those who plan to attend. However contact is made — through ads, bars, or clubs — further contact is possible through referrals (Palson and Palson, 1972).

VIEWPOINT 4.5

CONTACTING SWINGERS

Attention Swingers

Want to get together with other swingers, or would you like to start your own group? Isn't it frustrating to know that there are plenty of swingers just like you in your own city and yet you can never seem to meet each other, or even if you do, it ends up a disappointment?

How would you like to meet with other swingers in complete privacy on a twice-a-month basis where you won't be offended nor offend anyone else and meet other swingers to do just the things you like to do?

"Swingers Galore" travels to Regina, Saskatoon, Winnipeg, Calgary, Edmonton, and to points in Eastern Canada when we hear from you. There will be a cover charge only.

Act now! We could be in your city next week. We will be sure to invite you if you send us your telephone number. All replies strictly confidential. Those who reply to this ad with interest will be invited first. We will contact you by PHONE ONLY and will discuss the above with only yourself. No messages or call-back numbers will be left. Also swingers who enjoy cross-dressing, S/M, voyeurism, bondage, etc. No discrimination in these areas!

"Swingers Galore" is not an escort service nor does it supply people for these get-togethers. Only swingers like yourselves who answer this ad will be invited to attend. Send all replies to: "Swingers Galore," P.O. Box 8088, Saskatoon, Sask. S7K 4R7

Source: *Tab International*, 1985, September 7:13.

Who Swings and Why?

Several studies indicate that swingers are generally white, middle-class people who, outside the narrow realm of sexuality, hold conservative views on major issues (Bartell, 1971:24–46; Symonds, 1971:103; Jenks, 1985). Further, the swinging scene is dominated by married couples. Unmarried partners and single women are welcome, but men lacking a steady relationship with a woman are frequently avoided or discouraged (through extremely high fees) from attending swingers' events. One of the justifications for swinging is that it is believed to improve and expand one's marital relationship through new sexual experiences. As swingers say: "The family that swings together clings together." Footloose men are not part of this family orientation. Moreover, since single people of both sexes are often more promiscuous, they are, as a category, more likely to introduce AIDS and venereal disease into the local swinging scene.

The fact that unattached women, unlike unattached men, are desirable and justifiable is consonant with Bartell's (1971:57) observation that, at least in the United States, swinging fulfills male sexual fantasies and male interests in sexual variety. Henschel's (1973) study of 25 Toronto-area women showed that the initial decision to swing was made by the husband in 59 percent of the cases, by the couple in 28 percent of the cases, and by the wife in only 12 percent of the cases. Those who continue to swing have somehow reached the conclusion that swinging is good. But Henschel (1973:890) notes:

> In the context of decision making, swinging can be viewed as a male institution, and confirmations of the advent of a "sexual revolution" and of the abolition of the double standard should be reconsidered.

Most wives, it seems, swing chiefly to please their husbands.

The evidence to date indicates that some couples clearly come to enjoy swinging. Perhaps they are the ones who keep their sexual encounters from becoming so personal that a rift develops in their relationship (Thio, 1988:269–270). Swinging, partly because it is deviant, adds zest to a boring life; in the words of Lyman and Scott, it is another adventure. And some women believe that, by swinging, they have shed some of their sexual inhibitions and possibly developed a new self-image as sexually attractive to the opposite sex.

However, there are many dropouts from the swinging scene. Bartell (1971:273–275) believes that guilt plays little or no role in the decision to leave. Rather, it appears that a set of reactions develops that is opposite to those which keep some couples swinging. For instance, some drop out because their self-image deteriorates; they begin to see themselves as sexually loose, as sleeping with anyone who is handy. This reaction is probably more common among females than males. But it can lead to increased pressure on the husband to abandon swinging. Additionally, some men discover that their sexual fantasies are better than the real thing, that swinging is not what it is imagined to be. For the institution of the family, then, swinging is sometimes functional, sometimes dysfunctional.

Even where personality considerations are not at issue, Bartell (1971:257–259) says there is a definite involvement curve among those whom he studied. The typical couple took up to five months to find other swingers. After a few favourable experiences, they then used their contacts to pursue an active swingers' life. This stage lasted from 6 to 18 months. Somewhere between 18 months and 2 years, involvement waned, leading to a substantial reduction in swinging or to its complete abandonment. Some couples began to worry about venereal disease. Others found that the novelty had worn off, since they were beginning to meet the same people again. Stephenson's (1973) respondents said that the pace became too costly in time and energy.

CONCLUSIONS

This chapter has covered several forms of adjustive tolerable deviance, along with their work and leisure justifications. Psychiatrists no longer consider homosexuality a mental illness. Rather, it is seen as a matter of preference: in the language of this book, an adjustment in the development of the sexual value system. Sometimes the process of adjustment encompasses more than mere sexual practice. It may take in the entire range of thought and action that comprise the male and female sex roles of society.

Thus, the concept of sex role is important in a discussion of homosexuality. It is less significant in the sphere of male homosexuality than in the sphere of female homosexuality. In the case of most male homosexuals, deviance centres on an aberrant sexual preference. Outside the area of sex, they are quite inclined to think and act as other males in our society. The study of male homosexuality is, at bottom, the study of a deviant form of male sexual practice.

When the focus shifts to lesbianism, the concern with sex roles is sometimes as narrow as it is in the case of male homosexuality. Some women are sexually attracted to each other, just as some men are. Indeed, we have seen that some members of both categories may not even define themselves as homosexual, although they are aware that what they are doing is socially disapproved of.

However, when we consider the lesbian who rejects patriarchical society and the traditional woman's role, as well as the men who enforce that role's enactment in everyday life, we move from narrow deviant sexual practice to broad sex-role deviance. The latter is a much more encompassing form of deviance. A wide range of sex-role traits is rejected in lesbian sex-role deviance, in comparison with the narrow range of traits rejected in sexual deviance of all kinds (homosexual and heterosexual). The radical lesbian is the most visible expression of female sex-role deviance. But lesbian women who do not accept the radical title may still reject, in a more quiet way, significant aspects of the woman's traditional role.

A second theme underlying much of the preceding discussion of heterosexual deviance is that, at present in North America, mankind (and to a much lesser extent womankind) has been most inventive in the search for sexual variation in an era when sexuality is highly valued (Wolshok, 1971). But, for most men, that search fails to turn up anything substantial which could serve as a lasting substitute for our institutionalized ways of sexual expression. Those ways are the conventional sex acts conducted within a marital or a serious non-marital relationship. Watching strippers, cross dressing, swapping mates, and masturbating to pornography are, when considered from the standpoint of a lifetime, usually fleeting attempts to outflank the constraints of society.

But, as noted here and in the previous chapter, the deviant road to sexual bliss is indeed a rocky one. When one deviates, one strives at the same time to avoid detection. The effort must be worth the costs. The sex drive is among the most easily satiated of the human appetites (although it is also the quickest to reappear). Moreover, sexual prowess, as a type of achievement, counts for relatively little in our society. Hence, it is hardly surprising that attempts to profit from deviant heterosexual pursuits often fail. In addition, a declining sex drive is also a factor leading many men and women to abandon their goal of finding a richer sex life than society can conventionally offer.

Apparently, few people find it noticeably difficult to shake their desire for certain types of deviant sex. Those who do, keep a number of psychologists, psychiatrists, and sex counsellors in business. Others swell the ranks of such self-help organizations as Sex Addicts Anonymous and Sexaholics Anonymous (both based in the United States). For most heterosexual deviants, however, these measures are unnecessary. Their deviance lasts only a few years of their lifetime. Perhaps our present orientation of tolerance is as effective as any attitude in encouraging a return of sexual normalcy. At least tolerance avoids placing impediments that emerge when intolerance is the norm (e.g., criminal record, unfavourable community image).

NOTES

1 Social control is a broad process that is part of every social institution. It is not an institution in its own right. Rather, social control is achieved or at least striven for in each institution through its norms, values, groups, and organizations.

2 Heterosexual male prostitution does exist, but is rare (Rich, 1979:102). Heterosexual male prostitutes usually cater to wealthy, middle-aged women found at resorts, bars, and residential hotels. Male strippers performing for women have opportunities to prostitute themselves, which they occasionally take.

3 Laumann and associates (1994:288–290) have attempted to explain the differences in the estimated prevalence of homosexuality found by Kinsey et al. and by more recent researchers. They note, for example, that Kinsey's sample was recruited purposefully, rather than selected by means of modern probability techniques. The former procedure leads to overestimation.

4 Curiously, men who act or pose in pornographic productions and those who patronize prostitutes have historically not been seen as deviant.

5 This is a substantial modification of Super's (1957) classification of career stages. Neither his taxonomy nor that of Miller and Form (1980), the two most cited schemes in the literature, fit the work histories of tolerable deviants. This sequence is developed further for another form of entertainment, namely, Canadian professional football (Stebbins, 1993).

6 Actual sex acts before an audience (paying or not) are seldom mentioned in the scientific literature on pornography (but see Special Committee on Pornography and Prostitution, 1985:128–129). Nonetheless, to the author's best knowledge, there is no publicly available pornography of this sort in Canada.

SUGGESTED READING

Bartell, Gilbert D. *Group Sex.* New York: Peter H. Wyden, 1971. A classic field study by an anthropologist and his wife of middle-class swingers and their get-togethers in the Chicago area.

Bryant, Clifton D. (ed.) *Sexual Deviancy in Social Context.* New York: New Viewpoints, 1977. A collection of articles on various kinds of sexual deviance under modern study.

Christensen, F.M. *Pornography: The Other Side.* New York: Praeger, 1990. Christensen, a philosopher of science, argues that antipornography campaigns are themselves morally evil, that vehement opposition to pornography is a symptom of tragically mistaken beliefs about sex.

Plummer, Kenneth (ed.) *The Making of the Modern Homosexual.* London: Hutchinson, 1981. A collection of articles on developments in the sociology of homosexuality, directions of inquiry, and selected research reports.

Tripp, C.A. *The Homosexual Matrix.* (2nd ed.) New York: New American Library, 1987. An excellent and engaging review by a psychologist of the psychology, sociology, and politics of homosexuality.

Wolf, Deborah Goleman. *The Lesbian Community*. Berkeley, CA: University of California Press, 1979. A classic participant observer study of the San Fransisco lesbian community, a community well known for its radical stand on lesbian issues.

REFERENCES

Adam, Barry D. *The Rise of a Gay and Lesbian Movement.* Boston: Twayne, 1987.

Auger, Jeanette A. "Lesbians and Aging: Triple Trouble or Tremendous Thrill." In *Lesbians in Canada*, edited by Sharon D. Stone, pp. 25–34. Toronto: Between the Lines, 1990.

Bartell, Gilbert D. *Group Sex*. New York: Peter H. Wyden, 1971.

Bibby, Reginald. *The Moral Mosaic: Sexuality in the Canadian 80s*. Lethbridge, AB: University of Lethbridge, 1982.

Bindman, Stephen. "Military gives OK to Gays, Lesbians," *Calgary Herald*, 1992, Wednesday, October 28: A1.

Boles, Jacqueline and Albeno P. Garbin. "The Strip Club and the Stripper." In *Sexual Deviancy in Social Context*, edited by Clifton D. Bryant, pp. 111–123. New York: New Viewpoints, 1977.

Bond, Rene and Winston Hill. "Interview with a Pornographic Film Star." In *Sexual Deviance and Sexual Deviants*, edited by Erich Goode and Richard Troiden, pp. 68–72. New York: William Morrow, 1974.

Boswell, John. *Christianity, Social Tolerance, and Homosexuality*. Chicago: University of Chicago Press, 1980.

Brannigan, Augustine and Sheldon Goldenberg. "The Study of Aggressive Pornography: The Vicissitudes of Relevance," *Critical Studies in Mass Communications*, 1987, 4:262–283.

Brooks, Virginia. *Minority Stress and Lesbian Women*. Lexington, MA: D.C. Heath, 1981.

"Church Reaffirms Homosexual Policy," *Calgary Herald*, 1990, Wednesday, August 22:A1.

Clark, Rebecca. "Male Strippers," *Journal of Popular Culture*, 1985, 19, Summer: 51–56.

Committee on Homosexual Offences and Prostitution. *Report of the Committee on Homosexual Offences and Prostitution*. London: Her Majesty's Stationery Office, 1957.

Cooke, Amber. "Stripping — Who Calls the Tune?" In *Good Girls/Bad Girls: Sex Trade Workers and Feminists Face to Face*, edited by Laurie Bell, pp. 92–99. Toronto: The Women's Press, 1987.

Cronin, Denise M. "Coming Out Among Lesbians." In *Sexual Deviance and Sexual Deviants*, edited by Erich Goode and Richard Troiden, pp. 268–277. New York: William Morrow, 1974.

Dank, Barry M. "The Homosexual." In *Sexual Deviance and Sexual Deviants*, edited by Erich Goode and Richard Troiden, pp. 174–210. New York: William Morrow, 1974.

Davidson, J. Kenneth, Sr. "Autoeroticism, Sexual Satisfaction, and Sexual Adjustment among University Females: Past and Current Patterns," *Deviant Behavior*, 1984, 5:121–140.

DeLamater, John. "The Social Control of Sexuality." In *Annual Review of Sociology*, Vol. 7, edited by Ralph H. Turner and James F. Short, Jr., pp. 263–290. Palo Alto, CA: Annual Reviews, 1981.

Deschamps, Jean-Robert. "Sexual Offenses and Police Intervention," *Contact*, 1985, 4, Fall:6.

Dixon, Joan K. "Swinging." *Journal of Sex Research*, 1984, 20:71–90.

Donnelly, Peter. "Running the Gauntlet: The Moral Order of Pornographic Movie Theaters," *Urban Life*, 1981, 10:239–264.

Douglas, Jack D. and Frances C. Waksler. *The Sociology of Deviance*. Boston: Little Brown, 1982.

Dressel, Paula L. and David M. Peterson. "Becoming a Male Stripper," *Work and Occupations*, 1982, 9:387–406.

Ettore, E.M. *Lesbians, Women, and Society*. London: Routledge and Kegan Paul, 1980.

Faraday, Annable. "Liberating Lesbian Research." In *The Making of the Modern Homosexual*, edited by Kenneth Plummer, pp. 112–129. London: Hutchison, 1981.

Fischer, William A. and Azy Barak. "Pornography, Erotica, and Behaviour: More Questions than Answers," *International Journal of Law and Psychiatry*, 1991, 14:65–84.

Ford, Clellan and Frank A. Beach. *Patterns of Sexual Behavior*. New York: Harper and Row, 1951.

French, Carey. "Sexual Swinging in the Plague Years." *Globe and Mail*, 1988, Saturday, October 1:D5.

Fulford, Robert. "Crisis at the Victory Burlesk." In *The Underside of Toronto*, edited by W.E. Mann, pp. 255–258. Toronto: McClelland and Stewart, 1970.

Gallup Report. 1991, Wednesday, September 25.

Garrett, Laurie. "Report from the AIDS Front," *Newsday*, 1992, July 28:53, 56, 57.

Ginsburg, Kenneth N. "The Meat-Rack: A Study of the Male Homosexual Prostitute." In *Sexual Deviancy in Social Context*, edited by Clifton D. Bryant, pp. 160–176. New York: New Viewpoints, 1977.

Goffman, Erving. *Behavior in Public Places*. New York: The Free Press, 1963.

Goode, Erich. *Deviant Behavior*. (4th ed.) Englewood Cliffs, NJ: Prentice-Hall, 1994.

Greenberg, David F. *The Construction of Homosexuality*. Chicago: University of Chicago Press, 1988.

Greene, Beverly. "Lesbian and Gay Sexual Orientations." In *Lesbian and Gay Psychology*, edited by Beverly Greene and Gregory M. Herek, pp. 1–24. Thousand Oaks, CA: Sage Publications, 1994.

Hedblom, Jack H. "The Female Homosexual." In *Deviance*. (2nd ed.), edited by Simon Dinitz, Russell R. Dynes, and Alfred C. Clarke, pp. 235–247. New York: Oxford University Press, 1975.

Henshel, Anne Marie. "Swinging: A Study of Decision Making in Marriage," *American Journal of Sociology*, 1973, 78:885–891.

Herek, Gregory M. "Documenting Prejudice Against Lesbians and Gay Men on Campus: The Yale Sexual Orientation Survey," *Journal of Homosexuality*, 1993, 25:15–30.

Hesslund, Hans. "Masturbation and Sexual Fantasies in Married Couples," *Archives of Sexual Behavior*, 1976, 5:133–147.

Humphreys, Laud. *Tearoom Trade*. (Enlarged ed.) New York: Aldine, 1975.

Jahr, Cliff. "The All-Gay Cruise." In *Deciphering Deviance*, edited by Saul D. Feldman, pp. 401–405. Boston: Little Brown, 1978.

Jenks, Richard J. "A Comparative Study of Swingers and Nonswingers: Attitudes and Beliefs," *Lifestyles*, 1985, 8:5–20.

Kinsey, Alfred C. et al. *Sexual Behavior in the Human Female*. Philadelphia: W.B. Saunders, 1953.

Kinsman, Gary. *The Regulation of Desire: Sexuality in Canada*. Montréal: Black Rose Books, 1987.

Knox, David. *Human Sexuality*. St. Paul, MN: West Publishing Co., 1984.

Laumann, Edward O., John H. Gagnon, Robert T. Michael, and Stuart Michaels. *The Social Organization of Sexuality: Sexual Practices in the United States*. Chicago: University of Chicago Press, 1994.

Leslie, Gerald R. and Sheila K. Korman. *The Family in Social Context*. (7th ed.) New York: Oxford University Press, 1989.

Lewis, Sasha G. *Sunday's Women: Lesbian Life Today*. Boston: Beacon Press, 1979.

Lindquist, John and Howard L. Cane. "Myths and Realities of Dirty Book Buyers," *Free Inquiry in Creative Sociology*, 1979:7.

Linz, Daniel and Neil Malamuth. *Pornography*. Newbury Park, CA: Sage Publications,1993.

Livingood, J.M. (ed.) *National Institute of Mental Health Task Force on Homosexuality: Final Report and Background Papers*. Rockville, MD: National Institute of Mental Health, 1972.

Livsey, Bruce. "Aural Sex," *Financial Post Magazine*, 1994, July/August: 22–26.

Luckenbill, David F. "Entering Male Prostitution," *Urban Life*, 1985, 14:131–154.

Lyman, Stanford M. and Marvin B. Scott. *The Drama of Social Reality*. New York: Oxford University Press, 1975.

MacIntosh, Mary. "Homosexual Role." In *The Making of the Modern Homosexual*, edited by Kenneth Plummer, pp. 30–52. London: Hutchinson, 1981.

Martin, Del and Phyllis Lyon. *Lesbian/Woman*. New York: Bantam Books, 1972.

McCaghy, Charles H. and James K. Skipper, Jr. "Lesbian Behavior as an Adaptation to the Occupation of Stripping." In *Deviant Behavior*, edited by Delos H. Kelly, pp. 478–488. New York: St. Martin's Press, 1979.

McKay, Barry and L. Dolff. *The Impact of Pornography: An Analysis of Research and Summary of Findings*. Ottawa: Department of Justice, Research, and Statistics, Government of Canada, 1985.

McKinstry, William C. "The Pulp Voyeur: A Peek at Pornography in Public Places." In *Deviance: Field Studies and Self-Disclosures*, edited by Jerry Jacobs, pp. 30–40. Palo Alto, CA: National Press Book, 1974.

Miller, Delbert C. and William H. Form. *Industrial Sociology*. (3rd ed.) New York: Harper & Row, 1980.

Miller, Gale. *Odd Jobs: The World of Deviant Work*. Englewood Cliffs, NJ: Prentice-Hall, 1978.

Palson, Charles and Rebecca Palson. "Swinging in Wedlock," *Transactional/Society*, 1972, 9, February: 28–37.

Paquette, Carmen. "Personal Reflections on Lesbian Organizing in Ottawa." In *Lesbians in Canada*, edited by Sharon D. Stone, pp. 221–229. Toronto: Between the Lines, 1990.

Parker, Graham. *An Introduction to Criminal Law*. (3rd ed.) Toronto: Methuen, 1987.

Peterson, David M. and Paula L. Dressel. "Social Notes on the Male Strip Show," *Urban Life*, 1982, 11:185–208.

Plummer, Kenneth. "Homosexual Categories: Some Research Problems in the Labelling Perspective of Homosexuality." In *The Making of the Modern Homosexual*, edited by Kenneth Plummer, pp. 53–75. London: Hutchinson, 1981.

Polsky, Ned. *Hustlers, Beats, and Others*. Chicago: University of Chicago Press, 1985.

Ponse, Barbara. "The Problematic Meaning of Lesbian." In *The Sociology of Deviance*, edited by Jack D. Douglas pp. 25–33. Boston: Allyn and Bacon, 1984.

Potter, Gary W. "The Retail Pornography Industry and the Organization of Vice," *Deviant Behavior*, 1989, 10:233–251.

Rayside, David and Scott Bowler. "Public Opinion and Gay Rights," *Canadian Review of Sociology and Anthropology*, 1988, 25:649–660.

"Realities and Fallacies of Homosexuality," *Society*, 1993, 30, July/August:2–3.

Rich, Robert M. *The Sociology of Criminal Law*. Toronto: Butterworths, 1979.

Richardson, Diane. "Lesbian Identities." In *The Theory and Practice of Homosexuality*, edited by John Hart and Diane Richardson, pp. 111–124. London: Routledge and Kegan Paul, 1981.

Risman, Barbara and Pepper Schwartz. "Sociological Research on Male and Female Homosexuality." In *Annual Review of Sociology*, Vol. 14, edited by W. Richard Scott and Judith Blake, pp. 125–147. Palo Alto, CA: Annual Reviews, Inc., 1988.

Ronai, Carol R. and Carolyn Ellis. "Turn-Ons for Money: Interactional Strategies of the Table Dancer," *Journal of Contemporary Ethnography*, 1989, 18:271–298.

Rothblum, Esther D. "Introduction: Lesbianism as a Model of a Positive Lifestyle for Women." In *Loving Boldly: Issues Facing Lesbians*, edited by Esther D. Rothblum and Ellen Cole, pp. 1–12. New York: Harrington Park Press, 1989.

Russell, D.E.H. "Pornography and Rape: A Causal Model," *Political Psychology*, 1988, 9:41–73.

Saghir, Marcel T. and Eli Robins. *Male and Female Homosexuality*. Baltimore, MD: Williams and Wilkins, 1973.

Salamon, Edna. "The Homosexual Escort Agency," *British Journal of Sociology*, 1989, 40:1–21.

Salutin, Marilyn. "Stripper Morality." In *Deviant Behavior and Societal Reaction*, edited by Craig L. Boydell, Carl F. Grindstaff, and Paul C. Whithead, pp. 532–545. Toronto: Holt, Rinehart & Winston of Canada, 1971.

Scholfield, Michael. *Sociological Aspects of Homosexuality: A Comparative Study of Three Types of Homosexuals*. Boston: Little Brown, 1965.

Schur, Edwin M. *Labeling Women Deviant*. New York: Random House, 1984.

Skipper, James K., Jr. and Charles H. McCaghy. "Stripteasing: A Sex-Oriented Occupation." In *Studies in the Sociology of Sex*, edited by James M. Henslin, pp. 275–296. Appleton-Century-Crofts, 1971.

Slade, Joseph. "Pornographic Theaters Off Times Square," *Transactional/Society*, 1971, 9, November-December:35–43, 79.

Special Committee on Pornography and Prostitution. *Pornography and Prostitution in Canada*, Vol. 1. Ottawa: Canadian Government Publishing Centre, 1985.

Sproat, Ron. "The Working Day in a Porno Factory." In *Sexual Deviance and Sexual Deviants*, edited by Erich Goode and Richard Troiden, pp. 83–92. New York: William Morrow, 1974.

Stebbins, Robert A. *Canadian Football: The View from the Helmet.* Toronto: Canadian Scholars Press, 1993.
Stein, Michael. *The Ethnography of an Adult Bookstore.* Lewiston, NY: Edwin Mellen Press, 1990.
Steinem, Gloria. "Erotica and Pornography." In *Take Back the Night,* edited by Laura Lederer, pp. 35–39. New York: William Morrow, 1980.
Stephenson, Richard M. "Involvement in Deviance," *Social Problems,* 1973, 21:173–190.
Sundholm, Charles A. "The Pornographic Arcade," *Urban Life and Culture,* 1973, 2:85–104.
Super, Donald E. *The Psychology of Careers.* New York: Harper & Row, 1957.
Symonds, Carolyn. "Sexual Mate Swapping." In *Studies in the Sociology of Sex,* edited by James M. Henslin, pp. 81–112. New York: Appleton-Century-Crofts, 1971.
Talese, Gay. *Thy Neighbor's Wife.* Garden City, NY: Doubleday, 1980.
Tewskbury, Richard. "Patrons of Porn: Research Notes on the Clientele of Adult Bookstores," *Deviant Behavior,* 1990, 11:259–271.
Thio, Alex. *Deviant Behavior.* (3rd ed.) Boston: Houghton Mifflin, 1988.
Thompson, William E. and Jackie L. Harred. "Topless Dancers: Managing Stigma in a Deviant Occupation," *Deviant Behavior,* 1992, 13:291–311.
Tripp, C.A. *The Homosexual Matrix.* (2nd ed.) New York: Meridian, 1987.
Visano, Livy A. *This Idle Trade: The Occupational Patterns of Male Prostitution.* Concord, ON: VitaSana Books, 1987.
Weinberg, Martin S. and Colin J. Williams. *Male Homosexuals.* New York: Penguin Books, 1975.
Winick, Charles. "From Deviant to Normative: Changes in the Social Acceptability of Sexually Explicit Material." In *Deviant Behavior.* (2nd ed.), edited by Delos Kelly, pp. 712–743. New York: St. Martins, 1984.
Wolf, Deborah Goleman. *The Lesbian Community.* Berkeley, CA: University of California Press, 1979.
Wolschok, Ann. "The Emergence of Middle-Class Deviant Subcultures: The Case of Swingers," *Social Problems,* 1971, 18:488–495.
Wood, Floris W. (ed.) *An American Profile — Opinion and Behavior: 1972–1989.* Detroit: Gale Research, 1990.
Yaffé, Maurice and Edward C. Nelson. *The Influence of Pornography on Behaviour.* London: Academic Press, 1982.
Zillman, D. and J. Bryant. "Effects of Prolonged Consumption of Pornography on Family Values," *Journal of Family Issues,* 1988, 9:518–544.
Ziplow, Steven. *The Film Maker's Guide to Pornography.* New York: Drake Publishers, 1977.

5

ALCOHOL

Consuming alcohol is part of the way of life in Canada and many other countries around the world. According to figures compiled in 1991, Canadians and Americans drink 35 percent less than Europeans, who consume more than 10 litres of alcohol per year. Australians drink 20 percent more than North Americans (*The Journal*, 1991/1992:15). A recent *Gallup Report* (1994) estimated that 76 percent of Canadians imbibe; the figure has fluctuated between 75 and 80 percent since 1974.

In Canadian society, people drink alcoholic beverages in a variety of settings. For instance, alcohol is often a central ingredient in the celebration of the approaching weekend, the happy practice of the TGIF (thank God it's Friday) party. Soirees, weddings, receptions, and birthdays are commonly seen as events requiring alcohol, as most certainly are the weeks of the Christmas-Chanukkah-New Year's season. Between these and other customary and quasi-customary occasions that invite drinking, we can observe the use of alcohol on television, watch others imbibe at sidewalk cafes, and sense the joy of it all from countless advertisements in newspapers and magazines and on roadside billboards.

This is social drinking, or at least that is the definition promoted by the alcoholic beverage industry and by many of its customers. However, the physical condition resulting from strong dosage is seen as deviant. There are two major deviant extensions of widely accepted social practice: drunkenness, defined by many Canadians as a tolerable form of deviance in alcohol use; and alcoholism, an intolerable form. Both are covered in this chapter, since they are interrelated in several ways and since both rest on some of the same precipitating factors. For wine, beer, and spirits are **drugs**: substances or preparations which are narcotic and which, in moderate doses, induce sleep, relieve pain, and weaken sensitivity. In strong doses, however, alcohol, like many other drugs, is poisonous; it produces stupor, coma, and convulsions. While it is possible for specialists to define drunkenness and alcoholism in relatively precise physiological terms, these states are frequently given imprecise social definitions by the general public.

DEFINING ALCOHOLIC DEVIANCE

On the most general level, the public sees drunkenness and alcoholism as deviant because these conditions give the appearance that those affected have lost control over their actions. Willful loss of control in societies such as ours where rational behaviour is valued (behaviour motivated by distinct goals and pursued by efficient means) is scorned and discouraged. Loss of control is expressed in two ways (MacAndrew and Edgerton, 1969:13–14). First, it is believed that drink markedly impairs one's ability to perform sensorimotor skills. Examples are the inability to walk straight, talk clearly, or stand without wavering. Scientific research corroborates this common sense observation. Second, alcohol is believed to depress certain functions in the brain, thereby weakening one's moral and thought functions. This conventional belief has entered science under the name of the **disinhibition hypothesis**. MacAndrew and Edgerton (1969: Ch. 2) cite cross-cultural evidence that casts doubt on this notion. Akers (1992:42) cites survey and laboratory research demonstrating that both conforming and deviant behaviour enacted under the influence of alcohol "are more a function of sociocultural and individual expectations and attitudes than of the physiological effects of alcohol."

It is clear that Canadian laws about alcohol consumption are based, to some extent, on these conventional beliefs. The assumption of moral inhibition caused by alcohol is evident in the section of the Criminal Code that defines as disorderly conduct any act that causes a disturbance in or near a public place as a result of drunkenness. Further, a person who is habitually drunk in the home "and thereby endangers the morals of the child or renders the home an unfit place for the child to be in," is guilty of a more serious offence. In both instances, the assumption is that drunkenness is an important factor in disturbing or endangering the child's morals. It is assumed that people who are drunk are morally and rationally out of control. In the same vein, the law assumes that "intoxicating liquor" can be used to "stupefy or overpower" a person so that he or she will submit to sexual intercourse, an act the individual would presumably resist under conditions of sobriety. Thus, the Criminal Code, section 212(1)(i), also makes this act an offence. It is also an offence to be in the care or control of a motor vehicle while drunk. This law, however, is founded on the more scientifically defensible principle that sensorimotor skills are impaired by excessive drinking. Table 5.1 demonstrates how, as the percentage of alcohol in the blood increases, sensorimotor behaviour becomes impaired.

TABLE 5.1 BLOOD ALCOHOL LEVEL AND BEHAVIOURAL EFFECTS

Percent Blood Alcohol Level	Behavioural Effects
0.05	Lowered alertness, usually good feeling, release of inhibitions, impaired judgment
0.10	Slowed reaction times and impaired motor function, less caution
0.15	Large, consistent increases in reaction time
0.20	Marked depression in sensory and motor capability, decided intoxication
0.25	Severe motor disturbance, staggering, great impairment of sensory perceptions
0.30	Stuporous but conscious — no comprehension of the surrounding world
0.35	Surgical anesthesia; about LD (lethal dose) 1, minimum level causing death
0.40	About LD 50

Source: Ray Oakley and Charles Ksir. *Drugs, Society, and Human Behavior.* (5th ed.) St. Louis, MO: Mosby/Year Book, 1989, p. 154.

It should be no surprise, then, that legal definitions of drunkenness also follow the moral-rational inhibition assumption. Legally, a **drunk**, someone in the state of drunkenness, is a person who has lost personal control because of too much alcohol. **Habitual drunkenness** refers to the habit of getting drunk frequently, with sessions of sobriety in between (Rich, 1979:194). Kotarba (1984:154), for example, defines "heavy drinking" (i.e., habitual drunkenness) as the consumption of five or more drinks on a more or less daily basis.

The question of interest to those who view alcohol consumption from the labelling perspective is, Where on the scale of blood alcohol levels (Table 5.1) does one become morally and rationally drunk? Consider the following interpretation by Ray and Ksir (1989:154):

> At less than 0.03%, the individual is dull and dignified.
> At 0.05%, he is dashing and debonair.
> At 0.1%, he may become dangerous and devilish.
> At 0.2%, he is likely to be dizzy and disturbing.
> At 0.25%, he may be disgusting and dishevelled.
> At 0.3%, he is delirious and disoriented and surely drunk.
> At 0.35%, he is dead drunk.
> At 0.6%, the chances are that he is dead.

Is a particular individual drunk at 0.03 percent or must he or she reach 0.05 or 0.1? Ray and Ksir suggest that definite drunkenness sets in at 0.3 percent. The legal limit for driving is 0.08 percent. But much depends on the status of the person in question and the situation in which he or she is being judged. Different people will define that person differently, on the basis of their attitudes toward him or her and toward alcohol. Even though precise measurement of alcohol consumption is available and motor behaviour can be proved to be affected by it, the label of "drunk" is applied in everyday life with considerable looseness.

Defining **alcoholism** is no easier. One common conception is that it is a physically damaging disease resting on physiological dependency and uncontrolled consumption of alcohol. Perhaps the two best-known proponents of this definition are E.M. Jellinek (1960) and Mark Keller (1960). Some scientists reject the disease concept, however, arguing either that it is vague or that it is unsubstantiated by research evidence (for a review, see Conrad and Schneider, 1992:97–106; Fingarette, 1988). What *is* alcoholism, if it is not a disease? This question is seldom answered by the critics of the disease concept. We shall return to the definition of alcoholism later in the chapter.

CONSEQUENCES OF ALCOHOL USE

Directly or indirectly, the definitions of drunkenness and alcoholism reflect, in the minds of their creators and proponents, a concern with the consequences of excessive alcohol use. The popular view is that those consequences are inevitably unfavourable for the individual or for society or for both. Lemert (1972:73–74) lists three which are dysfunctional in many societies.

First, there are economic costs associated with drunkenness and alcoholism. People do squander money on liquor, money that could be invested in capitalist enterprise or given to charity, for example. Also, rehabilitation programs for problem drinkers absorb funds that could be spent elsewhere. Second, "[i]ntoxication and drunkenness levy critically higher costs in certain contexts of technologically mediated, interdependent, high-speed, high productivity, health-oriented societies" (Lemert, 1972:74). In other words, drunkenness and alcoholism contribute to death and injury rates, lower productivity, cause traffic accidents, and lead to absenteeism. Third, excessive consumption of alcohol leads to disorderly conduct. Although the rate of arrests for alcohol-related offences has been declining, they still constitute the largest category of all arrests in North America (Thio, 1988:377; Jackson and Griffiths, 1991:90). And driving while intoxicated remains a significant offence in Canada, even though it dropped from its place as fourth most common in 1989 to seventh in 1993 (Statistics Canada, 1993). Fewer Canadians than ever are driving while under the influence.

Does excessive use of alcohol lead to crime and violence? The general public and even some criminologists (e.g., Siegel, 1992:308, 310) are convinced that it does. Still, the U.S. Secretary of Health Services (1990:171–174), in an exhaustive review of the pertinent literature, concluded that "methodological weaknesses in much of the applied research conducted in these areas preclude firm conclusions about alcohol's role in specific types of violence." This report contains a similar caveat with respect to the possible link between alcohol and property crime. Should science be unable to find a causal link between alcohol and crime and violence, we would have further support for Akers' conclusion cited earlier that deviant behaviour enacted under the influence of alcohol is more strongly related to expectations and attitudes than to physiological effects of the drug.

It is much less widely recognized that drunkenness and even alcoholism may also be functional for a society or a significant segment of it. Lemert (1972:73) notes that political regimes have used alcohol to make native populations dependent on them. Further, alcohol is often used to create a sense of fellowship and to strengthen group bonds. Alcohol, perhaps because we believe it to be a disinhibitor, helps bring people together by "loosening them up" and allowing for free interaction (Brissett, 1978:120). Lastly, to the extent that cures for common diseases benefit an entire society, alcohol, in moderate doses, may work (a function) to inhibit chronic lung disease and myoclonic dystonia, a movement disorder (*The Journal,* 1984c:5). There is also evidence that moderate drinkers have a lower incidence of heart disease than teetotalers (*UC Berkeley Wellness Letter,* 1994:5).

As for society, there are favourable and unfavourable consequences for individuals stemming from excessive consumption of alcohol. Lemert (1972:72) notes that alcohol is valued in some societies "as a food, as a promoter of digestion and sleep, and as a protection against cold and fatigue". Brissett (1978) observes that one's public image as a "heavy drinker" is a social identity and, in certain circles, a badge of self-worth. He goes on to note that regular drinking bouts are part of the drinker's routine existence; they help give continuity to life. Finally, because drunkenness in our society promotes the feeling of being outside one's ordinary roles, it allows for enacting new lines of behaviour. In these circumstances, inebriation is a "prop" in the drama of social interaction where drunken interactants can play at being people they are not in reality.

Many of the unfavourable consequences of excessive drinking for the individual are well known. The hangover is one of them. Long-term heavy drinkers suffer from malnutrition, muscle weakness, and, when combined with smoking, certain forms of cancer. With a history of prolonged heavy drinking, organic brain damage is possible. Such damage is a condition of alcoholic psychosis, a form of mental disorder. Last, but not least, long-term drinking to excess damages the liver by way of cirrhosis, an alcohol-generated disease.

Whether heavy drinking leads to positive or negative social and personal consequences depends, in part, on the context within which this kind of deviance occurs. From the standpoint of those doing the imbibing, moderate drinking as well as heavy drinking may be seen as either leisure or adjustment, or both. These two definitions of one's own heavy drinking vary according to a number of social characteristics. We examine first the two contexts of heavy drinking, then the social characteristics.

HEAVY DRINKING AS LEISURE

Statistically, rates of heavy drinking among Canadians have been falling in recent years (Canadian Centre on Substance Abuse, 1994:18). In 1989, 15 percent reported that they consumed at least 8 drinks per week, and 6 percent reported that they consumed 15 or more drinks weekly (Eliany, 1991). Men continue to outnumber women as heavy drinkers (and even as social drinkers). For example, in the same year, 10 percent of the male drinkers drank 15 or more drinks in a week, compared with 1 percent of the female drinkers.

Heavy drinking takes place in a variety of leisure settings, among them parties, receptions, picnics, bars, restaurants, clubs, festivals, and informal gatherings. However, some heavy drinking is done in seclusion or in isolation, often in the home. Sociological research on heavy drinking is usually limited to studies of bars and taverns and to studies of skid row, where drinking occurs in both settings as well as in small gatherings known as "bottle gangs".

Public Drinking Houses

Downtown bars, neighbourhood taverns, licensed restaurants, and posh nightclubs are among the many public drinking houses in Canada and the United States. Most people who frequent them are moderate social drinkers. For instance, only 2 percent of the sample of Canadian public drinkers studied by Cosper and his associates (1987) went to a public drinking house chiefly for the purpose of buying alcohol. The proportion having this motive rose only to 5 percent among frequent drinkers at regular drinking places. Nevertheless, some excessive drinking does take place. A number of antecedent conditions and social patterns have been identified in connection with heavy drinking in public drinking houses.

Clinard (1975) studied heavy drinking in the United States, where he noted that the tendency to mingle with other patrons in a drinking establishment diminished as an individual drinker became more inebriated. Heavy drinkers became less interested in the conversation and games around them and more interested in being alone to concentrate on their alcohol consumption. Although the practice is often illegal, bartenders sometimes encouraged this transition by suggesting that the inebriate "have another." Heavy drinking was also facilitated for some of Clinard's sample by friendships with bartenders and by loans (also illegal) that they made to the drinkers. He found that many heavy drinkers had, at one time or another, cashed their paycheques at the drinking houses they patronized. It is no wonder, then, that such drinkers prefer public houses whose main purpose is to sell liquor over those providing a combination of liquor and food, entertainment, or amusements (Cosper et al.,1987).

Smart and Ogborne (1986:76–80) summarized several studies of patron behaviour in Canadian public drinking houses. In contrast to the drinking scene described by Clinard, Canadian researchers have observed that, during a typical evening, the isolated drinker drinks less than group drinkers. The latter also stay longer in the tavern, chiefly because of the conviviality of the group. On balance, whether one drinks alone or in the company of others is not a factor in heavy drinking. It is also clear that bar staff in Canadian drinking places are aware of the monetary benefits to be gained from encouraging people to buy another round even though they are intoxicated (Prus, 1983).

Students of bar culture have learned that regulars at public drinking houses may, in fact, be habitués at several establishments. For example, some people go to a particular bar for sexual liaison, as in the heterosexual pickup (Cavan, 1966:178–190) or the homosexual one-night stand (Read, 1980). Or, as Kotarba (1984) found in his study of working-class men, a man may go to one bar to gamble, another to drink with workmates, a third to relax with members of the softball team, and a fourth to meet with his ethnic group.

These observations suggest that public drinking houses, especially those serving a neighbourhood, become socially specialized; they draw a particular leisure, ethnic, socioeconomic, age-related clientele. Moreover, these functions may change over the course of the day or week. That is, a bar might be filled with office workers in the late afternoons Monday through Friday, but become a hangout for local swingers or lesbians on Friday and Saturday evenings. Although there is no research to confirm it, the impression is that heavy drinkers imbibe in places that are congruent with their interests and social background, even if they interact relatively little with other patrons.

Skid Row Drinking

Archard (1979:1–4) indicates that **skid row**, a term coined in the United States, is identifiable by its unique combination of physical, behavioural, and economic characteristics. North American skid rows are found in or adjacent to the downtown core of large cities.[1] They offer a distinctive lifestyle of drinking, idling, panhandling, and searching for the necessities of existence (food, shelter, and a place to sleep). All this takes place within an environment of cheap restaurants, second-hand shops, religious missions, dilapidated hotels and rooming houses, and last, but certainly not least, seedy bars and taverns. Skid row as a way of life is considered in Chapter 9. Here we cover only the part of it that bears on heavy drinking and alcoholism.

Research in Britain, Canada, and the United States reveals that many skid row denizens are not problem drinkers (Archard, 1979:4; McLaughlin, 1987; Snow and Anderson, 1993:44–45). These studies, among others, suggest that approximately one-third of the male skid row population in North America are problem drinkers, and that this proportion may be somewhat higher in Britain. The large majority of the remainder are moderate drinkers, and a small proportion are true teetotalers. Although the stereotype that all men on skid row are problem drinkers is clearly false, it is true that more problem drinkers are found here than in the overall population where, as we saw earlier, they make up only between 6 and 15 percent. On skid row, as in the general population, problem drinking among women is much rarer than among men.

Correspondingly, Mathew Dumont (1981) found that the skid row bar, like the neighbourhood bar, is more than a watering hole for transient drunks and alcoholics. The tavern he studied offered relief from police harassment, shelter from the weather, and support and friendship from others of similar status. It was the daytime social centre for many skid row men, that is, until around four o'clock, when workers began to arrive for their pre-dinner drinks prior to going home.

Perhaps the most colourful drinking arrangement on skid row is the **bottle gang** (Snow and Anderson, 1993:190). Earl Rubington (1981) describes this collectivity. The gang forms spontaneously on the street, when several skid row men decide that they would like to drink. To reach this goal, they first pool their meagre cash and then dispatch one from their group (the "runner") to buy a bottle of cheap wine. If the group lacks sufficient money for the purchase, its members may try to panhandle the needed amount. The runner is carefully chosen for his apparent reliability (to return with the bottle) and relatively respectable looks (to avoid police harassment). Once the bottle is in hand, a semi-private place is sought, such as an alley or doorstep, where consumption can take place without interruption. The contents of the bottle are consumed in rounds at a rate of two swallows per drinker starting with the leader, or organizer, and continuing with the runner. Drinking is done furtively; the bottle is always hidden in its brown bag. Between rounds the men smoke and talk about mutual interests on skid row. Once the bottle is empty, the gang disperses, unless the decision is made to drink further. Archard (1979:66–81) found that the British **drinking school** operates in much the same way and serves many of the same purposes as the North American bottle gang.

HEAVY DRINKING AS ADJUSTMENT

On the basis of Fingarette's (1988) book on heavy drinking, the heavy drinker may be defined as follows: A **heavy drinker** consumes alcohol in excess of community norms, doing so to the point where it becomes the central activity in what other people consider a deviant way of life. Three conventional definitions of alcoholism and heavy drinking are also pertinent to the present discussion. The **physical dependence** definition — an alcoholic is someone who experiences intolerable withdrawal symptoms when off the bottle — does not necessarily apply to the heavy drinker. The latter may drink a great deal, but somehow avoids becoming dependent on liquor. The **lack of control** definition espoused by E.M. Jellinek (1952) and Alcoholics Anonymous attempts to define both the heavy drinker and the alcoholic. Both are believed to be unable to control their alcohol consumption. The control definition shades off into the **disease** definition, which, as indicated earlier, is also endorsed by Alcoholics Anonymous, Jellinek, and Keller (1976), among others: alcoholism is a medical disease, and alcoholics are people who suffer from this disease.

By and large, these definitions all centre on the consequences and characteristics of heavy drinking and its most serious stage of development: alcoholism. In accordance with the theme of this book, heavy drinking may be defined in still another way — as a socially labelled deviant adjustment to certain problems, demands, or situations in life. In contrast to the definitions just presented, the conception of deviance as adjustment stresses the antecedents that lead to what the majority of society feels is morally reprehensible behaviour.

In scientific circles, the disease definition is the most controversial of the four conventional definitions presented. Conrad and Schneider (1992:102) report that the majority of practitioners and pure scientists still accept it. But there is also growing opposition to it. First, some critics say that the alcoholism-as-disease notion is an analogy that has outlived its usefulness. Its major contribution was historical and humanitarian; it encouraged the public to view alcoholism as something other than an immoral, deviant condition. These critics contend that the disease conception now hampers research on alcoholism by suggesting that one becomes an alcoholic involuntarily and that, as in other diseases, cure is largely out of the hands of the patient.

Second, the disease conception of alcoholism has not been supported by research. Conrad and Schneider (1992:103–105) have reviewed the evidence, and note that research has failed to substantiate the claim that alcoholics have predisposing characteristics that distinguish them from non-alcoholics (see also Fingarette, 1988). Research has also failed to confirm Jellinek's belief that alcoholic drinking is a form of progressive degeneration which inevitably culminates in destructive addiction. Nor does there seem to be adequate evidence for the hypothesis that chronic drinking results from loss of self-control, that alcoholics are physically incapable of saying "no" to their desire for liquor.

Perhaps most controversial of all is the hypothesis that absolute abstinence for the rest of one's life is required of the alcoholic if he or she is to remain sober. Conrad and Schneider (1992:105) discuss a review of 74 studies, all of which have failed to support this proposition. The alternative hypothesis, for which there is some evidence, is that at least a proportion of former alcoholics can become self-controlled social drinkers; that is, the career of an alcoholic is unpredictable and by no means unidirectional: he or she engages in troubled drinking at various points of a mostly unpredictable career. A researcher unaware of the variety and variability of alcoholic careers might easily conclude that a certain pattern exists where there is none (Gilbert, 1987:5). Thus, a study of heavy drinkers who recovered on their own which was carried out at the Addiction Research Foundation (Hollobon, 1990) reported the following: "The majority who recover naturally, like the treated, remain abstinent, but a few return to low levels of drinking. Some drink once or twice a year, while a few might drink six days a month but one to three drinks at most." Still, as one might suspect in so difficult an area, there is also recent evidence in support of the absolute abstinence principle (Helzer et al., 1985).

The controversy over the disease conception continues. Some argue, with Szasz (1972), that alcoholism is really a bad habit, not a disease. Long-time medical researcher Jules H. Masserman, a physician, seems to side with Szasz when he says that "no one has yet demonstrated any determinative, genetic, constitutional, dietary, infectious, or other solely physiological causes of 'alcoholism'" (Carpey, 1984:12; see also *The Journal*, 1989:6; Faulkner et al.,1988). Alasuutari (1992:54) calls alcoholism-as-disease a "modern myth". Even some lay people have been impressed with the lack of congruence of the disease conception of alcoholism with the actual characteristics and consequences of this form of deviance:

> Dear Ann Landers: We are hearing a great deal about the "disease" called alcoholism these days. Do you have the guts to print this?
>
> If alcoholism is a disease, it's the only disease that is bottled and sold.
> It is the only disease that requires a licence to keep it going.

It is the only disease contracted by the will of man.
It is the only disease that produces revenue for the government.
It is the only disease that provokes crime.
It is the only disease that is habit-forming.
It is also the only disease that causes violent death on the highways.
It is the only disease spread by advertising.
And the only disease not caused by a germ or a virus.
Can it be that it is not a disease at all?

I'm from the Show-Me State

Dear Missouri: The experts whose opinions I respect say alcoholism IS a disease. But you raise some interesting questions. Thanks for writing.

Ann Landers' response hints at the exasperation that many specialists in this area must also feel: if not the disease conception, then what? By what conceptual means do we direct the treatment of this widespread problem?

Alcohol Abuse and the Workplace

The conception of deviance as adjustment revolves around the antecedents leading to the deviant behaviour. For example, some people drink heavily to try to erase from their memory particular unpleasant emotional experiences. Others do so in the belief that drink will help them enjoy a social gathering, build their self-confidence, or aid their functioning ability at work or leisure. In the terminology of anomie theory, excessive use of alcohol is at times an act of retreatism, an escape from something, and at others times an act of innovation, a deviant means of reaching conventional goals. Both are ways of adjusting to life's demands.

With respect to the adjustive use of alcohol in the workplace, there is considerable debate about whether the unfavourable characteristics of a given workplace are related to excessive use of alcohol. Martin (1990) has reviewed the evidence for and against this proposition, only to come to the conclusion that the jury is still out. "The actual relationship," he says (1990:60), "is probably found between these opposing points of view. It is not the conclusion of this literature review that workplace factors are the primary causes of alcohol problems." Other factors such as genetic tendencies, personality attributes, and family relationships are significantly more important.

Still, the general public, as well as some scientists (Plant, 1979: Ch. 2), believe that certain occupations and levels of society do contain disproportionate numbers of problem drinkers. The following passage about alcohol use in Britain demonstrates how this view gets established:

The influence of an individual's occupation is another factor which has an effect on his drinking. This can be exerted in several ways. The most direct influence will be when the job makes alcohol specially available to him at little or no cost — the hotel chef or kitchen porter who is given as much drink as he wants, the barman who is repeatedly being stood drinks by his customers, the brewery worker who is granted or knows how to "fiddle" a daily ration of beer, and so on. Some people in such occupa-

> tions may of course be attracted to work where alcohol is available since they are drinking heavily already: the barman's choice of occupation may, for instance, be as much an effect of his drinking as a continuing support of his habit. The influence of occupation may also work in many other powerful but less direct ways, as in the cases of the executive or the travelling salesman with expense-account entertaining, the unmarried itinerant labourer whose only leisure activity is drinking with other men in the pub, the worker in the printing trade who is exposed to strong occupational traditions of drinking, the actor or entertainer, or the street photographer who always goes to the pub when it rains (Royal College of Psychiatrists, 1979:103–104).

These people drink frequently. But, according to research, they drink only small amounts at each sitting, for their average consumption and ratio of problem drinkers matches that of other occupational groups. The studies reported by Cosper and Hughes (1983) and by *The Journal* (1984b:11) demonstrate a similar pattern for journalists and members of the Canadian Forces, respectively.

Fillmore's (1990) and Maranda's (1991) studies of occupational drinking subcultures demonstrate that certain conditions can foster job-related use of alcohol. Working routinely in a team with colleagues promotes solidarity, which may be founded in part on drinking together both on and off the job. Moreover, some occupations, such as bartending, make alcohol routinely available to those working in them.

Nor does the fact that epidemiological studies show problem drinkers to be more prevalent in the working classes necessarily refute the proposition that problem drinking and occupation are unrelated. Archer (1977:22) points out that such studies derive their conclusions from the exceptional numbers of working-class employees in industrial alcohol-treatment programs. However, it is likely that there is a stereotype among the middle-class superiors of these workers that problem drinking is a distinctly working-class affliction. And, since working-class employees are more closely supervised than many white-collar ones, their alcohol-related problems are more readily identified. The result: a disproportionate number of working-class personnel are referred to company treatment programs and, subsequently, spurious conclusions are reported in the epidemiological research literature.

The foregoing should not suggest, however, that deviant use of alcohol in the workplace is unrelated to attempts to adjust to something. A minority of workers in a variety of occupations at all social-class levels may still use alcohol to cope with problems to which their colleagues adjust in other ways, some of which may also be deviant. In a summary of the risk factors at work that, so to speak, drive some people to drink, Plant (1979:38–40) lists the following: social pressures to drink; separation from normal social or sexual relationships or from both; poverty; and specific work-related stresses.

Heavy Drinking and the Elderly

As the average longevity of the population increases, more and more heavy drinkers are appearing in the ranks of the elderly, drinkers who are attempting to adjust to problems unique to their phase of the life cycle. In general, heavy drinking tapers off with advancing years (Pittman, 1990:22). But recently, there has been evidence that some people aged 65 and older are drinking in excess. Heavy drinking is frequently the way these people cope with depression, loss of friends and relatives, and loneliness and isolation (Atkinson, 1988; Hollobon, 1986:1). Older men may be more likely to adjust in this deviant manner than older women facing the same social and psychological conditions.

Data from the General Social Survey of 1991 demonstrates that the proportion of alcohol-related deaths in Canada rose significantly between 1987 and 1990 among males and females aged 65 and older (Canadian Centre for Substance Abuse, 1994:68–69). By contrast, other age categories generally showed a relatively stable rate or a moderate decline during the same period. The rate of increase for the elderly ranged from 12 to 42 percent, depending on the age category examined.

ALCOHOLISM AS DEVIANT CAREER

Whether alcohol is used as an aid to adjustment or as a vehicle for leisure, its addictive properties can force users into a special deviant career — that of the alcoholic. Jellinek's (1952) model of the four-stage process of alcoholism describes the progressive psychological and physiological changes that take place as addiction sets in.

In the **pre-alcoholic symptomatic stage**, the would-be alcoholic discovers, while drinking locally, that alcohol can relieve certain tensions. In Jellinek's scheme, continued drinking actually reduces the individual's tolerance for tension, which, nevertheless, he or she attempts to reduce by consuming more liquor. The more the individual drinks, the greater his or her tolerance for alcohol grows. Hence, a vicious circle is established. As the amount of alcohol increases, so does the psychological and physiological impact of the drug. This stage can last anywhere from six months to two years.

When early alcoholics begin to experience blackouts, Jellinek says they have entered the **prodromal** stage. A blackout is a lapse in memory caused by the over-ingestion of alcohol. After the drinking bout, the incipient alcoholic has no memory of what happened during it. A blackout is not the same thing as passing out from too much liquor. The prodromal stage is also characterized by solitary, clandestine drinking, as in sneaking a swallow or two in the morning. As the need grows for greater amounts of alcohol, more clandestine drinking occurs, accompanied by guilt for the problems caused by the secret drinking.

The onset of the **crucial** stage is marked by a lack of control over drinking. Consumption continues until the individual passes out, runs out of alcohol, or runs out of money to buy it. According to Jellinek, this stage is distinguished by the alcoholic's efforts to demonstrate to all who might care that the drinking is controllable. In this connection, there may be short periods of sobriety or changes in drinking patterns, such as consuming drinks more slowly. But, when even the alcoholic is unable to deny the lack of control, he or she begins to create rationalizations for it, which include blaming important people in the person's life for the condition: spouse, employer, workmates, and relatives. This behaviour, too, has its self-fulfilling tendencies: it engenders guilt and a desire to assuage it with liquor. Many alcoholics lose their interest in food at this time, preferring a steady diet of drink.

Such eating and drinking patterns propel alcoholics toward the **chronic** stage, in which they begin to display bizarre behaviour. Their strong dependence on liquor generates a terrible fear that their supply of it may somehow disappear or dry up. This is the time of binge drinking, sometimes lasting for several days. During this final stage, *delirium tremens* sets in, the manifestations of which include uncontrollable shaking and frightening hallucinations. Alcoholics in this condition may have deteriorated so much they find it difficult to get a drink to their mouths because of their violent shaking. When they finally manage to do so, and swallow the contents, they vomit immediately. Many people at this stage also suffer from progressive malnutrition. Acute liver damage (cirrhosis) and mental disorder (alcoholic psychosis) are among the conditions at the chronic stage that finally drive at least some alcoholics to seek help, to admit they have a problem that they are unable to solve alone and seek help. (See Viewpoint 5.1.)

The alcoholic career is, at every step of the way, a set of adjustments to circumstances, real and imagined, which have existed, presently exist, or will exist. The Jellinek model describes alcoholism as a progressive disease that inevitably worsens unless it is treated. As mentioned earlier, however, there are serious challenges in research to his assumptions of progressiveness and uncontrollability. Considered as a career, as we have done here, these challenges pose no problem. The labelling theory conception of deviant career includes the possibility of abandoning that career. For example, the alcoholic might be alarmed by his or her behaviour at the prodromal stage and find other ways to adjust to the critical problems. Whatever the nature of the career of the problem drinker, there are other factors underlying excessive drinking besides the need to adjust to something.

CULTURAL ANTECEDENTS

For certain segments of the population, sometimes referred to by practitioners as "high-risk groups", drinking is part of the way of life. Drinking blends with other aspects of the group's culture to produce exceptional rates of consumption, in comparison with other groups in society and with society as a whole. That is, the cultural milieu into which a person is born or which he or she enters at a later stage of life may encourage alcohol consumption in special ways.

Excessive alcohol use among Canadian native peoples, for instance, has reached epidemic proportions in certain parts of the country. Heavy drinking by Indians is concentrated among young males who consume liquor in small groups, in much the same manner as the skid row bottle gang described earlier (Lemert, 1982). From a cultural perspective, there is considerable tolerance for this behaviour — indeed, even peer pressure (McKenzie, 1994) — within the native community. Thomas (1981) observes that one of the problems faced by many

VIEWPOINT 5.1

HITTING THE BOTTOM AS AN ALCOHOLIC

I had no idea how depressing, lonely, even frightening, alcoholism could be. That is, I had no idea until I lost everything that I cherished — my job, my wife, and my self-respect. And, yet, looking back on it now, I had to "hit bottom", as recovered alcoholics call it, before I could gather enough courage to face my troubles head on.

I always liked to drink. It was the social thing to do, and getting drunk once in a while was all right, too. It all happened so gradually that it was hard to realize I was becoming an alcoholic. I just had more fights with my boss who didn't like the way I was managing his store. I hated him but still wanted to prove to him that I could do the job. The booze helped me forget; it calmed my nerves. At the bar and at home I could give my side of our disagreements and get support from those who listened.

But I guess everyone got tired of hearing about my troubles — after all, the boss and I were fighting over the same issues. The booze and the talk had been my therapy. But eventually I had only the booze. So I drank alone.

I got used to this style of life, getting soused alone, then coming home, often in a foul mood. I started taking secret nips on the job, too. Eventually my performance at work began to deteriorate, and my boss had no trouble finding a justification for firing me. In the middle of last winter, I suddenly was out of work.

My wife was furious. She felt the drinking had caused the firing. After a particularly bitter fight one night following my return from the bar, she took the kids and the car and drove to her mother's house in another city. There was no money coming in, and we would be unable to pay the rent on our apartment. She could also see that I was getting worse rather than better.

I was out on my ear shortly after the end of the month. I did have some money left over as severance pay from my job, but a lot of this went for drinks and bottles of liquor, so other living costs had to be cheap. I found a room in one of the seedier areas of town. I disliked the people who lived in the neighbourhood. They were not like me, I thought. Yet, because I wanted to talk with others about my problems, I soon came to know them.

As my money ran out, my situation worsened. I couldn't leave this area of the city, since it was the only place I could survive without money. I had learned from my acquaintances how to panhandle and generally how to scrounge a living. But since I would drink up all the cash that I could gather in, eating and sleeping became randomly met needs — eating at a nearby mission when food was available and sleeping when I found a protected doorway, park bench, or parking garage.

Finally, I was arrested on a public nuisance charge. I had eaten little in days and was sleeping in a back alley after an evening of drinking cheap wine. Someone called the police, and I wound up spending the night in jail with other misfits. It was quite a shock. I realized that I was now one of them.

The judge pointed out the next day that I could be sent to jail for up to 90 days. But in place of the jail sentence, he demanded that I attend Alcoholics Anonymous meetings for three months.

At this point I was ready to try anything. At A.A. I met other people who showed me how to stay sober. With sobriety I slowly regained my respect and got a new job. It has been a long and difficult road back, but one I am very glad to have taken.

North American Indian tribes is the breakdown of their traditional culture, which has engendered a retreatist orientation, particularly among young men. They have chosen to retreat through alcohol use.[2] Scott (1993) reports that native youths are at two to six times greater risk for every alcohol-related problem experienced by other Canadian youths, except cancer. The majority of native people in treatment are receiving it for excessive use of alcohol, narcotics, and hallucinogens.

The drinking habits of young Indian males parallel those of another high-risk group: young males in general. Particularly influenced are those between the ages of 10 and 24. Parental influence wanes considerably during these years and is replaced by peer-group influence. The peer group has its own image of adult masculinity, which often includes drinking alcohol and demonstrating a capacity for "holding one's liquor". The result is that, in Canada in 1990, men aged 20 to 24 had by far the highest average of drinks consumed per week in comparison with men in other age categories. The national average for men of all ages was 6.44 drinks consumed per week (Canadian Centre on Substance Abuse, 1994:38). Nevertheless, the proportion of young men and women drinking alcohol declined in the latter half of the 1980s (Eliany, 1992), a trend that has continued in the early 1990s (*Gallup Report*, 1994).

Historically, women of all ages, but particularly young women, have demonstrated lower rates of alcoholism and alcohol-related problems than men. They are also least often identified as heavy drinkers and less often arrested for public drunkenness. They generally drink less frequently than men and in smaller quantities.

Ethnicity is sometimes a powerful cultural antecedent of both excess and moderation in alcohol use. Jews, Italians, and Chinese, for example, are known for their low rates of alcoholism and related difficulties. Members of these groups drink alcoholic beverages, but they do so in moderation and with reference to various in-group customs and norms. For instance, the Chinese stress self-control. Drunkenness is regarded pejoratively as a lapse of this attribute. Unlike many Western Europeans and North Americans, the Chinese do not see drunkenness as cute (Trainor 1984:10). Jews, even those who are not Orthodox, learn to associate the consumption of alcohol with special, often sacred occasions. They define drunkenness as a Gentile practice (Glassner and Berg, 1980).

The Irish stand at the opposite pole. High rates of alcoholism have been observed in Irish populations both inside and outside Ireland. One cultural explanation of this pattern is said by Walsh (1979) to stem from the "heroic tradition" of Irish drinking. "Thus the heroic spirit of Ireland insisted that there was no more honorable way in which a man, be he rich or poor, might ruin his career and even his life than by drink" (Walsh, 1979:396).

In France, where alcoholism rates are among the world's highest, wine drinking is an everyday activity. Anderson (1979) says wine consumption there is part of socialization of the young. They learn that wine has nutritive value, although this value is sometimes inflated by the non-scientist. They also learn that it is impolite to fail to offer wine to guests in the home, that it is an important part of any social gathering. Wine is also believed to prolong muscular endurance. One should therefore consume it during physical labour. Lastly, the alcohol in wine is purported to nullify the unsanitary properties of other foods ingested along with it.

Clearly, religion may also be a cultural antecedent to the deviant use of alcohol. In addition to what has already been said, we must consider the differences in rates of drinking between fundamentalist Protestants, on the one hand,

and Roman Catholics and liberal Protestants, on the other. The former usually forbid drinking, and so have a lower proportion of heavy drinkers than the latter. But those fundamentalist Protestants who do drink are more likely to become problem drinkers than other Christians (Thio, 1988:381). There are two explanations for this. First, there is little cultural support for social drinking among fundamentalists; they have not learned to drink in moderation as part of leisure, as Catholics and liberal Protestants have. Second, having deviated from their religious teachings by drinking, they often feel intense guilt, which they try to assuage by consuming still more alcohol.

CONTROLLING ALCOHOLIC DEVIANCE

Any discussion of the control of alcoholic beverages and alcoholic deviance must incorporate certain facts of alcohol consumption in Canada. While 76 percent of Canadians consume alcoholic beverages, variations exist within Canada which must also be taken into account when considering control. According to the Canadian Centre on Substance Abuse (1994:36), the sales in 1990–1991 of alcoholic beverages in litres of absolute alcohol per person aged 15 and over run from lows of 6.64 in New Brunswick, 7.39 in Saskatchewan, and 7.54 in Prince Edward Island, to 9.44 in Alberta and 10.16 in British Columbia, to the high point of 16 litres in Yukon, where tourism is suspected of contributing significantly to sales (Canadian Centre on Substance Abuse, 1994:20). The sale of absolute alcohol in 1990–1991 in the Northwest Territories was 11.46 litres per person. In general, the largest amounts of alcohol in Canada are bought and consumed in the west and northwest, the next largest amounts in the centre of the country, and the lowest amounts in the Atlantic area. Moreover, larger amounts are drunk in urban areas than in rural ones.

Obviously, prohibition, a control strategy enforced before World War I (1914–1918) in Atlantic Canada and across the entire land by 1918, is unlikely to work today. As reported earlier, 76 percent of those polled in the *Gallup Report* (1994) responded that they use alcohol. Hence, there can be no doubt about the current widespread acceptance of moderate alcohol consumption. Yet the argument can be made that some kind of control is necessary since, as we saw earlier, 21 percent of the population consume eight or more drinks per week. Eliany (1991) reports that substantial numbers of Canadians have been disturbed, insulted, assaulted, injured, even killed by people who have been drinking.

Prohibition was one of the goals of the temperance movement, which has been striving to control the consumption of alcohol since the early nineteenth century. In Canada, the height of success for the movement came around the time of World War I, when first provincial and then federal laws were passed against the purchase and consumption of alcohol, although not against its manufacture. Exceptions were made for medical, sacramental, and scientific purposes. The gradual repeal of those laws between 1923 and 1927 and their replacement with the now familiar government-controlled liquor outlets should not be interpreted as evidence for the failure of prohibition as a control strategy (Decarie,

1988). In most provinces, prohibition was in force for too little time to demonstrate its effectiveness.

Decarie (1988) has pointed out that the repeal of prohibition was actually a response to changing attitudes. In the nineteenth century, when most Canadians were self-employed as farmers, fishermen, and small businessmen, it was believed, no doubt with some justification, that the excessive use of alcohol destroys initiative. Originally, the temperance movement urged either moderate (i.e., temperate) use of alcohol or complete abstinence from it. As Canada became urbanized, the number of self-employed people declined. The new urban population was much less optimistic about improving its lot by any means. Moreover, it was becoming clear that urban social problems were caused by political and economic forces rather than by excessive drinking.

Although interest in the principles of the temperance movement — moderation or abstinence — has declined since its peak around 1920, the movement lives on. Perhaps its best-known supporter is the Woman's Christian Temperance Union (WCTU). The WCTU originated in the United States and spread across Canada between 1875 and 1886. In 1982, there were 102 chapters in Canada, with a combined membership of 3787 (Sheehan, 1985).

In the meantime, the control of alcohol use has taken a different form. It, too, has a long history, stretching back to the introduction of the disease concept of alcoholism by Benjamin Rush, an American physician, in his 1785 publication *An Inquiry into the Effects of Ardent Spirits upon the Body and Mind.* From its inception, the temperance movement used the disease concept as a means of promoting its goals (Gusfield, 1963). Support for the concept within the movement waned during the momentary success of prohibition, but quickly regained popularity both inside and outside the movement following repeal.

As Gusfield (1982) notes, the disease definition has focused attention on the alcoholic person and urged treatment for his or her affliction. While some scientists have studied alcoholism from this perspective, its popularity in lay circles has undoubtedly come chiefly from Alcoholics Anonymous. This organization was founded in 1935 in Akron, Ohio, by a physician, Dr. Bob, and a stockbroker and alcoholic, Bill W. They organized themselves and others around the principle of group support and encouragement of fellow members, and pursued the goals of sobriety and abstinence. It is a tenet of Alcoholics Anonymous that members can rid themselves of the "disease" of alcoholism. The history and influence of A.A. since its establishment are well known. Its members consider it one of the most successful self-help groups for alcoholism in the world, although other such groups are also enjoying success by operating from principles which sometimes contrast sharply with A.A.'s principles of religion and of alcoholism as a disease. These organizations include Moderation Management (M.M.) and Secular Organizations for Sobriety, or Save Ourselves (S.O.S.) (*The Journal*, 1994:5–7). A more complete statement of A.A.'s principles is contained in Viewpoint 5.2.

While the disease concept continues to enjoy widespread acceptance, albeit with occasional and perhaps increasingly more frequent challenges, Gusfield (1982) says that there is also a "renaissance of prevention". Paralleling the concern

VIEWPOINT 5.2

THE TWELVE STEPS AND TWELVE TRADITIONS OF ALCOHOLICS ANONYMOUS

The Twelve Steps

1 We admitted we were powerless over alcohol — that our lives had become unmanageable.
2 Came to believe that a Power greater than ourselves could restore us to sanity.
3 Made a decision to turn our will and our lives over to the care of God, *as we understood Him.*
4 Made a searching and fearless moral inventory of ourselves.
5 Admitted to God, to ourselves, and to another human being the exact nature of our wrongs.
6 Were entirely ready to have God remove all these defects of character.
7 Humbly asked Him to remove our shortcomings.
8 Made a list of all persons we had harmed, and became willing to make amends to them all.
9 Made direct amends to such people wherever possible, except when to do so would injure them or others.
10 Continued to take personal inventory and when we were wrong promptly admitted it.
11 Sought through prayer and meditation to improve our conscious contact with God *as we understood Him,* praying only for knowledge of His will for us and the power to carry that out.
12 Having had a spiritual awakening as the result of these steps, we tried to carry this message to alcoholics and to practice these principles in all our affairs.

The Twelve Traditions

1 Our common welfare should come first; personal recovery depends upon A.A. unity.
2 For our group purpose there is but one ultimate authority — a loving God as He may express himself in our group conscience. Our leaders are but trusted servants; they do not govern.
3 The only requirement for A.A. membership is a desire to stop drinking
4 Each group should be autonomous except in matters affecting other groups or A.A. as a whole.
5 Each group has but one primary purpose — to carry its message to the alcoholic who still suffers.
6 An A.A. group ought never endorse, finance or lend the A.A. name to any related facility or outside enterprise, lest problems of money, property and prestige divert us from our primary purpose.
7 Every A.A. group ought to be fully self-supporting, declining outside contributions.
8 Alcoholics Anonymous should remain forever nonprofessional, but our service centers may employ special workers.
9 A.A., as such, ought never be organized; but we may create service boards or committees directly responsible to those they serve.
10 Alcoholics Anonymous has no opinion on outside issues; hence the A.A. name ought never be drawn into public controversy.
11 Our public relations policy is based on attraction rather than promotion; we need always maintain personal anonymity at the level of press, radio and films.
12 Anonymity is the spiritual foundation of all our traditions, ever reminding us to place principles before personalities.

Source: Alcoholics Anonymous World Services, New York. Reprinted with permission.

with alcoholism as a disease demanding treatment and cure is a recent emphasis on preventive measures. One of these is **case finding**, in which people in high-risk groups become targets of persuasion for changes in habit or for treatment. For example, recruits in the Canadian Forces take a ten-week course on life skills which includes information about substance addiction and the factors that contribute to alcohol and drug use (*The Journal*, 1984a:9).

Another preventive measure is education. Programs in industry and secondary schools, and interviews and advertisements on radio and television are aimed at segments of the population larger than a particular high-risk group. Preventive information about the dangers of driving while drunk is also presented in short messages on signboards and in newspapers and magazines.

There are, in addition, numerous situational attempts to prevent alcoholism and heavy drinking, many of which amount to a sort of partial prohibition. They are intended to control the context of drinking. Thus, in Canada, as in many other countries, there are legal age limits (18 or 19, depending on the province) below which one cannot purchase liquor. Furthermore, alcohol sales are restricted to certain hours, days, and places. Other regulations specify the maximum alcohol content for beer, wine, and spirits. Taxes have been used to drive up the price of alcohol as a means of keeping its purchase and consumption at a moderate level. Ornstein (1980) has found that this strategy is most effective for the sale of spirits and least effective for the sale of beer.

Legislative measures have also been enacted in the hope of controlling the delinquent and sometimes dangerous behaviour of drinkers. Gusfield (1982) points to the laws passed to control public drunkenness and driving while intoxicated as the two main examples. Having already discussed the legal aspects of public drunkenness, let us turn our attention to the legislated control of driving while intoxicated.

Ross (1984) observes that, as a social problem, driving while intoxicated is the recent creation of a social movement in North America, which hopes to eliminate it. According to Ross, attempts in the United States and certain European countries to deter it by means of punitive legislation have uniformly ended in failure. In these programs, drunken drivers are subjected to severe penalties on the basis of measurements of levels of blood alcohol concentration (the famous 0.08). One of the severest codes is found in Finland, where one may receive four years of imprisonment on conviction for driving while intoxicated with provisions for a six-year sentence if someone is injured and seven years if someone is killed. Research demonstrates that, while the number of alcohol-related automobile accidents decline immediately upon the implementation of such legislation, the long-term effect is nil. Eventually people become accustomed to the threat of severe penalties and return to their old habits of drinking heavily and then, in some instances, driving a motor vehicle.

But other strategies for prevention exist (see U.S. Department of Health and Human Services, 1990: Ch. X). Raising the legal drinking age has proven effective in the United States. Harsh legal penalties may be effective if police officers and the general public can be convinced of the importance of this approach to the problem. Evaluations of training programs for servers of alcoholic beverages suggest that they can help control the amount of alcohol their patrons consume. Finally, evidence is accumulating in support of equipping school-age children and youth with the social skills needed to resist peer pressure to drink while driving.

SUMMARY AND CONCLUSIONS

Heavy drinking and alcoholism are two deviant extensions of the widely accepted practice in Canadian society of social drinking. They are termed deviant because those who engage in them appear to have lost control over their actions. Loss of control is commonly expressed in two ways: inability to perform sensorimotor skills, and supposedly weakened moral and thought functions. The second way of losing control, known as the disinhibition hypothesis, has only tenuous empirical support.

Even though precise measures of alcohol consumption are available and motor behaviour can be shown to be affected by such consumption, the label of "drunk" is applied in everyday life with considerable looseness. Defining the nature of alcoholism is also difficult. One common conception is that it is a physically damaging disease which rests on physiological dependency and uncontrollable ingestion of alcohol.

The consequences of alcohol use may be favourable or unfavourable for a society: functional or dysfunctional. On the unfavourable side we find the squandering of money on alcohol and the diversion of funds for alcoholic rehabilitation and such problems as absenteeism, low productivity, traffic accidents, and, possibly, crime. Still, alcohol has also contributed positively to societies, by creating dependent populations, bringing a sense of fellowship, strengthening group bonds, and inhibiting certain diseases. Individual people are also positively and negatively affected by the use of alcohol.

Heavy drinking takes place in a number of leisure settings. One of these is the public drinking house, where only a small proportion of the clientele may be heavy drinkers. The latter tend to drink alone here at certain times of the day and week when the clients are compatible with their social background.

By no means are all the habitués of skid row problem drinkers. Some of those who do drink, whether moderately or heavily, patronize neighbourhood bars where they meet other vagrants. Alternatively, a group of skid row men may pool their money as members of a temporary bottle gang to buy and furtively consume a cheap bottle of wine.

Four definitions of "alcoholic" and "heavy drinker" are in use today in lay and scientific circles. A heavy drinker consumes alcohol in excess of community norms, doing so to the point where it becomes a central activity in a deviant way of life. An alcoholic is someone who is physically dependent on alcohol, who lacks control over its consumption, or whose consumption has become disease-like. These definitions centre largely on the consequences and characteristics of heavy drinking and alcoholism. A fifth definition of heavy drinking as adjustment stresses the antecedents that lead to what society regards as morally reprehensible behaviour.

Of all these definitions, the disease conception is presently the most controversial. Research has failed to support some of the claims associated with it. A.A., for example, strongly endorses the disease conception, even though, objectively, its success can be traced to group support for individuals who truly desire to take control of their lives and renounce alcohol.

Although people do adjust to problems at work by resorting to alcohol, research evidence indicates that excessive drinking on the job is unrelated to particular occupations, industries, or social classes. Members of occupations with a reputation for drinking appear to drink frequently, but in small amounts and in ways that fail to generate an addiction to alcohol. By contrast, age does appear, in some instances, to be related to excessive alcohol consumption. Young males and the elderly show disproportionately high rates of alcoholism in comparison with other age categories.

One conception of the deviant career in alcohol use is available in Jellinek's four-stage process of alcoholism. The stages are the pre-alcoholic symptomatic stage, prodromal stage, crucial stage, and chronic stage. A principal assumption underlying this model — that alcoholism is a progressive disease — is challenged in research.

Certain cultural antecedents also have a bearing on the rates of drinking in a society. Exceptionally high rates are found among North American native peoples and among the Irish and French, as well as in the age groups previously mentioned. Men, in general, have higher rates of alcoholism than women.

Numerous strategies have been undertaken to control alcoholic deviance: complete prohibition, case finding, education, situational limitations on purchases of alcohol, and legislation. The last of these has attempted, without demonstrated success, to stem the tide of driving while intoxicated. Its effectiveness appears to hinge on the willingness of the police and the general public to treat this approach to prevention seriously.

NOTES

1. Archard (1979) notes that British skid rows are not centrally located, but rather are diffused throughout the city in small pockets in the working-class and commercial districts.
2. An alternative hypothesis is presented by Lurie (1979). She argues that excess drinking among North American Indians is their way of validating their Indianness. That is, such behaviour is a form of protest that distresses whites who accept the stereotype of the drunken Indian and who are thereby reminded of the differences between the two racial groups.

SUGGESTED READING

Archard, Peter. *Vagrancy, Alcoholism, and Social Control.* London: Macmillan, 1979. A 15-month ethnographic study of British men on skid row, their institutions, and their problems with alcohol.

Denzin, Norman K. *The Alcoholic Self.* Newbury Park, CA: Sage Publications, 1987. Denzin explores the lived experience of the alcoholic from the assumption that alcoholism is a disease in which negative emotions divide the self into warring inner factions.

Fingarette, Herbert. *Heavy Drinking: The Myth of Alcoholism as a Disease.* Berkeley, CA: University of California Press, 1988. The author critically examines the questions of control, prevention, and treatment of heavy drinking as conventionally approached by science and the lay public.

Marshall, Mac (ed.) *Beliefs, Behaviors, and Alcoholic Beverages: A Cross-Cultural Survey*. Ann Arbor, MI: University of Michigan Press, 1979. A collection of articles on the beliefs and practices associated with alcohol in various societies around the world.

Roman, Paul M. (ed.) *Alcohol Problem Intervention in the Workplace*. New York: Quorum Books, 1990. A collection of statements centring on the development and implementation of employee assistance programs for alcohol-related problems.

Smart, Reginald G. and Alan C. Ogborne. *Northern Spirits: Drinking in Canada Then and Now*. Toronto: Addiction Research Foundation, 1986. A thorough survey of the historical and contemporary patterns of alcohol use in Canada. There are discussions of prohibition, taxation, policy, prevention, native drinking, and problem drinking.

REFERENCES

Adrian, Manuella. "Youth: Alcohol and Other Drug Use in Canada," *The Journal*, 1985, 14, June:11–12.

_________ "Older Canadians: Alcohol and Other Drug Use," *The Journal*, 1986, 15, May:9.

Akers, Ronald L. "Alcohol." In *Encyclopedia of Sociology*, Vol. 1, edited by Edgar F. Borgatta and Marie L. Borgatta, pp. 41–48. New York: Macmillan, 1992.

Alasuutari, Pertti. *A Cultural Theory of Alcoholism*. Albany, NY: State University of New York Press, 1992.

Anderson, B.G. "How French Children Learn to Drink." In *Beliefs, Behaviors and Alcoholic Beverages: A Cross-Cultural Survey*, edited by Mac Marshall, pp. 429–432. Ann Arbor, MI: University of Michigan Press, 1979.

Archard, Peter. *Vagrancy, Alcoholism, and Social Control*. London: Macmillan, 1979.

Archer, Janet. "Occupational Alcoholism: A Review." In *Alcoholism and its Treatment in Industry*, edited by Carl J. Schramm, pp. 2–29. Baltimore, MD: Johns Hopkins University Press, 1977.

Atkinson, R.M. "Alcoholism in the Elderly Population," *Mayo Clinic Proceedings*, 1988, 63:825–828.

Brissett, Dennis. "Toward an Interactionist Understanding of Heavy Drinking," *Pacific Sociological Review*, 1978, 21:2–30.

Canadian Centre on Substance Abuse and the Addiction Research Foundation. *Canadian Profile: Alcohol, Tobacco & Other Drugs, 1994*. Ottawa and Toronto: Canadian Centre on Substance Abuse and the Addiction Research Foundation, 1994.

Carpey, Sissy. "'Disease Concept' of Alcoholism Still Unproven Says Masserman," *The Journal*, 1984, 13, June:12.

Cavan, Sherri. *Liquor License: An Ethnography of Bar Behavior*. Chicago: Aldine, 1966.

Clinard, Marshall B. "The Public Drinking House and Society." In *Deviance*. (2nd ed.), edited by Simon Dinitz, Russell R. Dynes, and Alfred C. Clarke, pp. 172–180. New York: Oxford University Press, 1975.

Conrad, Peter and Joseph W. Schneider. *Deviance and Medicalization.* (Expanded ed.) Philadelphia: Temple University Press, 1992.
Cosper, Ronald and Florence Hughes. "So-Called Heavy Drinking Occupations: Two Empirical Tests," *Journal of Studies on Alcohol*, 1983, 43:110–118.
_________, Ishmael O. Okraku, and Brigitte Newmann. "Tavern Going in Canada: A National Survey of Regulations at Public Drinking Establishments," *Journal of Studies on Alcohol*, 1987, 48:252–259.
Decarie, Graeme. "Temperance Movement." In *The Canadian Encyclopedia.* (2nd ed.), pp. 2129–2130. Edmonton: Hurtig, 1988.
Dumont, Matthew P. "Tavern Culture: The Sustenance of Homeless Men." In *Down to Earth Sociology.* (3rd ed.), edited by James M. Henslin, pp. 103–111. New York: The Free Press, 1981.
Eliany, Marc. "Alcohol and Drug Use," *Canadian Social Trends*, 1991, 2, Spring: 19–26.
_________ "Alcohol and Drug Consumption among Canadian Youth," *Canadian Social Trends*, 1992, 26, Autumn:10–13.
Faulkner, William, Diane Sandage, and Brendan McGuire. "The Disease Concept of Alcoholism: The Persistence of an Outmoded Scientific Paradigm," *Deviant Behavior*, 1988, 9:317–332.
Fillmore, Kaye M. "Occupational Drinking Subcultures: An Exploratory Epidemiological Study." In *Alcohol Problem Intervention in the Workplace*, edited by Paul M. Roman, pp. 77–94. New York: Quorum Books, 1990.
Fingarette, Herbert. *Heavy Drinking: The Myth of Alcoholism as a Disease.* Berkeley, CA: University of California Press, 1988.
Gallup Report. 1994, Monday, May 9.
Gilbert, Richard. "UK's Addiction Research Unit," *The Journal*, 1987, 16, March:5.
Glassner, Barry and Bruce Berg. "How Jews Avoid Alcohol Problems," *American Sociological Review*, 1980, 45:647–664.
Gusfield, Joseph R. *Symbolic Crusade.* Urbana, IL: University of Illinois Press, 1963.
_________ "Prevention: Rise, Decline and Renaissance." In *Alcohol, Science, and Society Revisited*, edited by Edith L. Gomberg, Helene R. White, and John A. Carpenter, pp. 402–426. Ann Arbor, MI: University of Michigan Press, 1982.
Hollobon, Joan. "Older Alcoholics," *The Journal*, 1986, 15, May:1–2.
_________ "Solo Recovery Surprise," *The Journal*, 1990, October:4.
Jackson, Margaret A. and Curt T. Griffiths. *Canadian Criminology.* Toronto: Harcourt Brace Jovanovich, 1991.
Jellinek, E.M. "Phases of Alcohol Addiction," *Quarterly Journal of Studies on Alcohol*, 1952, 13:673–684.
_________ *The Disease Concept of Alcoholism.* Highland Park, NJ: Hillhouse Press, 1960.
The Journal. "Drug Dangers, Life-Skills Part of Basic Training," 1984a, March:9.
_________ "CF Personnel Drink More Often Than Civilians," 1984b, May:11.
_________ "Alcohol May Aid Myoclonic Dystonia," 1984c, June:5.
_________ "Letters," 1989, September:6.
_________ "Stats/Facts," 1991–1992, December/January:11.
_________ "Mutual Help Movements: A Special Report," 1994, September/October:5–7.
Keller, Mark. "Definition of Alcoholism," *Quarterly Journal of Studies on Alcohol*, 1960, 21:125–134.

_________ "The Disease Concept of Alcoholism Revisited," *Journal of Studies on Alcohol*, 1976, 37:1694–1717.

Kotarba, Joseph A. "One More for the Road: The Subversion of Labeling within the Tavern Subculture." In *The Sociology of Deviance*, edited by Jack D. Douglas, pp. 151–160. Boston: Allyn and Bacon, 1984.

Lemert, Edwin M. *Human Deviance, Social Problems, and Social Control*. (2nd ed.) Englewood Cliffs, NJ: Prentice-Hall, 1972.

_________ "Drinking Among American Indians." In *Alcohol, Science, and Society Revisited*, edited by Edith L. Gomberg, Helene R. White, and John A. Carpenter, pp. 80–95. Ann Arbor, MI: University of Michigan Press, 1982.

MacAndrew, Craig and Robert B. Edgerton. *Drunken Comportment*. Chicago: Aldine, 1969.

Maranda, Marie-France. "Alcool et drogue en milieu de travail dans une usine de pâte et papiers." *Recherches Sociographiques*, 1991, 32:55–68.

Martin, Jack K. "Jobs, Occupations, and Patterns of Alcohol Consumption: A Review of Literature." In *Alcohol Problem Intervention in the Workplace*, edited by Paul M. Roman, pp. 45–66. New York: Quorum Books, 1990.

McKenzie, Diane. "Aboriginal Substance Use: Research Issues." Proceedings of a Joint Research Advisory Meeting of the Canadian Centre on Substance Abuse and National Native Alcohol and Drug Abuse Program, 1994.

McLaughlin, Mary. "Homelessness in Canada — The Report of the National Inquiry." Ottawa: Canadian Council on Social Development, 1987.

Ornstein, Stanley I. "Control of Alcohol Consumption Through Price Increase," *Journal of Studies on Alcohol*, 1980, 41:807–818.

Pittman, David J. "The Impact of Macrosocial Forces on the Distribution of Alcohol Problems in the Workplace." In *Alcohol Problem Intervention in the Workplace*, edited by Paul M. Roman, pp. 19–26. New York: Quorum Books, 1990.

Plant, Martin A. *Drinking Careers: Occupations, Drinking Habits and Drinking Problems*. London: Tavistock, 1979.

Prus, Robert. "Drinking As Activity," *Journal of Studies on Alcohol*, 1983, 44:460–475.

"Rating Your Risks for Heart Disease," *UC Berkeley Wellness Letter*, 1994, May:4–5.

Ray, Oakley and Charles Ksir. *Drugs, Society, and Human Behavior*. (5th ed.) St. Louis, MO: Mosby/Year Book, 1989.

Read, Kenneth E. *Other Voices: The Style of a Male Homosexual Tavern*. Novato, CA: Chandler & Sharp, 1980.

Ross, H. Laurence. "Social Control Through Deterrence: Drinking-and-Driving Laws." In *Annual Review of Sociology*, Vol. 10, edited by Ralph H. Turner and James F. Short, Jr., pp. 21–35, Palo Alto, CA: Annual Reviews, 1984.

Royal College of Psychiatrists. *Alcohol and Alcoholism: Report of a Special Committee of the Royal College of Psychiatrists*. London: Tavistock, 1979.

Rubington, Earl. "Variations in Bottle-Gang Controls." In *Deviance*. (4th ed.), edited by Earl Rubington and Martin S. Weinberg, pp. 360–368. New York: Macmillan, 1981.

Scott, K. "Substance Abuse among Indigenous Canadians." In *Research Issues: Substance Use Among Indigenous Canadians*, edited by Diane McKenzie, pp. 21–42. Ottawa: Canadian Centre on Substance Abuse, 1993.

Siegel, Larry J. *Criminology*. (4th ed.) St. Paul, MN: West, 1992.

Smart, Reginald G. and Alan C. Ogborne. *Northern Spirits: Drinking in Canada Then and Now*. Toronto: Addiction Research Foundation, 1986.

Snow, David A. and Leon Anderson. *Down on Their Luck: A Study of Homeless Street People*. Berkeley, CA: University of California Press, 1993.

Statistics Canada. *Canada Yearbook*, 1985. Ottawa: Supply & Services, 1985.

__________ *The Control and Sale of Alcoholic Beverages in Canada*. (Cat. no. 63–202) Ottawa: Supply & Services, 1986.

__________ *Canadian Crime Statistics, 1993*. (Cat. no. 85-002) Ottawa: Industry, Science and Technology Canada, 1993.

Szasz, Thomas S. "Bad Habits Are Not Diseases: A Refutation of the Claim That Alcoholism Is a Disease," *The Lancet*, 1972, July 8:82–83.

Thio, Alex. *Deviant Behavior*. (3rd ed.) Boston: Houghton Mifflin, 1988.

Thomas, R.K. "The History of North American Indian Alcohol Use as a Community-Based Phenomenon," *Journal of Studies on Alcohol*, 1981, Supplement no. 9:29–39.

Trainor, Dorothy. "Chinese 'Immunity' to Alcoholism Being Tested," *The Journal*, 1984, June:10.

U.S. Secretary of Health and Human Services. *Alcohol and Health*. Seventh Special Report to the U.S. Congress. Rockville, MD: National Institute on Alcohol Abuse and Alcoholism, 1990.

Walsh, D. "Alcoholism and the Irish." In *Beliefs, Behaviors, and Alcoholic Beverages: A Cross-Cultural Survey*, edited by Mac Marshall, pp. 394–403. Ann Arbor, MI: University of Michigan Press, 1979.

6

CANNABIS AND PRESCRIPTION DRUGS

Of the psychoactive or mood-altering drugs that are used for deviant leisure, alcohol is by far the most widely consumed in Canada.[1] The honours of second and third place in drug consumption as deviant leisure go to certain prescription drugs and cannabis (e.g., marijuana, hashish), respectively (Canadian Centre on Substance Abuse, 1994:28, 117). Because cannabis is illegal, its use is not part of the routine lifestyle of the vast majority of Canadians. Likewise, the legal requirement of an authorized prescription helps prevent prescription drugs from becoming part of that lifestyle. Thus, unlike alcohol, the drugs considered in this chapter are not numbered among the institutionalized props that aid our meals, celebrations, holidays, and other social occasions. Any recreational use of any of the psychoactive drugs just mentioned is therefore deviant, although regular, dependent use is more seriously so than occasional, non-dependent use.

TOLERATED DRUGS

In Canada, the use of cannabis is regulated by the Narcotic Control Act (NCA). Despite its illegal status, a case can be made that simple possession and use of cannabis are effectively tolerated in Canada. Erickson and Murray (1988:319–320) conclude their examination of recent judicial practices in this sphere as follows:

> What these results point to is the inescapable conclusion that the system has learned to accommodate the large number of cannabis offenders processed through it each year. This particular pressure for reform — the overextension of police and court resources — would appear to have been defused. Other pressures, such as the youth of offenders

> and the costs they incur from criminalization, have not dramatically altered, but are now tolerated. It might be argued that the greater leniency of sentences and the social dilution of stigma as a "cannabis criminal" [have] tended to minimize the impact on offenders' identity and lives. Nevertheless, most respondents were quite similar at both times [interviewed in 1974 and 1981] in wishing to maintain secrecy about their criminal record as far as family and employers were concerned.

Another indicator of tolerance for simple possession of the marijuana form of cannabis comes from public opinion polls. A Gallup poll taken in July 1989 (*Gallup Report*, 1989) revealed that 49 percent of the sample favoured retaining criminal penalties for using the drug. Other respondents favoured either fines or removal of all penalties. Nonetheless, 49 percent opposition to any decriminalization of marijuana possession is the highest level in many years. Only 35 percent were opposed to decriminalization in a Gallup poll taken in 1977.

Perhaps because the public is not greatly concerned at present about cannabis use, the police are giving its control relatively low priority. Evidence for this comes, in part, from the rates of arrest for simple possession of cannabis, which declined approximately 21 percent from 1983 to 1993. However, they still account for 63 percent of all drug incidents reported by the police (Statistics Canada, 1993:20).

The possession of prescription drugs for personal use, whether medical or recreational, is not illegal. Still, prescription drugs are legally distributed only upon a physician's written instructions. They are therefore of concern to the police if they are acquired fraudulently. Public concern about this matter is at a low level, in part because of the perception that these drugs cause relatively little harm to those who use them.

Low public concern and low police priority with respect to both cannabis and illicit prescription drugs have been accompanied by a decline in consumption. Use of the former has been dropping for many years. For the period 1985 to 1990, the Canadian Centre on Substance Abuse (1994:112) reported a further modest drop of 0.6 percent in the number of people who consumed marijuana or hashish at least once during the previous year.

The decline in the illicit consumption of prescription drugs has been substantial. The number of persons arrested for possession of or trafficking in controlled drugs (one of the Food and Drug Act's classes of prescription drugs) dropped 75 percent between 1987 and 1990 (Royal Canadian Mounted Police, 1993:26).[2] Moreover, between 1985 and 1991, there was decline in the number of reported thefts of these drugs from pharmacies, with the sole exception of amphetamine. Reported forgeries of prescriptions diminished as well, including those for amphetamine (Canadian Centre on Substance Abuse, 1994:323, 326).

THE NATURE OF PSYCHOACTIVE DRUGS

Before proceeding with our discussion of cannabis and prescription drugs as deviant leisure, it will be useful to consider the properties and effects of these substances.

Cannabis

Cannabis is the generic term for four specific drugs prepared from the plant *Cannabis sativa,* a genus of hemp. Of the four, **marijuana** is the most common. It is variously known on the street as pot, grass, weed, joint, reefer, and ganja. Marijuana is typically rolled into a cigarette and smoked. **Hashish**, or "hash", is the dried, sticky resin of the cannabis plant. It, too, may be smoked, although some users prefer to bake it into or cook it with certain foods. **Hash oil** (also known as oil, honey oil) is obtained by purifying hashish with an organic solvent. The fourth drug is the euphorically active ingredient in cannabis. It is usually referred to as **THC**, the scientific abbreviation for tetrahydrocannabinol. It is sometimes sold on the street in a form diluted with one of the hallucinogens (e.g., PCP, LCD). Since THC is concentrated in the resinous, flowering tops of the cannabis plant, hash and hash oil are considerably stronger drugs than marijuana, which consists largely of the ground leaves, flowers, and seeds of the plant.

The acute, unpleasant effects of cannabis are well established. Intoxication impairs immediate memory and interferes with a range of intellectual tasks. All other relevant factors considered, students high on cannabis in the classroom will learn significantly less than if they were sober. Since reaction time is slowed by heavy doses of the drug, it is also dangerous to drive a car or fly a plane in this condition. Research demonstrates that decrements in performance are still evident many hours beyond the perceived limit of intoxication (Julien, 1995:344). Users unaccustomed to the drug may experience such reactions as nausea, dizziness, pains in the chest or throat, and loss of body coordination. Large doses can produce anxiety, confusion, and hallucinations in people who ordinarily use the drug in moderation.

Long-term effects are only now beginning to surface, partly because large numbers of long-term users have only recently accumulated in the general population. Research involving these people suggests that marijuana tobacco may impair lung functioning significantly more than ordinary tobacco. It is presumed that steady use of the former is at least as carcinogenic as of the latter. Respiratory problems, including bronchitis and sinusitis, are also common among heavy users. Additionally, a strong dependence (i.e., addiction) may eventually develop in some chronic users who take high doses. However, there is so far no evidence that continual use of cannabis leads to heroin use or use of other strong, more addictive drugs (Commission of Inquiry into the Non-Medical Use of Drugs, 1972:130). That is, no properties have been discovered in the cannabis itself that might cause this transition.

Cannabis is lucrative. Its sales were reported by the *Financial Post* (1986:2) to be one of the country's "biggest big businesses". Canadians were said to spend nearly as much on all illegal drugs as they do on automobiles. More than half this amount went for cannabis. In the United States, Schlosser (1994:46) says that 1993 estimates of the value of the nation's marijuana crop run as high as $24 billion, $8 billion more than corn, the largest legal crop.

Prescription Drugs

Three categories of prescription drugs will be considered here. The **barbiturates**, or "downers", are sedatives that slow the central nervous system. Medically, they were developed to treat tension, anxiety, convulsions, sleeplessness, and high blood pressure. They are available under such trade names as Luminal, Mebaral, Seconal, Nembutal, and Amytal. The **amphetamines**, popularly known as "uppers", stimulate the user and thereby increase alertness and energy. The result is a feeling of well-being. Their medical purpose is to treat obesity and depression. Cylert, Preludin, and Ritalin are among the trade names under which this drug is sold. In Canada, the Food and Drug Act (FDA) regulates the use of barbiturates and amphetamines, which fall under the heading of "controlled" or "Schedule G" drugs. The third category, the **tranquillizers**, are similar to the barbiturates, except that they induce a psychological calm without also inducing sleep. They, too, help reduce anxiety, nervousness, muscular tension, and the like. They are sold under such trade labels as Serax, Valium, Librium, and Halcion.[3] The FDA classifies them as "prescription" or "Schedule F" drugs. (Note: In this book the phrase "prescription drugs" refers to the drugs in both schedules, since all are available only on prescription.)

Chronic use of these drugs carries unfavourable consequences. They spring, in part, from the tolerance that develops from routine doses of the same strength, a condition which forces the user to increase the dosage to achieve the same level of effect. Chronic users of barbiturates often suffer from headache, depression, anemia, impaired vision, slurred speech, and impaired functioning of the liver. Babies of mothers who are chronic users are also adversely affected. Moreover, these drugs are powerful enough to be a leading means of suicide. Chronic users of amphetamines eventually suffer from malnutrition or, possibly, amphetamine psychosis, a disorder similar to paranoia. Some users are prone to violence. Still others damage their kidneys or develop lung and heart problems. **Physical dependence**, a condition wherein one suffers acute physiological withdrawal symptoms when administration of the drug is stopped, rarely accompanies even heavy amphetamine use. But **psychological dependence** is a problem: life seems dull when the effects have worn off; satisfaction and well-being are lacking.

Consequences for long-term users of tranquillizers appear to be fewer. Nonetheless, some mentally ill patients who have taken this drug for long periods develop a variety of involuntary movements of the mouth and chin, and possibly other parts of the body. Babies of mothers who have been chronic users may suffer withdrawal symptoms.

ACQUIRING PSYCHOACTIVE DRUGS

Because the psychoactive drugs considered in this chapter are either wholly illegal or legally available only by prescription, certain barriers must be overcome in acquiring them. Unlike with alcohol, one cannot simply go to a local store and buy what one wants. Rather, "connections" are necessary; users must learn who supplies their drugs, when and where they can be bought, and how to avoid detection by the authorities. The process of the illegal acquisition of cannabis is different from that of the acquisition of prescription drugs (for leisure rather than for medical use).

Cannabis

Of the various cannabis derivatives, Canadians by far prefer hashish, marijuana, and liquid hashish. The Royal Canadian Mounted Police (1993:3) report that, apart from temporary shortages, these drugs are readily obtainable in most parts of the country. Hashish is the most popular of the three, in good part because the most widely available marijuana in Canada grows wild but contains a disappointingly low level of THC. Still, hydroponic technology is now being applied to the cannabis plant to help overcome the limitations of the Canadian climate by growing high-quality marijuana indoors, particularly in British Columbia.

The most recent annual report from the Royal Canadian Mounted Police (1993:3) indicates that most of the cannabis derivatives available in Canada come from Afghanistan, Colombia, Jamaica, Lebanon, Mexico, and Pakistan. The largest quantities of hashish are smuggled in from Lebanon (mainly the Bekaa Valley, according to Blackwell, 1988:331) and Southwest Asia, arriving in all sorts of land, sea, and air conveyances disguised in nearly innumerable ways.

The average level of THC in marijuana available on North American streets has risen during the past two decades. Ray and Ksir (1989:301–302) report that the drug now commonly contains from 2 to 5 percent of psychoactive material. The narcotic strength of hash oil has also been increasing. Today, efficient methods of preparation can produce samples containing more than 50 percent THC.

To acquire the best cannabis, North American users must turn to a network of dealers who are clandestinely linked to a small set of importers. Studies by Sorfleet (1976) and the Commission of Inquiry into the Non-Medical Use of Drugs (1972) indicate that in a typical Canadian city, the importers supply the dealers with the more desirable, stronger material. This is accomplished, for example, by taping small amounts of it to one's body and passing through customs inspection at an airport or sending some through the mail in a hollowed-out souvenir. The imported cannabis is passed on first to large-scale dealers, then to small-scale dealers, and ultimately to non-dealing customers, some of whom may also distribute the drug within their own social circles. This they do as a favour, charging only enough to cover costs or pay for their own drug needs.

While competition among the importers and dealers helps control prices, they are nevertheless driven up by the number of middlemen involved in the distribution process. One consequence of this competition, in a market where the margin of profit is small, is the tendency for dealers to cut the quality of their product. In Canada, marijuana is most commonly cut with such inert plant material as grass, alfalfa, oregano, and parsley. Occasionally, a beef bouillon cube or brown sugar is substituted for genuine hashish. The Commission of Inquiry into the Non-

Medical Use of Drugs (1972:25) concluded at the time of their study that street cannabis in Canada was rarely diluted with other drugs.

Prescription Drugs

The acquisition of prescription drugs, when not done in the illicit street market, is markedly different. According to a series of articles in *The Globe and Mail* (Lavigne, 1986), illegal users often acquire them through a sympathetic physician who writes and rewrites the desired prescriptions. Some of these practitioners are gullible; they accept at face value the patient's complaint and prescribe the barbiturate or amphetamine requested. Other physicians — the number is unknown, though probably small — are well aware of the patient's false claims. The charge for each prescription is said by Lavigne to run from $50 to $100. Or these physicians ask sexual favours. Addicted patients and those who are wealthy are apparently willing to pay the price. Some patients threaten their physician with break-and-entry of their office, if the medicine is not prescribed. Others threaten to break into drugstores. Some do.

Less risky and more common is the tactic of forging prescriptions. Addicts steal blank prescription pads from physicians' offices and sell them to each other. Other recreational drug users, whether addicted or not, engage in double or multiple doctoring (an illegal practice discussed more fully in the final section); they seek out two or more physicians to treat and prescribe the desired medicine for the same faked ailment. It should come as no surprise that those who work with such drugs — nurses, physicians, and pharmacists — find their acquisition much easier. Some members of these professions are addicts or unaddicted regular users.

Users learn from each other and from medical literature available in public libraries which illnesses ordinarily call for the drugs they want. They learn how to manipulate a physician into making the right prescription, for instance, by maintaining that they are allergic to certain other regularly used drugs. A lie of this sort steers the unsuspecting doctor toward prescribing the desired medication. Regular users also share information about gullible or crooked physicians. According to Lavigne (1986), a group of prescription drug dealers is known to have set up a phoney doctor's office in Metropolitan Toronto through which they acquired prescription pads bearing the fictitious name of a physician and his telephone number.

Given the interest in prescription drugs, it is to be expected that there is street traffic in them as well. Dealers acquire their supply in one or more of the ways just mentioned, selling the drugs to customers who find this source more convenient and less risky than others. One ring of Toronto dealers was caught selling prescription drugs on the street for $12 per pill (Lavigne, 1986). The Royal Canadian Mounted Police (1993:28) have identified clandestine laboratories in Québec and Alberta, which make amphetamines for street trade. In 1987, police in the United States broke up a Québec-based drug ring that was engaged in manufacturing tranquillizers:

Miami — U.S. authorities said Tuesday they have smashed a drug ring that funneled millions of phoney Quaaludes into the United States from Quebec for five years.

Forty-nine people — twenty Canadians, twenty-seven Americans and two Colombians — have been indicted on a series of charges.

The indictment said the ring was responsible for distributing 13.5 million counterfeit Quaalude tablets — 70 percent of the illegal trade — throughout the United States.

The indictment was handed down by a Fort Lauderdale grand jury in December but kept secret to give police on both sides of the border time to plan a series of arrests dubbed Operation Avalanche.

The drug sold as Quaaludes, the brand name for methaqualone, was actually a potent derivative of diazepam — the principal ingredient in Valium and other tranquillizers. Police said each tablet was sold on the street for $6 or $7.

The indictment accuses the defendants of producing diazepam in laboratories set up in farmhouses in remote areas of Quebec, transporting the drug to Florida, and making it into tablets to be sold as Quaaludes.

Because of widespread abuse, Quaaludes and all methaqualone have been illegal to make or sell in the United States since 1984.

The indictment alleged pharmaceutical manufacturer Roger DuFour of Montreal headed the Canadian operation that altered legal manufacturing operations to supply diazepam to make the counterfeits.

Twenty-four people have been arrested or are already in custody. The rest, including DuFour, are at large.

The indictment included charges of possession and intent to distribute diazepam, operating a continuing criminal enterprise, failure to declare the drug at customs, and violation of U.S. patent and trademark laws.

Among those named was Nick Cotroni, member of a Montreal family that figured in a Quebec inquiry into organized crime in the 1970s. He surrendered Tuesday in Miami.

Also named is William Obront, 63, described by the same inquiry as the Montreal underworld's banker. Obront is serving 20 years in a Florida jail for drug offences. (*Calgary Herald*, 1987, Wednesday, March 18:A9)

PSYCHOACTIVE DRUG USE AS LEISURE

We have concentrated so far on the negative, acute, long-term effects of cannabis and prescription drugs. Among the main reasons for the deviant consumption of these drugs, however, is precisely the opposite condition: to achieve a pleasant alteration of one's *present* mood or, among long-term users, to ward off withdrawal symptoms. For those motivated in this way, caution about long-term consequences is of no consideration as they seek an unusual mode of leisure made possible by nature or by the manufacturers of pharmaceuticals.

Becoming a Cannabis User

Reginald Smart (1983:27) summarizes the principal desirable effects sought by cannabis users in leisure settings:

1. Euphoria or a "high". Users feel relaxed, happy, and floating in pleasurable experiences. Many report having important insights.

2 Hilarity. Users frequently laugh and talk more than usual, often in a rather silly, repetitive fashion. Later they lapse into a quieter, even sleepy state.
3 Heightened sensation. Many users report more pleasure in listening to music or looking at art.
4 Misperception of time. Users usually find that time is overestimated; a few minutes seem like an hour.

Hendin and his colleagues (1987:154–159) found that marijuana helped experienced users enhance their self-awareness and sexual relations. In some cases, they used the drug to maintain distance and restrict commitment in a particular primary relationship. The strength of these effects depends on, among other things, the concentration of THC and the method of consumption. For instance, effects appear more quickly and with greater strength when the cannabis is smoked than when it is eaten.

Users must learn how to consume cannabis in order to experience its special effects and to appreciate them. Becker (1963), Zinberg (1984), and Hirsch et al. (1990) have demonstrated that those who consume cannabis by smoking participate in a decidedly social experience. However, it is an experience many neophytes approach with a degree of apprehension about the unknown. They must be taught by seasoned users how to inhale the smoke to achieve the maximum effect of the THC. Furthermore, the effects themselves are not inherently pleasant. Therefore, newcomers to the drug must be convinced that the feelings of floating, heightened awareness, and misperception of time are enjoyable. Certain conventions must also be learned, such as passing the joint (marijuana cigarette) from person to person in the gathering until it is consumed.[4] Once this learning has taken place, the high from cannabis, say its devotees, is genuine euphoria. Viewpoint 6.1 presents one man's views on the benefits of cannabis.

VIEWPOINT 6.1

THE BENEFITS OF CANNABIS

Durie grinned. "Nobody can change my mind about pot. I think everyone should smoke it. I think if you're going to get off on something because you have some need to get a buzz, then pot is all right. It doesn't make you steal or want to get into a fight. But the law is the law and it takes a dim view of middle-class gangsters.

"But I'm absolutely against acid. I've done coke. I consider it dangerous. I've been offered to do coke runs. It's a dirty business operated by dirty people. The thing with coke is that it changes your nervous system. I've done it with lawyers and all kinds of upper-class people. Your mood really changes. It gives you verbal diarrhea. First it's yappity yap. It starts out as fun and then you start getting paranoid and your orbit begins to decay very quickly. Your lines keep getting bigger to achieve the same orbit. I've had a dozen friends die on coke or become severe epileptics. In six months, I've seen very intelligent people degenerate into complete nervous wrecks. It's disgusting. I think it's even more deadly than heroin. You'll do it till you die because you want the high. As for heroin, from what I hear it's extremely dangerous and lethal. Pot is laid back, mellow. The only side effect is you get the munchies. Pot cures glaucoma and anorexia."

Source: Victor Malarek. *Merchants of Misery*. Toronto: Macmillan of Canada, 1989, pp. 197–198.

Becoming a Prescription Drug User

Most prescription drugs are consumed as pills or capsules. Whether taken in this form or as an elixir or injection, the user does not ordinarily need to be instructed in how to take the drug and may not even need to be instructed in its effects and the pleasure they give. Still, there is a lore about prescription drugs, too, which is best learned through interaction with its regular consumers. That lore includes the slang names of the various drugs, the desirable and undesirable properties of each, and the most efficient means of acquiring the drugs. It includes knowledge of how to avoid official detection as a recreational user. Last but not least, it contains a set of justifications for engaging in this form of leisure.

Studies of the everyday lifestyle of the leisure-oriented prescription drug taker are rare, perhaps because, as Douglas and Waksler (1983:220) have observed, social scientists have ignored the pleasure principle as a motive for using these medications. Thus, it is not known whether white-collar pill parties similar to the one described in Viewpoint 6.2 still occur and, if they do, how common they are. The existence of such parties suggests that, apart from the social connections needed to acquire, learn about, and avoid problems with recreationally used drugs, the connections resulting from their actual use are desirable. These connections, which may develop into enduring relationships, are fostered to some extent by the effects of the drugs themselves.

Prescription drug use is not seen as seriously deviant by those who engage in it for the purpose of leisure (Douglas and Waksler, 1983:215). At the very worst, they see their special pleasure as a form of tolerable deviance. After all, they reason, millions of people in North America take all sorts of medicine for all sorts of ailments, both real and imagined. Recreational use of mood-altering drugs, although hardly the normal practice, is, in their eyes, no more than a minor extension of that practice. Indeed, many non-users have recreational users as friends and relatives, although they may sometimes be unaware of the extent to which they consume their drugs and the efforts they make to obtain a steady supply.

Moreover, the psychological states sought by recreational users are states that many people value, even though they reject drugs as a means of attaining them. In fact, the barbiturates produce psychological and behavioural effects similar to those produced by intoxicating doses of alcohol. For example, both drugs excite and stimulate their users in a general way, while promoting a certain lack of inhibition. Barbiturate users may become happy, pleasant, euphoric, and mellow, just as many alcohol drinkers do. They may, however, experience the opposite reaction, becoming hostile, suspicious, and aggressive (which sometimes happens with alcohol as well). Like alcohol, high doses of barbiturates slow reaction times and impair mental functions. Tranquillizers, when taken in normal doses, generally produce similar states: well-being, relaxation, and lowered inhibitions.

The effects of the amphetamines are different. With moderate doses, users typically experience alertness, wakefulness, improved concentration, feelings of clearer thinking, and greater responsiveness to the immediate environment. There is also a reduction in fatigue and boredom, along with an elevation in mood, euphoria, and sociability. There may be improvements in the performance of

VIEWPOINT 6.2

A WHITE-COLLAR PILL PARTY

Eddie, the host, a painter who has received some recognition, had been awake three or four days, he was not exactly sure. He consumes between 150 and 200 milligrams of amphetamine a day, needs a large part of that to stay awake, even when he has slipped a night's sleep in somewhere. The dose would cause most people some difficulty; the familiar diet pill, a capsule of Dexamyl or Eskatrol, which makes the new user edgy and over-energetic and slightly insomniac the first few days, contains only 10 or 15 milligrams of amphetamine. But amphetamine is one of the few central nervous system stimulants to which one can develop a tolerance, and over the months and years Ed and his friends have built up massive tolerances and dependencies. "Leapers aren't so hard to give up," he told me. "I mean, I sleep almost constantly when I'm off, but you get over that. But everything is so damned boring without the pills."

I asked him if he knew many amphetamine users who have given up the pills.

"For good?"

I nodded.

"I haven't known anybody that's given it up for good." He reached out and took a few pills from the candy dish in the middle of the coffee table, then washed them down with some Coke.

The last couple to arrive — a journalist and his wife — settled into positions. The wife was next to me on the oversize sofa, and she skimmed through the "Product Identification Section" of the *PDR*, dozens of pages of pretty color photos of tablets and capsules. "Hey!" she said to no one in particular. Then, to her husband, "Look at the pretty hexagonal. George, get the Source to get some of them for me." George, across the table, near the fire, nodded.

I had been advised to watch him as he turned on. As the pills took effect something happened to the muscles of his face, and the whole assembly seemed to go rubbery. His features settled lower and more loosely on the bones of his head. He began to talk with considerably more verve.

A distractingly pretty girl with dark brown eyes sat at the edge of our group and ignored both the joint making its rounds and the record player belching away just behind her. Between the thumb and middle finger of her left hand she held a pill that was blue on one side and yellow on the other; steadily, with the double-edged razor blade she held in her right hand, she sawed on the seam between the two halves of the pill. Every once in a while she rotated it a few degrees with her left index finger. Her skin was smooth, and the light from the fireplace played tricks with it, all of them charming. The right hand sawed on.

I got the Book from the coffee table and looked for the pill in the pages of color pictures, but before I found it, Ed leaned over and said, "They're Desbutal Gradumets. Abbot Labs."

I turned to the "Professional Products Information" section and learned that Desbutal is a combination of Desoxyn (methamphetamine hydrochloride, also marketed as Methedrine) and Nembutal, that the pill the girl sawed contained 15 milligrams of the Desoxyn, that the combination of drugs served "to both stimulate and calm the patient so that feelings of depression are overcome and a sense of well-being and increased energy is produced. Inner tension and anxiety are relieved so that a sense of serenity and ease of mind prevails." Gradumets, the Book explained, "are indicated in the management of obesity, the management of depressed states, certain behavioral syndromes, and a number of typical geriatric conditions," as well as "helpful in managing psychosomatic complaints and neuroses," Parkinson's disease, and a hangover.

The girl, obviously, was not interested in all of the pill's splendid therapeutic promises; were she, she would not have been so diligently sawing along that seam. She was after the methamphetamine, which like other amphetamines "depresses appetite, elevates the mood, increases the urge to work, imparts a sense of increased efficiency, and counteracts sleepiness and the feeling of fatigue in most persons."

After what seemed a long while the pill split into two round sections. A few scraps of the yellow Nembutal adhered to the Desoxyn side, and she carefully scraped them away. "Wilkinson's the best blade for this sort of thing," she said. I asked if she didn't cut herself on occasion, and she showed me a few nicks in her left thumb. "But a single edge isn't thin enough to do it neatly."

She put the blue disk in one small container, the yellow in another, then from a third took a fresh Desbutal and began sawing. I asked why she kept the Nembutal, since it was the Desoxyn she was after.

"Sometimes I might want to sleep, you know. I might *have* to sleep because something is coming up the next day. It's not easy for us to sleep, and sometimes

VIEWPOINT 6.2 *(continued)*

we just don't for a couple or three days. But if we have to, we can just take a few of these." She smiled at me tolerantly, then returned to her blade and tablet.

When I saw Ed in New York several weeks later, I asked about her. "Some are like that," he said; "they like to carve on their pills. She'll sit and carve for thirty or forty minutes."

"Is that sort of ritual an important part of it all?"

"I think it is. She seems to have gotten hung up on it. I told her that she shouldn't take that Nembutal, that I have been cutting the Nembutal off my pills. It only takes about thirty seconds. And she can spend a good half hour at it if she has a mind to. I told her once about the effect of taking a Spansule; you know, one of those big things with sustained release [like Dexamyl, a mixture of dextroamphetamine sulfate and amobarbital designed to be effective over a twelve-hour period]. What you do is open the capsule and put it in a little bowl and grind up the little pellets until it's powder, then stuff all the powder back in the pill and take it, and it all goes off at once. I'll be damned if I haven't seen her grinding away like she was making matzo meal. That's a sign of a fairly confirmed head when they reach that ritual stage."

Next to the candy dish filled with Dexedrine, Dexamyl, Eskatrol, Desbutal, and a few other products I hadn't yet learned to identify, near the five-pound box of Dexedrine tablets someone had brought, were two bottles. One was filled with Dexedrine Elixir, the other with Dexamyl Elixir. Someone took a long swallow from the latter, and I thought him to be an extremely heavy user, but when the man left the room, a lawyer told me he'd bet the man was new at it. "He has to be. A mouthful is like two pills, and if he was a real head, he'd have a far greater tolerance to the Dexedrine than the amobarbital, and the stuff would make him sleepy. Anyhow, I don't like to mess with barbiturates much anymore. Dorothy Kilgallen died from that." He took a drink from the Dexedrine bottle and said, "And this tastes better. Very tasty stuff, like cherry syrup. Make a nice cherry Coke with it. The Dexamyl Elixir bitter."

Source: Bruce Jackson, "White-Collar Pill Party," *Atlantic Monthly,* 1966, August:35–40.

athletic skills and simple mental tasks. But such effects are not found in all users. Some people become nervous, irritable, restless, and confused instead. Their ability to concentrate may also be weakened. Clearly, amphetamines are no quick route to leisure for this latter group.

The amphetamine users who have gained the most public notoriety as well as the most scientific attention are the "speed freaks": the heavy-dose, chronic users who get high quickly through injections taken every four to eight hours. Speed freaks on a "run" continue in this way without sleep for up to a week. They talk incessantly, are full of boundless energy and unpredictable, and, as a result, are shunned by others, including regular drug users of all kinds, who want to sleep from time to time. Speed freaks, although they may be enjoying themselves, make poor company. Their sole interest during a run is their private experience of the effects of the amphetamines. In the shadowy world of illicit drugs, their unpredictability threatens other users.

To the extent that users of cannabis and prescription drug develop either a physiological or psychological dependence on their drugs, they move into the deviant career stage of secondary deviance. With dependence, they develop a significant degree of loss of control over their actions. Further, their quest for drugs begins to take precedence over most, if not all, other aspects of their lives, indicating that they are moving out of the sphere of tolerable deviance into that of intolerable deviance.

Multiple Drug Use

Multiple drug use for pleasure occurs in two ways. Some users consume different drugs on different occasions, say alcohol one evening and cannabis two nights later. This is *serial* consumption. Such a pattern is based on preference, availability of the drug, and its acceptance by others in the setting. Other users engage in *simultaneous* consumption of two or more psychoactive drugs. This practice may develop from the persuasiveness of other users, who contend, for example, that a particular barbiturate enhances one's high when taken along with alcohol or an amphetamine. Or users who have a tolerance for large doses of one drug may try another drug at the same time in an attempt to achieve a satisfactory high.

Those who had used alcohol and cannabis together told the Commission of Inquiry into the Non-Medical Use of Drugs (1970:84) that the former suppresses the psychoactive effect of the latter. They reported that, for this reason, they rarely used them simultaneously, but did use them serially. More recent research by Siemens (1980:170) reveals that some experimental subjects found the reverse — that cannabis antagonizes the effects of alcohol. Other subjects in Siemens' studies held that there was no difference between taking the two drugs together and using them separately. Still others said that the effects of both were enhanced when they were taken at the same time.

Alcohol, barbiturate, and tranquillizer users may try combinations of these three on the same occasion. Their combined effects are sometimes muted, however, owing to a cross-tolerance generated from chronic use of any one of them. The idea is to double the pleasure of each drug. But the practice can be lethal. Barbiturates are also sometimes used with amphetamines to reduce the irritation- or tension-producing effects of the latter. More common, however, is the practice of alternating the two, using barbiturates to overcome the insomnia caused by amphetamines, then using amphetamines later for stimulation during the hangover and drowsiness caused by depressants. This pattern of use has been observed among otherwise socially respectable users (Commission of Inquiry into the Non-Medical Use of Drugs, 1970:36). Speed freaks may also take a barbiturate to terminate their run on amphetamines. Marc Schuckit (1989:240) has commented:

> The concomitant administration of two [or more] substances over an extended period of time very likely does increase the risk of the development of medical consequences.... The specific problems depend on the specific drugs involved, as well as the individual's age, preexisting medical disorders, and concomitant nutritional status and experience of stress.

PSYCHOACTIVE DRUGS IN THE WORKPLACE

Cannabis is most widely used as a means of leisure. Nonetheless, some of its devotees hold that it is also an aid to their occupational pursuits, while others see it as an escape route from those same pursuits (Hendin et al., 1987:157–158). Those whose work demands a high level of artistic creativity — painters, musicians, and authors, for instance — sometimes turn to cannabis for help with their work. It is said to heighten their capacity to imagine, to generate unusual cognitive and ideational associations, and to allow them to perceive otherwise unnoticed aspects of the environment. Whether these claims are valid is a question that science is currently trying to answer. The following passage describes the psychedelic world that one artist sees when under the influence of cannabis:

> First of all, you suddenly notice as if for the first time in your life, how fantastically beautiful everything in the world is — even little things you hardly thought worth looking at before... all colours become incredibly bright and intense, and sounds and touches full of beauty.... But there is much more than just the heightening of the senses. You begin to think think think. More profoundly and more interestingly than ever before. You have fantastic ideas thrown up by your imagination which knows no bounds or restraints. And you feel an intense physical exhilaration that makes you want to leap around. Everything in the world suddenly becomes true and real — you can see deep into people's minds by just looking at their eyes — you can tell everything about them, their thoughts, characters, dreams and secrets. You can see what people are really like, their "image" is shattered — and so is yours — you start behaving as you really are. Politeness for the sake of politeness is impossible, or if tried, it is completely unconvincing. You become obsessed with the beauty of everything around you — a small noise made with your mouth is wonderful — you repeat it over and over again. To any observer you appear crazy but this is nothing to you — you are in your own lovely world creating thoughts and visions and sounds and sights — creating whatever you like — doing whatever you like — you have woken up at last and start seeing the world as it really is for the first time.... (Auld, 1981:149).

Information about the use of barbiturates and tranquillizers on the job is scanty. Since their psychological and behavioural effects are similar to those of alcohol, when taken in subhypnotic doses, the possibility certainly exists that some employees might try to escape the boredom or tension of their work by these chemical means. After all, barbiturates, since they are odourless, present less risk of detection than alcohol. They are also easier to conceal on one's person than a bottle. And users can always claim that the pill they are taking is an aspirin, a vitamin, or a prescribed medication.

Not much more is known about the occupational use of amphetamines. Smart (1983:65) writes that they were prescribed on a limited basis during World War II, for counteracting fatigue and increasing alertness. Students, restaurant serving staff, long-haul truck drivers, and others who must stay awake and be alert for longer than normal periods may turn to this medication. Finally, athletes, both amateur and professional, have been known to use amphetamines for the boost in energy and confidence they provide (Leonard, 1993:152).

In the conceptual language of anomie theory, the routine use of psychoactive drugs at work is an instance of deviant innovation. The user has rejected some of the conventional means for reaching ordinary success goals in the belief that cannabis or amphetamines, for example, will help him or her reach them more quickly and efficiently. Just how realistic this belief is remains to be determined scientifically.

PSYCHOACTIVE DRUGS AS ADJUSTMENT

With the exception of cannabis, which is a derivative of a naturally growing plant, the psychoactive drugs considered in this chapter are manufactured chemical products designed to effect some sort of adjustment to everyday life circumstances. Their medical use is what legitimates them. Their deviant use is often, though not always, an extension of their role in a medical treatment program.

Medically, amphetamines have been used to treat such ailments as epilepsy, parkinsonism, pregnancy nausea, and nasal congestion. Psychiatrists sometimes administer the drug intravenously to stimulate untalkative patients to speak more freely about their problems and their past. And, since amphetamines suppress hunger, they have become a common ingredient in modern diet pills.

Through such legitimate uses, some patients have become dependent on or addicted to these drugs. This happens when, for example, they begin to take them in doses larger than those recommended by their physician, perhaps under the misguided assumption that such doses will help them adjust better to the problem under treatment, or because they like the way the drug makes them feel. The services of gullible and crooked physicians and street dealers enable the patient to drift toward deviant use of the medication. Some physicians, recognizing this possibility, prescribe amphetamines only as a last resort or not at all.

A similar transformation can occur in treatment programs that incorporate tranquillizers and barbiturates. Tranquillizers are widely used in medicine to treat anxiety, tension, insomnia, and behavioural excitement. They are also used to relieve convulsions, lower back pain, and withdrawal symptoms from opiate and alcoholic addiction. Likewise, barbiturates can be used to treat insomnia (the common sleeping pill), convulsions, and certain psychiatric disorders. Even though dependence on these drugs can develop after as little as one month of daily use, many physicians fail to take the same precautions needed to ward off a deviant drug career with tranquillizers as they do with amphetamines.

To the extent that cannabis and prescription drugs produce a euphoria similar to that of alcohol, they too can be seen as a way of retreating from the unpleasant circumstances of everyday life. In such anomic circumstances as failure at work, enduring poverty, lack of social support, low self-esteem, or inadequate coping skills, these drugs offer an adjustment, or more accurately, an escape (Hendin et al., 1987:158; O'Malley and Mugford; 1991). The adjustment is, in effect, a retreat to another psychological level where, to be sure, the problems are not solved. But at least they do not have to be confronted for the moment.

A critical difference between cannabis and other psychoactive drugs is that cannabis found its way into Canada and the United States not as a medication but as a deviant means to work, leisure, and adjustment. Even today, the medical uses of cannabis are largely limited to the treatment of physical problems such as the nausea and vomiting that accompany chemotherapy. But there are social uses of cannabis, which include easing interpersonal relations, since cannabis often makes people more convivial and talkative and less inhibited. Further, as Zinberg (1984:88) reports, some users hold that cannabis affords an improvement in sexual relations:

> R: I find that sex is better when I'm stoned.
> I: How come? What's the difference?
> R: Well, because I can do more things with grass. I can, well when I'm straight there's just too much goin' on, you know, in my head. If I wanted to kiss a girl while I was straight, there'd be too much going on in my head for me to really get into the kiss, whereas with grass I can get into the kiss much more easily, I can really *feel* the kiss, the energy in the mouth, and that's all I feel. Like a blending of energies... more into body feelings rather than thinking. "Well, am I doing this right, will she like this, will I like this?" Everything just happens naturally, and you are only in that experience, not in another and not in your head. You can even feel what the other person is feeling, I mean in her body. You can feel with your body when her body is close to orgasm and then you begin to feel it too. There's something like a merging of feelings, body feelings, and every touch, every movement, is like magnified a hundred times. Touches even on the hands or even toes become intense. The only problem is that usually after such an intense experience I just want to fall asleep. But that's OK, too. There's this sense of timelessness. Nothing exists but this moment.

DEVIANT DRUG CAREERS

To the extent that the drugs discussed here are addictive — and they all are to some degree — a career of progressive dependence similar to that involving alcohol is possible. What starts out as either medical treatment or recreational use is continued for the psychological and physical benefits the drug in question is seen to provide. As it becomes more important to the person's work, leisure, or adjustment to some problem, he or she begins to devote more time to acquiring it. Acquisition means developing connections, finding money for purchases, persuading physicians to prescribe the drug, and so on. Meanwhile, continued use leads to tolerance of the current dose, so that larger doses must be taken to get the same effect. Thus, the drug's centrality to the individual's way of life increases, a trend that is accelerated if and when psychological dependence sets in. It is at this point that the regular user moves from primary to secondary deviance.

Long use of the drug in increasingly heavier doses may eventually produce physical dependence. Now, like the alcoholic, the user moves into the sphere of intolerable deviance and may require professional help. He or she may experience "bad trips", problems with possible or actual detection, and adverse physical and psychological reactions during periods of sobriety.

Yet only a small proportion of the users of the psychoactive drugs considered in this chapter have a deviant career of the sort just described. A survey in *The Journal* (1991/1992:12–13) presents data on the use of illicit drugs among Ontario students, 13 to 19 years of age, in 1989. Of the total sample, 14.1 percent had used marijuana at least once during the previous year. A much smaller proportion would have used the drug on a regular basis. The same survey revealed that, at least once during the previous year, 2.5 percent of the students used amphetamine, 2.4 percent used tranquillizers, and 2.2 percent used barbiturates for non-medical purposes.

The Cannabis Career

The only psychoactive drug career on which we have any significant amount of information is that involving cannabis.[5] Neophytes who have drifted far enough from conventional mores to be willing to try the drug go through the learning process described earlier. Yet it is clear that, among those who try cannabis, many ultimately reject it as a regular component of their lifestyle. Eliany (1991:24) reports that, in 1989, only half of those who used the drug at least once during the past year actually used it once a week or two to three times a month.

Those who come to enjoy the cannabis experience, however, often continue to the next career stage, that of occasional user. Here users learn the justifications for using the drug in a society that treats as deviant those who do so. These users consume cannabis freely and uncompulsively, usually for reasons of leisure. The tolerable deviance status of occasional cannabis use is evident in the fact that such users are less anxious today about arrest and public exposure than ever before. Nevertheless, it is often considered prudent to keep their deviance secret from employers and, for younger users, parents. Personal crises caused by the drug, such as discovery by an employer or an adverse reaction to an overdose, may lead some occasional users to end their involvement with cannabis at this point.

Those who move on to heavy regular use, even if not dependent on the drug, are often forced by circumstances into a form of secondary deviance that is publicly defined as intolerable. Heavy users require extensive and costly supplies of cannabis, a situation that usually brings them into some sort of direct contact with the drug underworld. They often penetrate it deeply enough to be able to acquire the drug wholesale, and, in this manner, they come by the opportunity to retail it and partially offset their own expenses. Some heavy users take prescription drugs as well, a practice which presents another set of supply and secrecy problems. Should a user develop a criminal record in connection with cannabis, this official label can add another career contingency which, among other things, can affect his or her chances of legitimate employment.

CORRELATES OF USE

There are correlates of deviant psychoactive drug use, just as there are of deviant alcohol use. The former, however, are of a standard demographic nature, unlike many of the correlates of the problematic use of alcohol, which are cultural.

We turn first to the correlates of cannabis use. According to the overview of the 1989 National Alcohol and Other Drugs Survey provided by Eliany (1991), males are more likely than females to use cannabis regularly, by a ratio of slightly higher than 2 to 1. Regardless of the sex of the user, heaviest consumption of the drug is found among younger people, aged 15 to 34. Cannabis use among men and women over 55 years of age is virtually nil. As for regional differences, use is highest in British Columbia (9.6 percent of those surveyed), then in Nova Scotia (7.4 percent), and lowest in Newfoundland (4.5 percent); the average is 6.5 percent.

Although there are plenty of recent data on the correlates of legitimate, or medical, use of prescription drugs, data on the correlates of their non-medical or recreational use are difficult to gather and, for this reason, unavailable. Earlier studies have found that most recreational users are under 30 years of age. Smart (1983:69) believes that the peak year for amphetamine use was 1970, and that the proportion of regular users of the drug has been declining ever since. Studies done in Ontario in the late 1970s by the Addiction Research Foundation (1981:110–111) indicate that males were more likely than females to experiment with both barbiturates and amphetamines, especially the latter. Both sexes were equally likely to use tranquillizers for recreational purposes.

CONTROL

As noted earlier, legal control of the tolerable deviance discussed in this chapter falls under the Narcotic Control Act for cannabis and the Food and Drugs Act for prescription drugs. Possession of cannabis can lead to a summary conviction, with a maximum sentence of six months in jail and up to a $1000 fine. Subsequent offences may bring up to a year in jail and as much as a $2000 fine. These penalties are the same as for possession of such drugs as opium and cocaine. To be found guilty of "possession of cannabis", it must be proved in a court of law that one had smoked a joint, had cannabis on one's person, or had knowingly consented to permitting it to be placed in one's home or on one's property. Trafficking cannabis, like trafficking other narcotic drugs, is an indictable offence punishable by up to seven years in prison.

We certainly could not conclude from the last paragraph that cannabis use in Canada is a form of tolerable deviance, since the penalties for possession and trafficking are the same for all narcotic drugs. The evidence for tolerance at the official level comes from the patterns of arrest and conviction for possession presented earlier in the chapter. These rates have been declining for over a decade. Moreover, at least in Calgary, simple possession rarely provokes a jail sentence. A fine between $100 and $300 is the most common penalty. Dealers in that city, if convicted, can expect to get 30 to 90 days in jail (Lee, 1985). Erickson and Murray (1988:318) note the trend toward greater leniency and the preference of judges for absolute discharges:

> In 1981, a greater proportion of the respondents (58%) received this outcome than in 1974 (42%), while the proportion being convicted and fined was reduced from 24% to 8%. The awarding of conditional discharges, which imposes a probationary period, remained constant as the outcome for one-third of both samples.

Possession of a controlled drug (an amphetamine or a barbiturate) for the purpose of trafficking is a summary offence punishable by up to 18 months in jail. Possession is defined in the same way as it is for cannabis and the other narcotic drugs. Trafficking, which includes selling, exporting, importing, transporting, or manufacturing the drug in question, or "offering" to do any of these, is punishable by up to ten years in prison.

Tranquillizers are prescription drugs rather than controlled drugs. Selling them without a verbal or written prescription may lead to a summary conviction which, for a first offence, can bring up to three months' imprisonment and up to a $500 fine. Second and subsequent offences may result in as much as six months in jail and up to a $1000 fine. If the prosecutor decides to proceed by indictment, the penalty could be as high as three years in prison and a $5000 fine.

Simple possession of tranquillizers, amphetamines, and barbiturates is not in itself a violation of the Narcotic Control Act. Nevertheless, it is illegal to "prescription shop" or "double doctor", forge prescriptions, or steal psychoactive drugs from pharmacies and doctors' offices.

Do threats of fines and jail sentences for possession and trafficking deter use of the drugs examined in this chapter? The general answer, according to existing evidence, is "no": attempts to deter drug crime by such means have been largely unsuccessful (Teevan, 1976; Blackwell and Erickson, 1988:446). Part of the problem is that deterrence is most likely to occur when punishment is both certain and swift (Griffiths and Verdun-Jones, 1994:488). But it seldom is, in instances of the use and trafficking of cannabis and prescription drugs. What does keep people from violating the law is a respect for the law (not for the penalties), together with an abhorrence for the proscribed behaviour, and a desire to remain respectable. People rarely reach the point in thought or behaviour where they consider the legal reprisals. In other words, the internalization of conventional social values has so far been the most effective means of controlling deviant drug use.

It seems that we are faced with a paradox. The recreational consumption of cannabis and prescription drugs is declining, but apparently for reasons other than stiff legal penalties. Judicial leniency and slack law enforcement are not among these reasons, for they too fail to account for the decline. If anything, we might predict that such leniency and slackness would lead to an increase in the use of these substances. Perhaps, then, a significant number of would-be users *have* internalized social values that lead them to initial avoidance or subsequent renouncement of all psychoactive drugs. I know of no research aimed at discovering these values. We might speculate, however, that the contemporary high value of health and fitness for many Canadians may be curbing their appetite for drug-based leisure.

Clearly the law and the enforcement of the law are out of step with each other. With respect to the drugs considered here, the law provides for jail sentences in every instance of its violation. By contrast, enforcement agents rarely use these powers, even though there is ample opportunity. They are influenced by a small majority of the public that favours some degree of decriminalization of cannabis possession (public opinion on prescription drugs is unknown). Various federal governments have said that reform of the NCA and the FDA is long overdue. The last major change in Canadian drug legislation occurred in 1969. At the time of writing, the Chrétien government has introduced Bill C-7, the Controlled Drugs and Substances Act, which is much the same as an earlier draft formulated by the preceding Mulroney government. Bill C-7 is presently mired in controversy, with the forces for the status quo — such as the RCMP and the Canadian Association of Chiefs of Police — supporting it, and the forces for change — such as the Canadian Bar Association and the Criminal Lawyers Association — opposing it. The latter see the bill as relying too heavily on the courts and law enforcement, as the NCA and FDA do (see Garlick, 1994, for further details). As of the summer of 1995, Bill C-7 was on its way to third reading in the House of Commons.

Thus we have still another example of sociological conflict: in this instance, between decriminalization of the possession of cannabis and opposition to decriminalization. Among supporters of the latter are those who also oppose the consumption of alcohol, those who believe that cannabis is or may be proved to be seriously harmful, and those who oppose the non-medical use of all drugs other than alcohol, tobacco, and caffeine.

SUMMARY

After alcohol, prescription drugs and cannabis are the second and third most widely consumed psychoactive drugs in Canada. Public tolerance appears to be behind a decline in the rate of arrest for the illegal use of these drugs since 1975. But these substances are not completely harmless. Cannabis impairs immediate memory, interferes with a range of intellectual tasks, and slows reaction time. Among its long-term effects on heavy users are impaired lung functioning and possible mild dependence.

Tolerance and dependence are also among the consequences of long-term use of prescription drugs. Dependence may be either psychological or physical or both. Reactions to the chronic use of barbiturates include headache, depression, anemia, impaired vision, slurred speech, and impaired liver functioning. Babies of mothers who are chronic users may also be affected. Heavy use of amphetamines can lead to malnutrition, amphetamine psychosis, kidney damage, and lung and heart problems. Tranquillizers, though generally lacking long-term negative consequences, produce a variety of involuntary body movements in some patients.

Cannabis can be gathered locally in fields or acquired from dealers who sell either local or imported material. Importing cannabis requires an elaborate network of importers, large- and small-scale dealers, and customers, some of whom also sell to their friends. Heavy competition leads some dealers to cut marijuana with such material as alfalfa or oregano, or to substitute a beef bouillon cube or brown sugar for genuine hashish.

Illegal users of prescription drugs acquire them by misrepresenting the condition of their health to gullible physicians or by dealing with crooked practitioners. Less common acquisition strategies are forging prescriptions and breaking into pharmacies and doctors' offices. Prescription drugs may also be purchased at high prices from street dealers.

Most deviant psychoactive drug use is for leisure purposes; the object is to pleasantly alter one's present mood. Cannabis users seek the euphoria, hilarity, heightened sensations, and misperceptions of time that this drug can offer. To achieve these effects, neophytes must learn from experienced users how to inhale the cigarette and how to appreciate the sensations that follow. Prescription drug users learn from other users the properties of each drug, ways to acquire them, ways to avoid official detection, and justifications for engaging in this kind of leisure. The effects sought by barbiturate users are similar to those sought from alcohol: pleasant, happy, mellow, euphoric feelings. Tranquillizers produce a similar frame of mind. Those who use amphetamines typically seek alertness and wakefulness. Speed freaks value this condition so highly that they will run on amphetamines for up to a week, during which time they eat and sleep little.

Through contact with other drug users, multiple drug users learn about the benefits of taking two or more psychoactive drugs at the same time. The exact effects experienced depend on the user and the drugs taken. Some users prefer to use different drugs in sequence; they may, for instance, take amphetamines to counteract the hangover and drowsiness caused by barbiturates.

Certain psychoactive drugs are seen as an aid to work. Artists and others involved in creative work sometimes argue that cannabis heightens the imagination and allows them to perceive previously unnoticed aspects of the environment. Amphetamines are occasionally used by those who must stay awake and be alert for longer than normal hours. Athletes have been known to use them to boost their confidence and energy.

The psychoactive drugs considered in this chapter are designed to effect some sort of adjustment for medical patients. But some patients experience either psychological or physical dependence on these medications, which may lead them to use unethical if not criminal means to supply their deviant habit. Even cannabis is used at times to facilitate adjustments in social relations.

Deviant careers involving prescription drugs start out as either medical treatment or recreational use. The non-medical uses made of these drugs encourage their users to continue with them. When tolerance develops and some sort of dependence follows, the deviant moves toward secondary deviance, which is judged by the community with varying levels of intolerance. The career of the cannabis user is similar. Heavy use requires extensive contact with the drug underworld and carries certain risks of apprehension and possible official labelling.

Males are more likely than females to use cannabis. High school and university students and non-students of the same ages form the largest category of cannabis users in Canada. As of the early 1990s, perhaps 5 percent of the Canadian population aged 15 and over used it at least once in a year.

Possession and trafficking of cannabis and trafficking of prescription drugs are illegal under the Narcotic Control Act and the Food and Drugs Act, respectively. But fines and jail sentences seem to have little effect as deterrents. Indeed, even the enforcement of the relevant laws is out of step with their content. To correct this woeful situation, the Chrétien government is presently trying to maneuver the highly controversial Bill C-7, the Controlled Drugs and Substances Act, through the House of Commons.

NOTES

1 Technically speaking, caffeine and nicotine are also psychoactive drugs, although we are unaccustomed to thinking of them as such. Certainly they are not as powerful as alcohol, cannabis, and prescription drugs.

2 In 1991, the number of persons arrested for possession of these drugs shot up by nearly the same proportion by which it had dropped during the preceding four years. We shall have to wait several more years to determine whether this is a mere blip or the beginning of a new trend.

3 Excluded from consideration here are the various "look-alike", "act-alike", and "designer" drugs, which have the appearance and some of the effects of the prescription drugs, but which are sufficiently different chemically to fall outside the laws controlling them (Royal Canadian Mounted Police, 1991:44–45).

4 Note the similarity between this ritual and that of the bottle gang discussed in Chapter 5.

5 This section draws substantially from the works of Howard Becker (1963) and the Commission of Inquiry into the Non-Medical Use of Drugs (1972:188–196).

SUGGESTED READING

Blackwell, Judith C. and Patricia G. Erickson (eds.) *Illicit Drugs in Canada: A Risky Business.* Scarborough, ON: Nelson Canada, 1988. A collection of readings on illicit drug use and its control from the perspectives of law, history, sociology, psychology, criminology, and pharmacology.

Commission of Inquiry into the Non-Medical Use of Drugs. *Cannabis.* Ottawa: Information Canada, 1972. A somewhat dated but still useful review of the chemical nature, social history, and legal standing of marijuana use in Canada.

Commission of Inquiry into the Non-Medical Use of Drugs. *Other Drugs.* Ottawa: Information Canada, 1973. All drugs other than cannabis are covered, including prescription drugs.

Giffen, P.J., Shirley Endicott, and Sylvia Lambert. *Panic and Indifference: The Politics of Canada's Drug Laws.* Ottawa: Canadian Centre on Substance Abuse, 1991. An examination of the evolution of Canada's drug laws, the failure of law reform in this area, and the national Drug Strategy, put into effect in 1987.

Ray, Oakley and Charles Ksir. *Drugs, Society, and Human Behavior.* (5th ed.) St. Louis, MO: Mosby/Year Book, 1989. A textbook treatment, from a sociological point of view, of all drugs including alcohol, nicotine, and caffeine. The focus is chiefly on the American drug scene.

REFERENCES

Addiction Research Foundation. *Statistical Supplement to the Annual Report, 1979–80*. Toronto: Addiction Research Foundation, 1981.

Auld, John. *Marijuana Use and Social Control*. London: Academic Press, 1981.

Becker, Howard S. *Outsiders*. New York: The Free Press, 1963.

Blackwell, Judith C. "Canada in a Global Setting: Notes on the International Drug Market." In *Illicit Drugs in Canada: A Risky Business,* edited by Judith C. Blackwell and Patricia G. Erickson, pp. 326–335. Scarborough, ON: Nelson Canada, 1988.

_________ and Patricia G. Erickson (eds.) *Illicit Drugs in Canada: A Risky Business.* Scarborough, ON: Nelson Canada, 1988.

Canadian Centre on Substance Abuse. *Canadian Profile: Alcohol, Tobacco & Other Drugs*. Ottawa: Canadian Centre on Substance Abuse, 1994.

"Cannabis: A Big Business," *The Financial Post,* 1986, January 25.

Commission of Inquiry into the Non-Medical Use of Drugs. *Interim Report*. Ottawa: Information Canada, 1970.

_________ *Cannabis*. Ottawa: Information Canada, 1972.

Douglas, Jack D. and Frances C. Waksler. *The Sociology of Deviance*. Boston: Little Brown, 1982.

Eliany, Marc. "Alcohol and Drug Use," *Canadian Social Trends,* 1991, 20, Spring:19–26.

Erickson, Patricia G. and Glenn F. Murray. "Cannabis Criminals Revisited." In *Illicit Drugs in Canada: A Risky Business,* edited by Judith C. Blackwell and Patricia G. Erickson, pp. 314–321. Scarborough, ON: Nelson Canada, 1988.

Gallup Report, 1989, Monday, July 3.

Garlick, Richard. "Bill C-7 Hearings Reveal Sharply Divided Opinions," *Action News* (Canadian Centre on Substance Abuse), 1994, 5, May/June:1–2.

Griffiths, Curt T. and Simon N. Verdun-Jones. *Canadian Criminal Justice*. (2nd ed.) Toronto: Harcourt Brace, 1994.

Hendin, Herbert, Ann P. Haas, Paul Singer, Melvin Ellner, and Richard Ulman. *Living High: Daily Marijuana Use Among Adults*. New York: Human Sciences Press, 1987.

Hirsch, Michael L., Randall W. Conforti, and Carolyn J. Graney. "The Use of Marijuana for Pleasure: A Replication of Howard S. Becker's Study of Marijuana Use." In *Journal of Social Behavior and Personality* (Special Issue), edited by J.W. Neuliep, 1990, 5:497–510.

Julien, Robert M. *A Primer of Drug Action*. (7th ed.) New York: W.H. Freeman, 1995.

Lavigne, Yves. "Prescription Addicts: Trading Sex and Money for Drugs,"*The Globe and Mail,* 1986, September 27:A1–A2.

_________ "Theft of Prescription Drugs by Nurses Viewed as Threat to Hospital Patients,"*The Globe and Mail,* 1986, September 30:A8.

_________ "Underworld Uses Cunning Schemes to Obtain Drugs," *The Globe and Mail,* 1986, October 1:A9.

_________ "Prescription Drug Addicts Cut Across Social Lines," *The Globe and Mail,* 1986, October 2:A12.

Lee, Gordon. "Blindness to Drug Use Bemoaned," *Calgary Herald,* 1985, February 2:B1.

Leonard, Wilbert M., II. *A Sociological Perspective of Sport*. (4th ed.) New York: Macmillan, 1993.

Malarek, Victor. *Merchants of Misery.* Toronto: MacMillan of Canada, 1989.

O'Malley, Patrick M. and Stephen Mugford. "The Demand for Intoxicating Commodities: Implications for the War on Drugs," *Social Justice,* 1991, 18:49–74.

"Quebec Drug Ring Smashed," *Calgary Herald,* 1987, Wednesday, March 18:A9

Ray, Oakley and Charles Ksir. *Drugs, Society, and Human Behavior.* (5th ed.) St. Louis, MO: Mosby/Year Book, 1989.

Royal Canadian Mounted Police. *National Drug Intelligence Estimate, 1984–1985.* Ottawa: Ministry of Supply and Services, 1986.

_________ *National Drug Intelligence Estimate, 1990.* (Cat. no. JS61-1/1990) Ottawa: Supply and Services Canada, 1991.

_________ *National Drug Intelligence Estimate, 1992.* (Cat. no. JS61-1/1992) Ottawa: Supply and Services Canada, 1993.

Schlosser, Eric. "Reefer Madness," *The Atlantic Monthly,* 1994, August:45–63.

Schuckit, Marc A. *Drug and Alcohol Abuse: A Clinical Guide to Diagnosis and Treatment.* (3rd ed.) New York: Plenum, 1989.

Siemens, Albert J. "Effects of Cannabis in Combination with Ethanol and Other Drugs." In *Marijuana Research Findings: 1980,* edited by Robert C. Petersen, pp. 167–198. Rockville, MD: National Institute on Drug Abuse, 1980.

Smart, Reginald G. *Forbidden Highs: The Nature, Treatment and Prevention of Illicit Drug Abuse.* Toronto: Addiction Research Foundation, 1983.

Sorfleet, Paul. "Dealing Hashish: Sociological Notes on Trafficking and Use," *Canadian Journal of Criminology and Corrections,* 1976, 18:123–151.

"Stats Facts," *The Journal,* 1991/1992, 20, December/January.

Teevan, James J. "Deterrent Effects of Punishment," *Canadian Journal of Criminology and Corrections,* 1976, 18:152–160.

Zinberg, Norman E. *Drug, Set, and Setting.* New Haven, CT: Yale University Press, 1984.

7

GAMBLING

Robert Herman (1990:264) defines **gambling** as "the voluntary risking of a sum of money called a *stake, wager,* or *bet,* on the outcome of a game or other event." The American Commission on the Review of the National Policy toward Gambling (abbreviated here as CRNPG) concluded that the practice is inevitable: "No matter what is said or done by advocates or opponents of gambling in all its various forms, it is an activity that is practiced, or tacitly endorsed, by a substantial majority of Americans" (CRNPG 1976:1). In the following decade, Jan McMillen (1989:397) made the same observation for Canada. Canadian gambling has seen considerable change since the year of McMillen's paper, as it continues to move away from the traditional charity-oriented games to those bringing substantial profits to provincial governments and private entrepreneurs. Difficult economic times are partly to blame for this trend: governments are faced with dwindling resources with which to meet the increasing demands for services. In the ensuing hype, the voices of the moralists and critics have been all but drowned out.

Gambling in Canada, as in many other Western countries, is a favourite pastime of many. In a sample of Canadians surveyed in 1980, 78 percent had gambled for money in one way or another during that year (Canadian Institute of Public Opinion, 1980). This proportion did not change appreciably in 30 years. But a 1993 survey found that 89 percent of Albertans gamble at least once a year, compared with 75 to 80 percent of Americans (Haynes, 1993). This, the sole survey in Canada on the matter since 1980, suggests that the proportion of gamblers in the country may be rising. *The Globe and Mail* (1992:A4) reported that in 1992 Canadians spent over 9 billion dollars gaming, nearly 3 billion of which went for the most popular games of chance in North America, lotteries. They spent approximately another 3.7 billion on bingo and horse racing. In that year, per capita wagering ran from a high of $433 in Alberta to a low of $193 in Newfoundland, for the eight provinces for which complete revenue figures were available.

LEGITIMATE GAMBLING

Perhaps the main difference between the American and Canadian gambling scenes is the somewhat greater uniformity of gaming laws in Canada. Federal law in Canada prevents the provinces from establishing certain games. They may, however, license, regulate, and operate the games which are legal in whatever manner they choose. While there is also federal control in the United States, the states appear to have more freedom than the Canadian provinces to choose the games they wish to operate.

Five types of legal gambling are available on some basis in North America: casinos, parimutuel betting, off-track betting, lotteries, and bingo.[1] The three main illegal types — numbers, bookmaking, and illegal casinos — operate in much the same manner on either side of the Canadian–U.S. border owing, in good part, to the fact that the same crime syndicates are believed by the police to be running the games in both countries. We turn here to the legal types; the illegal forms are examined in the next section.

In the United States, the casinos organize several forms of wagering, such as blackjack, keno, roulette, and slot machines, for the profit of the owner. Legal casinos, which are found in Nevada and New Jersey, supplement play with ample amounts of food, drink, lodging, and entertainment. Recently North Dakota legalized casino gambling (with a betting limit of two dollars), which is run by charities in much the same way as in some Canadian provinces (Lidz, 1986: 64–65). The CRNPG found that more stringent legislation and its enforcement in the 1960s have virtually eliminated the large illegal casinos that once served many American cities.

In Canada, the amount of casino gambling has grown considerably in recent years, as one province after another discovers this rich source of revenue. By and large, Canadian casinos offer the same games as those in the United States. The main exception is the prohibition of slot machines that discharge slugs or tokens. With regulations similar to those in Britain, the Criminal Code of Canada, section 197(2) indicates that a "common gaming house" is legal

> while it is occupied and used by an incorporated genuine social club or branch thereof, [and] if (a) the whole or any portion of the bets on or proceeds from games played therein is not directly or indirectly paid to the keeper thereof, and (b) no fee is charged to persons for the right or privilege of participating in the games played therein other than under the authority of and in accordance with the terms of a licence issued by the Attorney General of the province in which the place is situated or by such other

person or authority in the province as may be specified by the Attorney General thereof.

In his history of legal gambling in Canada, Campbell (1991) notes that, prior to substantial changes in the Criminal Code made in 1969, this form of leisure was limited to sporadic charity bingos and raffles, midway games of chance, and parimutuel betting on horse races. The 1969 legislation broadened the conditions of charity gambling. Subsequent legislation in 1985 gave the provinces the right to control their own lotteries and manage and operate mechanical gambling devices. Alberta has been a pioneer in this field; it introduced new forms of gaming and strict but workable regulatory controls. Its comprehensive licensing and accounting regulations for charity gambling have been copied in many jurisdictions across North America.

It was also Alberta that laid the foundation for legal casino gambling in Canada, starting with the roulette, blackjack, and crown-and-anchor games offered on green felt tables at the 1975 Edmonton Exhibition (Campbell, 1991:157). An efflorescence of charity-based casinos followed, first in Alberta, then in other provinces. For the moment at least, Alberta has officially pledged to stay on this course (Cunningham, 1994). But other provinces, notably Manitoba, Québec, and British Columbia, have already introduced for-profit casinos conceived in a manner avoiding violation of the federal Criminal Code (e.g., Campbell, 1993; Dougherty, 1994). The slot machines described earlier are unavailable in these establishments.

Parimutuel wagering is legal in some form in 33 states (U.S. Bureau of the Census, 1993:307), and in all provinces. In this system, players wager against each other instead of against a bookmaker. Roughly 80 to 90 percent of all bets are returned to the bettors. "Payoffs" are made on the first three winning horses or dogs (win, place, and show). The "takeout" or remaining portion is then split among the owners of the animals, the track, and the state or province in which the event occurs. The takeout is somewhat smaller in Canada than in the United States. Legal parimutuel wagering is also conducted on jai alai in Florida, Nevada, and Connecticut. Horse racing is by far the most popular form of parimutuel gambling in North America.

Off-track betting (OTB) at a location distant from the racetracks is a recent modification of the parimutuel gambling system. It is lawful in New York, Nevada, and Connecticut, but illegal in all other states and in Canada. However, a betting arrangement similar to OTB is found in Alberta, where one may bet on a horse race by telephoning the track. There is no remote intermediary in this procedure. Where it is lawful, OTB is a government-based attempt to make money and, and at the same time, entice customers away from illegal bookmaking operations. This presumably enables government to better control customer exploitation, which is inevitable when a private third party comes between the bettor and the racetrack. Although New York's off-track betting system is the oldest in the United States. Rosencrance (1988:46) notes that it is not achieving one of its goals: "While illegal race bookies suffered an initial setback with the passage of OTB, they have adjusted and have made a substantial comeback by catering to customer needs through credit extension and improved services."

Fourth on our list of types of legal gambling — though first in popularity — are the government-run lotteries. They are legal in 33 states (U.S. Bureau of the Census, 1993:307), while raffles (a kind of lottery) are legal in 21. Both lotteries and raffles are legal throughout Canada; the former are now played on video screens in some parts of the country. In a lottery, chances to win a share of a prize, usually cash, are sold at a set price. Raffles tend to differ only in the form of the prize offered; they normally award goods instead of money and tend to be smaller in scope. They are a common source of funds for religious and charitable organizations.

The fifth type is bingo, which is legally available across Canada and in a large majority of states. Bingo sessions are so common in churches, charitable organizations, service clubs, and the like that they are not defined as gambling at all by many players (CRNPG, 1976:160). Yet, at least in the United States, there is considerable illegal bingo, because of tax licensing and reporting procedures. But the average player knows nothing of it, since he or she has little to do with the management of this form of entertainment.

CRIMINAL GAMBLING

Running concurrently with legitimate gambling operations are the three criminal types. All three are understood to be controlled by organized crime. The details of the numbers game (also known as policy, mutuel, or bolita) are too complicated to present here. In brief, a person selects a number to bet on, based on almost any conceivable criterion, including superstitions, hunches, dreams, and favourite numbers. Most common is the use of a three-digit system in which players wager on any of 1000 numbers. Their bets are then placed with a runner (sometimes called a writer or seller) who delivers them to one or more functionaries in the local numbers network. The daily winning number may be selected in a variety of ways, the favourites being those which can readily be verified by the players. Thus, numbers are often selected from data on the financial page of the local newspaper, parimutuel handle figures, or racetrack payoffs, all of which are publicly available. Payoffs are such that 49 to 52 percent of the total wager remains as profit for the operators (Christiansen, 1985:246–247). In the survey conducted by the CRNPG (1976:75), 3 percent reported participating in numbers games.

In bookmaking, bookies collect clandestine wagers on horse races and sports events, and on a variation of the latter known as pool, sports, or parlay cards. These middlemen facilitate betting by those who are personally unable to attend the contest on which they bet. More importantly, American bookies offer tax-free winnings to their customers (at the time of writing, there is no tax on gambling winnings in Canada), and both Canadian and American bookies offer credit to those who need money to continue gambling. By taking bets on sports events, bookies offer a service unavailable in OTB. Their function is to gather the wagers, determine a profit, and pay off the winners. The profit is around 11 percent (Christiansen, 1985:246–247). In pool-card betting the bookmaker, who prefers a bigger monetary volume, is replaced by a runner who passes out cards, collects wagers and card stubs, and delivers payoffs. Surveys (CRNPG, 1976:75; *Weekend Magazine*, 1979:3) show approximately 4.3 percent of Americans and 2 percent of Canadians betting with bookies on horse races and sports events, especially football, hockey, basketball, and baseball.

Despite tougher legislation dealing with interstate gambling violations, a few small illegal casinos known as "flat stores" still exist in the United States (CRNPG, 1976:176). They are movable operations specializing in blackjack and dice — and in the art of quick relocation, should their whereabouts become known to the police. The wide availability of legal casinos in Canada has virtually eliminated the flat store in this country.

TOLERANCE OF GAMBLING

The public's perception of gambling as deviance varies considerably, depending on the specific type. Many people think that bingo, for example, is exciting, respectable entertainment, while wagering through a bookie is downright criminal. As a broad category of deviant behaviour, gambling has every possible legal status. We have seen that some of it is legitimate (lotteries, bingo, parimutuel betting), some of it criminal (numbers, bookmaking), and some of it non-criminal (neighbourhood poker games).

On the criminal side, police enforcement of the law is often "very difficult" (CRNPG, 1976:35, 39). John Rosencrance (1988:100–101) describes the current situation:

> Both the public and agents of social control maintain that legal sanctions will not stop gambling, that people will continue to gamble regardless of the legality of such activities, and that enforcement is an ineffective deterrent. Police and prosecutors talk of enforcement as fingers in the dike, while the public maintains that it is impossible to legislate morality. This perspective has led to reduced enforcement, light sentences for those actually charged, and massive violations of gambling laws by the nation's bettors.

Effective tolerance of gambling by both officials and the public is highly evident in the gambling and betting incidents enumerated in the *Canadian Uniform Crime Reports*. Between 1975 and 1992, their numbers declined by approximately 70 percent.[2]

What, then, is tolerated in gambling, and what is not? Only a partial answer is possible at present, since there has been no research on the matter. In general, people seem to regard as deviant, but tolerably so, those who gamble regularly, three or more times a week (Joyce, 1979:155; Dickerson, 1984:38), for large stakes with money that perhaps could be better used for their families. According to Walker (1992:153) this constitutes "heavy gambling". It is analogous to heavy drinking as described in Chapter 5, inasmuch as neither is substantially problematic even though both are stigmatized as deviant. Accompanying the relative tolerance of heavy gambling is lingering support for the Protestant work ethic and the principle that one should earn one's livelihood through conventional work (Devereux, 1968:58). Big winnings through gambling appear to violate this principle. Gambling as tolerable deviance, whatever its legal status, becomes intolerable deviance when it grows either compulsive or pathological, or shows close connection with the criminal underworld.

TYPES OF GAMBLERS

In this section, we consider seven types of gamblers: the professional, the percentage gambler, the cheater, the economic gambler, the thrill gambler, the functional gambler, and the pathological gambler. Though there exists a variety of typologies from which to draw, the one best suiting our purposes is that of Joseph Scimecca (1971).

The Professional

Professional gamblers, most of whom are men, are skilled, knowledgeable players for whom gambling is a way of life. Both Scimecca (1971) and Morehead (1950) recognize the distinctiveness of the professional attitude: a preference for contests of ability among peers. Preferred games include poker, blackjack, craps, and pool, games in which skill and knowledge are important factors in the outcome and house takeout is minimal or non-existent. It is for this reason that professional gamblers say they "play" rather than "gamble". Professionals also avoid cheating. They maintain composure at all times and demonstrate gamesmanship even when losing (Martinez and La Franchi, 1969:52). They are honoured in gambling circles for their commitment to the occupation as a livelihood and for their knack of making a living at it without underhanded tactics.[3]

Hayano (1984:158) cautions that the term "professional" as applied to gamblers should not be confused with the same term used with reference to doctors and lawyers. Like "professional" deviants of other sorts, gamblers are best regarded as *experts* in a given line of marginal work (Stebbins, 1979:24). This *caveat* frees us from having to search for such trappings of professionalism as codes of ethics, formal and certified training, and provision of services meeting major social values. The term "professional" when used in this context will, in fact, denote an expert who makes either a full-time or a part-time living from gambling; in this discussion, from poker (Walker, 1992:51) and blackjack.

Hayano (1984:158–161) identifies four types of professional poker and blackjack players. The **worker-professional** is a man or woman who holds a non-deviant job, but who is dedicated to a career in gambling and spends a good deal of time pursuing it. The non-deviant job, however, provides the steady income needed to live from day to day. Playing poker or blackjack is thus a hobby, a form of seriously regarded leisure (Stebbins, 1992) that encourages commitment and perseverance.

The **outside-supported professional** has an even better extragambling income, derived from savings, investments, retirements funds, or a similar source. In this category we find retired people, housewives, and the independently wealthy. Hayano (1984) also places students who, presumably, use their gambling winnings as a source of pin money, into this group.

The **subsistence professional** is a consistent winner, but only of relatively small bets. He or she uses the winnings to live on, to pay the bills of everyday living. There is little interest here in a career in gambling, or in moving on to higher stakes and stiffer competition.

This, however, is precisely the orientation of the **career professional**. Such a person is much more likely to be a man than a woman, when compared with the first three types, and is most highly committed to gambling as an occupation. Even when broke, he prefers to borrow money in order to return to gambling. Hayano (1977) found in his study of poker professionals in Gardena, California (one of the few places in North America where commercial poker gambling is legal) that they see their occupation as arduous. They emphasize a work ethic, including a commitment to poker, honesty, and integrity in borrowing and lending money to pay their own or others' gambling debts. They also pride themselves on "class" personal demeanour, whether winning or losing. Table 7.1 summarizes the key characteristics of the four types discussed above.

The Percentage Gambler

Percentage gamblers lack the degree of devotion to gambling shown by the professionals. They treat it as a part-time enterprise in which, given their consid-

TABLE 7.1 THE PROFESSIONAL GAMBLER: SUBTYPES AND CHARACTERISTICS

Subtype	Estimated Male/Female Ratio	Non-gambling Income	Degree of Career Commitment	Usual Game Stakes	Desire for Upward Mobility
Worker-Professional	15-20:1	Yes	None	All stakes	Moderate
Outside-Supported Professional	15-20:1	Yes	None to moderate	All stakes	Moderate
Subsistence Professional	30-40:1	Usually no	Little to moderate	Small to medium	None or little
Career Professional	40-50:1	Usually no	Moderate to high	Medium to high	Moderate to high

Source: David M. Hayano, "The Professional Gambler: Fame, Fortune, and Failure," *The Annals of the American Academy of Political and Social Science*, 1984, 474, July:160.

erable knowledge of the odds, they bet only when the chances of winning are relatively high. Unlike the professionals, these players are more interested in the money than in the "action" itself and are inclined to seek games with "suckers" while avoiding those with peers.

Percentage gamblers, as their name implies, are chiefly concerned with the money that gambling can potentially bring in as a moonlighting form of employment, rather than with its leisure qualities. Playing against accomplished opponents threatens these gamblers' livelihood.

The Cheater

The **cardsharp** and the **dice mechanic** constitute two special categories of the third type of gambler, who is known more broadly as the cheater. Cheating appears to be an entirely male form of deviance. Like the percentage gambler's, the cheater's goal is to make money. Therefore it is better to play against inferiors than against peers. But the skills of the cheater are different from those of either the percentage gambler or the professional. This individual uses the sleight of hand and gimmicked equipment of the entertainment magician. Indeed, in gambling circles, cardsharps and dice mechanics are alternatively known as "magicians" (Lesieur, 1984:179).

Prus and Sharper (1991:21–47) differentiate between two kinds of systematic cheats in gambling, the **rough hustle**, or semiprofessional, and the **professional**. The former possesses fewer manipulative skills than the latter and, in general, knows less about "hustling" or cheating at cards and dice. He also has fewer interpersonal skills to charm unsuspecting players into accepting him as an ordinary gambler. He is less dedicated to cheating as a livelihood, possibly because he is less successful at it. The rough hustle is more likely to work alone than the professional, since he is not good enough as a cheater to attract a partner. The professional cheater is, in many ways, the opposite of the rough hustle. He is much more likely to have polished interpersonal and manipulative skills and a level of expertise that enables him to continue in this line of work as a full-time livelihood.

Working up the action is no mean task. "Spots" must be found to "spread" (introduce or enter) card or dice games. Spots include a myriad of charities, conventions, local stags, benefit dinners, golf outings, and banquets. Once a party is chosen, the delicate assignment of entering the action must be carried off as unobtrusively as possible. The skilled hustler blends like a chameleon with his marks, whatever their social status, to convey an impression of respectability and innocence. Sometimes the hustler's act fails or comes close to failure, most commonly because of the suspicion generated by being a stranger and winning. Even here his glib tongue often smooths things over peacefully.

Cheating is a form of criminal deviance; it is illegal. Its status as intolerable deviance is not in doubt; even other gamblers regard the cheat as a criminal. In Canada, cheating at gambling is an indictable offence leading to imprisonment for two years.

The Economic Gambler

The fourth of our types is the economic gambler, whose principal end is also to make money. He wants to get rich quickly without resorting to what he regards as the evil of legitimate employment. Such gamblers have little commitment to gambling as a way of life. Nor do they possess much skill at it (unlike the aforementioned types). Rather, the economic gambler relies on superstition. James Henslin (1967) recorded the ways in which off-duty taxi drivers used verbal and non-verbal gestures to try to control the dice in their craps games. Some forms of "magic", as he called them, are presumed to maximize one's control over the dice; other forms are presumed to regain the control that is momentarily lost; still other forms are presumed to minimize opponents' control over the dice.

It is likewise among bingo players. Rachael Dixey (1987:211) cites some of the superstitions she observed among her sample of British women:

> I won the link one night on a Saturday wearing a green blouse and a green jumper, and funny enough I won the link again the next night, and people said, "Oh, are you wearing your lucky stuff?" ...Some people won't buy a ticket as soon as they come in, or they won't go after a certain person to get a ticket. Some think the first ticket is going to be lucky.

In another study, blacks in New York's Harlem district were observed to use religious charms from Hoodoo to generate good luck when betting on numbers (McCall, 1964). Hoodoo is an urban version of a black religion from Haiti and Trinidad. In itself it has no link with gambling. Nonetheless, urban blacks in the United States have converted its charms to good luck symbols that are used to (magically) ensure success in their numbers games.

The economic gambler is possibly the best example of William Eadington's (1987) hypothesis that wealth is the primary motive for gambling. He studied the allocations and expenditures of bettors and concluded that gambling is commonly seen as a way to rise into a higher social class.

The Thrill Gambler

The thrill gambler relieves the boredom of everyday life by throwing dice, playing the horses, wagering on numbers, and engaging in similar kinds of betting. There is a moderate level of ego involvement here, but little skill to accompany it. Hence, superstitious acts and beliefs are a prominent aspect of this type of play. Bingo players reach for such talismans as wishbones, rabbits' paws, plastic elephants (that must face the caller), and locks of hair to guide fate in a favourable direction (Carlyle-George, 1981).

Zurcher (1983) studied the "friendly" poker game, a semi-monthly event held on a rotating basis at the homes of a group of upper-middle-class men. One of the functions of the sessions was to allow the players to unwind and regenerate themselves after a day's work. But, Zurcher (1983:145) found, a leading attraction was the thrill of each hand of poker:

> The poker group did not tolerate disruption of the "pace" of the game. Some players commented about the rapid series of "thrills" that were strung together in a night's playing — the thrill of the "chance" and the "risk". A regular explained, "We don't eat sandwiches and things like that during the game, and we don't shoot the bull, because it causes a break in the action." Another remarked, "It's like a new game every hand. There's a new dealer, you get a new set of cards, and it's a whole new ball game. You get your new cards dealt to you and you've got to think all over again what you are going to do with this hand." Each player was a broker of events potentially thrilling to himself and his colleagues.

The Functional Gambler

The functional gambler demonstrates especially well an aspect of the functional approach to deviance previously not considered — the function of deviance within a small group, even while the same deviance is generally regarded by the society as a whole as dysfunctional. In a study that has never been repeated, Zola (1964) observed off-track betting through a bookie in a working-class bar in a large New England city. Of the several men who patronized and gambled at Hoff's Place, few were unemployed. Nonetheless, many of them managed to assemble approximately ten minutes before race time each day to place their bets with the bookie, follow their favourite horse on a radio broadcast, and help those who won celebrate their good fortune.

The bookie seemed to create gambler solidarity, a sort of "we" — the working-class men at Hoff's — against "they" — the local racing system, as personified by the bookie. A win by any one of the gamblers was defined as a victory for all at Hoff's. That is, the win functioned to heighten group solidarity and to give these men a rare sense of being in control of their lives, instead of the other way around, the normal outlook for many working-class people. An outlook of control could prevail because most of the men avoided superstitions and used some sort of rational means to place their bets. Most would either handicap — use available information about past performances of horses, jockeys, post positions, and so on — or use a "hot tip", insider information about the race not generally known to the public.

The study by Light (1977) of the numbers-gambling banks in urban black communities demonstrates the functionality of this form of gambling for another small segment of the larger society. Conventional banking institutions have never been able to provide adequate service in poor areas. Light (1977:896) noted that among the favourable or functional consequences of the black numbers bank is the fact that, once the money has been bet, it serves as a form of forced savings:

> The bettor's justification for this seemingly preposterous misconception arises from unsatisfactory experiences with depository savings techniques. Once a numbers collector has a man's quarter, they aver, there is no getting it back in a moment of weakness. If, on the other hand, the quarter were stashed at home, a saver would have to live with the continuing clamor of unmet needs. In a moment of weakness, he might spend the quarter. Therefore, in the bettor's view, the most providential employment of small change is to bet it on a number.

The small change is rarely missed. But should one "hit a payoff", the win is usually big and most useful to the winner. This system also provides credit for regular gamblers who participate in it. Light learned, too, that numbers racketeers are sometimes large investors in black-owned businesses in the ghettos.

The Pathological Gambler

Scimecca's label for this member of his typology was "compulsive gambler", a term which has now fallen out of favour with many researchers in the interdisciplinary field of gambling studies. "Pathological" is believed to encompass better than "compulsive" the initial pleasure that draws future problem gamblers into excessive wagering. While we are on the subject of types, note that "problem gambler" — another terminological newcomer — is a broader concept than pathological gambler; the problem type is buffeted by certain negative consequences of his or her gambling. But even though this person is no longer merely gambling heavily, he or she is not gambling pathologically. In the words of Lesieur and Rosenthal (1991), the various types fall along a continuum anchored at one end by occasional gambling and at the other by pathological gambling. "The essential feature of pathological gambling," according to the DSM-IV (1994:617), "is persistent and recurrent maladaptive gambling behavior... that disrupts personal, family, or vocational pursuits."

The pathological drive to gamble makes it difficult to say "no" to the next opportunity to bet on the horses, buy a lottery ticket, play a hand of poker, or pull the lever of a slot machine. Many pathological gamblers borrow heavily to continue their habit; some even resort to criminal means to acquire gambling money. Pathological gambling, at its worst, is a form of secondary intolerable deviance that consumes large amounts of time and energy and dominates the individual's life.

The stark fact is that few people can consistently win at gambling (Kusyszyn, 1979). Those who do profit over the long run — the professionals and percentage gamblers — do so by sticking to those few games which require skill and knowledge — but not the intervention of a "house" or other intermediary: notably poker, blackjack, and pool and billiards. An intermediary organization or individual (e.g., bookie) will take a set percentage of the money bet, leaving relatively little for distribution among the winning gamblers.

Some pathological gamblers will bet on virtually anything. Waller (1974: 45–46) reports on interviews with men who had bet on when a fly would land on a table, or on which raindrop would be the last to reach the bottom of a train window. Others specialize in games such as roulette, craps, or horse racing, where they believe they can "crack" the system and win significant amounts of money. (See Viewpoint 7.1 for a discussion of the appeal of lotteries.) But because these people gamble indiscriminantly and with little real skill, they are destined in the long run to lose more than they win. This situation, as we shall see, leads to a lifestyle distinct from that of other deviants and even other gamblers.

VIEWPOINT 7.1

THE APPEAL OF LOTTERIES

Lottery Mania

H. Roy Kaplan: By 1990, lotteries should gross $20 billion dollars. They are already one of our leading industries. Our present experience with lotteries in twentieth century America raises several issues worth investigating. 1) Their effect on the work ethic. 2) Do they increase compulsive gambling? 3) Are the poor heavy gamblers? 4) What is their impact on states' economies, on both earmarked categories and on the general revenue? 5) Why do people buy lottery tickets? 6) What is the impact of lotteries on society? Kaplan's responses range from his position that lotteries are "the least pernicious form of gambling... a cheap high that feeds the dream," to "the escapist dreams and desires of people are a manifestation of a deeper malaise that courses through the veins of our social system." Kaplan recommended, however, that government which sanctions gambling, should "provide funds for educating the public, for treating abusers and for researching the impact of gambling policies."

Vicki Abt: Disagreed with Kaplan's characterization of the lotteries as "least pernicious." The odds against winning make lotteries a "sucker's game," which the state should not be pushing. Unlike other forms of gambling, which involve at least a redeeming minimum of calculation, work and know-how, the lotteries contradict the belief that, "reward is based upon effort and character and knowledge." Abt applied to lotteries Terry Kellogg's criteria for addiction and concluded that lotteries are a highly addictive form of gambling. Lotteries also fail to meet three standards of the wealth of nations: brainpower; physical labor; capital investment. "The lottery does not produce any real wealth... it is a transfer tax, and the state, in promoting it, is being at best, disingenuous and at worst, greedy."

Dan Bower: Told some surprising stories of "Lottery Mania," anecdotes about lottery lines and huge jackpot stories designed to illustrate that people like success — particularly the success of the lottery, that everybody has their "greed level," that they tend to band together, be drawn to a place, a spectacular event and "do crazy things." Witness the extremes of soccer games in Great Britain or the opening of a supermarket. Bower did not judge lottery mania, either morally or psychologically. "I don't know whether it's good or bad. There's both sides to a story... I don't know how to stop the Lottery Mania; or if I want to stop it." He did however, evaluate the lottery politically: "The people vote for the lottery, they also vote every week, when they step up to buy a lottery ticket, that's another vote in favor of Lottery Mania."

Ron Nabakowski: "People who spend $1.50 on the lottery spend two hours that day talking about it... and that's the point. The lottery is fun and people want it for that reason. Seventy of Ohio's residents play lottery, most just occasionally. "When you compare a rollover jackpot of $9 million or more, I think we've got a good product... Most of the compulsive gamblers I know are also looking at the Wall Street Journal... But we do have problem gamblers and we are addressing that problem and will do more... The more lottery tickets we sell, the more compulsive gamblers there will be... Anybody in this industry who says lotteries don't create compulsive gamblers is naive as hell or a damn liar... We are attempting to institute the policy to set aside 1% of the advertising budget for public education."

Source: Gordon T. Graves, H. Roy Kaplan, Daniel W. Bower, Ronald Nabakowski, and Vicki Abt, "Lottery Mania," *Quarterly News from the National Council on Compulsive Gambling,* 1989, 4, Winter:15. Publication of The National Council on Problem Gambling, NY. By permission.

GAMBLING SCENES

Gambling scenes have four important components: people, places, equipment, and action. They vary considerably from one type of gambler to another in their specific details.

The People and Places

For the devotee, the people of the gambling world constitute a set of acquaintances and friends who staff and patronize the racetracks, lottery stands, poolrooms, betting shops, and poker parlors which they regularly frequent. These establishments offer an opportunity to express skill and knowledge, for instance, in poker or in betting on horses. Or they may merely be places where one can experience the thrill of gambling and get a chance to win something; at bingo or the slot machine, for example. Some gambling establishments, notably the Nevada and New Jersey casinos, embellish the gambling experience by offering a lavish atmosphere of restaurants, entertainment, and lodging:

> The idea, of course, is not only to render the casino area itself timeless (a casino never has a clock or alteration in lighting, which makes it socially comfortable for a gambler to risk money at any hour of the day or night), but also to allow a touring gambler to spend his entire bankroll within the confines of the given casino. A gambler located in one casino complex can purchase wardrobes several times over, pick up an elegantly designed fur coat, dine on escargot, gefilte fish, canneloni, sukiyaki, drink Chambertin '61 or 1966 Dom Perignon as well as assorted spirits, smoke Havana cigars, play tennis, swim, golf, sweat in dry or wet heat, be massaged and coiffured, be entertained by the likes of Frank Sinatra. Ann-Margret, and Sammy Davis, and never feel sexually deprived (Skolnick, 1978:36).

The social interaction that occurs in these places is of two major kinds. The first, and for many the most important, is that which is necessary to conduct games of chance. Gamblers interact in a businesslike manner with croupiers, bookies, money changers, ticket sellers, bingo callers, numbers runners, and others. Poker and pool gamblers interact with each other, extracting subtle information from actions to determine any bluffing or cheating.

A special language has arisen around the common problems and situations faced by all who participate. According to Prus and Sharper (1991:71–75), card hustlers "spread" or start a card game at large social functions. At the start, the game is likely to include "deadheads", players not inclined to bet much money. Among the manipulations used during such a game are "false cutting", "false shuffling", "running up the deck" (stacking it), and such techniques as "peeking" and dealing "seconds" and "bottoms".

In addition, before and after a gambling stint, there are opportunities for the second type of social interaction, shoptalk. Roulette players, for instance, may discuss the various predictive theories for winning at their game (Oldman, 1974). Poker players pride themselves on not being "tight-assed chickenshits" who are afraid to help other regulars. They openly discuss matters of mutual interest, calling such talk "weather reports", "scorecards", or "daily news" (Rosencrance, 1986:366–367). Bingo players sometimes discuss the differences between the callers at the halls where they play (Pratt, 1980). Finally, there is the unusual interaction between a "big winner" of a lottery and other lottery participants who hope to attract some of the winner's luck. This is achieved, it is believed, by touching the winner. Winners report being mobbed, rubbed, and touched to such an extent that they have been bruised and clawed (Kaplan, 1978:14–15).

Equipment

To most gamblers, the artifacts associated with their work or leisure are not problematic or in any other way special. The lottery ticket, the bingo card, the roulette table are simply means to the gambler's ends and do not have to be carefully attended to during the process of reaching those ends.

But the same is not true of certain items of equipment in other games of chance. Cards, for example, can be marked or subtly printed on the back in order to convey their value on the front. Poker and blackjack players, always wary of cheaters, are constantly on the watch for gimmicked equipment. Craps players always check for loaded "cubes", dice that are overbalanced with a small metallic weight called a "slug". Gamblers in pool and billiards (Polsky, 1985: 36–40) are concerned with the resilience of the cushions lining the edges of the table.

Concern with equipment in horse racing sometimes takes the form of handicapping. As mentioned earlier, handicappers attempt to amass sufficient knowledge about the horses in a race, the jockeys riding them, and the conditions of the track to make a rational bet on the winner. The horse player correlates these data with other information that he or she is able to obtain, which often includes trainer intentions (e.g., whether this is a preparatory race for the horse), earlier betting patterns, and tips from those who know (Rosencrance, 1985:39).

Slot machines are another kind of equipment that must be carefully considered. Downes and his colleagues (1976:193) observed that regular slot machine players in Britain frequently attempt to "read" the machines. They pass from one to another until they find one that "feels" right. Or they will play one until they "get to know" it, then return to play it repeatedly.

Action

One central quality of gambling as leisure is conveniently summed up in a single loaded word — *action*! There is action when the risk of loss is possibly avoidable (Lesieur, 1984:44). As Goffman (1967:156) puts it:

> The distinctive property of games and contests is that once the bet has been made, *outcome is determined and payoff awarded all in the same breath of experience* [instead of being separated by a long period of time]. A single sharp focus of awareness is sustained at a high pitch during the full span of the play.

This excitement is the number one motive for the thrill gambler. Indeed, it stands as a major attraction of betting for all types, though some games are more absorbing than others. A recent study of Alberta gamblers sheds light on this area (Wynne Resources Ltd., 1994:88):

> How they felt during play varied by game preference. For lottery ticket buyers and Sport Select players, the anticipatory thrill comes after the wager has been made. The ticket purchase itself is a rather perfunctory act, but the tension level rises prior to watching the draw or the sports results on TV.

> For those who enjoy rapid-fire, continuous games such as bingo, casino games, and VLTs, the excitement comes from playing the game. Just being in action is pleasurable in itself.

In other words, gambling sometimes amounts to more than the mere hedonism of action. Even as leisure, it offers its skilled and knowledgeable practitioners a way of developing and expressing abilities and cultivating a favourable self-image within their special subculture. Leisure studies specialists (e.g., Abt et al., 1984; Saunders and Turner, 1987; Filby and Harvey, 1989) have explored in detail the leisure nature of the various games of chance.

In Czikszentmihalyi's (1990:49, 67, 72–77) terms, gamblers who experience action are in "flow". (Gamblers refer to the feeling as a "rush".) Flow, as a frame of mind, is possible when there is a wide range of potential outcomes, all of them uncertain. The individual gambler, whether by skill or by chance or by a combination of the two, places a bet on one or a few of these outcomes. As the gambling event unfolds, the bettor becomes totally absorbed with the process and its possible outcomes, to such an extent that he or she is aware of nothing else. Clearly, the event must unfold in such a way (a horse race or a spin of the roulette wheel) that the unfolding can be observed. Certainly the gamblers who were at Caesar's Palace, Las Vegas, in April 1981 and continued to play despite a fire in the tower overhead were in flow (*Calgary Herald*, 1981:C20). Viewpoint 7.2 portrays the nature and course of the action found nightly in the countless bingo halls across Canada.

GAMBLING CAREERS

The social science literature on gambling is perhaps richest in articles and books attempting to identify the motives for gambling. Smith and Preston (1984) have classified motives into 11 categories. The first and most prominent category contains the psychoanalytic theories, which propose guilt and masochism as the two primary reasons for gambling. Edmund Bergler's (1957) book provides an example. The main theme running through his study and those of other psychoanalysts is that the antecedent personality development of gamblers is an important factor in the initiation and maintenance of their wagering habits. Such analyses of the male compulsive gambler are especially common. He is seen as striving to prove his masculinity, impatient, narcissistic, and power-hungry, with a fetishistic attachment to money. Above all, he is seen as having an unconscious desire to lose.

Second is the motive of economic gain. Eadington's (1987) work exemplifies this approach. Gambling is viewed from this perspective as a means of either upward mobility or conspicuous consumption. Through it, the gambler can demonstrate his or her affluence to others. The professional, economic, and compulsive types of gamblers frequently have this motivation.

The third motive is play, leisure, and recreation. Igor Kusyszyn (1984:139), a psychologist, argues that gambling offers an escape from reality and helps satisfy

VIEWPOINT 7.2

THE COURSE OF THE ACTION IN BINGO

Then there are the bingo rituals, the comfort of repetition. As the caller settles in at the mike, and the first hush rustles through the crowd, people wait, as one, for each shiny, colored ball to pop out of the machine into the caller's hand, for the deadpan voice proclaiming, "Under the N... 36... N... 36...."

Nobody of good taste talks at bingo. Socializing is confined to intermissions. The caller is king, each with his (or her) own style and catchphrases, telegraphing the mysteries, the clues, the code of bingo: "Top of the house... O... 75"... "Bee-nine-ah"... "Heinz 57"... "And the little one... B... one"... Quack, quack, two little ducks... I... 22"....

If a coveted game goes number after number without a winner, the crowd begins to mutter, murmur, roar with impatience and suspense ("It's going to go, it's going to go," is heard from the next table)... with a huge collective sigh of relief and disappointment when someone "bingos". The games continue, and a worker discreetly places a pile of experienced bills at the winner's elbow. (But the winner barely blinks, as he or she intensely plays the next game.)

And of course there are myriad permutations of numbers in winning designs: straight lines, four corners, kite, sputnik, star, postage stamp, baseball, the letter T, half a house, picture frame, sandwich, garbage game, the Richmond R, the Kilarney K, the West Hillhurst W.... If your mind wanders, you may forget which pattern you are playing. Bingo is exhausting.

But that is another aspect of bingo: the wandering mind. Amazingly, it has been described as a form of meditation, relaxing a tense soul. "The mindless moment," states one observer. "Hung in space, totally free, waiting for the next number." Are the hordes of people not only aiming for big bucks, but experiencing inner peace, as well? Granted, there is an odd sort of calm that allows one's mind to travel effortlessly through clouds of thought (and smoke) while pondering the numbers in a reverie of reflex, ritual and relaxation.

Source: Linda Kupecek, "Bingo," *Calgary Herald Sunday Magazine*, 1985, September 27:8–9.

various needs, including that of play. Gambling activities have also been interpreted as allowing people to act different roles, such as the high roller and the cunning winner.

Zola's (1964) study illustrates the fourth motive: gambling behaviour as a learned role. He observed that gambling in bars and other social situations was a tradition among immigrant men who internalized this role as part of the primary socialization in their families.

Both Zola's research and Zurcher's (1983) more recent study of the neighbourhood poker game illustrate the fifth motive for gambling: to be with friends for a social gathering.

The sixth motive is prestige. It differs from the economic motive to the extent that the gambler wants to be seen by others as an important or "big time" person, not just someone who is rich. Thompson and Dombrink (1988:354–359) describe a prototypical European casino, an opulent setting for high-status gamblers only. The passage by Skolnick presented earlier in this chapter portrays the American type of casino, which differs from the European setting by being open to all social classes, among other ways. (See Thompson and Dombrink, 1989:338–340, for a more detailed comparison of the two.)

The seventh gambling motive is escape from economic frustration. Several studies carried out in the 1960s (e.g., Devereux, 1968:56–57) dealt with this aspect of gambling. Analysts believe some gamblers are trying to beat the dominant capitalistic system, which they feel has deprived them of certain goals.

Gambling as an occasion to use one's intellect is the eighth motive. Games such as poker and horse racing can be played using rational calculations to reduce the risk of loss. Rosencrance's (1985) study of the racetrack demonstrates this motive.

The ninth motive stems from the belief held by some gamblers that they are lucky people. According to Bergler (1957), these individuals are neurotic. They view themselves unrealistically as clever possessors of a special kind of luck. They "know that they will win", even if the objective probability of their doing so is very low.

The desire to experience the action is the tenth motive in Smith and Preston's list, a motive we have already considered in connection with the gambling scene. It is frequently joined with the eleventh motive: curiosity or a desire for new experiences. In the study of Alberta gamblers conducted by Wynne Resources Ltd. (1994:43), 39 percent of the respondents said they gambled to satisfy their curiosity about participating in games of chance. In this spirit, people may play the roulette wheel, bet on a horse, or try the slot machines. It is unlikely, however, that they would enter into a clandestine poker game or pool match out of curiosity, since these require some prior knowledge and skill.

Two observations should be made with reference to this list of motives. One is that, usually, several of them are operative at the same time. For instance, someone may believe that he or she is lucky and gamble for the money and action inherently possible in games of chance. The other observation is that all these motives are objective; they have been identified by scientists, not only by the gamblers themselves. The Alberta study (Wynne Resources Ltd., 1994:43) suggests that people gamble primarily for fun or entertainment, to win money or, given the role of charities in Canadian gambling, to support a worthy cause. Many respondents also said that they gambled because games of chance are exciting or pose a challenge.

Career Development

Once established, the interests of many gamblers — particularly thrill, functional, economic, and percentage gamblers — manifest little continuity in a particular direction. They gamble for set reasons that are either satisfied or not in specific episodes of betting. They experience the action, win or lose money, or enjoy the company of the other players or the environment of the gambling establishment. The next episode will be more or less the same.

Other gamblers, however, do have careers that progress and sometimes regress in a definite direction. The professional is one of these. Skill and knowledge are key elements in this gambler's career, but, since the takeout is so high, ups and downs are inevitable. Even the professional poker player, who normally works in a setting where there is no takeout, faces this problem (Hayano, 1984:159–160). Thus, from game to game and year to year, many professionals drift back and forth among worker-professional, outside-supported professional, and career professional.

Progressive continuity for poker and pool professionals appears to follow the four contingencies identified by Prus and Sharper (1991:28–30) for card and dice hustlers. First, both the professionals and the hustlers must get connections that provide routes to partnerships for the latter and games for the former. Second, their playing abilities must be favourably evaluated by more established members of the "profession". Third, players must be willing to invest the time, effort, and money to cultivate certain skills and acquire necessary equipment (in hustling and pool). Fourth, recognition as an accomplished player must eventually be won, a sort of "certification" that gives access to playing opportunities in the most prestigious places, with the best players, for the highest stakes.

The Pathological Gambler

The pathological gambler has the most distinctive career. Martinez (1983:129–130) has developed a "naturalistic theory" of compulsive gambling which contains the principal elements of the deviant career in this area. In the beginning, the pathological gambler develops a total commitment to gambling. At this point he or she is still in control of the deviance and is tolerated by the wider community. Gradually, male compulsives, in particular, begin to view themselves as cunning, powerful, moneyed playboys who live in the lofty reaches of the entertainment world and who do not have to be bothered with a mundane nine-to-five job. Commitment to gambling is enhanced by a commitment to this associated self-conception. These individuals see and identify themselves as gamblers, although at this stage they deny any implications that they are pathologically tied to betting.

Eventually, losses which publically and privately threaten this image begin to accumulate. Still, the action, the gambling scene, and the dream of being a success combine to keep the pathological gambler wagering habitually. At this point, the individual's deviance becomes intolerable, both to the community and to himself or herself. The outcome of this condition has already been discussed.

The DSM-IV (1994:617) estimates that pathological gamblers comprise 1 to 3 percent of the population. In a review of 22 surveys done as part of the study of gambling in Alberta by Wynne Resources Ltd. (1994:17–18), it was found that the prevalence rate of pathological gambling is generally higher in the studies conducted after 1990.

The classification of some gamblers as pathological is an example of the medicalization of deviant behaviour. Walker (1992:150), among others, rejects this approach:

> From the point of view of the sociocognitive theory, the problem gambler is neither sick nor compulsive. There is no pathology, only the damage caused by financial loss. There is no addiction, only false beliefs and irrational thinking.

Irrational thinking is evident in the gambler's illusion that he or she is in control — that more skill is needed to win than is objectively true. It is also apparent in the gambler's biased evaluation of outcomes, where wins are seen as an expression of ability, and losses discounted as evidence of failure. Finally, irrational thinking manifests itself in the gambler's entrapment in the belief that, despite many heavy losses, gambling will eventually pay off, and handsomely.

Stigma

The stigma attached to official labelling as a gambler is possible only if one is apprehended for playing the numbers, wagering through a bookie, or gambling in an illegal casino. But informal labelling is a major contingency for all gamblers, except those who play bingo and the lotteries. Justifiably or not, gambling is regarded by many as a social problem (Newman, 1975; Brenner and Brenner, 1987:16–21).[4]

Career professionals at poker have been described by Hayano (1977:561) as concerned about the image their family and friends may have of them as compulsive gamblers, cheats, or thieves. They adjust by stressing the skill, poise, honesty, and commitment that characterize career professionals in this "occupation". For some, the most dreaded image is that of failure, of being so unsuccessful as a gambler that large debts accumulate which confute the image they are striving for (Livingston, 1974:81–82; Lesieur, 1984:196).

CONTROLLING GAMBLING

There are three aspects of the control of gambling. First, there are legal and judicial attempts to limit the criminal side of this form of deviance, particularly the service component, which is believed to be organized and operated by the underworld. Second, the state has an interest in controlling gambling in order to gather in some of the revenue generated in this lucrative business. Third, there are attempts to control pathological gambling and to rehabilitate those who suffer from it. Only the last of these three is considered here.

Walker (1992: Ch. 7) reviews a range of treatment approaches to problem gambling: group support, group or individual therapy, behaviour modification, aversion therapy, and individual or marital counselling. None enjoys a high success rate, not even the most celebrated, Gamblers Anonymous (G.A.) (Walker, 1992:242). Patterned after Alcoholics Anonymous, with its disease model, Gamblers Anonymous holds frequent meetings where members discuss their gambling-related problems and recount their betting careers. Sympathy and group support for gambling abstinence and the problems encountered in attaining this goal help account for the effectiveness of G.A. Honesty and self-responsibility are cardinal personal traits demanded for all G.A. members; they are clearly expressed in the G.A. motto: "God grant me the serenity to accept the things I cannot change, the courage to change the things I can, and the wisdom to know the difference."

Recovery is no easy task. There are inevitable relapse problems. In a rare evaluation of G.A., Stewart and Brown (1988) found that, when using its success criterion of prolonged and unbroken abstinence, only 7 percent of the members refrained from gambling during a two-year period. One of the weaknesses of the various treatment approaches is a lack of first-hand understanding of gamblers and gambling (Lesieur and Custer, 1984). The gambling and recovery phases of the pathological gambling career are illustrated in Figure 7.1.

SUMMARY

According to public opinion and records of gambling expenditures, gaming in North America is at an all-time high, with indications of gaining even further popularity. This trend is largely restricted, however, to the five legitimate forms of gambling: casinos, parimutuel betting, off-track betting, lotteries, and bingo. Criminal gambling — bookmaking, illegal casinos, and the numbers game — is likely to continue, but not to expand appreciably in popularity.

The high public appeal of betting and the large amounts of money spent on it, coupled with the declining rates of arrest for gambling infractions throughout North America, suggest a general tolerance for gambling. The activity is tolerably deviant when participants gamble three or more times a week, for large stakes, with money that perhaps should be spent elsewhere. It is tolerably deviant when done with an air of seriousness unheard of among ordinary recreational gamblers, and when it is seen as an attempted subversion of the work ethic. It is intolerable when it either becomes compulsive or shows signs of being too closely connected with the underworld.

Several types of gamblers operate within this atmosphere of tolerance and widespread public betting. They include professionals, or, more accurately, experts who can be sorted into the categories of worker-professional, outside-supported professional, subsistence professional, and career professional. There are also the percentage gambler and the cheater. The latter may be either a cardsharp or a dice mechanic. The economic gambler strives to get rich quickly through gambling, to avoid the slower, seemingly more painful, route to success via an ordinary job. Bingo and neighbourhood poker games offer two examples of thrill gambling as a type of wagering. The functional gambler is someone whose efforts at betting contribute to the solidarity of a small group or subcommunity. The pathological gambler is someone who becomes addicted to gambling in general and continues at it to the point of personal ruin.

Although they vary considerably in their specific details, all gambling scenes contain four important components: people, places, equipment, and action.

Scientists have discovered many motives accounting for a gambler's entry into the betting world: guilt and masochism; economic gain; play, leisure, and recreation; role playing; socializing; prestige; escape from frustration; intellectual expression; belief in personal luck; desire for action; and curiosity and desire for new experiences. Gamblers themselves say they gamble primarily for fun or

FIGURE 7.1 CAREER OF PATHOLOGICAL GAMBLING AND RECOVERY

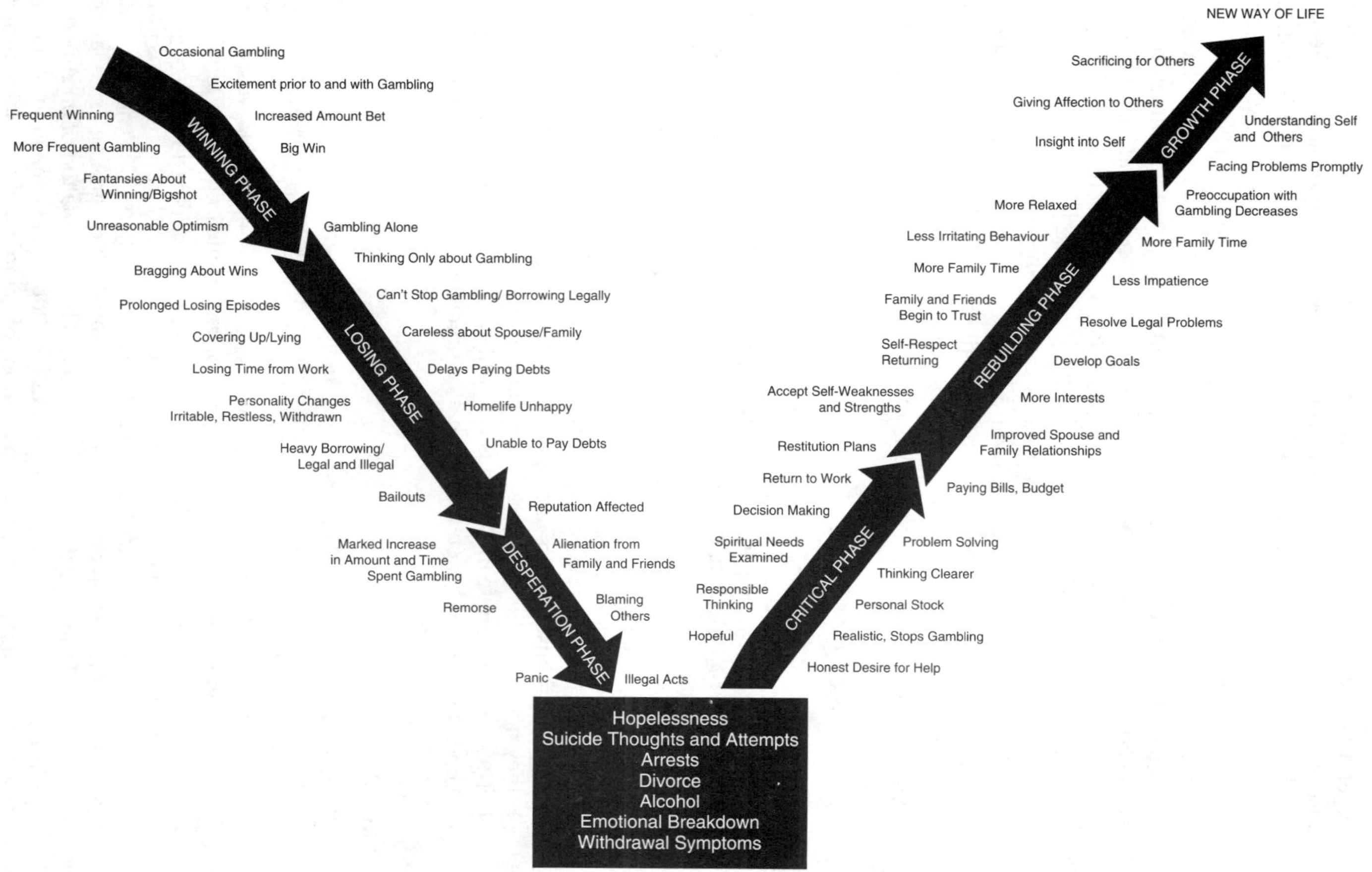

Source: Robert L. Custer, "Pathological Gambling." In *Patients with Alcoholism and Other Drug Problems,* edited by A. Whitfield. New York: Year Book Publishers, 1982.

entertainment, to win money or, in Canada, to support a worthy cause. Some are also attracted to games of chance which are exciting or pose a challenge.

The professional makes a career of gambling, although one characterized by frequent ups and downs. The best professionals are constantly developing their skills and looking for opportunities to play with other gamblers in increasingly prestigious settings. Pathological gamblers hope to follow a similar career. But they gamble indiscriminately, without much skill, to the point where they become addicted to the action and the dream of success, which consistently eludes them as they slide deeper into financial and social difficulty.

All gamblers except those who play bingo and the lotteries must cope with the stigma attached to their deviant interests. Still, gambling in general is not considered threatening enough to enforce widespread use of the formal social control measures that exist. The most concerted effort at control is exerted only in extreme cases of pathological gambling. It takes the form of group therapy, group support (G.A.), and, less frequently, individual professional therapy or other kinds of treatment.

NOTES

1 Some states have legalized forms that continue to be illegal elsewhere in North America. For instance, commercial poker is legal in Gardena, California, while pinball machines for gambling purposes are legal in Illinois (Rich, 1979:186).

2 See the annual volumes of *Crime and Traffic Enforcement Statistics,* which was recently retitled *Canadian Crime Statistics,* both of which are published by Statistics Canada, Cat. no. 85-205.

3 Some sociologists (Morehead, 1950) extend the category of professional to cover gambling-house owners and operators. Scimecca (1971:58), however, argues that they never gamble; the odds or "vigourish" are always in their favour.

4 These authors argue that there is no justification for the claim made by the general public and experts alike that gambling is a social problem.

SUGGESTED READING

Kaplan, H. Roy. *Lottery Winners: How They Won and How Winning Changed Their Lives.* New York: Harper & Row, 1978. An interview study of a sample of lottery winners in the United States.

Lesieur, Henry R. *The Chase.* Cambridge, MA: Schenkman, 1984. A sociological study of the careers of compulsive gamblers and their effects on family and work.

Prus, Robert C. and C.R.D. Sharper. *Road Hustler: Grifting, Magic, and the Thief Subculture.* New York: Kaufman and Greenberg, 1991. Observations of and interviews on the occupation of card and dice hustlers. This expanded edition contains chapters on entertainment magicians and on grifting as a way of life.

Rosencrance, John. *Gambling without Guilt: The Legitimation of an American Pastime.* Pacific Grove, CA: Brooks/Cole, 1988. An examination of the gambling scene, past and present, the explanations of gambling, the social worlds of gambling, and the problems of illegal and compulsive gambling.

Walker, Michael B. *The Psychology of Gambling.* New York: Pergamon, 1992. A review of the field of the psychology of gambling, including psychological explanations for gambling, Walker's own sociocognitive theory of gambling involvement, and treatments for problem gambling.

REFERENCES

Abt, Vicki, Martin C. McGurrin, and James F. Smith. "Gambling: The Misunderstood Sport — A Problem in Social Definition," *Leisure Sciences,* 1984, 6:205–220.

Bergler, Edmund. *The Psychology of Gambling.* New York: Hill & Wang, 1957.

Brenner, Gabrielle A. and Reuven Brenner. *A Profile of Gamblers.* Montréal: *Centre de recherche et développement en économique, Université de Montréal,* 1987.

Campbell, Colin S. "Gambling in Canada." In *Canadian Criminology,* edited by Margaret A. Jackson and Curt T. Griffiths, pp. 153–166. Toronto: Harcourt Brace Jovanovich Canada, 1991.

Campbell, Don. "Gambling in Manitoba Pays Off for Some," *Financial Post,* 1991, July 3:8.

Canadian Institute of Public Opinion. 1980, November 19.

"Canadians are Hooked on Gambling," *Globe and Mail,* 1992, May 9:A1, A4.

Carlyle-George, Peter. "When the Chips Are Down," *Maclean's,* 1981, February 9:18a–20a.

Christiansen, Eugene M. "Illegal Gambling." In *The Business of Risk,* edited by Vicki Abt, James F. Smith, and Eugene M. Christiansen, pp. 29–52. Lawrence, KS: University of Kansas Press, 1985.

Commission on the Review of the National Policy Toward Gambling (CRNPG). *Gambling in America.* Washington, DC: U.S. Government Printing Office, 1976.

Cunningham, Jim. "Gambling on Gambling," *Calgary Herald,* 1994, August 21: B1–2.

Czikszentmihalyi, Mihaly. *Flow: The Psychology of Optimal Experience.* New York: Harper & Row, 1990.

Devereux, Edward C., Jr. "Gambling." In *International Encyclopedia of the Social Sciences,* Vol. 6, edited by Edward Sills, pp. 53–62. New York: Crowell, Collier Macmillan, 1968.

Dickerson, Mark G. *Compulsive Gamblers.* London: Longman, 1984.

Dixey, Rachael. "It's a Good Feeling When You Win: Women and Bingo," *Leisure Studies,* 1987, 6:199–214.

Dougherty, Kevin. "Montreal Casino Hits the Jackpot," *Financial Post,* 1994, January 29:6.

Downes, D.M. et al. *Gambling, Work and Leisure.* London: Routledge & Kegan Paul, 1976.

Eadington, William R. "Economic Perceptions of Gambling Behavior," *Journal of Gambling Behavior,* 1987, 3:264–273.

Filby, Mike and Lee Harvey. "Recreational Betting: Individual Betting Profiles," *Leisure Studies,* 1989, 8:219–228.

Goffman, Erving. *Interaction Ritual.* Chicago: Aldine, 1967.

Hayano, David M. "The Professional Poker Player: Career Contingencies and the Problem of Respectability," *Social Problems,* 1977, 24:556–564.

_________ "The Professional Gambler," *The Annals,* 1984, 474, July:157–167.

Haynes, Dave. "More Canadians Gamble than do People in the U.S.," *The Journal,* 1993, April:3.

Henslin, James M. "Craps and Magic," *American Journal of Sociology,* 1967, 73:316–330.

Herman, Robert D. "Gambling." In *Encyclopedia Americana,* Vol. 12, pp. 264–266. Danbury, CT: Grolier, 1990.

Joyce, Kathleen M. "Public Opinion and the Politics of Gambling," *Journal of Social Issues,* 1979, 35:144–165.

Kaplan, H. Roy. *Lottery Winners: How They Won and How Winning Changed Their Lives.* New York: Harper & Row, 1978.

Kusyszyn, Igor. "Compulsive Gambling: The Problem of Definition," *International Journal of the Addictions,* 1979, 13:1095–1101.

_________ "The Psychology of Gambling," *The Annals,* 1984, 474, July:133–145.

Lesieur, Henry R. *The Chase: Career of the Compulsive Gambler.* Cambridge, MA: Schenkman, 1984.

_________ and Robert L. Custer. "Pathological Gambling: Roots, Phases, and Treatment," *The Annals,* 1984, 474, July:146–156.

_________ and Robert Rosenthal. "Pathological Gambling: A Review of the Literature," *Journal of Gambling Studies,* 1991, 7:5–40.

Lidz, Franz. "A Truly Friendly Game of Chance," *Sports Illustrated,* 1986, October 27:64–65.

Light, Ivan. "Numbers Gambling Among Blacks: A Financial Institution," *American Sociological Review,* 1977, 42:892–904.

Livingston, Jay. *Compulsive Gamblers.* New York: Harper & Row, 1974.

Martinez, Thomas M. *The Gambling Scene: Why People Gamble.* Springfield, IL: Charles C. Thomas, 1983.

_________ and Robert La Franchi. "Why People Play Poker," *Trans-action,* 1969, 6, July/August:30–35, 52.

McCall, George J. "Symbiosis: The Case of Hoodoo and the Numbers Racket." In *The Other Side,* edited by Howard S. Becker, pp. 51–66. New York: The Free Press, 1964.

McMillen, Jan. "The Future: Golden Goose or Trojan Horse? — Symposium Summation." In *Gambling in Canada: Golden Goose or Trojan Horse?,* edited by Colin S. Campbell and John Lowman, pp. 371–410. Burnaby, BC: School of Criminology, Simon Fraser University, 1989.

Morehead, Albert H. "The Professional Gambler," *The Annals,* 1950, 269:81–92.

Newman, Otto. "The Ideology of Social Problems," *Canadian Review of Sociology and Anthropology,* 1975, 12:541–550.

Oldman, David. "Chance and Skill: A Skill of Roulette," *Sociology,* 1974, 8:407–426.

Polsky, Ned. *Hustlers, Beats, and Others.* Chicago: University of Chicago Press, 1985.

Pratt, Sheila. "Every Card Can Be a Winner on the Bingo Circuit," *Calgary Herald,* 1980, January 11:B4.

Prus, Robert C. and C.R.D. Sharper. *Road Hustler: Grifting, Magic, and the Thief Subculture.* (Expanded ed.) New York: Kaufmann and Greenberg, 1991.

Rich, Robert M. *The Sociology of Criminal Law.* Toronto: Butterworths, 1979.

Rosencrance, John D. *The Degenerates of Lake Tahoe: A Study of Persistence in the Social World of Horse Race Gambling.* New York: Peter Lang, 1985.

_________ "Why Regular Gamblers Don't Quit," *Sociological Perspectives,* 1986, 29:357–378.

_________ *Gambling without Guilt: The Legitimation of an American Pastime.* Pacific Grove, CA: Brooks/Cole, 1988.

Saunders, D.M. and D.E. Turner. "Gambling and Leisure: The Case of Racing," *Leisure Studies,* 1987, 6:281–299.

Scimecca, Joseph A. "A Typology of the Gambler," *International Journal of Contemporary Sociology,* 1971, 8:56–72.

Skolnick, Jerome H. *House of Cards: The Legalization and Control of Casino Gambling.* Boston: Little Brown, 1978.

Smith, Ronald W. and Frederick W. Preston. "Vocabularies of Motives for Gambling Behavior," *Sociological Perspectives,* 1984, 27:325–348.

Stebbins, Robert A. *Amateurs: On the Margin Between Work and Leisure.* Beverly Hills, CA: Sage Publications, 1979.

_________ *Amateurs, Professionals, and Serious Leisure.* Montréal and Kingston: McGill-Queen's University Press, 1992.

Stewart, Ruth and Iain Brown. "An Outcome Study of Gamblers Anonymous," *British Journal of Psychiatry,* 1988, 152:284–288.

"Ten Injured in Caesar's Palace Fire," *Calgary Herald,* 1981, April 2:C20.

Thompson, William N. and John D. Dombrink. "A Politically Acceptable Model of Casino Gambling for American Jurisdictions." In *Gambling in Canada: Golden Goose or Trojan Horse?,* edited by Colin S. Campbell and John Lowman, pp. 337–366. Burnaby, BC: School of Criminology, Simon Fraser University, 1989.

U.S. Bureau of the Census. *Statistical Abstract of the United States: 1993.* (113th ed.) Washington, DC: U.S. Government Printing Office, 1993.

Walker, Michael B. *The Psychology of Gambling.* New York: Pergamon, 1992.

Waller, Adrian. *The Gamblers.* Toronto: Clarke Irwin, 1974.

"Weekend Poll: Gambling," *Weekend Magazine,* 1979, 29, February 10:3.

Wynne Resources Ltd. *Gambling and Problem Gambling in Alberta: Final Report.* (Prepared for Alberta Lotteries and Gaming) Edmonton: Wynn Resources Ltd., 1994.

Zola, Irving K. "Observations on Gambling in a Lower-Class Setting." In *The Other Side,* edited by Howard S. Becker, pp. 247–260. New York: The Free Press, 1964.

Zurcher, Louis A., Jr. *Social Roles.* Beverly Hills, CA: Sage Publications, 1983.

8

MENTAL DISORDER

The term "mental disorder" is used in this chapter and elsewhere in this book as a synonym for madness and insanity (both organic and functional), and as the term designating this kind of behaviour and thought. Conrad and Schneider (1992: Ch. 3), in their review of the history of mental disorder as it applies to present-day Western conceptions, point out that this psychological condition has been recognized for centuries. The ancient Palestinians identified behaviour that was impulsive, uncontrolled, or unreasoned as madness. The ancient Greeks and Romans thought madness was caused by divine possession.

During the Middle Ages, religious explanations of mental disorder dominated. In consonance with church dogma, mental illness was thought to be caused by God as punishment for the sin of faithlessness. It was believed that God was testing the individual's strength (as in the tribulations of Job) while administering a warning to repent. People whose behaviour seemingly put them in league with the devil were branded as witches. In the later Middle Ages and Renaissance, madness called for an inquisition and, if the defendant was found guilty (which was nearly always the case), for burning at the stake.

The Renaissance brought a renewed interest in ancient Greek and Roman thought, specifically, in some of their medical ideas on insanity. The result of this interest was a gradual shift in treatment from torture (to drive out evil spirits presumed to exist in the insane) and burnings to confinement in chains. By the eighteenth century, the practice of chaining up people largely became abandoned in favour of mere confinement. Conrad and Schneider (1992:46–47) point out that confinement came to be justified as a means of ensuring conformity and of resocialization. Because physicians were the only practitioners who had the legitimate authority to dispense medical treatment and medication, they were given the authority to identify and treat mental disorder.

During the eighteenth and nineteenth centuries the concept of **mental illness** gradually emerged as Western society's modern designation for madness. Conrad and Schneider (1992:47) describe the process: "Illness came to include misconduct and the deviant behaviour commonly known as madness, first by its use as a metaphor that was later reified into a myth, and second as a justification for the medical involvement and authority over madness."

CONTEMPORARY DEFINITIONS OF MENTAL DISORDER

Understanding mental disorder from a sociological perspective requires us to recognize two kinds of definitions of the condition: the *scientific* and the *common sense*. There is possibly more agreement on the latter than on the former.

Scientific Definitions

Because of the extensive disagreement among scientists about the nature of mental disorder, formal definitions are difficult to find. Perhaps the most influential and clear-cut is the definition developed by the American Psychiatric Association for its standard reference, *Diagnostic and Statistical Manual of Mental Disorders,* presently in its fourth edition:

> In DSM-IV, each of the mental disorders is conceptualized as a clinically significant behavioral or psychological syndrome or pattern that occurs in an individual and that is associated with present distress (e.g., a painful symptom) or disability (i.e., impairment in one or more important areas of functioning), or with a significantly increased risk of suffering death, pain, disability, or an important loss of freedom. In addition, this syndrome or pattern must not be merely an expectable and culturally sanctioned response to a particular event, for example, the death of a loved one. Whatever its original cause, it must currently be considered a manifestation of a behavioral, psychological, or biological dysfunction in the individual. Neither deviant behavior (e.g., political, religious, or sexual) nor conflicts that are between the individual and society are mental disorders unless the deviance or conflict is a symptom of a dysfunction in the individual, as described above (American Psychiatric Association, 1994:xxi-xxii).

Among the key psychiatric criteria for defining mental illness are the presence of *distress* and *disability,* which must be present in any diagnosis of mental disorder. Being deviant is not, in itself, sufficient, particularly when the deviant in question is a member of a subgroup whose values conflict with those of the larger society. Rather, says Endleman (1990:138), people are held to be mentally disordered because their "'weird' and 'crazy' way of perceiving and reacting to the world is seen as at least disturbing and unsettling to others, as violating... expectations of how people are supposed to think and act in society." The criterion of disability comes close to our conception presented in Chapter 1 that mental disorder, as the individual patient sees it, constitutes an adjustment to certain of life's problems.

The disease conception of mental disorder implies that a physical lesion of some sort can be identified as an important cause of the individual's psychological condition. Certainly, the **organic** mental disorders would lend themselves to such an interpretation — for instance, senility, which is caused to some extent by bodily deterioration; or paresis, which may be caused by syphilis. Organic disorders are brought about by some sort of physiological imbalance.

Although the disease concept was once applied to the **functional** mental disorders, the tendency today is to treat them as a distinct class of mental disorder. The functional disorders have no known organic or physiological antecedents. Rather, they are believed to be caused by maladjustments that are interpreted by the deranged person as functional or adjustive to his or her problems in life.

Thomas Szasz (1987) argues, largely alone among psychiatrists, that mental illness with only a functional basis is a "myth". That is, there is no such thing, since there is no biological basis for it. According to Szasz, the use of the term "illness" here is a psychiatric value judgment, usually a conservative one supporting the conventional social order.

Common Sense Definitions

The common sense definitions of mental disorder coincide in that the behaviour in question is deviant. They have, in William Eaton's (1986:1) words, *bizarre* qualities: they are seen by ordinary members of the society as "(1) odd in manner, (2) marked by extreme incongruities and contrasts, and (3) unexpected and unbelievable." Such behaviour is unusual in any society.

Scheff (1984:36–40) notes that there are many rules in a society on which consensus is so complete that nearly everyone takes them for granted — until someone violates them. There are labels for some of these rule violations, such as crime, perversion, and drunkenness. But there is also a residue of diverse kinds of violations for which no explicit label exists. The violation of these norms is referred to by Scheff (1984:38) as residual rule breaking (discussed in Chapter 2 of this book). The behaviours referred to in psychiatry as "symptoms" — withdrawal, posturing, hallucinations, continued muttering — are transgressions of residual rules or, in the theoretical language of this book, residual moral norms.

Scheff (1984:91) and Goffman (1961:131–146) indicate that bizarre behaviour is first noticed by the everyday associates of the mentally disordered person: the person's friends, relatives, neighbours, and workmates. When the behaviour becomes intolerable, a medical solution is sought. Psychiatrists often validate the complainants' judgment of the behaviour as bizarre (residually deviant), and define the behaviour in professional terms, describing it by the aforementioned symptoms and calling it mental illness. In short, the mentally disordered are labelled, first informally by everyday associates and later formally by the medical profession.

Common sense definitions of mental disorder also include judgments about the *immorality* of such behaviour. Disordered, bizarre behaviour is a violation of moral norms. Whether scientifically valid or not, the popular conception is that the mentally disordered are responsible for their actions (Francis, 1985:3). In this sense at least, bizarre behaviour may be considered wrong behaviour. Moreover, conformity to residual rules, as we have already noted, is not optional. When those rules are violated, they bring sanctions. Often the label of "crazy" or "nuts" is sanction enough. Threat inheres in the violation of residual rules because such behaviour is incongruous, unexpected, and unbelievable in places and situations where such aberrations are unwelcome. As D.L. Rosenhan (1973:254) puts it: "There is by now a host of evidence that attitudes toward the mentally ill are characterized by fear, hostility, aloofness, suspicion, and dread. The mentally ill are society's lepers." And this despite the mental health movement, which hopes to change these attitudes to ones more benign.

Mental Disorder in Other Societies

Up to this point, we have been discussing contemporary definitions of mental disorder in Western societies. Although all societies recognize certain forms of bizarre behaviour, the actual behaviour defined as bizarre varies widely from one society to another. Of significance is the fact that cultures having no contact with Western civilization rarely define bizarre behaviour as mental illness (Conrad and Schneider, 1992:38). Indeed, such behaviour may not even be defined as deviant.

A case in point comes from the Bena Bena of the Eastern Highlands of New Guinea, where some men suffer from episodes of deafness and aggressiveness lasting up to a day. While in this state, they randomly threaten others with clubs and arrows and run around in circles, but speak very little. These attacks are not scorned, however. They are also quickly forgotten once past. The attacks are believed to be caused by ghosts, who are intensely feared by the Bena Bena. Hence the unlucky victim is more to be pitied than censured; certainly he is not considered deviant (Langness, 1965). In Bali, madness is considered a psychological state in which people have the opportunity to communicate with the divine (Connor, 1982). It is a means of transcending everyday life and therefore cherished.

Still, there is a consensus among psychiatrists that the bizarre behaviour found in non-Western societies, such as that just described, is classifiable as some kind of mental illness (deReuck and Porter, 1965; Gallagher, 1987:23). Only the symptoms and distributions of the illnesses vary. At present, most of the evidence suggests that mental disorders may be somewhat less prevalent among people in non-industrialized societies than among those in industrialized societies (Gallagher, 1987:218–219). But estimating cross-cultural prevalence is fraught with methodological difficulties; we must therefore treat this observation as hypothetical.

PREVALENCE

Measuring the prevalence of mental disorder in industrial societies is nearly as difficult as measuring it elsewhere if, by prevalence, we mean the proportion of the population that is afflicted in this way. Part of the problem is that by no means all the people suffering from psychological aberrations come to the attention of the specialists trying to estimate their prevalence. And, since the very definition of mental disorder is not easily applied, the registration of cases is inconsistent. For these reasons and others, I will not attempt to present data on the number of Canadians or Americans believed to be suffering from noticeable mental distress or disability, apart from observing that the incidence of these conditions in the population is not insignificant. As evidence, note that in 1990 suicide was the third most frequent cause of death among Canadians under the age of 75 (Statistics Canada, 1994:132).[1]

While the actual prevalence of mental disorder may be increasing — a hypothesis on which there is disagreement (see later in this chapter) — there is a demonstrable trend toward the de-institutionalization of mental patients in Canada. Table 8.1 shows that the rates of admission and separation (discharges, death, and transfers) have dropped between 1975 and 1988–1989. Curra (1994:408) summarizes data going back to 1955 that indicate a similar trend in the United States. In that country, however, admission rates have been rising over the years, even while the number of mental patients in hospitals has been falling. What is happening is that they are presently staying in hospital for shorter periods than was the case before the 1950s — and for rehabilitation and treatment, rather than for segregation from the larger population.

TREATMENT

Until about the mid-1950s, hospitalization remained the prevailing method of treatment for the mentally disordered in twentieth-century North America. The

TABLE 8.1 ADMISSIONS AND SEPARATIONS IN CANADIAN PSYCHIATRIC HOSPITALS (SELECTED YEARS BETWEEN 1975 AND 1988–1989

Year	Number of Hospitals	Admissions	Separations
1975	59	49 696	51 469
1976	58	45 697	47 384
1979–1980	46	39 276	38 629
1987–1988	20	19 503	19 166
1988–1989	19	18 988	18 666

Source: Statistics Canada. *Mental Health Statistics,* Vol. 1: *Institutional Admissions and Separations* (Cat. no. 83-204) Ottawa: Minister of Supply and Services Canada, 1977; Statistics Canada. *Health Reports: Hospital Annual Statistics,* Vol. 1 (Cat. no. 82-003S20) Ottawa: Minister of Supply and Services Canada, 1991.

reputation of such places as barrackslike human warehouses for segregating those whose bizarre behaviour the community could no longer tolerate generally appears to be well deserved. Goffman (1961) described one such establishment in Washington, DC, where he spent a year as a participant observer. As in prisons, patients lived almost entirely apart from staff, even though staff were supposed to be "treating" and "curing" them so they could resume their normal roles in the outside world. The patients were stripped of their personal possessions and identification and submerged in the anonymity of over 7000 inmates, all of them dressed and treated alike. In this setting, where conformity to institutional rules was regarded as evidence of psychological improvement, patients learned how to adapt to a unique social environment in which all necessary decisions were made for them. The more they adapted to this environment, the more unfit they became to live on their own in the larger community.

Mental hospitals have not vanished, although their numbers have declined more or less steadily since the 1950s, as Table 8.1 demonstrated. Rosenhan's (1973) study, conducted in the early 1970s in the United States, indicated that such places still created many of the same problems that Goffman noted over a decade earlier. In the mid-1980s, some of my own students, after learning of the Rosenhan study, said they encountered similar circumstances in the mental hospitals where they worked. Others, however, have said that, in their experience, Rosenhan's depiction is out of date. There appears to be considerable empirical work showing that life in the modern mental hospital (as opposed to the psychiatric ward in a general hospital) is humane and well oriented to care and, where possible, rehabilitation. However, this work has been "increasingly overlooked and buried beneath the burgeoning claims for community care" (Prior, 1993:37).

Lacking more recent research, we must ask whether the conditions prevailing in the 1980s in Canadian mental hospitals still hold. John Marshall (1982:49–50), writing about mental hospitals in Ontario, pointed out that low staff pay, severe budget reductions, and poor staff training resulted in an ineffective staff–patient ratio at a time when the only people sent to such places were those who were violent or highly disturbed. Richman (1988:1778) made the same point in a more general way for all of Canada when he wrote: "The psychiatric treatment of patients with long-term schizophrenic and major depressive disorders is still inadequate." And in 1984, Marnie Rice (1984:17) reported on a consensus among observers that assaults by patients on other patients and staff were increasing in Canadian mental hospitals.

Community Mental Health

The community mental health movement in North America was born in the early 1950s. Bernard Bloom (1973) has described the nature of the changes in treatment that it spawned. "Community mental health" refers to all activities undertaken in the wider community that are related to mental disorder. The goal is to effect treatment in the natural setting of everyday community life, rather than in the socially sealed environment of the locked ward or asylum. Community mental health stresses prevention, as distinguished from therapeutic intervention. The therapy that is given is brief and often takes the form of intervention into a crisis. In accordance with the movement's goals of integration into the wider community, workers in the field strive to use paraprofessionals as well as formally trained professionals, and those in the movement believe that community health services should be directly responsive to the needs of the local community.

The community mental health movement was made possible by a number of factors. Possibly the most prominent was the introduction in the early 1950s of psychotherapeutic drugs, especially the barbiturates and tranquillizers. "Stabilized" with medicine, many patients could remain and function at home rather than languish in a psychiatric ward or hospital. But social science research on the deleterious consequences of isolation in such places may also have played a role, for it may have stimulated the psychiatric profession to look for alternatives. Finally, as Scull (1984: Ch. 8) points out, mental hospitals are expensive places to operate. From a practical, economic point of view, the fewer of them the better. These factors, among others, were also at the root of the de-institutionalization trend discussed earlier.

The mental hospital, which had been the principal treatment centre for mental disorder for over 100 years, began to be replaced during the second half of this century with a variety of alternatives, including general hospitals, halfway houses, nursing homes, supervised apartments, and board-and-care homes. In the United States, community mental health centres sprang up everywhere. New psychoactive drugs and an emphasis on care and rehabilitation (instead of custody in an asylum) made it possible to return many patients to the community following in-patient treatment in a hospital or out-patient treatment at an alternative facility.

The North America-wide neoconservative backlash of the 1980s had the effect of significantly reducing the funding for all mental patients. The result was a sharp increase in the number of mentally disordered homeless people (Kearns and Taylor, 1989; Mechanic and Rochefort, 1990:322; O'Reilly-Fleming, 1993:24–25). Speaking about the United States, Silverstein (1990:149–150) is convinced that the community health movement was successful to this point. He (1990:148) notes that it faltered, however, "when it [was] applied to the small but significant number of chronically mentally ill persons who [needed] *long-term inpatient treatment,* traditionally a function of the state mental hospital."

Self-Help Groups

Workers in community mental health and psychiatric hospitals are classified by Grusky and Pollner (1981:356) as **service providers.** The **consumers**, namely, the patients, potential patients, and friends and families of patients, receive their services. It should be clear by now that they do not always like what they receive. In response they have organized to pursue their own interests.

Grusky and Pollner discuss two categories of this pursuit. One is political advocacy for the rights and interests of mental health patients. The other pursuit is therapeutic: self-help groups assist the patient in overcoming mental disorder and the problems of adjustment that accompany it.

One such self-help group is the Schizophrenic Society of Canada (formerly Canadian Friends of Schizophrenics). It was organized in 1978 in Oakville, Ontario by Bill Jefferies, a man who, though not himself a schizophrenic, had brothers and children who were (Belford, 1984). In 1983, Jefferies helped found and became president *pro tem* of the World Schizophrenia Fellowship, which works internationally to educate people about and promote research on this disorder. Today there are branches of the SSC in eight provinces. Over the years it has changed its focus from advocacy and therapeutic self-help to primarily advocacy. A recent issue of *Canada's Mental Health* (1993a:24–25) said the following about the SSC:

> Services/Activities for Members: The SSC provides information and support to its members through public awareness initiatives, advocacy initiatives, and research initiatives. The SSC determined at its September 1992 strategic planning exercise that public awareness would be the first priority for SSC during the next five years.

Among its principal goals are advocacy for increased funding for research on schizophrenia through the appropriate federal and provincial funding bodies; the development and implementation of a nation-wide public awareness campaign; the expansion of knowledge of the issues surrounding schizophrenia; and the development of stronger partnerships with allied organizations.

The Society for Depression and Manic-Depression of Manitoba is both an advocacy and a therapeutic self-help group (*Canada's Mental Health*, 1993b: 23–24). Its mission statement contains three purposes:

1. Offer support to those afflicted and their loved ones, helping them to understand and accept their illness, its treatment, and their role in recovery.
2. Develop a public awareness of the social, biochemical, and psychological factors in mania and depression.
3. Assist those suffering from mania and depression to obtain help from qualified professionals.

The Society runs a resource centre, provides monthly self-help support meetings across Manitoba, and trains volunteers to work with mental patients and their families. It also furnishes books, articles, video and audio tapes, and public speakers.

St.-Armand and Clavette (1992:33) would classify these two organizations as "[self]-help groups that work closely with professionals". Other self-help groups are "a-professional", inasmuch as they work with their own resources, while also being willing to work with professionals. A third category — "the anti-professional self-help groups" — are staunchly opposed to professional services. They constitute the foundation of the anti-psychiatry/psychiatric inmates' liberation movement, which got its start in the late 1960s and early 1970s (Burstow and Weitz, 1988; Silverstein, 1990: Ch. 4). Members of groups in the third category tell of psychiatric abuse in practice, which they hope to stamp out for themselves and others. Among the Canadian groups are the Mental Patients Association and the Ontario Coalition to Stop Electroshock. (See Viewpoint 8.1.)

VIEWPOINT 8.1

PSYCHIATRISTS AND CONSUMERS IN CONFLICT

At times it seems that psychiatrists and their patients have an adversarial relationship and that there is a tug of war going on. On one hand there is the growing consumers' movement with disgruntled patients and on the other hand is the traditional and sometimes autocratic psychiatric profession who view the clamour of consumers for more rights and better treatment with a jaundiced eye.

It has been my impression, after having been in the mental health system for the last twenty-five years, that it seems to be part of the psychiatrist's role to keep some vital information shrouded in mystery. Take for example the side-effects of the medication — I have found that either the psychiatrist is not willing to divulge this information or else he/she may not be very aware of the side-effects. Many mental health consumers complain to me that their doctor will not tell them about the possible adverse effects of the psychotropic drugs.

Being a journalist, I am a curious person. I sometimes read the Compendium of Pharmaceuticals and Specialities (CPS), psychology texts, or various pill books. It is important to me to know what the medication is doing to my body. If I have a certain side effect, I want to know if it is caused by the medication or some kind of physical illness. For instance, if I have blurry eyes I might go and get my glasses changed needlessly, when instead of my eyes being worse it is a medication side-effect. Since it just happens to be *my* body that the pills are going into, I feel that I should make informed choices. However, it has been my personal experience that most psychiatrists feel some hostility if a patient gets too curious about drug side-effects, the designated diagnosis, or the treatment.

I've gotten the distinct impression that doctors tend to prefer passive patients — the ones that don't ask too many questions. The idea of a doctor-patient partnership seems to be foreign to most psychiatrists. Rather, it appears to be a hierarchical relationship, with the "top dog" role assigned to the doctor.

I sense there is a general mood among consumers that they want to be informed about their illness and medication, while being consulted about the type of treatment that they receive. Consumers would like a partnership between doctor and patient. Many that I have talked to feel that for years they have suffered under a mental health system that has dominated them and often treated them like children. Not surprisingly, consumers are now demanding to be treated with dignity. But are mental health professionals willing to listen, or are they just interested in butting heads with the consumers' movement, which they perceive as a threat?

Today, it seems that there are extremes in both the professionals' and the consumers' camps. On one extreme there are patients' rights groups who say that doctors should not have the power to drug or confine patients in mental hospitals, labelling this "psychiatric oppression" and abuse. Some radicals even say that it is the mentally ill person's ultimate right of self-determination to commit suicide, and that no psychiatrist should be allowed to intervene.

I disagree with the idea of doing away with medication, hospitals, and suicide prevention. I really think that is going too far out on the lunatic fringe. However, I also find repugnant psychiatrists who believe that they are next to God and can wantonly control the lives of their patients. Some do this by over-drugging their patients, so that the zombie-like consumers cannot complain. Others do it by withholding information or adopting a condescending attitude. I feel that the anger among consumers at some in the psychiatric profession stems from the fact that the mentally ill are often made to feel frightened and powerless — like a persecuted minority.

I think that the only way to down-scale the conflict between psychiatrists and consumers is for both sides to try a meeting of the minds. Doctors should show more humility and be sensitive to the rights of patients. They should realize that there is a legitimacy to the

(Continued)

VIEWPOINT 8.1 *(Continued)*

need of consumers to network and to have a voice, so that psychiatric abuses can be curbed. History is full of examples of inhumane treatment of the mentally ill, and the modern mental health care system leaves much to be desired as well. At one meeting I heard a psychiatrist get up and imply that the mental health system is perfect. It made me very angry as I remembered the abuse I received in psychiatric hospitals and the lack of mercy and compassion that was exhibited by many of the staff when I was at my sickest. Psychiatrists can learn from the consumers' movement.

Conversely, consumers should realize that, although some have feet of clay, there are professionals who do care and who want to serve the mentally ill to the best of their ability. When choosing a good therapist, consumers can look to general practitioners, family, friends, or the yellow pages. For therapists in private practice there are directories available from their professional associations. Bryan M. Knight, in a column on "Mind Matters," advises, "Do not be misled by reputation alone. Trust your reaction when talking with the therapist. Does he or she seem interested in your problems? Do you feel welcome?" He says you should also ask about what experience the therapist has with your type of problem, how long he or she has been in practice, and about the therapist's professional qualifications. Since differences in personality and ideology may interfere with the therapeutic relationship, the consumer has the right to go to another therapist if things are not working out.

If there is the will, both fractious sides, psychiatrists and consumers, can learn and benefit from each other. After all, both want the same thing — good mental health care.

Source: Katherine E. Tapley, "Psychiatrists and Consumers in Conflict," *Canada's Mental Health*, 1994, 42, Summer:17–18. Reproduced with the permission of the Minister of Supply and Services Canada, 1995. By permission. Katherine Tapley, B.A., Master of Theological Studies, is a mental health consumer and freelance writer whose work has appeared in over 60 magazines.

Treatment as Control

Many members of the psychiatric profession and the public believe that psychiatric treatment, whether in hospitals or in the community, is beneficial for those who suffer from mental disorder. It is said to provide a cure for treatable disease. Still, it is also possible to view treatment as a means of social control. This view may be either conservative or radical.

The conservative view of treatment as control is functionalist (cf. Parsons, 1951:312–314, 429–432). The functionalists theorize that residual deviants, to the extent that they are disabled, threaten the community because they are wards of the state and fail to contribute to its smooth running and to its maintenance. A systemic imbalance is thereby created, which is corrected by placing the disordered individual in the "sick role", a legitimate deviant status from which it is expected that he or she will eventually recover and return to a productive life. Professional psychotherapy tries to facilitate this transition by resocializing these patients in a way that re-establishes them in conventional society.

In the radical (anti-psychiatry) view, psychiatric treatment, particularly hospitalization, is seen as an effective way of isolating those who threaten the functioning of some part of society with their bizarre, residually deviant behaviour. The object of isolation, according to this line of reasoning, is not treatment, but removal and punishment. Practitioners who collaborate in the isolation process are referred to as **institutional psychiatrists** by Szasz (1970:xxiii).

These professionals control unwanted social behaviour by presiding over the involuntary commitment of patients to mental hospitals or, more generally, by pronouncing people "insane". Szasz says that psychiatrists who are paid by an organization, such as a government, prison, court, or military unit, control behaviour in the interest of their employer (rather than the suffering patient) and thereby become institutional psychiatrists. As anthropologist and psychiatrist Ernest Becker (1962:172) puts it: "Psychiatry, in sum, is at present little more than a pseudoscientific discipline which directively manipulates individuals in the interests of the social *status quo* and the personal aggrandizement of the psychiatrists." The most extreme use of institutional psychiatry was said to have been widespread in the U.S.S.R., where political dissidents were labelled insane and then sequestered in prisons euphemistically identified as mental hospitals.

On a related note, Gabe and Lipshitz-Phillips (1984) raise the question of whether sedatives might not be instrumental in preserving hierarchical relations. They studied the use of tranquillizers in Britain, where they learned that anxiety and insomnia were in part caused by social structural factors. Their data suggest that these medications make people more docile; rather than trying to throw off the yoke of domination and exploitation, they become complacent and accept the status quo. In the collection organized by Burstow and Weitz (1988: Part 4), ex-mental patients, taking an anti-psychiatric point of view, tell their stories about "mind control" through drugs.

Understandably, many psychiatrists reject the radical view of treatment as social control. Others, according to Sedgwick (1982:213–214), have incorporated some of the ideas of labelling theory (which is said to be part of the radical view) into their own medical framework. Kenig (1992:47), for instance, notes that, in response to the radical critique, there is "inside even the most elite halls of psychiatry and inside medicine as a whole... a new appreciation of the social control and political implications of therapy." Whatever the future response to the radical view, the psychiatric profession seems destined to be the target of scrutiny and critique for many years to come, if for no other reason than the fact that its members hold power over others:

> In its claims to veracity both in the diagnoses declared by its clinicians and in the symptoms offered by its clients; in its work of custody, guardianship, and behavioral control, where an unthinking paternalism is often the easiest way out; above all, in its hegemony over systems of care, where often its role should be that of an adjutant among concerned helpers — in all these aspects psychiatry invites a continuing interrogation (Sedgwick, 1982:221).

MENTAL DISORDER AS DEVIANT CAREER

However one views the nature of psychiatric and other professional treatment of mentally disordered deviants, the deviants themselves must cope with their careers in this status. One contingency in this career is the considerable stigma that is still attached to being psychologically disturbed, especially to being labelled as such by a medical authority. But there are other contingencies as well. The most prominent characteristics of the deviant career of the mentally disordered are presented here within the three-stage framework of the moral career of the mental patient (Goffman, 1961:125–170).

Pre-Patient Stage

In any mental hospital, there are a small number of inmates who ask to be admitted (Thoits, 1985) and a larger number who have recidivated and are forced to return. The purest instance of the "pre-patient", however, is the person who has never been hospitalized for mental disorder and who now resists the possibility of this happening. We shall concentrate here on the most numerous among these patients, the unwilling pre-patient, and also to some extent on the unwilling "re-patient", or re-admitted patient. Moreover, we shall only consider civil commitment, as opposed to criminal commitment.

Schafer (1985) notes that the Canadian and American courts have established the legal right of the **competent** patient to refuse medical treatment of any kind. But if the person in question is judged (by a psychiatrist) to be incompetent, then that individual can be committed to treatment against his or her will. The medical reasoning behind this legal arrangement is paternalistic: people suffering from severe mental disorder are presumed to be unable to make rational decisions. It is the obligation of the state to care for those unable to care for themselves.

Edward Keyserlingk (1985) has summarized the provincial statutes bearing on involuntary commitment to treatment for a mental disorder. Only two provinces, Nova Scotia and Ontario, explicitly or implicitly provide the right for an individual to refuse commitment. The other provinces explicitly or implicitly exclude that right, while the Northwest Territories are silent about it. Since Keyserlingk wrote, the new Canadian Charter of Rights and Freedoms has been proclaimed. It states that everyone

- has the right to life, liberty and the security of the person and the right not to be deprived thereof except in accordance with the principles of fundamental justice. (Section 7)
- has the right not to be arbitrarily detained or imprisoned. (Section 9)
- [is] to be presumed innocent until proved guilty according to law in a fair and public hearing by an independent and impartial tribunal[.] (Section 11(d))
- has the right not to be subjected to any cruel and unusual treatment or punishment. (Section 12)

But these rights are guaranteed only within "reasonable limits" that can be "justified in a free and democratic society" (Section 1). In other words, do these rights apply in instances of homicidal or suicidal behaviour, or behaviour that is dangerous to others? If yes, how do they apply? It is now up to the federal and provincial governments to put these principles into action.

It is the issue of involuntary commitment around which Goffman organizes his discussion of the pre-patient stage of the moral career of the mentally disordered. According to pre-patients, they slide down a sort of "betrayal funnel", characterized in general by abandonment, disloyalty, and bitterness. This process is often started by a complainant who is familiar with the deviant's behaviour and who takes action that eventually leads to his or her hospitalization.

The complainant brings the pre-patient into contact with a set of agents and agencies, including police, clergy, lawyers, social workers, general medical practitioners, institutional psychiatrists, and sometimes even school teachers. Since family members and other complainants may have their ulterior motives for wanting to institutionalize the pre-patient, they, too, undergo an examination:

> A complaint to a third party, whether in the form of an accusation or a request for mediation, marks only the starting point for ensuing intervention. Complaints are subject to scrutiny and to possible revision by troubleshooters, who proceed with some awareness that allegations may be distorted or false, that the proposed allocation of blame and responsibility may be misleading or invalid, that the remedial action sought may be exploitative, subversive, or illegitimate (Emerson and Messinger, 1977:130).

Gradually, the pre-patient becomes aware of the coalition which has formed against him or her. Holstein (1987) found that judges in civil proceedings usually presume the pre-patient is mentally disordered, leading them to pass judgments consistent with this bias. When resisting the efforts to hospitalize him or her, the pre-patient is subjected to various persuasive messages from the complainant, relatives, and third-party agents. Those in the coalition contend that hospitalization will be beneficial, describing an unrealistically benign picture of life in mental institutions. Although noted by Goffman over 30 years ago, Gallagher (1987:299–319) describes a similar set of processes and steps in the pre-patient stage of the contemporary mental patient.

In-Patient Stage

Once inside, the in-patient is stripped of many important aspects of his or her external existence. In an institution, patients cannot play the social roles that formerly made them singular individuals and perhaps contributing members of the community. Moreover, they are often denied even the small personal items of everyday living: comb, cosmetics, shaving kit, bracelet, and the like. There are no special privileges; all must dress alike and follow set rules and routines. Finally, the personal history of each in-patient is recorded in detail by the hospital staff, information that is used to interpret his or her bizarre behaviour.

In-patients have the least authority of anyone around the hospital. Their movements are substantially restricted. Daily habits must be fitted into the institutional schedule and the fact of communal living in wards. They must learn to accommodate their thoughts and actions to those of many others, some of whom are from different social classes and ethnic groups.

The newly arrived in-patient is made to understand by staff and other inmates that he or she is just as qualified to be institutionalized as the rest of the patients. Newcomers are often inclined to maintain that they are really sane, that they "do not belong in this place." But such opinions are quickly discounted by veteran inmates, with remarks such as: "If you are so sane and healthy, then why are you here?" (See Prior, 1993:162.) They, too, have gone through the betrayal funnel, but have come to accept the judgment of those who betrayed them and those who run the hospital. Indeed, they have little choice, for there is no role that they may play other than that of mentally disordered person. For playing that role, they are rewarded; for trying to play the role of normal person, they are castigated for being pretenders (Scheff, 1984:65).

Richard's (1984) study of a small modern private facility indicates that the stripping process just described is still part of the routine treatment of patients in at least some present-day hospitals. Nevertheless, Goldstein (1979:401) concludes, after reviewing the literature in this area, that the worst aspects of mental hospitalization are found in large, bureaucratic, understaffed, and underfunded institutions and in those serving the poor. Prior (1993:163) concluded from his study of a British public mental hospital that "it was overwhelmingly clear that patients were quite content with their material and social environments in the hospital world."

Post-Patient Stage

Goffman did not examine the post-patient stage of the mental patient's career. His study focused on the hospital experience itself and the conditions leading up to it. Still, the troubles of the mentally disordered are rarely over once they leave the hospital. This is true even for those who depart with the psychiatric certification that they are "cured".

The problem post-patients encounter can be summed up in the term **continuance commitment**: "the awareness of the impossibility of choosing a different social identity... because of the imminence of penalties involved in making the switch" (Stebbins, 1976:35). Continuance commitment helps explain a person's persistent involvement with a deviant identity, even though he or she would prefer to renounce it. This continued involvement is enforced by the various penalties that accrue from attempting to renounce it and trying to adopt a conventional, non-deviant identity: in the case of the mentally disordered, the identity of a psychologically healthy person.

Recently, Jeffery Ulmer (1994) coined the term "structural commitment" to draw attention to the structural locus of constraints of this sort. That is, the penalties associated with trying to renounce a deviant identity have a structural basis; the societal reaction toward the ex-mental patient is such that his or her exclusion is built into the fabric of everyday interpersonal relations at work, in the family, among friends, and possibly in other spheres of life.

These structurally based penalties are often more objectionable than enduring the stigma of being labelled an ex-mental patient. Clausen's (1981) research suggests that stigma may be more a product of the individual's self-doubts than a consequence of the response of the people with whom he or she is associating. Experimental research (Link et al., 1987) suggests, however, that the saliency of the stigma is directly related to the degree of perceived threat the ex-patient poses for people with whom he or she is interacting. Scheff (1984:66–67) and Gibson and Groeneweg (1986) point out that ex-mental patients are often rejected when they try to find employment or assume other significant responsibility. Jeanette Cochrane and her colleagues (1992) note that employers are most concerned about absenteeism, recurring illness, violent or bizarre behaviour, and lack of interest in or slowness on the job.

But trying to assume significant responsibility runs counter to ex-mental patients' stereotyped role. Rather, they soon discover that they will at least be tolerated in conventional circles if they "keep their place". Care in one of the community mental health services, whether subsequent to hospitalization or in place of it, is apparently no solution to these problems either (Kirk and Therrien, 1975; Richman, 1988). Nancy Herman (1985; 1993) points out that individual ex-mental patients, when they are reasonably well recovered or stabilized by medication, sometimes directly fight the battle of stigma on their own. Others, believing that being an ex-convict is better than being an ex-mental patient, invent a personal history that identifies them as reformed criminals. Still others take the line of the mental health movement, which states that mental disorder is only a disease, and one that is frequently curable and not deviant. Viewpoint 8.2 presents a variety of accounts by ex-mental patients about their experiences in the larger community.

VIEWPOINT 8.2

EX-MENTAL PATIENTS IN THE COMMUNITY

Insider Accounts of Community Experience

Narrative data obtained from the interviews provide an insider perspective into the lives of those most affected by changes in mental health policy. This material allows us to ponder the proposition that the community experience of mentally disabled people is often shaped by circumstances beyond their own choosing.

1. Employment

Those who accept social assistance on the basis of disability forego the possibility of employment, but are able to participate in sheltered workshops. The tokenism of this situation is keenly felt and for many, as their comments show, the full-time employee in society is a yardstick against which self-worth is measured.

> The trouble is our entire society is geared to working people.
>
> Sometimes there's the odd dollar to make clearing the snow in the neighbourhood. On a good snowy week I can make $!0-15. But this is a bad year for snow. Last summer I made some money strawberry picking. It wasn't much but it was better than doing nothing.
>
> I'm happy, I guess. I accept it. My greatest skill is talking to people. So I might as well enjoy it. If there's nothing but Industrial Therapy (I.T.), then what's the point in looking?
>
> I just want to get some hard work and get adjusted. Not Mickey Mouse work. There's no pride in that.
>
> Four and a half years ago I was a Bell Canada operator and loved it. But then the system changed and they didn't need me. Two years ago I was a short order cook for two days but couldn't cope. March last year I was in the Registered Nursing Assistant (RNA) program, but dropped out. Last summer I was a volunteer here at St. Joseph's filling ice water glasses on the surgical ward. It was great. I enjoyed helping the elderly.

(Continued)

VIEWPOINT 8.2 *(Continued)*

2. Income

Poverty is central in limiting the types of community experience encountered by many mentally disabled people. It is a centripetal force drawing clients towards public and inexpensive points of congregation in the city. Lack of money contributes to the reduction of meaningful activity and restricts the range of potential meeting places for disabled people in the city.

> I usually run out of money. But it doesn't bother me much. It's tough but you learn to live with it. I don't like drinking and movies anyway. But I do like smoking and coffee. You learn to think of things that don't cost much. Main Street Coffee Shop is like a second home.

> I get by. I tend to keep friends who can buy me coffee.

> If I run out, I can usually find money in the street. You know, phone booths, newspaper stands. I can even make tips by running errands for Care Centre people. It's hard to do much around this town if you don't have any dollars. It's impossible. And they expect you to live on $77 a month. I mean it's not that anyone's looking for hand-outs or anything. If someone was to come and offer me a constructive way of living my life, then I would take it. I can't stand sitting around hoping when I should be out doing.

Poverty also restricts the spending choices of mentally disabled people in other important ways.

> I'd buy more clothes if I had the money. Right now I have no chance of a job. If you go for an interview, you should look good.

> Basically we have enough money. But that's very basic. It's rough. There's no room for luxuries like Christmas presents.

3. Psychiatric services

Clients speaking of the Care Centre refer to its role as a refuge and source of asylum from the stresses of the inner city. When the Care Centre closes, however, its closing will further restrict the activity options for many of its patrons. Those who offered comments on the two case management programs valued the role of the therapists as confidants and advocates. These services extend the radius of a person's social circle either directly or indirectly. Still, some service users express a desire for places more exclusively their own.

> I like meeting new people here. It's good just having a place to drop in to, sit down and relax for a while. But it's open and people who aren't schizophrenic and have nothing to do come here. Some are out to cause trouble. That makes it harder.

> This is really the only place in the community to go when you're low on energy. It takes a lot for people here to get out and do things. It's like a big boarding house. It's all right. It serves its function. But the after hours for people leave a lot to be desired.

> I don't want to see people at the Care Centre. They're just bums.

> It's good for me to have someone to talk to so that I won't end up back in the hospital. You try to keep out as long as you can. This time I'm not going off the needle, otherwise I'll be back up there. There should be something to do on the weekend. Nothing's open.

> If it wasn't for John (my social worker) keeping in touch, I don't know what I'd do. I need a push.

4. Social support

The following comments show how factors such as limited housing options, shared psychiatric experience and material poverty combine to limit social networks. While having numerous other psychiatric clients as friends can promote a social environment of mutual empathy that buffers the stresses of urban life, for many it compounds the difficulties of befriending people in the wider society.

> The problem with having other ex-patients as friends is that when they're down it rubs off on me.

> Too much time on your hands can drive you crazy. But it's good to have the freedom to do what we want everyday. We have a couple of good friends. We meet for coffee three times a week. But it's not good having too many friends from the hospital.

> I'm always running into someone from the psychiatric hospital to say hello to. I know quite a network of people. I suppose they are friends.

(Continued)

VIEWPOINT 8.2 *(Continued)*

We mostly go to the Eastside Coffee Shop and talk and smoke. There are usually a lot of people with psychiatric problems there.

I go to the James Street Baptist Church. It's a coffee house sort of thing and there's lots of drop-outs and ex-patients there. You might as well call it the street's psychiatric centre. The only other place I used to see people was at a bar on King St. But I've decided not to go there anymore. I don't want people like that as friends. The friends I want don't have to be rich, but I want them to be people who aren't psychiatric patients. I think I know what to say, but I just don't know where to meet them.

5. Housing

Sampled clients who had housing arrangements other than lodging home accommodation (e.g. those living with family) did not offer many comments on this topic. While for some the residential environment of boarding homes has appeal, others commonly express the desire for independence. This is not surprising. An adult living with up to 25 unrelated others recognizes the situation as abnormal. The variability of opinions about boarding homes is a reflection of the differences in both client expectations and the physical, social and managerial conditions of the individual homes.

There's no curfew and this allows me to come and go as I please. The meals are good and the people there are settled. They're older, but I get along with them. Boarding houses are a lot better here than they were in St. John's.

I'd be much happier in an apartment of my own. But even if I could afford it, I lack the proper housing skills like budgeting, cooking and cleaning. When I moved in, I expected to be taught skills to get an apartment on my own. But you find out that they don't overfeed you and the meals are nothing special. They don't care if you're having living difficulties. They're just there to do their job.

I've found that if I don't have a good living situation, I end up back in hospital. I'm serious when I tell people I get suicidal if I don't have a good place to live.

It would be nice to be able to participate in the way the house is run.

I was in the North End for five and a half years. That place was really bad. People stealing, bumming cigarettes, not enough food. The manager kept me there. He said I was perverted and that no one else would take me. He said I was the last straw of society, just an animal. But then I heard of CES from another client at the place.

6. Life-style

The life-styles of persons with long-term mental disabilities are frequently marked by boredom and repetition. Common expressions such as "spare time" and "leisure" take on new meaning for a population whose life-style is shaped by unrestricted time but restricted access to places in the city.

The days are too long. There's too much spare time. Then nights are a problem. It's just TV and nothing else to do in the evenings.

Some days are better than others, but generally I'm pessimistic. When the Care Centre's closed I generally stay in and feel very bored. Sometimes I go to the library or the art gallery. I try to find as many free places as I can. But part of my social problem is that I only know people who've been part of the St. Joseph's Day Program, the Care Centre or the house. People tend to look down on people with mental illness and think that we don't contribute to society. But you can't control that.

I don't know what to do. I just sit around and walk the street. I go to the Eastside Coffee Shop three times a day. Us guys talk a lot. Sometimes it's nonsense. But it kills a little boredom.

It seems like there are 48 hours in a day sometimes. Some days are really long. Most days I'll take a walk up to the psychiatric hospital. 'Course I wouldn't stay there, I'd just go there and come back. Walking is nothing to us types, you know. We've got all day. It's good to get out and see nature. It keeps you smiling and fit.

I hate the idle time. It's the emptiness of the days. For four years I've been off and on in the community but haven't been working. I paint sometimes, but you don't get much inspiration from boredom. But I suppose it's a challenge.

(Continued)

VIEWPOINT 8.2 *(Continued)*

7. Beliefs

While the era of community mental health has led to improved public understanding of mental illness, the stigma attached to it is still particularly tenacious. To those who have experienced psychiatric hospitalization and rejection by friends, minor events can reinstate the experience of isolation.

> People give you funny looks — the neighbours on our street, even here at the Centre. It gives you a funny feeling — we're all isolated from the rest of society. They say "look at those guys in there. They're sitting around drinking coffee all day." You have to be sick yourself to know what it's really like.
>
> On Wentworth Street there was discrimination against mental patients, because there are so many boarding homes in the area. In one coffee shop, they'll keep you waiting just to discourage you. In another, they wouldn't even give me a glass of water. Three years ago I had a run-in with a manager. I ended up with trespassing fines for refusing to leave.
>
> I don't like all the put-downs from people. It gives me the impression I'm being stereotyped. For instance, last month a manpower counsellor said to me, "You've got no chance of a job, admit it." Not earning any money gets under my skin. I need the incentive to get my life together.
>
> I don't like being in the East End. The people here are sick. It's a nursing home. I don't need to be here.
>
> I try to keep busy and feel meaningful. A man's meant to feel important through having a job. If a guy's disabled, they figure he loses his competitive spirit and urge to work. But I feel there should be more stress on people going back to a regular routine. Not just medications and the attitude that "you'll be OK until next week." That destroys your confidence for sure.

Source: Robin A. Kearns and S. Martin Taylor, "Daily Life Experience of People with Chronic Mental Disabilities in Hamilton, Ontario," *Canada's Mental Health*, 1989, 37, December:2–4. Reproduced with the permission of the Minister of Supply and Services Canada, 1995. By permission.

By no means are all those who are discharged from mental hospitals in Canada cured in the sense that they are unlikely to relapse into their old disorder. Some are, in fact, physically disabled by the medicine they must take to maintain a minimally acceptable level of psychological control. O'Reilly-Fleming (1993:24–26) and Snow and Anderson (1993:330, n.16) are among the many sociologists to observe that ex-mental patients are found in significant numbers in the poorer areas of Canadian and American cities where the homeless are trying to survive. Here they collect in boarding houses, skid-row flop houses, and cheap single-room-occupancy apartment buildings. In difficult financial times, these people are not threatening enough to lock up in hospitals. They can be released on their own (meagre) resources to save the state money. But in this environment, disabled and stigmatized as they are, some cannot survive financially and others cannot survive socially or psychologically. Both categories are apt to return to the mental hospital or to jail or, in sequence, to both.

Although it is yet to be specifically studied, the career of the community mental health patient (not the discharged post-patient) is undoubtedly much less dramatic and eventful. Perhaps certain coercive or persuasive measures must be used at the pre-patient stage to bring the individual to the point where he or she maintains regular contact with a therapist or out-patient facility. But it is in the nature of contractual psychiatry to respect the dignity of the client and somehow give him or her the impression that a genuine psychological service is being rendered. Hence, the in-patient career stage is something the community health patient never really experiences.

The stigma of out-patient treatment or private therapy may be reduced because it is easier to keep secret in the anonymity of large cities than is hospitalization, where one is conspicuously absent for a long period. Still, ex-community health patients are **discreditable** (Goffman, 1963:4); they must manage carefully the secrecy of their deviance or, if discovered, face the reactions of a community largely unsympathetic to mental disorder.

CORRELATES OF MENTAL DISORDER

Several attributes and conditions correlate with mental disorder, some of which may ultimately prove to have a causal link to it. The empirical support for these relationships is reviewed by Gallagher (1987: Ch. 9–11). The five correlates we shall examine here are sex, migration, place, age, and social class.

Sex

Perhaps the most controversial of all correlates is the sex of the mentally disordered person. Ortega (1992:1265–1267) writes that it is unclear whether sex differences exist in the overall rates of mental disorder. It is clear, however, that males and females differ in how much they suffer from particular disorders. For example, using standard psychiatric diagnostic tools, women have been found to suffer more from anxiety and major and minor depression; men have been found to suffer more from anti-social personality disorders. These differences are most pronounced among married people; evidence on the rates among the unmarried is inconclusive.

The usual explanation for these findings is that married women who remain at home with their children encounter a great deal of stress in their role as homemakers. Women who are married, have children, and work outside the home are subject to even greater pressures. They become frustrated with raising children in a relatively unstructured setting while at home and, in many instances, with working at low-paying, low-status jobs while away from home (Mowbray, Lanir, and Hulce, 1985).

The question of women reporting more mental disorder than men has become a major target of debate. Does this pattern result from the possibility that women are under greater stress or from the possibility that they are more likely than men (who often like to give the appearance of strength and control) to admit that they have psychological problems? Gove and Tudor (1973) argue that women's often frustrating, relatively non-rewarding position in Western society is ample ground for developing deviant adjustments to life's problems. Dorothy Smith (1975) contends that psychiatry is not substantially scientific, but rather ideologic. It contains a male understanding of reality, rather than an understanding based on the viewpoint of both sexes. Science sees women as passive and dependent, as people whose psychological problems are caused by personal rather than social conditions (Schur 1980:39). Resentment and despair at their subordinate position in society are not regarded by male psychiatrists (who predominate) as legitimate, non-deviant emotions — being unhappy or dissatisfied with one's situation in life is not the same as psychological depression. Miedema and Stoppard (1993) found that many of the hospitalized New Brunswick women whom they interviewed had experiences consistent with Smith's explanation.

Migration

International migrants are over-represented among mental hospital inmates. There are two standard explanations for this pattern. One is that international migration is stressful; the other is that the mentally disordered are more likely to migrate. Yet the most accurate explanation may be Ortega's (1992:1269) observation that people with the fewest resources and the least power, whether economic or social, are the most likely to experience psychological problems. This is often the situation in which immigrants find themselves.

Place

Sociologists have long held that the rates of mental disorder are lower in rural than in urban areas. This belief, it turns out, is more fiction than fact. Wagenfield (1982) found little evidence for rural superiority in this respect. Research results indicate that rural life is less blissful than previously thought, in significant part because of declining economic fortunes, inadequate mental health services, and substantial migration to the cities.

Age

The older we become, the less likely we are to need help for a mental disorder (Ortega, 1992:1267). The opposite is true, however, for some of the organic brain disorders. The elderly are most likely to experience depression, which affects a significant proportion of this age group. Nevertheless, depression is not easily distinguished from dementia and the other organic brain disorders. Approximately half of the elderly who suffer from these disorders are diagnosed as having Alzheimer's disease (Ortega, 1992:1268).

Social Class

The lowest socioeconomic class accounts for the highest proportion of all psychiatric patients. The other classes — working, middle, and upper — are under-represented here. There are, however, at least two reasons to suspect the validity of these generalizations. One is that the mentally disordered in the higher social strata are better able to afford private therapy than those in the lower social strata. The former are therefore likely to be omitted from public surveys of mental patients. Second, middle- and upper-class patients suffer more from internally oriented disorders and less from externally oriented ones than patients from lower classes. Thus, it is possible that the latter, because their disorders are more often violent and uncontrollable, must be hospitalized more often than those in the higher socioeconomic classes. Nevertheless, the inverse relationship between social class and rate of mental disorder does square with the observation presented earlier that those with the fewest resources and the least power are most likely to have psychological problems.

Apart from this statistical picture of social class differences in mental disorder are questions of the nature and quality of treatment. Hospitalization for those in lower social classes is much more likely to be custodial than therapeutic. Such treatment, and treatment on a mass basis in community mental health centres, also tends to rely heavily on psychotropic medications. Psychotherapy is, in effect, reserved for those who can pay for it. While some medication may be prescribed for those in psychotherapy as well, it is usually supplemental to direct personal counselling. Moreover, historically, psychotherapists have preferred to work with people of high social status, like themselves. Still, there is evidence from a study done in Chicago (Greenley, Kepecs, and Henry, 1982) that private psychiatric care is increasingly reaching patients of lower socioeconomic status.

TRENDS

The question frequently asked these days is whether mental disorder is increasing. Unfortunately, there is presently no definitive answer. William Eaton (1986:212–225) concludes for the United States that, as a sort of "educated guess", the rate of psychosis — the most serious of the mental disorders — has doubled or tripled over the past century. The trend for the milder disorders is shorter, but steeper. In both rural and urban areas, the pressures of social change — continual urbanization, industrialization, and computerization, in conjunction with declining economic fortunes, inadequate mental health services, and rural-to-urban migration — may be taking their toll on our mental health.

Bruce Dohrenwend (1975) takes precisely this stand. He contends that mental disorder is on the rise. But others, such as Gallagher (1987:217–218), disagree. Modern psychiatry, they say, has broadened its definition of mental illness, thereby redefining as psychotic individuals previously looked on only as eccentric or criminal. Moreover, at least in the United States, blacks and the poor are more likely to receive treatment today than in the past.

In the meantime, the general trends are clouded by a sort of "revolving door" pattern of release from hospital, failure to adjust in the wider community, and re-admission to hospital. Financial pressures are forcing major reductions in mental hospital services, which, it was hoped, would be offset by the services offered by community mental health facilities. There is evidence throughout North America that this adjustment is not taking place. Community mental health facilities are too few in number. Some are too expensive for poorer post-patients. Many are understaffed. The result is the career situation of the post-patient described earlier. In financially troubled times, it is probably only realistic to predict that the mentally disordered poor will languish in the slums of the large North American cities, when they are not languishing in the asylums.

Still, after a review of the literature on the nature and prevalence of mental disorder in other societies, Murphy (1982) concluded the following: "The non-Western way of life does not offer protection against mental illness to the point of making a marked difference in frequency. The rates of mental illness patterns I have discussed are much more striking for similarity from culture to culture than for difference." One thing is safe to say: the future rate of mental disorder in North America is anything but unambiguous.

SUMMARY

Madness, insanity, mental disorder — terms we have used synonymously in this chapter — have been an identifiable part of human life since at least the days of ancient Palestine. During the Middle Ages, religious explanations of madness predominated; it was believed to be punishment by God for the sin of faithlessness. The late seventeenth century brought a shift in treatment from torture and burnings as reactions to disorder to confinement in chains. As the concept of mental illness gained ascendancy in the eighteenth and nineteenth centuries, hospitalization without chains became the norm.

Possibly the most clear-cut scientific definition of mental illness is provided by DSM-IV. It emphasizes the presence of a behavioural syndrome associated with distress and mental disability. Mental illness may have an organic basis or a functional basis, or both. Szasz rejects as a myth the notion that functional mental disorders are true illnesses.

In common sense terms, mental disorder refers to behaviour that is bizarre and immoral: odd in manner, marked by extreme incongruities and contrasts, and unexpected and unbelievable. Such behaviour is in violation of residual rules or residual moral norms. The violations are first noticed by the disordered person's everyday associates. In non-Western societies, bizarre behaviour is not always considered deviant, even if it is possible to classify it as mental illness in accordance with modern psychiatric theory.

Measuring the prevalence of mental disorder is fraught with difficulty. Suffice it to note that its rate is not insignificant. It may be, too, that its rate is rising as a manifestation of the exceptional stress of our times.

Until about the mid-1950s, hospitalization remained the prevailing mode of treatment for mental disorder. Treatment in hospital was negligible; the function was largely custodial. Such places still exist, many of which follow the same practices that made them infamous as "asylums". But, as mentioned, the trend is toward less institutionalization, for a smaller proportion of the mentally disordered population.

Although hospitalization is considered appropriate, if not necessary, for violent and highly disturbed people, the tendency today is to try to keep the mentally disordered within the community and to treat them at community mental health centres. With the help of modern medications, it is believed that many patients can remain and function reasonably well in the community rather than stay committed in a psychiatric ward or hospital. Various self-help groups augment the community health effort by assisting their members in overcoming psychological problems.

It is possible to view psychiatric treatment as a form of social control. The conservative view of treatment as control is an expression of functionalism. Mental deviants enter the legitimate sick role and professionals rehabilitate them for return to productive life in the social system. In the radical view, institutional psychiatrists serve the interests of the status quo by sequestering threatening individuals in hospitals, where they can do no harm to established society.

The deviant career of mental patients follows three stages. In the pre-patient stage, they are unwillingly subjected to a change of status from private citizen to hospital patient, a transformation accomplished by a coalition of people through the process of the betrayal funnel. Involuntary commitment, and hence many of the characteristics of the pre-patient stage, are made possible by legal arrangements that give psychiatrists the power to send those diagnosed as mentally disordered to treatment facilities.

During the in-patient stage, the individual is stripped of the physical and social supports that made it possible to enact specific roles in society. In-patients learn, initially against their will, to define themselves as mentally disordered persons.

Subsequently, as post-patients, they learn that they are forced into a continuing commitment to the role of mental patient, resulting from self-doubts and from public fear and misunderstanding about mental disorders. Some post-patients, disabled and stigmatized, find they cannot survive financially, socially, or psychologically in the larger community and return to hospital or jail or, in sequence, to both.

There are several correlates of mental disorder. Turning first to the variable of sex, it is unclear whether differences exist here in the overall rates of mental disorder. It *is* clear, however, that males and females differ in the extent to which they suffer from particular disorders. Frustrations attendant on raising children and working at low-paying, low-status jobs outside the home help explain the higher rates among women.

International migrants are over-represented among mental hospital patients. Place of residence — rural or urban — seems to have little bearing on the rates of mental disorder. Age, however, does; older people are less likely to need help in connection with some form of mental disorder. Finally, the lowest socioeconomic class accounts for the highest proportion of all psychiatric patients. This pattern, too, may be biased, inasmuch as private treatment is less visible than hospitalization, the most common form of treatment for the lowest social strata.

Is mental disorder increasing in our society? Difficulty in defining this form of deviance and a lack of solid knowledge about its causes prevent a definitive answer. Despite the tenuousness of predictions, some students of mental disorder believe that increases are taking place and will continue to do so. Others contend it is impossible to determine future trends.

NOTES

1 This statistic is subject to qualification, inasmuch as a small proportion of all suicides are not related to mental disorder. As Gallagher (1987:255) observes: "Although some consider it risky to assume that a person who commits suicide is mentally ill, it is safe to assume that a suicidal person is at least temporarily disturbed."

SUGGESTED READING

Becker, Ernest. *The Birth and Death of Meaning: A Perspective in Psychiatry and Anthropology.* New York: The Free Press, 1962. A psychiatrist and anthropologist attempts to answer the question of why people act the way they act. In the second edition, published in 1971, Becker further explores this question and the general theory of human nature.

Canada's Mental Health. A quarterly periodical published in English and French by Health and Welfare Canada. It is directed to mental health professionals and informed laypersons.

Eaton, William W. *The Sociology of Mental Disorders.* (2nd ed.) New York: Praeger, 1986. A textbook that reviews much of the sociological literature on mental disorder, with particular reference to the United States.

Gove, Walter R. (ed.) *Deviance and Mental Illness.* Beverly Hills, CA: Sage Publications, 1982. A collection of original articles on mental disorder, some of which critically examine the labelling perspective and the research done from it.

Prior, Lindsay. *The Social Organization of Mental Illness.* London: Sage, 1993. An analysis of the changing definitions of mental illness and the ways they are reflected in the social organization of health care. The pre-patient, in-patient, and post-patient phases of mental health care are studied empirically.

Torrey, E. Fuller. *Nowhere to Go: The Tragic Odyssey of the Homeless Mentally Ill.* New York: Harper & Row, 1988. A psychiatrist examines the policy of deinstitutionalization, the course of its development, and the changes that must be made to render it humane.

REFERENCES

American Psychiatric Association. *Diagnostic and Statistical Manual of Mental Disorders.* (4th ed.) Washington, DC, 1994.

Becker, Ernest. *The Birth and Death of Meaning: A Perspective in Psychiatry and Anthropology.* New York: The Free Press, 1962.

Belford, Jeanne. "The Growth of Canadian Friends of Schizophrenics," *Canada's Mental Health*, 1984, 32, December:16–17.

Bloom, Bernard L. *Community Mental Health: A Historical and Critical Analysis.* Morristown, NJ: General Learning Press, 1973.

Burstow, Bonnie and Don Weitz (eds.) *Shrink Resistant: The Struggle against Psychiatry in Canada.* Vancouver: New Star Books, 1988.

Clausen, John A. "Stigma and Mental Disorder," *Psychiatry*, 1981, 44:287–296.
Cochrane, Jeanette, Joy Rogers, and Paula Goering. *Employment for Persons with a History of Mental Illness: Problems and Benefits — A Critical Literature Review.* Report from the National Health Research and Development Program. (Cat. no. NHRDP R-6606-4053-MHL) Ottawa: Health and Welfare Canada, 1992.
Connor, Linda H. "Ships of Fools and Vessels of the Divine: Mental Hospitals and Madness — A Case Study," *Social Science and Medicine*, 1982, 16:783–794.
Conrad, Peter and Joseph W. Schneider. *Deviance and Medicalization: From Badness to Sickness.* (Expanded ed.) Philadelphia: Temple University Press, 1992.
Curra, John. *Understanding Social Deviance.* New York: Harper Collins, 1994.
deReuck, A. and R. Porter (eds.) *Ciba Foundation Symposium: Transcultural Psychiatry.* London: Churchill, 1965.
Dohrenwend, Bruce P. "Sociocultural and Social Psychological Factors Affecting Personal Responses to Psychological Disorder," *Journal of Health and Social Behavior*, 1975, 16:365–392.
Eaton, William W. *The Sociology of Mental Disorders.* (2nd ed.) New York: Praeger, 1986.
Emerson, Robert M. and Sheldon L. Messinger. "The Micro-Politics of Trouble," *Social Problems*, 1977, 25:121–134.
Endleman, Robert. *Deviance and Psychopathology: The Sociology and Psychology of Outsiders.* Malabar, FL: Robert F. Krieger, 1990.
Francis, Ruth. "Residual Prejudice in the Helping Profession," *Canada's Mental Health*, 1985, 33, September:2–3.
Gabe, Jonathan and Susan Lipshitz-Phillips. "Tranquillizers As Social Control," *Sociological Review*, 1984, 32:524–546.
Gallagher, Bernard J., III. *The Sociology of Mental Illness.* (2nd ed.) Englewood Cliffs, NJ: Prentice-Hall, 1987.
Gibson, David and Gerrit Groeneweg. "Employer Receptivity to the Developmentally Handicapped: When 'Yes' Means 'No'," *Canada's Mental Health*, 1986, 34, June:12–16.
Goffman, Erving. *Asylums: Essays on the Social Situation of Mental Patients and Other Inmates.* Garden City, NY: Doubleday, 1961.
_________ *Stigma.* Englewood Cliffs, NJ: Prentice-Hall, 1963.
Goldstein, Michael S. "Sociology and Mental Health and Illness." In *Annual Review of Sociology*, Vol. 5, edited by Alex Inkeles, James Coleman, and Ralph H. Turner, pp. 381–409. Palo Alto, CA: Annual Reviews Inc., 1979.
Gove, Walter R. and Jeannette F. Tudor. "Adult Sex Roles and Mental Illness," *American Journal of Sociology*, 1973, 78:812–835.
Greenley, James R., Joseph G. Kepecs, and William E. Henry. "Changing Characteristics of Psychiatric Patients: Private and Public," *International Journal of Social Psychiatry*, 1982, 28:210–212.
Grusky, Oscar and Melvin Pollner (eds.) *The Sociology of Mental Illness.* New York: Holt, Rinehart and Winston, 1981.
Herman, Nancy J. "Crazies in the Community: An Ethnographic Study of Ex-psychiatric Clients in Canadian Society." Ph.D. dissertation, McMaster University, 1985.
_________ "Return to Sender: Reintegrative Stigma-Management Strategies of Ex-Psychiatric Patients," *Journal of Contemporary Ethnography*, 1993, 22:295–330.

Holstein, James A. "Mental Illness Assumptions in Civil Commitment Proceedings," *Journal of Contemporary Ethnography*, 1987, 16:147–175.

Kearns, Robin A. and S. Martin Taylor. "Daily Life Experience with Chronic Mental Disabilities in Hamilton, Ontario," *Canada's Mental Health*, 1989, 37, December:1–4.

Kenig, Sylvia. *Who Plays? Who Pays? Who Cares? A Case Study in Applied Sociology, Political Economy and the Community Mental Health Centers Movement.* Amityville, NY: Baywood, 1992.

Keyserlingk, Edward. "Consent to Treatment: The Principles, the Provincial Statutes and the Charter of Rights and Freedoms," *Canada's Mental Health*, 1985, 33, September:7–11.

Kirk, S.A. and M.E. Therrien. "Community Mental Health Myths and the Fate of Former Hospitalized Patients," *Psychiatry*, 1975, 38:209–217.

Langness, L.L. "Hysterical Psychosis in the New Guinea Highlands," *Psychiatry*, 1985, 28:258–277.

Link, Bruce G., Francis T. Cullen, James Frank, and John F. Wozniak. "The Social Rejection of Formal Mental Patients: Understanding Why Labels Matter," *American Journal of Sociology*, 1987, 92:1461–1500.

Marshall, John. *Madness: An Indictment of the Mental Health Care System in Ontario.* Toronto: Ontario Public Service Employees Union, 1982.

Mechanic, David and David A. Rochefort. "Deinstitutionalization: An Appraisal of Reform." In *Annual Review of Sociology*, Vol. 16, edited by W. Richard Scott and Judith Blake, pp. 301–327. Palo Alto, CA: Annual Reviews, Inc., 1990.

Miedema, Baukje and Janet M. Stoppard. "Understanding Women's Experiences of Psychiatric Hospitalization," *Canada's Mental Health*, 1993, 41, March:2–6.

Mowbray, Carol T., Susan Lanir, and Marilyn Hulce. *Women and Mental Health: New Directions for Change.* New York: Haworth Press, 1985.

Murphy, Jane M. "Cultural Shaping and Mental Disorders." In *Deviance and Mental Illness*, edited by Walter R. Gove, pp. 49–82. Beverly Hills, CA: Sage Publications, 1982.

"The NGO Profiles," *Canada's Mental Health*, 1993a, 41, Summer:24–25.

"The NGO Profiles," *Canada's Mental Health*, 1993b, 41, Fall:23–24.

O'Reilly-Fleming, Thomas. *Down and Out in Canada: Homeless Canadians.* Toronto: Canadian Scholars Press, 1993.

Ortega, Suzanne T. "Mental Illness and Mental Disorders." In *Encyclopedia of Sociology*, Vol. 3, edited by Edgar F. Borgatta and Marie L. Borgatta, pp. 1261–1271. New York: Macmillan, 1992.

Parsons, Talcott. *The Social System.* New York: The Free Press, 1951.

Prior, Lindsay. *The Social Organization of Mental Illness.* London: Sage, 1993.

Rice, Marine E. "Review of Assaults Within Psychiatric Facilities," *Canada's Mental Health*, 1984, 32, December:17–18.

Richard, Michel P. "*Asylums* Revisited: 1957–1982," *International Social Science Review*, 1984, 59:171–178.

Richman, Alex. "Psychiatry," *The Canadian Encyclopedia.* (2nd ed.), pp. 1976–1978. Edmonton: Hurtig Publishers, 1988.

Rosenhan, David L. "On Being Sane in Insane Places," *Science*, 1973, 179:250–258.

St. Armand, Néré and Huguette Clavette. *Self-Help and Mental Health: Beyond Psychiatry.* Ottawa: Canadian Council on Social Development, 1992.

Schafer, Arthur. "The Right of Institutionalized Psychiatric Patients to Refuse Treatment," *Canada's Mental Health*, 1985, 33, September:12–16.

Scheff, Thomas J. *Being Mentally Ill: A Sociological Theory.* (2nd ed.) New York: Aldine, 1984.

Schur, Edwin M. *The Politics of Deviance.* Englewood Cliffs, NJ: Prentice-Hall, 1980.

Scull, Andrew. *Decarceration: Community Treatment and the Deviant — A Radical View.* (2nd ed.) Cambridge, England: Polity Press, 1984.

Sedgwick, Peter. "Antipsychiatry from the Sixties to the Eighties." In *Deviance and Mental Illness*, edited by Walter R. Gove, pp. 199–224. Beverly Hills, CA: Sage Publications, 1982.

Silverstein, Max. *Vital Connections: Integrated Care for the Seriously Mentally Ill.* Lexington, MA: Lexington Books, 1990.

Smith, Dorothy E. "Women and Psychiatry." In *Women Look at Psychiatry*, edited by Dorothy E. Smith and Sara J. Davids, pp. 35–49. Vancouver: Press Gang Publishers, 1975.

Snow, David A. and Leon Anderson. *Down on Their Luck: A Study of Homeless Street People.* Berkeley, CA: University of California Press, 1993.

Statistics Canada. *Canada Yearbook, 1994.* Cat. no. 11-402E/1994) Ottawa: Ministry of Industry, Science & Technology, 1994.

Stebbins, Robert A. *Commitment to Deviance.* Westport, CT: Greenwood Press, 1976.

Szasz, Thomas S. *The Manufacture of Madness.* New York: Dell, 1970.

_________ *Insanity: The Idea and Its Consequences.* New York: John Wiley, 1987.

Thoits, Peggy A. "Self-Labeling Processes in Mental Illness," *American Journal of Sociology*, 1985, 91:221–249.

Ulmer, Jeffery T. "Revisiting Stebbins, Labeling and Commitment to Deviance," *The Sociological Quarterly*, 1994, 35:135–157.

Wagenfield, Morton O. "Psychopathology in Rural Areas: Issues and Evidence." In *Handbook of Rural Community Mental Health*, edited by P.A. Keller and J.D. Murphy, pp. 123–164. New York: Human Sciences Press, 1982.

9

DEVIANT LIFESTYLES

A **lifestyle** is a distinct set of shared patterns of behaviour, whether individual or collective, which, when combined with their associated values, attitudes, and orientations, constitute a special identity for the participants.[1] It is evident in the mode of living characteristic of people who speak of their lifestyle as a collective phenomenon. It is evident, too, in the participants' organization of their everyday existence.

Social and economic conditions play key roles in shaping the wide range of lifestyles that abound in modern Western societies. For instance, several different lifestyles have developed around the various levels of wealth. Age category, race and ethnicity, and location (urban vs. rural) are all among the significant factors shaping different lifestyles. Moreover, all these lifestyles are largely respectable. They diverge from the lifestyles of certain deviants.

The concept of lifestyle indicates that the people who share it organize a substantial proportion of their routine lives around it. The forms of deviance discussed up to this point, even secondary deviance, fall short of being true lifestyles. They are more accurately viewed as special pastimes (e.g., deviant sex) or adjustments to personal problems (e.g., alcoholism, compulsive gambling, mental disorder). To be sure, these deviant, often self-defeating adjustments monopolize the lives of those who have developed them, but they do so more on an individual basis than on a group basis. As for the three deviant belief systems discussed in the next chapter, they are not a sufficiently pervasive part of the lives of those who espouse them to meet our definition of lifestyle.

The deviant ways of the homeless and of those who pursue social nudism —

the two forms covered in this chapter — are sufficiently encompassing to warrant their classification as deviant lifestyles. The lifestyle of the former is, however, more pervasive than that of the latter. As we shall see, the two lifestyles differ in many other ways as well.

HOMELESS STREET PEOPLE

Homeless street people, Snow and Anderson (1993:36) write, are "the most destitute and degraded of all the homeless". They live in the marginal space of North American cities, with no home, no permanent or even temporary place of their own in which to eat and sleep. Snow and Anderson contrast marginal space with prime space. They define the latter as space which is routinely used for residential, commercial, recreational, or navigational purposes, or which is endowed with symbolic value. In comparison, they (1993:103) say, marginal space

> is of little value to regular citizens. In most communities, abandoned buildings, isolated weed patches, alleys, the roofs of buildings, the space under bridges, vacant lots, impoverished, run-down residential areas, warehouse districts, and skid rows are all marginal spaces.

Thus, skid row, as defined in Chapter 5, is but one part of a city's overall marginal space, albeit perhaps its most conspicuous and infamous part.

The people who inhabit these areas of the city are distinguished by their presence there, and further distinguished by their shabby attire and their undeniable poverty. Yet, since 1972, following a revision of the Criminal Code, it has not been an offence to be poor and homeless, to have no apparent means of support and, if one chooses to do so, to wander about the country in this condition, mostly by bus these days (Ward, 1979:100). It is an act of disorderly conduct, however, to fight, scream, shout, and swear; to insult others; to be drunk; to impede or molest others; to loiter; and to disturb others when in a public place. Since the homeless sometimes do these sorts of things, they are watched with suspicion by the authorities and sometimes arrested. Shlay and Rossi (1992:138–139) report that approximately one-third of the homeless in the United States have been jailed on misdemeanor charges.

Before 1972, street people in Canada were illegal persons, referred to in the law books as **vagrants**. Legally speaking, only two types of vagrant remain today. One is the person who supports himself or herself, in whole or in part, by gaming or crime and who has no means of legitimate work. The other is someone who was previously convicted of a sex offence and who has been found "loitering or wandering in or near a schoolground, playground, public park, or bathing area" (Criminal Code, s. 179[1][b]).

Who Are the Homeless?

Whether rightly or wrongly, society commonly regards homeless street people as deviant, albeit tolerably so. They are *absolutely* homeless. Another, larger group of the homeless, whom Baxter (1991:7) calls **people at risk**, is made up of the growing number of homeless families and parts of families. According to the United Nations, both families and individuals can be considered homeless when their dwelling fails to meet basic standards for physical adequacy and security of person and tenure. These homeless people are not, however, on the street. They are not absolutely homeless. Nor are they deviant, for poverty is not conventionally defined as a willful violation of the community's moral norms.

Although smaller in number than the people at risk, absolutely homeless street people still constitute a significant segment of the urban population. Moreover, they are by no means a homogeneous group. Following the classification developed by Snow and Anderson (1993: Ch. 2), they can be categorized as one of five types: the recently dislocated, straddlers, and three subtypes of outsiders referred to as tramps, bums, and the mentally disordered. Similar terminology has been used from the first study of homeless street people conducted by Nels Anderson (1923) to the present, including studies by Spradley (1970:66–68, 95) and Hoch and Slayton (1989:37–38).

The **recently dislocated** are conspicuous on the street by their adaptive behaviour, which is a response to the unfamiliarity of their new surroundings. They are frightened by what they see: the deterioration of the built environment, the slovenly appearance of those whose company they must now keep, and the institutions that serve them or control them (e.g., the missions, Salvation Army, local police). This category contains the youngest inhabitants of a city's marginal space, most of whom are single males. But recently, being unable to find shelter, the number of females, children, and teenagers in this group has been increasing (Shlay and Rossi, 1992:135). Many of the children and adolescents are runaways, although some of those in their late teens and most of those in their early twenties are rural-to-urban migrants searching for work. Finally, some of the recently dislocated are immigrants, native peoples, or people with drug and alcohol problems. All in all, a highly diverse group.

If the recently dislocated continually meet with failure to get off the street — in most instances failing to find adequate employment — they become **straddlers**. They have by now become substantially more familiar with the marginal spaces they inhabit. Snow and Anderson (1993:52) describe the orientation of people in this group:

> There is a desire, on the one hand, to tie the future to the past by escaping from street life. On the other hand, planned ways of getting off the street tend to become increasingly unclear, and there is a tendency to slip into lassitude, letting the days flow by without taking any action. Frequently, at this stage talk and action are inconsistent.

Straddlers are at a turning point in their lives. Although in principle they would like to return to the domiciled world, they are at the same time pushed toward the street by circumstances well beyond their control. Many of these people are on the verge of joining the ranks of the chronically homeless, of becoming true outsiders.

The **outsiders** have adapted to street life to such an extent that their orientation is toward it, rather than toward trying to return to a domiciled life sustained by sufficient employment. They have become caught up in the daily routine of survival in the marginal spaces of Canadian and American cities. Now little else matters; their existence here is taken for granted.

The subtype of **tramp** is the most honoured among those who fall into the category of outsider. The modern meaning of the term has a history extending back into the early twentieth century, when some tramps were members of the revolutionary labour union, the Industrial Workers of the World (Anderson, 1923). Then and now, tramps have been and are willing and able to work for various lengths of time. Local temporary work and migrant labour are their specialities:

> "I'm beginning to learn that," I said, "if all your stories are true, which it seems they are after today, you're the hardest working sonofaguns...."
>
> "Bitches," Carl corrected me, "one of the hardest working sonofabitches you ever saw. And I could take you to Minneapolis and show you fifty guys just like me. They might look like bums or derelicts, but they're workers. You thought being a tramp meant being just a no-good — well, I hope I've showed you, showed you how to tell the working men from the rest. Their clothes and their gear. You got to look at their hands; their hands give it away every time." (Harper, 1982:116–117)

The tramps are the most mobile, independent, and self-controlled of the outsider category. They also tend to be the oldest. The popular image of adult street people is that they are **bums**, an image that the tramp tries hard to deny. There is good reason for this denial. A bum, in the public's mind, is someone who lacks self-control, is unpredictable, drinks too much, and is highly dependent on society, and who therefore frequently winds up in jail. The labels "derelict", "wino", and "transient" have similar meanings. And the popular image is not all wrong; there are bums on skid row who are separate from the tramps.

Many more street people are thought to be bums than actually fit the popular image. Why? Lyman (1989) points out that sloth is one of the seven deadly sins in Western culture (along with lust, anger, envy, pride, greed, and gluttony). Sloth is sinful because it mocks the work ethic, and street people are bums in the public mind because they have elected sloth in a work-oriented world and get away with it. They are seen as people who have fallen below society's standards of economic morality (Parker, 1983:84–85).

Unlike tramps, some street people cannot work, because of a congenital or acquired physical disability or a chronic and incapacitating disease. Some cannot work because they are mentally handicapped. And some suffer one or more of these conditions as a result of old age. Given their disabilities and their dependency on alcohol, it is hardly surprising that these outsiders are much less mobile than the tramps.

Wright's (1989:49) evaluation of the Health Care for the Homeless program in the United States revealed that, among those street people who were capable of working, more than half did so. While most found part-time or sporadic employment, a few actually held full-time jobs. But in no case did any of them earn enough to sustain themselves in stable housing. Only 5 percent could be considered genuine bums, people who could work but nonetheless steadfastly refused to do so.

The **mentally disordered** who live on the street are classified in popular thinking as another genre of bum. Although their number is difficult to estimate and extensive surveys are lacking, a review of 60 studies undertaken by Shlay and Rossi (1992:138) suggests that this category constitutes from one-quarter to one-third of all the people on the street. Furthermore, Mechanic and Rochefort (1990:318) found little evidence to support the claim that de-institutionalization is the principal cause of homelessness among the mentally disordered (but see Elliot and Krivo, 1991). Indeed, Johnson (1990:150–151) and Lee (1992:845) suggest that the causal link may, in a significant proportion of the cases, be the other way around. Mental illness, notes Johnson (1990:150), may be adjustive tolerable deviance, an adaptation to highly distressing circumstances:

> Living on the street or in a shelter, as many homeless people do, cannot possibly have a positive effect on one's self-esteem or provide much in the way of gratifying experience; and homelessness itself is a state of such unremitting crisis that one would expect it to provoke some kind of emotional or mental disorder, in and of itself.

Snow and Anderson (1993:67–68) have estimated that perhaps 10 percent of their Texas sample were truly mentally disordered.

Legal Status of the Homeless

In Canadian legal terms, street people constitute a **public nuisance**; they are actual or potential violators of the laws pertaining to disorderly conduct. Because of their low economic status and homeless situation, they are, as the police see it, likely to cause trouble. They are believed to have no commitment to public order in the community since they own no property and have no attachments to local institutions and relationships. In the eyes of the law (Giffen, 1966; Wiseman, 1970), street people are identifiable by dress, location, the company they keep, the smell of alcohol, and their activity (loitering, staggering). Given this evidence, the police must decide whether to make an arrest and the court must determine whether sentencing is justified. Legal action is based on the likelihood of the person in question making trouble for himself or herself in the immediate future; for example, he or she is drunk and could possibly get injured, or has no place to sleep and will therefore sleep illegally in a park or bus depot.

Demographic Characteristics of the Homeless

The demography of homeless street people revolves around the conditions of homelessness and poverty. For a variety of reasons, certain members of society find themselves with so little money that they are unable to afford a home of any kind. The initial problem, then, is a lack of income so acute that these people can live nowhere other than the street. This is an adjustment made with reference to few alternatives. The people who wind up on the street are nearly always alone; they are usually unmarried, divorced, widowed, or separated and, in general, estranged from all but the most superficial human relationships.

Historically, Canadian skid rows have chiefly been populated by the disadvantaged and stigmatized ethnic groups who have immigrated to the street, and by urban Indians. Stigma and linguistic inadequacy combine into a formidable barrier that prevents an escape from poverty in general and skid row in particular. To these factors is added a sizable educational deficiency: a significantly lower proportion of today's denizens of the street hold a high school diploma than the national average (Cohen and Sokolovsky, 1989:70; Fortier, 1991:35; Snow and Anderson, 1993:278–279).

The employable on the street mingle with the unemployable. For reasons discussed previously, disabilities of one sort or another force the latter onto skid row as the only possible response to destitution. Today, the physically handicapped are joined by the mentally handicapped who, as noted in Chapter 8, drift onto the street because they are unable to manage the demands of everyday living, including those of finding and holding a job. Previously, they were retained in hospitals. With the current trend toward de-institutionalization, they are being released in increasingly greater numbers to community health programs, which are unable to manage the overload.

Other street people are employable, but, in difficult economic times, they find it impossible to get enough work to maintain even a minimal residence. They are what Karl Marx (1977:481) called the "industrial reserve army", which, in good economic times, is part of the labour force of capitalist societies. In bad economic times, its members are left to fend for themselves with neither work nor money. They are also part of the "relative surplus population", whose minimal skills and level of education qualify them for only the most menial jobs.

Another demographic component which has changed substantially over the years is age. Wallace (1965) noted that, during the course of the twentieth century, skid row has changed from an employment pool of able-bodied young men (i.e., tramps) to a dumping ground for the aged. Though it is true that, with age, some people become unemployable, this change is exaggerated in the public's mind, for many people beyond age 60 do not grow infirm, lose stamina, or in some other way become handicapped (McPherson, 1990:390–391). But the myth persists that aging is tantamount to infirmity of mind and body — a myth leading to discrimination against the elderly. Those who are old or who look old — and many middle-aged street people look old — are rejected as employees. Rejection may take the form of mandatory retirement. Or it may be an outright refusal to hire elderly people, on the grounds that younger people are available and can fill the position in question better and for a longer period of time.

The age structure of the street has recently undergone yet another change — many runaway teenagers are now found there (McLaughlin, 1987:4–6). Economic recession is partly to blame for this trend, inasmuch as young people are unable to find jobs with which to support themselves. But unlike many of the older people on the street, these youths lack the education and work skills needed to gain steady employment (Parrish, 1985).

Finally, the sex component on the street is also different today. What was once a nearly all-male community is now increasingly composed of women. The middle-aged and elderly women are the "bag ladies" who carry their possessions about in a shopping bag or its equivalent. In addition, mothers with young children, who together constitute homeless families, sometimes spend periods of time on skid row. In this situation, the children are placed in some sort of government-supported care, while the mothers eke out an existence in the inner city, searching for work (O'Reilly-Fleming, 1993:43–53).

One force behind the new age and sex composition of contemporary street life is the decline in the availability of cheap lodging: hostels, missions, single-room hotels, and the like. As part of their attempt to redevelop their central business districts, many European and North American cities have destroyed these establishments, replacing them with office towers or high-rise apartment buildings. The poor in Europe and North America face a more acute shortage of lodging than ever (Shlay and Rossi, 1992:152; Begin, 1993:9–12). Unemployment and severe reductions in welfare spending also help account for the new demographic trends among homeless street people.

THE STREET AS A WAY OF LIFE

When one lives on the margin, surviving is the main activity. For homeless street people in Canada, the struggle to live is somewhat less acute because they receive small but regular pension, social assistance, or disability cheques. Tramps can often locate seasonal and part-time work. McLaughlin (1987) reported that, in that year, over 51 percent of all homeless people were benefitting from some kind of social assistance, a figure that would be considerably lower for the absolutely homeless. Many of the men and women without such income panhandlle, while those with some means of support panhandle as a supplement. Some find a partial livelihood in collecting salable objects such as cans and bottles. In the United States, some find it in selling their blood. Younger women frequently and younger men sometimes prostitute themselves, a commerce they carry out in the city's prime space. Younger men and women may also sell drugs. Ironically, an unknown proportion of the population on the street is eligible for welfare payments, but, with no permanent address and little knowledge of how the welfare system works, they never receive it.

With money, a street person can purchase a cheap meal at a nearby restaurant. Without it, he or she must line up for a handout from a soup kitchen in the area, go to a mission where free meals are served following a sermon, or hope there is something left at the nearest food bank. Some resort to digging around in dumpsters and garbage cans.

When street people are not waiting in line for food, they are often waiting to claim one of the scarce beds in the area to spend the night. According to the description of New York's flops presented by Cohen and Sokolovsky (1989:23–24), the ones which remain are as seedy as those bulldozed by urban redevelopment. Visitors rent a 1.3 m by 2 m cubicle for the night; they get a bed, a small table, and possibly a hot plate and some eating and cooking ware. Some of these places also have large dormitories equipped with several dozen cots. Whether in cubicles or dorms, the occupants confront filth and vermin at every step.

Alternative places to spend the night are parks, doorways, depots, shopping malls, underground garages, even garbage bins. Heating grates are coveted in the winter. Churches located near the marginal areas of the city sometimes contribute financially to nearby street agencies or operate meal- and church-service programs of their own (Cooper, 1987:144; Snow and Anderson, 1993:304–307). Sheila Baxter (1991), in her examination of homelessness in Vancouver, mentions that the First United Church maintains sleeping accommodations for a limited number of local street people.

The remaining time on the street is used for leisure. Participating in bottle gangs and hanging out in skid row taverns are two popular pastimes. Many street people simply sit or lie near a busy street or sidewalk and watch the comings and goings of the city's inhabitants while sharing a cigarette and some conversation. In the winter, some seek refuge in bus and train terminals and subway stations. Some head for downtown libraries, which provide warmth. Inner-city museums serve a similar purpose.

However, in these places, loitering and sleeping are prohibited. Everyone has a right to use them, but only for the purposes for which they are intended. Shabby appearance and lethargic gait quickly alert security personnel and provoke an unceremonious eviction.

A substantial portion of each day is spent walking from one place to another and standing in line in search of money, food, shelter, and leisure. Indeed, one of the most wearisome aspects of the lifestyle of the absolutely homeless is the boredom and idleness enforced by this routine. Those who can work escape the monotony to some extent. The rest accommodate themselves to a situation which for many shows no sign of change. In Viewpoint 9.1, Toronto freelance writer M.L. Allen sketches a typical day in the lives of Canadian street people living on skid row.

One might ask how these people maintain their self-respect. A study by Snow and Anderson (1987) suggests that they do so, in part, during their everyday conversations. Some distance themselves from the other habitués of skid row by arguing that they are somehow special or uncommitted to the street person's way of life. Other hold that being a tramp or bum is a modestly honourable status. Still others tell stories designed either to enhance personal identity or to paint a rosy picture of the narrator's future:

> Tomorrow morning I'm going to get my money and say, "Fuck this shit." I'm going to catch a plane to Pittsburgh and tomorrow night I'll take a hot bath, have a dinner of linguini and red wine in my own restaurant... and have a woman hanging on my arm (Snow and Anderson, 1987:1362).

VIEWPOINT 9.1

A TYPICAL DAY ON SKID ROW

During the night, one man repeatedly screamed in his sleep. Another man carried on a lengthy conversation with an imaginary friend, while a third moaned quietly to himself. At one point, someone fell out of a lower bunk, but didn't wake up, and continued to sleep on the floor. Another man had his shoes stolen. In the hallway outside, there were fights and near-fights....

Alone on the street, without work or friends or family, the daily job is one of merely surviving — of trying to get food during the day and shelter for the night. Most hostels turn their clients out at seven in the morning, supposedly to look for work. But, asks the pastor of a Toronto church that provides winter shelter, "what happens when there's no longer any work out there? It means that people live on the streets in the wintertime, and it's cold out there."

"We do a lot of walking, and a lot of waiting in line," says a homeless man in Vancouver, describing his day. They walk to a soup kitchen or a depot distributing free food. Because it's often necessary to arrive early to be sure of getting something, they may spend several hours waiting in line. If they're too late, or there's nothing available, they may have to resort — as was reported of many young people in Montreal — to digging through garbage in search of something to eat.

In the afternoon, they begin to drift back to the hostels, again arriving very early to be sure of getting a place. Many of the better hostels — those offering showers, a change of clothes, a TV room — can only be used a few nights a month. This means it's necessary either to keep moving between hostels, or to find somewhere else that offers protection from the elements, such as an underground garage or a parked car. In Halifax, a derelict was nearly crushed to death in a garbage truck after he went to sleep in a trash bin. Every winter in Toronto, according to Alderman David Reville, "people are found frozen in abandoned buildings and cars."

Life on skid row is endlessly difficult and sometimes dangerous Some of the older men accept that kind of life, but few of the younger ones do. "I'm too young to be in a place like this," says a young man in a Toronto hostel. "It breaks my heart to be without a job," says another; "I feel dead inside. How will I survive? Will I ever find a job?"

Worst of all, the longer someone is on skid row, the more difficult it is to get out. "They get caught up in a lifestyle, in a vicious downward spiral," a hostel manager explains.

"They end up in one of these hostels and they never leave the system again." Or, as one young man put it, "Being like this for three years, I feel like an old man, but without a cane."

Source: M.L. Allen, "Down and Out," *Canada and the World*, 1985, 50, April:26–28. Reprinted with permission of *Canada and the World*, Waterloo, Ontario.

HOMELESSNESS AS A WORLD PROBLEM

With its many social programs, Canada should have a significantly smaller number of skid rows and street people than countries without such programs. This is undoubtedly true when Canada is compared with some of the developing nations, where one in two people live in slums or homeless conditions (*Urban History Review*, 1986:278).

Still, as reported in the *Financial Post* (1984:25–26), medical and hospital facilities, dental treatment, and good nutrition are far from equally distributed in Canada. Nor are our other social programs sufficient to eliminate or even significantly reduce the size of the homeless population (Begin, 1993). One of the problems is that Canadian skid rows, as part of urban marginal space, are less visible than those in, say, the United States. They are smaller, more scattered, and possibly less blighted. As a result, the street and its inhabitants may be harder to define as a problem in Canada than in many other Western nations.

The General Assembly of the United Nations established 1987 as the International Year of Shelter for the Homeless (IYSH). The principal goals of the IYSH were to help the poor and disadvantaged improve their living accommodations and neighbourhoods, to search for affordable improvements for large numbers of people, and to establish shelter and settlement programs. A guarded estimate places at one-quarter of the world's population the number of people living in inadequate housing. The potential here for conflict, if they were capable of organizing in their own interest, is great. In North America, the homeless population is largely passive. At present, it is unlikely to become the seat of discontent against the rest of society.

SOCIAL NUDISM

According to St. Augustine, human nakedness was natural and unproblematic until it provoked sexual intercourse between Adam and Eve. This "sinful" act indicated that nakedness stimulated lust; therefore, Augustine reasoned, humanity should always be clothed in public places (Lyman 1989:55–57). The moral basis for wearing clothes in Western society (as opposed to various practical and decorative bases) was greatly reinforced by this pronouncement.

Judeo-Christian tradition is also the moral basis for the passage in the Canadian Criminal Code, Section 174, that reads: "Every one who, without lawful excuse, is nude in a public place, or is nude and exposed to public view while on private property... is guilty of an offence punishable on summary conviction." A person is defined as nude when he or she is clad in a way that offends public decency or order. Legally, public nudity is an act of disorderly conduct.

Despite such legal and moral proscriptions, nudism and naturism have existed throughout this century. In the past two to three decades, both have begun to attract large numbers of followers. Gary Page (1971) writes that naturism began as an organized movement in Germany in 1903. It spread rapidly across Europe, particularly to Switzerland and Britain. Social nudism in Canada began in 1939 with the formation of the Van Tans nudist club of Vancouver. A rustic camp was established in 1946 near North Bay, Ontario. Today there are clubs throughout most of Canada.

Before proceeding, it will be useful to consider the difference between nudism and naturism. As it turns out, the usage of the two terms is most complicated. Historically and presently, "naturism" is the term chiefly used in Europe, whereas "nudism" is preferred in North America, Australia, and New Zealand (Kamphorst, 1989:7). Today, in Europe and increasingly in the latter countries, however, members of the movement use "naturism" to refer to adherence under all possible circumstances to certain ideals of health, such as going nude, benefitting from the rays of the sun (but avoiding its cancerous potential), remaining in good physical condition, avoiding unhealthy habits (e.g., smoking), and maintaining a healthy diet. From this standpoint, nudity is to be practised wherever one can get away with it: at home, beaches, camps, resorts, parties, swimming pools, and so forth. Nudism, by contrast, is now often seen as primarily recreational, as reflected in the 1994 renaming of the American Sunbathing Association to the American Association for Nude Recreation. Adherents of both naturism and nudism value the sense of being at one with nature when nude, which means, among others things, that no part of the body is to be considered shameful or vulgar. Moreover, everywhere today, both are emphasizing the social and recreational components of going nude (c.f. American Sunbathing Association, 1987; Kamphorst, 1989). Still, those who identify themselves as naturists place greater emphasis on health principles than those identifying themselves as nudists. I will try to respect this distinction in this chapter, even if the sociological literature on nudism/naturism, much of which is old, does so only rarely.

Sociologically speaking, the foregoing also describes an ideology which serves as a set of justifications for a lifestyle regarded as deviant by many members of the larger society. This lifestyle involves more than an occasional episode of skinny-dipping in a local pond or a few trips to a nude beach somewhere. It is the practice of going without clothes while interacting with other people of all ages and both sexes in areas and places reserved for this purpose. Those who identify most strongly with the nudist movement justify social nudity on the basis of its health, relaxation, and social benefits, not in terms of sexual excitement or exhibitionism. The movement rests on the aforementioned orientation that there is nothing shameful or vulgar about any part of the body; it is to be appreciated in its natural state.

THE NUDIST LIFESTYLE

A brief methodological note is in order at this point. Sociological research on nudism in Canada is both dated and limited; it presently rests on studies of a few clubs conducted approximately 30 years ago by Weinberg and Page. To offset this lack of research, five leaders in the Canadian nudist movement were interviewed by the author in January 1987 and November 1994. In addition to answering a number of questions about the contemporary Canadian and American nudist scene, they read drafts of this section, indicating, from their experience, where the observations and findings of Weinberg and Page no longer apply. Their views have been incorporated in various places throughout the remainder of this chapter and are sometimes, but not always, acknowledged.

Nudity of the sort considered here takes place openly in designated places and areas. In its promotional literature, the American Association for Nude Recreation (which has several Canadian affiliates) classifies these places and areas into two categories. **Landed clubs** have privately owned, co-operatively owned, or leased grounds with facilities ranging from rustic to luxurious. They are variously referred to as clubs, parks, camps (a rather outmoded term), resorts, or beaches. The members of **non-landed clubs** sometimes use the facilities of landed clubs, as a group. Alternatively, they may hold social events, nude or clothed, at restaurants, private homes, or entertainment centres. A non-landed club may also rent a local YMCA or health centre for a swimming party. There are also urban non-landed clubs, where members join in nude swimming, court games, and saunas.

The lifestyle of club nudists revolves around couples (married or unmarried) and children. In principle, anyone who is interested in nudism, is willing to pay the membership fee, and meets membership requirements may join a club. However, single men and women are regarded with suspicion; the former, in particular, may be flatly prohibited from membership or charged especially high fees to test their attachment to nudist principles. Research done three decades ago suggested that between 70 and 80 percent of club members are married, while most of the remainder are unmarried couples (Ilfeld and Lauer, 1964:88; Weinberg, 1967).

The people who patronize the landed clubs often do so as part of their holidays. Depending on the size of the grounds and the facilities, a variety of activities is available, from sports to dancing (clothing usually required) to conversation. Special competitions are held for the children. The activities of both the landed and the non-landed clubs continue through fall, winter, and spring, when most North American outdoor facilities are closed. The club organizations often hold Halloween, Valentine's Day, and New Year's Eve parties, as well as such monthly gatherings as pot-luck suppers. (Viewpoint 9.2 describes the amenities of an alternative to the two types of clubs, the nudist resort.)

There is nothing illegal about any of these arrangements, as long as the nudists remain out of public view. The development of nude or "free" beaches in North America, such as Wreck Beach in Vancouver and Black's Beach near San Diego, California, poses certain legal problems. For the moment, the question of the legality of these areas in Canada is being overlooked:

VIEWPOINT 9.2

THE AMENITIES OF A NUDIST RESORT

A typical nudist resort offers something approaching a complete vacation package for its clients, many of whom are likely to spend two to three weeks there participating in a variety of activities in the nude. Sports activities are extremely popular, particularly tennis, swimming, and volleyball. Resorts established on large tracts of land may offer walking trails and opportunities for nature study, while those established on the shore of a lake or an ocean count boating and fishing among their amenities. These activities are commonly augmented by saunas, hot tubs, and exercise facilities.

Whereas many nudists view sport and exercise as central to their lifestyle, the full range of activities at the typical nudist resort extends far beyond this. Thus, there is often a game room as well as another much larger space where dances, meetings, and entertainment events are held. Some resorts are equipped for camping in recreational vehicles. Nor is the family side of nudism overlooked: the children invariably have their own play and swimming areas. Many resorts maintain a reading library; some, a videocassette library. The more upscale establishments offer a restaurant, while snack bars are available at all resorts.

In the end, the goal is much the same at every nudist resort: to promote a healthy, wholesome physical and moral lifestyle based on the principles and practices of social nudism.

> "The understanding is that if nobody's creating problems and if there aren't any public complaints, we don't arrest anybody down there [Wreck Beach] for public nudity," says Sergeant Fred Hardy, commander of the RCMP detachment that patrols the beach. Vancouver parks and recreation superintendent Victor Kondrosky agrees: "I guess you could describe our policy as looking in the other directions." (Masters, 1981:12)

More recently, Wreck Beach has moved closer to legality, through its official recognition by the Vancouver city council as a free beach whose surveillance falls within the jurisdiction of the Vancouver police.

Research done in the 1960s by Page (1971) and Weinberg (1967) indicated that between 50 and 68 percent of landed club nudists in Canada and the United States visit formally or informally among themselves, as often as once a month. The same two studies indicated that nudists in Canada and the United States hold a wide range of occupations, though professionals and craftspeople were found to be somewhat over-represented. The general impression then was that nudism appeals primarily to those in the middle- and upper-middle classes. The informants interviewed for this chapter believe that, today, the working class is significantly better represented than previously. In both countries, fewer Catholics and more religious non-affiliates become nudists than their proportion in the general population. Otherwise, the distribution of nudists by religion more or less coincides with the general population. The panel of interviewees add that there are few non-white club nudists.

The discussion in the older sociological studies of nudist club norms which sustain an acceptable level of moral conduct is now out of date. Today, use of alcohol is permitted, although in moderation. Photography is allowed as long as the subject consents. Videotaping, however, is often proscribed. There are no longer formal rules about body contact. People are expected to comport themselves on club premises as they would in any public place when clothed. But there is variation: Smith (1980) observed considerably more touching of various sorts on a French free beach than on a German one. Additionally, it is expected that members will strive to maintain the confidentiality of other members by refraining from revealing to outsiders the others' association with the club. In nudist/naturist circles everywhere, a fundamental expectation is that people will be nude on club premises and at many club functions, unless such conditions as cool weather or sunburn dictate otherwise.

Verbal or physical conduct that offends or embarrasses others is grounds for suspension or termination of membership, though the occasional sex joke or discussion is not ruled out. Seductive postures and adornments, however, *are* ruled out. Indeed, bodily modifications and adornments are considered contrary to nudist philosophy, which holds that the body is an object to be appreciated in its natural state. In this connection, Smith (1980) found in his comparison of two nude beaches that those on the French beach adorned their bodies or shaved their pubic areas significantly more often than those on the German beach.

These norms are undoubtedly violated from time to time. From the studies and the interviews, it is clear that they are upheld often enough to avoid routine problems. The fear is that relaxation of the norms could lead to a situation that would drive many families from the clubs, the very people who form the backbone of club membership.

For various reasons, people do drop out of the clubs. The drop-out rate appears to be higher in American clubs than in Canadian ones (cf. Page, 1971:402; Weinberg, 1967:99). In both countries, however, the principal reasons for leaving the club aspect of the nudist movement are boredom and loss of interest. A dislike for the relatively primitive facilities of the rustic clubs drives away some Americans, but few Canadians. Single or unaccompanied men and socially isolated couples leave most quickly, largely because of the social pressure they experience from other members. It is also a fact of nudist life that any titillation derived from seeing members of the opposite sex in the nude quickly wears off, eliminating that reason for staying in the movement. Some grow weary of routinely trying to conceal their deviance. Some leave because of changes in their families: divorce, new positions, changing interests of teenaged family members, and so on. (The shyness of adolescents about their changing bodies seems to be universal; Smith (1980) rarely saw them on the beaches he observed.)

BECOMING A NUDIST

Martin Weinberg's (1966) study of Canadian and American nudists focused on the process of becoming a nudist. As David Matza (1969:111–117) explains, newcomers to any form of deviance must "be willing" to participate in it before they will actually try it for the first time. The pre-deviant must either have developed a tolerant, if not sympathetic, attitude toward the deviance in question or have transformed his or her outlook more or less on the spot to enable immediate participation. It appears that approximately 50 percent of Weinberg's respondents were willing, whereas the remainder harboured negative attitudes or had given no thought to joining a nudist group. The latter had to be persuaded, a task usually carried out by the husband.

Accordingly, the initial interest in nudism for female respondents came chiefly from their husbands. As sources of interest for women, another person and nudist magazines ranked as the second and third most frequent. For men, the rank order of sources of initial interest was roughly the reverse: nearly half the sample became interested through the magazines, while another person was the second most prevalent source. My five interviewees said that newspaper and news magazine articles, which have become common in the past two decades or so, are also significant sources of information leading to initial interest.

Thus the early stages of the female nudist's career are typically characterized by reluctance to go to a club and disrobe. Weinberg reported that, in the couples he surveyed, 79 percent of the men were more interested in going to a club for the first time than the women. No woman said she wanted to go more than her husband. Among the women, 21 percent said they were as interested as their husbands in visiting a club. These proportions changed dramatically on the return visits: 40 percent of the men wanted to go more than their wives, 51 percent of both members wanted to go, and 9 percent of the women wanted to go more than their husbands.

The nudist leaders interviewed for this chapter in 1994 believe that the proportions of men and women embracing nudism/naturism, whether for the first time or subsequently, are now less dissimilar than in the older studies. In an age of female liberation, going unclothed among friends and acquaintances appeals to more women than before. Still, Vingerhoets and Buunck's (1987) study of nude beaches in the Netherlands suggests that, in general, women are still significantly less enthusiastic about the nudist/naturist program than men.

For both men and women, reluctance is changed to acceptance by a set of conditions that reads very much like the definition of nudism set up at the beginning of this discussion. The most frequently mentioned attraction of club nudism in Weinberg's study was the friendliness and sociability found there. Relaxation and escape from the city were the next most attractive aspects. The attractions of sunbathing, outdoor activities and sports, freedom from clothing, and physical health were all approximately third in importance. Only 1 percent of the sample said that seeing others in the nude was what they liked most about nudism.

The tenet of nudist ideology that nudism brings the family closer together was not borne out in Weinberg's research. Roughly 80 percent of his sample reported no change in family relationships as a result of their involvement in nudism in general and club nudism in particular. Just 11 percent of the respondents stated that the principal attraction of nudism was that it informs children about the human body, and only 4 percent said that its principal attraction was that it generates family cohesiveness. Still, it may be that nudist families are already so cohesive and informed about the body that club membership can do little to enhance these qualities. On the basis of its own surveys, the American Sunbathing Association (1987) reported that the divorce rate of its members is lower than the national average in the United States.

THE NUDE BEACH

Douglas, Rasmussen, and Flanagan (1977:49–52), in their study of a California nude beach, report similar psychological problems surrounding the initial unwillingness to participate at a nude beach. Many men and women who went to the beach for the first time had to be persuaded to remove their clothes. Some never did remove them. Vingerhoets and Buunk (1987) observed a similar reluctance on the beaches in the Netherlands.

At the nude beach, there are relatively few children, numerous married and unmarried couples, and single men and women. Douglas et al. estimated from questionnaires that 55 percent of the "beachers" were single, 39 percent were married, and 8 percent were divorced. Of their respondents, 72 percent did not consider themselves nudists of the club mentality.

Nude beaches are large, impersonal stretches of sand, many of which serve metropolitan areas. Vancouver's Wreck Beach is about 1.5 km long and is reputed to accommodate 8000 on a fine weekend (Masters, 1981); the one studied by Douglas et al. was over 3 km in length and drew 40 000 people on a hot summer day. By contrast, the largest club that Page (1971) observed had 400 members. Lee Baxandall's *World Guide to Nude Beaches and Recreation*, 1991 edition, lists 44 areas along and around Canadian rivers, lakes, and hot springs that are routinely used for nude recreation. Most are located in Québec and British Columbia. A brochure from the *Fédération québécoise de naturisme* boasts of over 50 such sites in that province alone.

On a scale of morality, the California beach studied by Douglas and his colleagues fell roughly between the conservative family orientation of the typical nudist club and the radical behaviour of an open-air sex orgy. In this milieu, some of the club rules discussed earlier simply did not apply. Although such activities are by no means the norm, the Douglas research team observed the occasional sexual act (petting, fellatio, masturbation, and, still more rarely, actual intercourse). The norm was to engage in sex privately, if at all, in the hills behind the beach. Related activities such as body painting and seductive posturing — both contrary to nudist principles — are also occasionally found on nude beaches.

The sight of erect male organs was to some extent expected and apparently not very upsetting. They were defined as normal body parts reacting in normal fashion to the presence of attractive nude women. More disturbing to the regulars of the beach than erections or open displays of sex were open displays of voyeurism, an activity that is completely legal (Douglas et al., 1977:112–140). Voyeurs used binoculars from the cliffs above the beach or stood on the beach (clothed or unclothed) and leered at the sunbathers. The French beach studied by Smith (1980) showed many of the same characteristics as the California beach in Douglas et al.'s study.

The nude beach is a place where men and women can meet each other for heterosexual ad homosexual liaisons; the latter are arranged on a separate part of the beach. Couples who swing search the sands for like-minded pairs with whom they can subsequently spend the evening in a spousal exchange. To be sure, not everybody participates in these casual sexual encounters; many are there for the sun and the freedom from clothing.

But even the nude beach, despite its more liberal code, eventually brings satiation and boredom to many of its frequenters:

> We have seen that the initial feeling is excitement — the unseen exposed is exciting. But then one becomes mellow, especially in a public situation in which one cannot consummate the erotic desire and where even erotic responses like erections are still shamed. One comes to have less erotic feeling for nude scenes — one mellows (Douglas et al., 1977:223–224).

The result, according to the Douglas study, was a high rate of turnover, even among old-time regulars. Many of those who remained became less natural, partially clothing themselves or covering up in some other way. Covering, the authors argue, produces ambivalence and titillating erotic feelings. With such feelings, the boredom often vanishes and the nude beach once again becomes an interesting place.

SOCIAL ORGANIZATION

Nudism, as we have seen, is made possible by a variety of organizations. Even the free beaches have some social organization to them. The nudist clubs in North America usually belong to one of the large associations which act as promotional agents for the movement and publish magazines and newsletters containing information of interest to members. In Canada, the principal such associations are the Federation of Canadian Naturists and the Western Canadian Nude Recreation Association. The latter is an affiliate of the American Nude Recreation Association which itself organizes over 200 clubs containing approximately 43 000 members — an increase of 43 percent from the 30 000 members of just seven years before. Both clubs and individual club members may join these organizations or the various smaller regional organizations that also exist. There are approximately 25 nudist/naturist clubs in Canada, according to Baxandall's 1991 edition of *World Guide to Nude Beaches & Recreation* and the American Sunbathing Association's 1990 edition of the *North American Guide to Nude Recreation.*

Both Weinberg and Page discuss the organizational careers open to the most involved camp members and camp owners. Involved members may become camp leaders and move on from there to become members of an association executive or, alternatively, start, purchase, or manage a camp of their own. At the camp level, some involved members gain enough support from and influence over other members to be given a say in camp operations.

The nude beaches are generally much less organized. Those in California do have a promotional and lobbyist organization known as Beachfront U.S.A. Morality. Douglas (1984) describes how the nude beachers there organized in order to direct local television crews to the more innocent sections of the beach so that a safe, wholesome image of it could be communicated to the public. On Vancouver's Wreck Beach, cleanliness and beach access are monitored by the Wreck Beach Preservation Society, a group of volunteer ecologists and naturists. Still, the vast majority of free beaches are organized only insofar as users behave according to the norms of nudism and naturism that enthusiasts the world over tend to share.

TOLERANCE AND STIGMA

The popularity of nude beaches in Canada and the United States, their tacit legality, and the visible formal organizations of club nudists are all evidence of the modern tolerance of nudism and nudity in North America. So is the finding in 1983 by the Gallup Poll that 72 percent of an American sample approved of the concept of "clothes-optional" beaches (*California Naturist,* 1986). Gone are the days when members in primitive camps used only first names to identify themselves. Coverage of the clubs and beaches by the mass media often contains full names and perhaps pictures of regular members. Clubs are commonly listed in local telephone books, while municipal councils and citizens' groups appear to have adopted a live-and-let-live attitude toward them.

Nonetheless, nudists, especially those who patronize the landed clubs, perceive a lingering degree of social stigma. Even in the Netherlands, where nudism/naturism is enjoying immense popularity, the practice is still regarded "as more or less deviant" (Vingerhoets and Buunk, 1987:14). In North America, practitioners must put up with sporadic legal and moral challenges to their way of life from local opponents (see *The Bulletin*, American Association for Nude Recreation, various issues). One recently divorced nudist wrote:

> When I was looking for a new mate, I made no bones about being a nudist. I usually worked it into the first conversation I had with a woman. That way, if the woman agreed to go out with me, it was clear from the start that nudism was not a taboo subject. I have heard more than a few single fellows say that they would never mention the "N" word amongst their lady friends for fear of being thought weird (American Association for Nude Recreation, 1994:8).

Still, it is clear that this form of tolerable deviance is becoming more popular (and thereby less deviant). Between the first and second editions of this book, the American Association for Nude Recreation grew by 13 000 members, as noted earlier. The International Naturist Federation, with affiliates in 26 countries in Europe, North America, and South America, as well as in Australia and New Zealand, now counts 250 000 members (Kamphorst, 1989:4) and is said to be growing as well. The *Fédération québécoise de naturisme* (FQN) is a member of the *Regroupement Loisir Québec*, an organization that speaks for the vast majority of leisure associations in that province. At the International Leisure Studies Conference held in November 1994 in Trois-Rivières, Québec, I picked up the FQN's brochure from among a variety of booklets and pamphlets on such leisure activities as amateur astronomy, community music, and craft-making.

SUMMARY

A lifestyle is a distinct set of shared patterns of behaviour, whether individual or collective, which, when combined with their associated values, attitudes, and orientations, constitute a special identity for the participants. Lifestyles develop around the categories of wealth, age, race, ethnicity, and, in some instances, deviant interests.

One lifestyle is that of the absolutely homeless. These people are not in themselves doing anything illegal, although they are closely watched for possible disorderly conduct. The absolutely homeless can be classed as one of five types: the recently dislocated, straddlers, and three subtypes of outsiders referred to as tramps, bums, and the mentally disordered. The recently dislocated are conspicuous on the street by their adaptive behaviour, which is a response to the unfamiliarity of their new surroundings. If they continually meet with failure to get off the street and find employment, they become straddlers. The straddlers are by now substantially more familiar with the marginal spaces they inhabit than previously.

The outsiders have adapted to street life to such an extent that their orientation is toward it rather than toward trying to return to a domiciled life sustained by sufficient employment. The most honoured among outsiders is the tramp, who is willing and able to work at temporary local and migrant jobs. The popular image of the absolutely homeless, however, is different. They are seen as slothful, dependent, alcohol-prone bums, known by their shabby dress, alcoholic breath, and lethargic behaviour. What is not understood by the public is that many homeless men and women cannot work because of chronic disease or mental or physical disabilities.

The demography of homeless street people revolves around the conditions of homelessness and poverty. Lack of money leaves some people with little choice but to make a life for themselves in some big city slum. Among the factors that contribute to their displacement are ethnic stigma, linguistic inadequacy, unemployability, and lack of jobs. In combination, these factors today draw a more diverse population to the marginal space of cities than ever before. A growing proportion of middle-aged and elderly women is now found among the ranks of the homeless.

Skid rows are distinct, poverty-stricken geographic areas within cities and towns; they contain certain institutions important to the survival of their inhabitants and their peculiar culture. Today, skid rows are just one part of the marginal space of a city, since urban renewal has eliminated many former sites near the downtown core.

Wherever it is found, skid row enforces a unique daily routine on its inhabitants. The main activity is survival. Finding money, buying or otherwise acquiring food, and arranging for shelter at night are the key components. Leisure here consists of drinking, relaxing, conversing, sleeping and, for some, reading. On the whole, everyday life on skid row is numbingly tedious. Yet, as bad as it is in Canada and the United States, homelessness and its attendant poverty are worse and more widespread in many other countries.

Another deviant lifestyle is nudism. The basis for the judgment in our society that nudism is deviant was much reinforced by St. Augustine's pronouncement that nakedness stimulates lust and the sin of sexual intercourse. To counteract this point of view, also expressed in the law, nudists and naturists contend that their ways promote relaxation, sociability, and health, based on the orientation that there is nothing shameful or vulgar about any part of the body.

Nudism is practised openly in designated places and areas: in the main, clubs, parks, resorts, and beaches. Club nudism centres on the couple (married and unmarried) and to a lesser extent their children. People without partners are less welcome. A variety of outdoor activities and sports fills the days at the landed clubs, which are supplemented with off-season meetings and informal gatherings at non-landed facilities. All this appeals primarily to a middle- and upper-middle-class, largely white clientele.

Club nudists maintain a variety of moral rules. They include no nude photography without permission of the subject, no videotaping, no suggestive verbal or physical conduct, and no covering of the body other than for protection from sun and cold. These proscriptions undoubtedly help explain why some people leave nudism; most of them are likely to be single, unattached members who are unattracted to the family-oriented ethos of club nudism.

Those interested in organized nudism first try the nudist life at a park, resort, or beach. Initially, men are more willing than their wives to try this form of deviance. Nudism/naturism becomes attractive for its relaxation, sunbathing, escape from the city, appreciation of the body, and promotion of healthful activities. Research suggests, however, that nudism fails to bring the family closer together, as is sometimes claimed by its apologists.

The nude beach is noticeably more liberal than the nudist club. Over half of the beachers are single. Beach nudists flock to stretches of publicly owned sand that serve large urban populations. Seductive actions and open sexual activities are occasionally observed in this impersonal milieu, although most beachers reportedly disapprove of them. The beaches are places where unattached men and women can meet each other for fleeting sexual liaisons, which, however, are usually consummated off the beach.

Club nudism is more organized than beach nudism. Short organizational careers are possible in the former, whereas social organization in the !atter is more apt to be temporary and related to a particular threat to the beachers' lifestyle. One of the problems affecting all nudists is stigma. Tolerance of nudism is high today compared with the past, but it is still regarded as a deviant activity by society in general.

NOTES

1 This definition was abstracted by the author from various theoretical discussions of lifestyle, many of which occurred in the course of leisure studies (see Stebbins, 1994).

SUGGESTED READING

Douglas, Jack D., Paul K. Rasmussen, and Carol A. Flanagan. *The Nude Beach.* Beverly Hills, CA: Sage Publications, 1977. An extensive study done by means of participation, observation, and questionnaire interviews of a large California free beach. It is the only study of this kind to date.

Harper, Douglas A. *Good Company.* Chicago: University of Chicago Press, 1982. A young doctoral student in sociology joins the world of the tramp, rides the rails, picks fruit as a migrant labourer, sleeps in the hobo jungles, and learns first-hand about this kind of life.

Hoch, Charles and Robert A. Slayton. *New Homeless and Old: Community and the Skid Row Hotel.* Philadelphia: Temple University Press, 1989. An interview study of the lifestyles of a sample of skid row residents living in single-room hotels in Chicago.

Ilfeld, Fred, Jr. and Roger Lauer. *Social Nudism in America.* New Haven, CT: College and University Press, 1964. The two Yale University students spent several months inside five nudist parks in Southern California. Although somewhat dated now, this is still the most thorough sociological study of the nudist movement in North America.

Page, Gary S. "Social Nudism: The Social Organization of Southern Ontario Nudist Camps." In *Social Deviance in Canada,* edited by W.E. Mann, pp. 390–405. Toronto: Copp Clark. This replication of Weinberg's research on Canadian and American nudist parks is more thorough with respect to the Canadian parks.

Snow, David A. and Leon Anderson. *Down on Their Luck: A Study of Homeless Street People.* Berkeley, CA: University of California Press, 1993. This study reports data from systematic observations of the activities of street people and face-to-face interviews with a sample of them.

REFERENCES

"All Canadians Are not Created Equal," *Financial Post,* 1984, April 14:25–26.

American Association for Nude Recreation. *The Bulletin,* 1994, 43, October:8.

American Sunbathing Association. "Let Yourself Be Free: A Look at the Nudist Lifestyle." (Video) Kissimmee, FL: American Sunbathing Association, 1987.

Anderson, Nels. *The Hobo: The Sociology of Homeless Men.* Chicago: University of Chicago Press, 1923.

Baxter, Sheila. *Under the Viaduct: Homeless in Beautiful B.C.* Vancouver: New Star Books, 1991.

Begin, Patricia. "Homelessness in Canada," *Current Issue Review,* Research Branch, Library of Parliament. (Cat. no. YM32-1/89-8-1993-11E) Ottawa: Minister of Supply and Services, 1993.

Cohen, Carl I. and Jay Sokolovsky. *Old Men of the Bowery: Strategies for Survival Among the Homeless.* New York: Guilford, 1989.

Cooper, Mary A. "The Role of Religious and Nonprofit Organizations in Combating Homelessness." In *The Homeless in Contemporary Society,* edited by Richard D. Bingham, Roy E. Green, and Sammis B. White, pp. 130–149. Newbury Park, CA: Sage Publications, 1987.

Douglas, Jack D. "Saving People from the Truth: The News on the Nude Scene." In *The Sociology of Deviance,* edited by Jack D. Douglas, pp. 91–98. Boston: Allyn & Bacon, 1984.

Douglas, Jack D., Paul K. Rasmussen, and Carol A. Flanagan. *The Nude Beach.* Beverly Hills, CA: Sage Publications, 1977.

Elliot, Marta and Lauren J. Krivo. "Structural Determinants of Homelessness in the United States," *Social Problems,* 1991, 38:113–131.

Fortier, Alain. "D'où viennent nos clochards," *Interface,* 1991, 12, janvier/février:34–35.

Giffen, P.J. "The Revolving Door," *Canadian Review of Sociology and Anthropology,* 1966, 3:154–166.

Harper, Douglas A. *Good Company*. Chicago: University of Chicago Press, 1982.
Hoch, Charles and Robert A. Slayton. *New Homeless and Old: Community and the Skid Row Hotel*. Philadelphia: Temple University Press, 1989.
Ilfeld, Fred, Jr. and Roger Lauer. *Social Nudism in America*. New Haven, CT: College and University Press, 1964.
Johnson, Ann Braden. *Out of Bedlam: The Truth about Deinstitutionalization*. New York: Basic Books, 1990.
Kamphorst, Teus. "Naturism: An Interview with Bart Wijnberg," *Leisure Newsletter*, 1989, 16, 1, Summer:3–24.
Lee, Barrett A. "Homelessness." In *Encyclopedia of Sociology*, Vol. 2, edited by Edgar F. Borgatta and Marie L. Borgatta, pp. 843–848. New York: Macmillan, 1992.
Lyman, Stanford M. *The Seven Deadly Sins: Society and Evil*. (Revised and expanded ed.) Dix Hills, NJ: General Hall, 1989.
Marx, Karl. *Karl Marx: Selected Writings*. (Edited by David McLellan) Oxford: Oxford University Press, 1977.
Masters, John. "Bare Encounters with the Sun-Worshipping Set," *Maclean's*, 1981, 94, August:12–13.
Matza, David. *Becoming Deviant*. Englewood Cliffs, NJ: Prentice-Hall, 1969.
McLaughlin, MaryAnn. "Homelessness in Canada — The Report of the National Inquiry." Ottawa: Canadian Council on Social Development, 1987.
McPherson, Barry D. *Aging As a Social Process*. (2nd ed.) Toronto: Butterworths, 1990.
Mechanic, David and David A. Rochefort. "Deinstitutionalization: An Appraisal of Reform." In *Annual Review of Sociology*, Vol. 16, edited by W. Richard Scott and Richard Blake, pp. 301–327. Palo Alto, CA: Annual Reviews, Inc., 1990.
Page, Gary S. "Social Nudism: The Social Organization of Southern Ontario Nudist Camps." In *Social Deviance in Canada*, edited by W.E. Mann, pp. 390–405. Toronto: Copp Clark, 1971.
Parker, Graham. *An Introduction to Criminal Law*. (2nd ed.) Toronto: Methuen, 1983.
Parrish, Carolyn. "Life in the Sidewalk Hotel," *Canada and the World*, 1985, 51, December:23–24, 26.
O'Reilly-Fleming, Thomas. *Down and Out in Canada: Homeless Canadians*. Toronto: Canadian Scholars Press, 1993.
Shlay, Anne B. and Peter H. Rossi. "Social Science Research and Contemporary Studies of Homelessness." In *Annual Review of Sociology*, Vol. 18, edited by Judith Blake and John Hagan, pp. 129–160. Palo Alto, CA: Annual Reviews, Inc., 1992.
Smith, H. W. "A Model Test of Cross-Cultural Differences in Sexual Modesty, Embarrassment, and Self-Disclosure," *Qualitative Sociology*, 1980, 3:223–241.
Snow, David A. and Leon Anderson. "Identity Work Among the Homeless: The Verbal Construction and Avowal of Personal Identities," *American Journal of Sociology*, 1987, 92:1336–1371.
__________ *Down on Their Luck: A Study of Homeless People*. Berkeley, CA: University of California Press, 1993.
Spradley, James P. *You Own Yourself a Drunk: An Ethnography of Urban Nomads*. Boston: Little Brown, 1970.
Stebbins, Robert A. "Lifestyles as a Generic Concept in Ethnographic Research." Paper presented at the Qualitative Methods Conference, University of Waterloo, Waterloo, ON, May, 1994.

Urban History Review, 1986, February 14:278–279.
Vingerhoets, Ad and Bram Buunck. "Attitudes Towards Nudists and Public Beaches: Some Evidence of Dissonance Reduction and Gender Differences," *Journal of Leisure Research*, 1987, 19:13–21.
Wallace, Samuel E. *Skid Row As a Way of Life*. Totowa, NJ: Bedminster Press, 1965.
Ward, Jim. *The Street Is Their Home: The Hobo's Manifesto*. London: Quartet Books, 1979.
Weinberg, Martin S. "Becoming a Nudist," *Psychiatry*, 1966, 29:15–24.
__________ "Nudist Camp: Way of Life and Social Structure," *Human Organization*, 1967, 26:91–99.
Wiseman, Jacqueline P. *Stations of the Lost: The Treatment of Skid Row Alcoholics*. Englewood Cliffs, NJ: Prentice-Hall, 1970.
Wright, James D. "Address Unknown: Homelessness in Contemporary America," *Society*, 1989, 26, September/October:45–53.

10

DEVIANT BELIEF SYSTEMS

A **belief** is any proposition about the social, physical, or supernatural world that is considered true, regardless of whether there is supporting scientific evidence. Thus, some beliefs are little more than assumptions about the world, whereas others have basis in empirical fact. Some beliefs, especially those about the supernatural, are not even empirically verifiable. Whatever their level of actual correspondence in experience, all beliefs are considered real by those who hold them. Beliefs are made credible to the believer through experience or by external authority. Further, those who hold them evince an enduring commitment that affects behaviour in everyday life. Unlike opinions, beliefs have a long life, although even they can be changed or abandoned.

A **belief system** is a coherent, more or less logical interrelationship of a set of beliefs, shared by members of a particular group. A belief system is part of a group's culture. Indeed, the presence of this kind of collective representation is often taken as evidence of the existence of the group itself.

A large-scale belief system is an important component of each social institution of a society. Such a system is usually a standard, respectable, inevitably conservative way of looking on social, physical, and supernatural reality. While all forms of deviance are seen by members of society as significant aberrations from one or more social institutions (see Chapter 1), only some forms revolve around alternative belief systems. Three of the latter are covered in this chapter: deviant religion, science, and politics. At the group level of analysis, these belief systems serve as the ideational foundation for sects and cults, occult groups, and extreme political organizations.

Since all belief systems change over time, it is instructive to inquire whether deviations from the established, institutionalized systems are *reactionary* or *radical*. Is the deviant system a generally unacceptable throwback to some outmoded pattern of belief, or does it contain new beliefs which have rarely been considered or beliefs which have been rejected as too extreme or bizarre? Reactionary and radical positions are evident in the three deviant systems discussed in this chapter.

RELIGION

Many sociologists still consider Yinger's (1970:256–280) sixfold typology and continuum established over 25 years ago a valid tool for analyzing organized religion (Weckman, 1987). Yinger's first type is the **universal church**, a historical form that no longer exists today (e.g., the Roman Catholic Church of the thirteenth century). Another is the **ecclesia**, or state church (e.g., Anglicanism in Britain, Catholicism in Italy). More familiar to Canadians are the various **denominations**, such as United Church, Presbyterianism, Lutheranism, and Catholicism (in Canada). All these systems fall within the realm of institutionalized religion in the societies where they exist. To be sure, there are liberal and conservative variants of each that may be regarded with suspicion by those outside them. But by and large, these variations are not sufficiently different to warrant the label of deviant religion.

Sects and cults, however, *are* deviant. Following Yinger's (1970:266) typology, an **established sect** differs only in degree from a **pure sect**. The former "is somewhat more inclusive, less alienated, and more structured than the pure sect, and therefore closer to the denominations." The Amish, Mormons, and Hutterites are examples of established sects. Both types of sect develop rather rigid, usually reactionary, doctrines that leave little room for compromise or tolerance of religious difference in the society. The appointment of leaders, their acts of leading, and the religious practices they establish are more formal in the established sect than in the pure sect. In both instances, though, leaders are lay members rather than trained specialists. Finally, pure sects are more likely to gain their adherents through religious conversion than are their established counterparts, where birth into a family of adherents is often the basis for membership.

Stark and Bainbridge (1981) describe sects as schisms from mainline faiths, whereas **cults** are innovations. Bromley and Shupe (1981:23–24) describe them as small, short-lived, religiously iconoclastic groups. A cult may succeed and eventually go on to become a sect, denomination, and even a world religion. Hinduism, Islam, and Christianity all began as cults. Or, more commonly, the cult fails and disappears. Bromley and Shupe hold that

> a cult is the starting point of every religion. Its organization is extremely simple. There is no bureaucracy or priesthood. In fact, there is barely any structure at all except for the single charismatic leader and his or her small band of devoted followers. Jesus and his twelve disciples offer a classic example of a cult. Nor are there scriptures, not only because the cult rejects all or part of society's dominant religious traditions but also

> because it is simultaneously engaged in the act of creating its own traditions out of which later generations will record "gospel" truths. The cult is thus nonconformist for two reasons. First, it struggles to start a radically new religious tradition, and, second, it exists in tension and conflict with what it regards as a corrupt, troubled world.

Among the active cults in North America today are the Unification Church, ("Moonies"), Children of God, Hare Krishna Movement, Church of Scientology, Divine Light Mission, and the Satanist groups. Perhaps the most celebrated cult in recent times was David Koresh's wing of the Branch Davidians, whose standoff in 1993 in Waco, Texas with 200 law enforcement officers made international headlines.

Two Cults

What is aberrant about deviant religion? To help us find an answer, we shall examine two cults, or new religions, as illustrations of the kinds of religious differences that society labels deviant. Both are radical, inasmuch as both bring dramatically new elements to the contemporary religious scene in North America.

The first to be considered is the Church of Scientology. It was founded in the United States in 1951 by L. Ron Hubbard, following the publication of his book *Dianetics: The Modern Science of Mental Health.* The book describes a system known as "processing" by means of which converts strive to erase the "engrams", the scars of bad experiences, that come from the soul and the psyche. The object of the dianetics system is to gain clear-thinking happiness in this life and eventual freedom from death of the "thetan", or soul. Engrams, according to Hubbard, are the cause of all aberrations in human behaviour.

Processing is aided by an "auditor" who helps the convert locate and deal with engrams. Psychological conditioning and discussion are the means by which this is achieved. The auditor is equipped with an "E-Meter" or psychogalvanometer (lie detector) to help him or her and the convert locate the engrams. During processing, the convert relives the traumatic events in his or her present and past life, thereby gaining freedom from them and their negative effects. The result is improved self-understanding, which is believed to increase awareness of basic capabilities and enable greater control of one's environment.

The Church of Scientology is a considerable success; Melton (1992:196) reports that in 1988 it had approximately 7 000 000 members throughout the world, organized in 600 churches, missions, and groups. Members are defined by the Church as those who have received training. How many of these people define themselves as Scientologists is unknown.

The Church of Scientology has been mired in controversy for years. Its international headquarters is located in Los Angeles. From here it has defended itself since 1958 against the Internal Revenue Service, the taxation branch of the Government of the United States, over charges that it is not a church and therefore not tax exempt. (Sociologists have made similar charges; cf. Barker, 1986:333.) It has also been embroiled in extensive litigation with other branches of the same government, as well as with branches of governments in Australia and Canada. Melton (1992:197) briefly reviews several exposés of the Church written either by unaffiliated writers or by former members. Yet, when not at the front defending itself against these enemies, the Church manages to grow and develop its programs. At present, one of its most formidable problems is overcoming its unsavory image.

The International Society for Krishna Consciousness, known as the Hare Krishna Movement, is an Eastern religion that has taken root in North America and elsewhere in the Western world, albeit in considerably modified form. Its adepts are conspicuous on city streets where, with heads shaven (except for a tuft of hair), wearing traditional clothing, and chanting their mantra, they solicit money for the religion. The Movement was founded in New York in 1965 by his Divine Grace A. C. Bhaktivedanta, Swami Prabhupada. The Hare Krishnas are followers of the Vaisnava tradition of the Hindu religion. Lord Krishna is believed to be the ultimate manifestation of the creator god, Brahman, who is the central godhead figure in all forms of Hinduism. Down through the centuries the belief became established that chanting, singing, and dancing are the best ways to rid the soul of ignorance and bad karma (predestined failure) and thereby to gain salvation. Chanting, singing, and dancing are seen as direct expressions of love for Lord Krishna.

When Swami Prabhupada brought the Vaisnava tradition to the United States in the 1960s, the atmosphere generated by the counterculture of the time was ripe for his message, according to Stoner and Parke (1977:44–45); Melton, 1992:234). The swami taught that the world is in an inevitable process of decline, which, however, will not culminate for nearly a half million years. The singing and dancing of the Hare Krishnas will help them avoid the decline. In the end, Lord Krishna will return to Earth and save his devotees; the rest of humanity will be destroyed.

Unlike the practice in India, where followers are born, North American Hare Krishnas are recruited from the general population. They follow a strict spiritual life in the centres and special farms of the International Society for Krishna Consciousness (ISKCON) of which there are nine in Canada and several in cities and towns around the world (*Back to Godhead*, 1982:30–31). Food is an important part of the Hare Krishna credo, and a Krishna vegetarian restaurant or two is usually established in larger cities.

By chanting the *maha-mantra* — Hare Krishna, Hare Krishna, Krishna Krishna, Hare Hare/Hare Rama, Hare Rama, Rama Rama, Hare Hare — the Krishnas hope to reach the mature stage of the love of God, where believers and God come together. Other principles of the religion are as follows:

1. By sincerely cultivating a bona fide spiritual science, we can be free from anxiety and come to a state of pure, unending, blissful consciousness.
2. We are not our bodies but eternal spirit souls, part and parcel of God (Krishna). As such we are all brothers and sisters, and Krishna is ultimately our common father.

3 Krishna is the eternal, all-knowing, omnipresent, all-powerful, and all-attractive personality of the Godhead.
4 The absolute truth is contained in all the great scriptures of the world. However, the *Bhagavadgita* is the literal record of God's actual words.
5 We should learn Vedic knowledge from a genuine spiritual master.
6 Before we eat, we should offer to the Lord the food that sustains us. Then the offering becomes Krishna and purifies us.
7 We should perform all our actions as offerings to Krishna and do nothing for our own sense of gratification.

Cult Conversion

To speak of a religious career for members of state churches and denominations is meaningless. A person is either born into one of these religions or joins it at some later point in life. As a practising member, he or she lives or tries to live by its principles while enacting a variety of secular roles. There is ordinarily little sense of continuity in the institutionalized religious roles; that is, there is little sense of turning point, career contingency, or status passage.

Not so with sect and cult involvements. People become members of a sect or cult, and hence religious deviants through the process of conversion. This is a major turning point in their lives. Subsequently, they may become disenchanted and renounce the cult: another turning point. Joining a sect or a cult is a deliberate act in which one embraces a new religious commitment. John Lofland (1981:31–62) offers a model of conversion composed of three predisposing conditions (tension, problem-solving perspective, religious seeking) and four situational contingencies (turning point, cult-affective bonds, extracult-affective bonds, intensive interaction).

Predisposing Conditions Before they get in touch with a religious group, pre-converts must experience the predisposing conditions:

1 Acute and enduring tension in the form of strain, frustration, or deprivation develops in response to an imagined ideal state of affairs in life, as opposed to current circumstances. Tension could arise in almost any segment of a person's life. The individual might be lonely and fearful somewhere in a large city or be drained by the oppressiveness of his or her job.
2 Pre-converts have a special problem-solving perspective with which they handle this tension; it is a religious, rather than a political or psychiatric, perspective. Religious meaning is therefore imposed on the events of everyday life. For pre-converts, conventional religious solutions failed to solve the tension.
3 Accordingly, they become seekers, people in search of solutions to their problems, solutions which are more radical than institutionalized religion can offer.

Without contact with the religious group, no conversion can occur.

Situational Contingencies Before direct contact with the cult or sect can lead to successful conversion of individuals predisposed toward it, they must pass through the four situational contingencies:

1. When they make contact with the group, pre-converts are at or close to a major turning point in their lives, such as loss of a job, graduation from college, or relocation to another part of the country. Individuals at a turning point are aware of the need to do something with their lives and of the relevant opportunities that make one action or another possible.
2. Contact with the sect or cult also leads to the development of cult-affective bonds; such bonds imbue the contact with a personal touch. Positive emotional relationships with existing members help swing the pre-convert's allegiance toward the group.
3. Meanwhile, there are either no influential extracult-affective bonds (say, because the pre-convert recently migrated), or bonds of this sort are with persons who have a similar religious interest.
4. Eventually, total conversion occurs, following a period of intensive interaction between the pre-convert and core members of the sect or cult.

Through this sequence, pre-converts acquire the ideological, intellectual, ritualistic, and experiential components of commitment, a process which transforms them into true converts.

The conversation process may appear to suggest that a career in deviant religion is largely a social psychological process involving the pre-convert and his or her cult. In harmony with this conclusion, Galanter (1989) and Hexham and his colleagues (1988:1481) have found considerable evidence that joining a cult depends on personal choice. But people also seek cult memberships because they are pushed, so to speak, by certain perceived shortcomings of the society in which they live (Barker, 1986:336–337). Two conditions encouraging them to seek an alternative spiritual outlet are their weak ties to the religion of their parents or dissatisfaction with that religion (Melton, 1992:12). Another condition is the impersonality of modern, urban society, which can be counteracted by the strong sense of belonging that comes with membership in a small and distinct group.

Profile of Religious Deviants

Melton and Moore (1982:29–35) write that the new religions of today are an urban phenomenon. The Hare Krishna Movement got its North American start in New York. L. Ron Hubbard's founding church was in Washington, DC, though he later moved its headquarters to Los Angeles. The Canadian outlets for these religions are, with the exception of the Krishna farms, found entirely in medium-sized and large cities.

Members of the cults are predominantly white, educated, middle- and upper-middle-class people. They are generally young (between 18 and 28 years of age) and unmarried. They are at a stage in life where many crucial, long-range decisions are being made about marriage, religion, and occupational career. They are, in the language of the conversion model, likely to be facing some sort of acute tension along these lines and inclined to seek a religious solution to that tension. In this connection, Melton and Moore (1982:30) note that the cults draw members from all established religions in proportion to the presence of those religions in the population. Cult members' commitment to the established religions is low or nominal; many also come from families that are non-religious.

Tolerance of Religious Deviance

It was argued in Chapter 1 that religious deviance is, at bottom, a combined form of deviance as leisure and deviance as adjustment. Kelly (1987:163–165) concludes that all religion is fundamentally a leisure activity. It is, he points out, *one* possible use of discretionary time and resources. Moreover, it can be argued that engaging in religious practices helps regenerate those who follow them. That is, practising religion may help reduce stress and renew dedication to the pursuit of the individual's secular roles. Other forms of leisure often serve the same purpose. Further, religious contemplation may be relaxing or leisurely for those who do the contemplating. Finally, normal religion may be conceived of as a basis for re-evaluation of the self and for setting a course toward the realization of personal potential. The adjustive aspects of religion in general and of deviant religion in particular are evident here, as well as in the earlier discussion of conversion.

Turning to the tolerable aspect of religious deviance, it should be noted that in both Canada and the United States freedom of religious thought and practice is guaranteed (so long as it does not violate other laws). Religious deviance, in our framework, is legitimate deviance. But the existence of the anti-cult movement is evidence that some people in North America are threatened by the new religions and have taken measures to try to control if not eliminate them. Thus, Stephen Kent (1990) explains in detail that we are now witnessing (often acrimonious) negotiations in which pro-cult and anti-cult camps attempt to portray the new religions as tolerably deviant or different on the one hand, or intolerably deviant or criminal on the other.

The anti-cult movement got its start with parents of young converts, disillusioned ex-converts, and some clergy (Shupe and Bromley, 1980). They constituted a loosely organized interest group whose purpose was to disseminate information about the "evils" of the cults, to offer advice and counselling to converts and their parents, and to lobby government for controls on cult activities. Whatever their specific approach to the cult "problem", all anti-cultists believe that the new religions recruit their members by "brainwashing" them, that is, by controlling their minds (Shupe and Bromley, 1980:29–31). The individual's free will is believed to be subverted by means of subtle techniques to the point where he or she is compliant and submissive to the demands of the cult leaders.

The first anti-cult organization was founded in the United States in 1971 in response to the perceived excesses of the Children of God cult (Shupe and Bromley, 1980:89). Although it grew throughout the 1970s, the movement gained most of its power, influence, and adherents following the Jonestown mass suicide in Guyana in 1978.[1] It was during this period that anti-cult organizations also began to take root in Canada; examples are the Toronto-based Committee on Mind Abuse (Hexham et al., 1988:1481) and the Cult Awareness Network (CAN). Yet despite the moral entrepreneurial-style pressures from the anti-cult movement for investigation into and legislation against the new religions, cults continue to operate and recruit ever larger numbers of members throughout North America:

> While the membership in various groups fluctuates year by year, the number of alternative religions and of people involved in them continues steadily to grow. Many former members retain a positive appraisal of the group(s) with which they were affiliated and form a base of positive support in the larger culture. In fact, the anti-cult movement seems to have doomed itself to failure in that it set itself the task of reversing a major trend in American society toward radical religious diversity (Melton, 1992:355).

Part of the problem of the anti-cultists appears to lie in their credibility. Most sociologists reject as false the proposition that the cults brainwash their converts (Barker, 1986:335; Petranek, 1988). The sociological position is indirectly supported by the testimony of those who have left the cults of their own accord, as opposed to being kidnapped and/or "deprogrammed" (counterbrainwashed) by the anti-cultists. The former are not so condemning (see Beckford, 1985:156).

The anti-cult movement has succeeded in constructing a negative image of the new religions which, as we have seen, has not stemmed the growth in the overall number of members. Obviously the issue is complicated and in need of further study (Hall, 1990:87). Further, the extent to which anti-cultists have been successful with their deprogramming techniques may only reflect the weakness or ineffectiveness of the original brainwashing. Nevertheless, their claimed successes have enabled them to argue that cult conversions are, in fact, superficial (Shupe and Bromley, 1980). More recently, the propensity for joining cults has been medicalized (e.g., American Psychiatric Association, 1989). Medicalization of the problem of the convert has bestowed an aura of respectability on the anti-cult effort (Robbins and Anthony, 1982), and also may be working to discredit the new religions in the minds of some potential converts. Still, Marc Galanter (1989), himself a psychiatrist, failed to find an exceptional number of psychologically troubled people among cult members.

SCIENCE

Deviation from the institution of science usually means acceptance of some aspect of the occult that challenges a regular scientific paradigm (Ben-Yehuda, 1985:114–115). Although not related etymologically (the words come from different Latin roots), the cults and the occult are frequently intertwined today, as they were in the past when religion and magic went hand in hand. The dividing line between science, religion, and the occult is sometimes vague, a situation that has spawned considerable disagreement over the true nature of the occult. As Truzzi (1974:245) put it: "In many ways, the occult is a residual category, a wastebasket, for knowledge claims that are deviant in some way, that do not fit the established claims of science or religion."

One distinguishing aspect of the occult is its tendency to focus on concealed or secret phenomena while making the claim that such phenomena are real and valid. The claim that something is real and valid, but that only one or a few special people are aware of it, challenges the public validation procedures of science. Hence the categorization of the occult as deviant science. Both science and the occult strive to identify and validate real phenomena, but the latter departs from the former in its procedures.

Another distinguishing aspect of the occult is its focus on *anomalous* things or events. According to Truzzi (1974:246),

> an anomalous object consists of the existence (or claimed existence) of some thing or event which is somehow a deviation from the usual, credible order of things; e.g., the sighting of an abominable snowman, a levitated fakir floating in the air, or a giant sea serpent. An anomalous process, however, can consist of quite ordinary things or events in some extraordinary conjunction. Thus an occultist may believe that a pin placed in a wax image will lead to the death of someone.

What is anomalous and what is not depends, in short, on how we define that which is abnormal.

Our interest here is in secret belief systems that deviate from regular science and thereby challenge it. As Ben-Yehuda (1985: Ch. 5) notes, there are also people who violate the norms of science by forging data or stealing others' ideas, for example. Some scientists espouse what the scientific establishment considers a bizarre hypothesis or methodology, but are otherwise respectable practitioners of their profession. In all these cases we are speaking of deviants *in* science (Bechtel and Pearson, 1985) rather than of deviants *from* science, the subject of this chapter. And even one or two deviants from science would fail to constitute deviant science as defined here, for they would not have generated a large-scale belief system shared by many other people. In common sense terms, we would likely identify the lone deviant from science as someone who is mentally disordered (a residual deviant). But if that person shared a set of strange beliefs about the natural world with others, then he or she would be identified by some sort of collective label as one of them.

Types of Occultism

Truzzi (1972) identified five areas of the occult which he believed were particularly salient in the United States in the early 1970s and which, together, constituted a modern revival of interest in occult phenomena that is still going on (Ben-Yehuda, 1985:74–76). With some modifications to Truzzi's typology, the five are divination, witchcraft-Satanism, extrasensory perception, Eastern religious thought, and a residual category of scientifically unexplained individual phenomena that are not part of any belief system. All five are still in vogue in the mid-1990s, and all have found adherents in Canada as well as the United States.

Divination Divination is the practice of trying either to foretell the future or to discover hidden knowledge. It is sometimes done by interpreting omens or portents (e.g., the flight of birds, a clap of thunder) or by making use of the psychical properties of a diviner. In the latter case, the diviner is assumed to have the cooperation of certain supernatural powers. Among the forms of divination found in Canadian society are astrology, palm reading, crystal gazing, spiritualism, and reading tarot cards. In all these, a diviner, who is an occult expert, is needed to mediate between the client and the system of knowledge in order to foretell the future or to discover hidden knowledge.

Astrology is the practice of foretelling the future by means of a theory about the positions of the stars and their supposed influences on human affairs and terrestrial events. This system of thought has ancient roots, but is now scientifically discredited. It is a reactionary form of scientific deviance, a return to an earlier belief system.

Truzzi (1972) identifies three levels of involvement with astrology. The first is most superficial. Here we find the tens of thousands of people who read their horoscope in the daily newspaper or one of the monthly astrological periodicals, or who use one of the telephone services now available. For many of them, their horoscopes and those of others make interesting subjects of casual conversation. That is, astrology is a genre of entertainment rather than a serious, valid guide to the future. The proportion of true believers is relatively small here. At the second level are those who have enough knowledge of the "mechanics" of astrology to seek a special casting of their personal horoscope. They visit a consulting astrologer or request a computer analysis of their horoscope. Those in the second level are believers. The same may be said for those at the third level. They not only cast their own horoscopes from their considerable knowledge of astrology, but also delve deeply into the theory itself to achieve a profound view of the universe and their place within it.

Palm reading and crystal gazing are often combined in the work of the fortuneteller who, these days, is more likely to go by the title of "reader" or "adviser". Tatro (1974) writes that people of all ages, both sexes, many religious backgrounds, and every race enter fortunetelling. Though started by the Rom (gypsies), it is no longer their exclusive domain. By and large, fortunetellers come from lower-class families and, finding upward mobility blocked, choose to adapt to their anomic situation by innovating in this unusual way.

According to Heeren and Mason (1981:173), the interaction between reader and client progresses through three types of conversation. The first centres on such everyday matters as the weather, eating habits, and social problems of the day. Once the reader has established rapport with the client, he or she asks a set of questions designed to learn about the client's personality and personal background. In the third type of conversation, the reader expresses his or her vision of or insights into the client, followed by a recommended course of action.

The reader progresses as far as possible through a series of routines with each client (Boles et al., 1983). The backstage preparational routines and the corresponding frontstage client-oriented routines are summarized in Viewpoint 10.1,

VIEWPOINT 10.1

ROUTINES, DEFINITIONS, AND ALIGNMENTS IN FORTUNETELLING

Backstage Routines	Frontstage Definitions	Client Alignments
1 Gleaning [in the outer office]: Assistant gets whatever information possible on client; room sometimes bugged.	1 The reader is busy: Client waits to see reader and chats with others.	
2 Sizing up client: Delivers opening spiel; assesses prospects for return visit.	2 The reader can help: Client meets reader, who then engages in conversation and prayer.	1 Unwitting moves: Client employs religious problem-solving perspective; relatively unguarded in approaching reader for action or remedy.
3 Convincing client: Torn pellet or use of information gathered in waiting room.	3 The reader has powers: Client is amazed at how reader knows details of personal life.	2 Uncovering moves: Client may express doubt, test and quiz reader.
4 Casing trouble: Deciphering the problem that brought client; sensing how much money reader can charge.	4 The client has a problem: Client receives a character reading amidst traditional accoutrements — crystal ball, cards, etc.	
5 Demonstrating trouble: Reader creates evidence that client is "hexed"; dying chicken, snake in egg, strong reliance on trick hardware.	5 The problem is occult and severe: Client realizes real reason he is having so much trouble; he is polluted, his luck is crossed.	
6 Holding client down: Sliding fees arranged and reader instructs and coaches client on need to return; gives him expendable hardware accounts for failure.	6 The work is helping: Client learns that psychic work costs and takes time; hardware can't be completely consumed and still be effective; bishops and reader working for him in his absence.	3 Control moves: Client elects to have work done; may keep reader accountable; interprets events as confirming reader's powers.

Source: Jacqueline Boles, Phillip Davis, and Charlotte Tatro, "False Pretense and Deviant Exploitation: Fortunetelling as a Con," *Deviant Behavior,* 1983, 4:375–394. By permission.

along with the client's adjustment to each frontstage routine. By employing these routines, the reader hopes to convert the client to his or her definition of the latter's problems and the recommended procedure for solving them. Still, some clients refuse to accept the reader's authority, which means that the entire set of routines may not be completed with them.

For both the fortuneteller, who claims to reveal hidden knowledge about a client's past, present, or future, and the astrologer, divination constitutes a deviant occupation. Money is exchanged for services rendered. As for the clients who seek these services with serious expectations, theirs is a form of deviant adjustment to the failure, as they see it, of scientifically guided, conventional practitioners to solve their problems.

Spiritualism is a good example of a combination of occult and religious (cultistic) elements. Melton (1992:118) defines spiritualism as "a religion based upon the belief that mediumship, the ability demonstrated by a few select persons to contact the world of spirits [of the dead], proves that the individual survives bodily death." It is believed that, through mediums, communication can be made with dead ancestors, friends, and relatives by "rapping", or pounding on a table. Spiritualists estimate that there are between 800 and 1000 believers in Canada (Townsend, 1988).

The fifth type of divination considered here is reading tarot cards. It, too, is a reactionary belief system, since its origin is traced to fifteenth-century Europe and even as far back as ancient Egypt. There are various decks of tarot cards. In the deck known as the higher arcana, each of the 22 cards bears symbols and drawings, and each may be combined with the others. The symbols and drawings represent laws and lessons. There is also a larger deck of 40, 52, or 56 cards called the lower arcana. In their various suits, the cards of the lower arcana represent ideas, problems, emotions and values, and everyday affairs. By combining cards, it is believed, people can discover attitudes, problems, and lessons of their present and future life. People can learn to read the cards for themselves and their friends, although expert readers are also available (see Zurowski, 1986).

Witchcraft-Satanism In Truzzi's (1972) view, modern witchcraft (which is different from earlier forms) and Satanism are two separate belief systems. Modern witches do not ordinarily view their beliefs and practices as heretical offshoots of Christianity, whereas Satanists, as worshippers of the Judeo-Christian Devil, have precisely this outlook.

The major distinction in witchcraft is that between white and black magic. The former involves the use of mystical magic (as opposed to entertainment magic (Stebbins, 1993:1–4) for socially beneficial ends. The latter uses the same form of magic to reach malevolent ends. The techniques by which either kind of goal is achieved are largely the same. They include positive thinking and intuition — two psychic powers — in combination with spells, formulas, and symbolism derived from the tradition of mystical magic as it has come down to the present (Scott, 1983:30–34). Modern witches then use this magic to make their wills powerful, which they do, in part, by learning to focus and project their consciousness. With a focused will, they call on various entities from the spiritual realm (archangels, nature spirits, demons, and deities such as Diana and Isis), who represent the power of the goddess. According to Moody (1971) this system is based on the belief that all elements in the...

> natural world are animate, have unique and distinct vibrations that influence the way they relate to other natural phenomena. It is the manipulation and the modification of these vibrations, forces, or powers, that is the basis of all magic.

Some witches operate individually; others join small groups called "covens", which meet semimonthly.[2] Most witches, who incidentally may be men or women, are members of a coven.

Although Truzzi pairs Satanism and witchcraft in the same type, most contemporary observers identify the former as a religious cult, as we did earlier in this chapter. Through their worship of the Christian Devil, Satanists mock various Christian forms and rituals, particularly those of Roman Catholicism (e.g., the Black Mass) (Melton, 1992:108–117). Satanists are often organized in short-lived groups of teenagers and young adults. Perhaps 1000 members claim adherence to Anton LaVey's Church of Satan. A third set of Satanists subscribes to the New Satanism, an offshoot of LaVey's Church that is centred on child abuse. Not surprisingly, sociologists have been able to document a Satanism scare and a corresponding anti-Satanist movement (Richardson et al., 1991).

Extrasensory Perception Extrasensory perception (ESP) is perception claimed to operate without the use of the senses of sight, smell, touch, taste, and hearing. It takes four forms. **Clairvoyance** is the ability to know objects and real events by means other than use of the senses. It is closely related to **precognition**, knowledge of — not just speculation about — future occurrences. Both are exemplified by the divination practices just considered. **Psychokinesis** is the ability to influence the movement of objects by willing them to move. Spoon bending is an entertaining example. **Telepathy**, or mind reading, refers to thought transference from one person to another. It is believed by some members of the audience to explain the magical wonders of the mentalists.

The term "extrasensory perception" was coined by J.B. and Louisa Rhine. These two psychologists also founded the field of parapsychology, the branch of psychology that investigates this phenomenon, in the 1930s. J.B. Rhine popularized his speciality during the 1960s and early 1970s with such books as *Reach of the Mind* (1961) and *Progress in Parapsychology* (1972). Nonetheless, study of the psi — that which relates to and is concerned with parapsychological or psychic events or powers — has always been regarded as, at best, a marginal branch of the science of psychology. The failure to replicate, the use of inadequate experimental controls, and other weaknesses have contributed to this status within the profession. "More important," says Cornell (1984:30),

> ...parapsychologists and proponents of the paranormal are hard pressed to produce any incontrovertible examples of their phenomena. This is true despite efforts by devoted and often quite sincere researchers as well as attempts to link parapsychological claims with quantum mechanics to explain the apparent leaps over the constraints of time and space.... While parapsychologists have failed to prove their case, the community of skeptics has provided ample evidence of how supposed supernatural... phenomena can be explained as the result of sloppy experimental procedures, misinterpretation, or ignorance of data and pure trickery.

People who believe in paranormal phenomena have difficulty recognizing that some events in everyday life occur by chance rather than by design.

Eastern Religious Thought In countries such as Canada, where established religion and science have worked out an ideological accommodation, religious belief systems that are seen as openly questioning this arrangement are considered deviant, albeit tolerably so. Thus, although it has been argued that Buddhist ideas are consistent with science (Swearer, 1987:399), Eastern religious thought is generally held to be anti-scientific. Moreover, the Eastern religions are characterized by a strong teacher orientation (Melton, 1978:308; Smithers, 1987:33–36). The key to their structure is the guru (known by different names in different groups), who possesses mystic truth and teaches the techniques leading to its acquisition. In broadest terms, these are yoga, dancing, meditation, study, and community with other believers.

An Eastern religion which has attracted considerable attention in North America since the 1960s is Zen Buddhism, an offshoot of mainstream Buddhism that developed in China in the sixth century A.D. It is the mystical school of Buddhism, revolving around the practice of the art of zazen, which is a form of meditation. Zazen is conducted in a quiet chamber in accordance with the stipulation that the meditator eat and drink in moderation. There he or she sits cross-legged on a small round pillow, which is itself placed on a larger, thick pillow. It is necessary to maintain a strictly upright position, tongue against the palate, lips and teeth firmly closed, and eyes continually open. In this state, the meditator regulates breathing and tries to achieve the full and perfect equilibrium of the organism. This is said to be accomplished by freeing oneself of all attachments and desires. One must not think of good or evil, right or wrong, but rather maintain the flow of mind, will, and consciousness. The end result, if all procedures are properly followed, is reaching the Dharma gate of great rest and joy.

Soto Zen is a Western expression of Zen practice that was founded in California and has since spread to Canada (Kawamura, 1988:293). Blends of Zen, Confucianism, and Taoism exist in Canada as well. They rest on meditation and parapsychological processes.

Residual Occult Phenomena Truzzi (1972:18) placed a variety of people and occurrences in the residual category of scientifically unexplained individual phenomena that are not part of a belief system such as those discussed in the preceding paragraphs. These phenomena include prophets, strange monsters (sea and lake serpents, werewolves, vampires), unidentified flying objects (UFOs), dowsers, or people who witch water (Vogt and Hyman, 1979), and many others. Canada has its share of such phenomena, including Ogopogo, the monster of Okanagan Lake in British Columbia, and Sasquatch, the "abominable snowman" of the same province. Memphré is believed to have found a home in Southeastern Québec in the depths of Lac Memphrémagog, on whose shores you will find the offices of an organization devoted to the study of underwater monsters, the International Dragontology Society.

In the 1970s, Melton (1978) identified 14 formally organized religious cults centred on UFOs, with further mention of numerous informal groups found in the metropolitan areas of the United States. These groups are, however, fluid and ephemeral, and in the early 1980s were starting to decline in number (Ellwood, 1987:717). Balch and Taylor (1977) studied a formally organized group in Oregon: a middle-aged man and woman who called themselves Bo and Peep offered their followers eternal life in the "literal heavens" if they would abandon their friends, families, jobs, and material possessions. If they could then overcome all their human emotions and worldly attachments, they would be taken to heaven in a UFO by means of a process called "Human Individual Metamorphosis". Each follower who went to heaven in this conveyance would become a new creature with an indestructible body. Cults abo.t and individual believers in UFOs exist in Canada as well (see Gavrakis and Bocquet, 1983).

Tolerance of Deviant Science

Deviant science, that is, belief in the occult, is yet another form of legitimate deviance in Canada and the United States. We are free to believe what we wish. And, as Table 10.1 indicates, we do just that.

As for tolerance, a Canadian Press release (*Calgary Herald,* 1979:B12) indicates that some observers of and practitioners in the occult perceive a somewhat heightened acceptance of their belief systems. Certainly, there is evidence that some forms of the occult are quite publicly accessible; practitioners may be found listed in the yellow pages of metropolitan telephone books under the headings "psychics", "psychic consultants", "psychic science practitioners". They are legally organized in such associations as the Academy of Psychic Arts and Sciences, Awareness Research Foundation, Association for Research and Enlightenment, and B.C. Society for Skeptical Inquiry. Most general bookstores have a section devoted to the occult, not to mention the specialized retailers of this literature.

Still, where clients are served in exchange for money, the possibility and actuality of fraud exist. In a rare instance of official action, in 1985 the Metropolitan Toronto police laid 90 charges of fraud or attempted fraud against 36 fortunetellers (*The Sunday Star,* 1986:A1, A8). Some professional entertainment magicians contend that in their midst are those who claim to have occult powers, but are mixing, for personal profit, some of the standard techniques of entertainment magic with a few shrewd observations of human psychology (Stebbins, 1993:14). How the threat of fraud affects the general level of public tolerance has yet to be determined.

TABLE 10.1 PERCENTAGE OF CANADIANS WHO BELIEVE IN SELECTED OCCULT PHENOMENA

Phenomenon	Percentage of Believers	Source
UFOs	46	*Gallup Report* (1989a)
Devil	30	*Gallup Report* (1989b)
Loch Ness Monster	13	*Gallup Report* (1989b)
Witches	11	*Gallup Report* (1989b)
Astrology	35	Bibby (1990:74)
Psychic powers	63	Bibby (1990:74)
Communication with the dead	22	Bibby (1990:74)

POLITICS

What constitutes political deviance must be defined with reference to the established political system in a given country at a given time. On the one hand, political reactionism in English Canada might include such elements as loyalty to the British Empire, allegiance to the nineteenth-century laissez faire economic liberalism of Edmund Burke, or the embracement of the social Darwinist policies of Aryan superiority. On the other hand, political radicalism in either English or French Canada might include proposals for a more or less completely socialized economy, a Marxist-style government of proletarian rule, or a society modelled on anarchism. Under the Constitution Act, 1982, these belief systems are legal, as is the right to assemble peacefully to discuss and promote them.

Sedition, however, is illegal: one may not speak, write, or act against the government or seek to overthrow it by *unlawful* means. A reactionary or radical political belief system that hopes to gain ascendancy through the normal channels of democracy is not seditious. In a word, it is tolerably deviant. Moreover, all this must be seen against a background of established Canadian conservatism and liberalism, the two political belief systems that generally accept the status quo, although each has a different blueprint on how to improve it.

Reactionism

A variety of contemporary political groups would seem to be tolerably deviant in a reactionary sense when viewed by the majority of Canadians. These include the separatist groups in Newfoundland and the West, to the extent that they espouse a return to an earlier stage in their histories when they were autonomous political entities. Ethnic supremacist groups, where they have a political platform, also fall in this category. Among them are the Aryan Nations in Alberta; the Ku Klux Klan in Ontario, Alberta, and British Columbia; and the anti-French Alliance for the Preservation of English in Canada.

Reactionism is the ideology of the radical right, the extreme right wing in politics. According to Stanley Barrett (1987:4–12), the right wing has been growing in reaction to the Western world's drift toward liberalism since World War II. That is, today's right wing finds most distasteful the humanitarian accommodations that Western societies have made in trying to solve capitalism's most intractable problem: inequality, particularly as expressed in poverty, ethnic and gender discrimination, and unequal access to education. Accordingly, the ideology of the far right consists of strains of racism and anti-Semitism. The former is based on the extreme view that the Christian religion defines blacks and other non-white peoples as inferior, indeed, subhuman. This point of view justifies dividing the world's population into two great classes: the privileged and the underprivileged. As for the Jews, those on the radical right say that Christianity identifies them as children of the Devil.

Bruce (1989) writes that the Christian Right is now losing ground in the United States, in the wake of effective countercampaigns by various liberal organizations.

President Clinton's strong electoral showing in 1992 could be interpreted as further evidence of this trend. In Canada, the picture is hazier. On the one hand, Canada has always been more liberal than its southern neighbour (Goldberg and Mercer, 1986:14); as a result, the far right has had much less ground in which to take root. On the other hand, the decline in 1993 of the federal Progressive Conservative Party and the concomitant rise of the Reform Party suggest that a Canadian right wing clearly exists in the mid-1990s, even if, on a national scale, it is a minority position. Still, this position is not generally that of the extreme right, but that of what Barrett (1989:9–10) calls the "fringe right". Members of the fringe right fear socialism, while opposing Third World immigration, foreign aid, homosexual rights, the liberalization of sexual norms, and so on. But they stop short of being reactionary, inasmuch as they eschew use of physical violence and reject accusations that they are fascist, racist, or anti-Semitic.

Radicalism

In our discussion of radical political deviance, we could consider such expressions as the Green Party or the *Parti Québécois* (as viewed in 1994 in Québec). However, the Communist Party of Canada is the longest-lived Canadian radical political group and has been the object of the greatest amount of analysis,[3] and so it will serve as our example. The party was founded in Guelph, Ontario in 1921, and became a legal party in 1924, following the repeal of the War Measures Act, which was in force during World War I. Over its history, the party has undergone a number of name changes in response to the stigma of communism in Canada and to acts of official harassment that are now impossible because of changes in the Criminal Code. Communists have occasionally won seats on municipal bodies. They have won provincial seats only three times (in Manitoba in 1936 and Ontario in 1943) and a federal seat only once. Since 1954, the party has succeeded only at the aldermanic level in Winnipeg and Vancouver.

Marchak (1988:12) describes some of the differences between socialism and communism:

> Communism within Canada has been closely associated with an international communist movement. As an ideological position, this is similar to socialism, arguing that capitalism is an avaricious system built on the... [backs] of exploited labour. Although communists anticipate that at some distant stage, centralized governments will become obsolete, they are normally hostile to syndicalist arguments. Their view of the improved society is one in which all production is socialized and all workers, or their direct representatives, have a say in how the society is managed. Communism differs from socialism and even more from social democracy in its argument that capitalism must be destroyed by force, and that a vanguard of advanced thinkers may be required to lead a workers' revolution. Thus, communism is hostile to democratic procedures even though, in reality, communist parties have participated in democratic elections.

The slogan of the Communist Party of Canada, as of other branches of the party around the world, is "Dictatorship of the Proletariat". Although this dictum implies overthrow of the bourgeoisie and the end of capitalism — in a word, revolution — the Canadian party has never tried to implement this goal. As Marchak (1988:141) points out, it has traditionally followed the lead of the Russian party, whose policy has not been to pursue the theoretical line but rather to pursue a practical one of promoting the long-term goal of world revolution. (Viewpoint 10.2 discusses the possible effects of the end of the Soviet Union on the Communist Party of Canada.) The Canadian party's small membership, which has never exceeded 8000, and its sporadic organizational problems have also forced it to reduce its aims and thereby remain tolerably deviant.

VIEWPOINT 10.2

THE OUTLOOK OF CANADIAN COMMUNISM

The collapse of Soviet communism now finally makes it possible to rid the Canadian left-wing labour movement of the false doctrines and harmful policies of Joseph Stalin's Marxism-Leninism. The purpose of this book is to help promote that result.

The end of Soviet communism may spell the end of the Communist Party of Canada. This party was subservient to Moscow leadership from its very beginning in 1922 (*sic*). There was no democracy in the party. Debate and controversy over doctrines and policies — with various groups and factions putting forward differing viewpoints, which is essential in an effective left-wing organization — was stifled. This was "justified" by the Leninist-Stalinist doctrine of "democractic centralism," which really meant dictatorship of the leaders, more often one "great leader," who automatically expected life tenure. What a strange product to come out of Marxism, which had exploded the "great man" theory of history.

Even after the Khruschev revelations at the Soviet communist party's Twentieth Congress in 1956, the Canadian Stalinists still kept on preaching the old Marxist myths. In Karl Marx's day it was fashionable in scientific writing to find "iron laws" and "inevitabilities" everywhere. We are indebted to Earl Browder, the former leader of the U.S. communist party, for his insight into why Marx erroneously believed socialist revolution to be inevitable.

In following Moscow's leadership, the Canadian Stalinists, led by Tim Buck and Sam Carr, turned the party onto the path of perpetual war against all other socialist and social reform groups, particularly the Cooperative Commonwealth Federation (CCF) and its successor, the New Democratic Party (NDP). Instead of considering itself as the left wing of one labour movement, striving for the common goal of winning a labour-socialist majority in parliament, the Canadian communists acted as if theirs was the mass party of the working class, which the NDP and all other reform groups should support and follow. In elections, instead of helping to elect NDP candidates, they ran candidates to oppose them.

When, in the 1920s, I and others proposed that in Canada's situation we should advocate and fight for Canadian independence and the completion of Canada's national structure and unity, the Stalinists opposed this as "colonialism" and laid down a policy of fighting only on straight "class" issues. They opposed the fight for Canadian independence for at least twenty years after that.

It is hard to think of a more harmful doctrine, especially now, in the 1990s, when the new social movements for women's equality and to save our planet earth are in the forefront, demanding the left wing's support. The future of the entire labour movement will be in doubt if it fails to give priority support to these non-class causes.

Had the left wing taken up the cause of Canadian independence at that time, it would have achieved an honoured place in the fight to save Canada from U.S. domination. Now, in the 1990s, with the U.S. seeking to annex Canada via the back door through the so-called Free Trade Agreement, this has become a life-and-death struggle. The Mulroney government is handing control of Canada, piece-by-piece, over to the U.S. In the 1988 elections, the pro-Canada vote was split between the NDP and the Liberals. Ed Broadbent, the NDP leader at the time, flunked the fight against the Free Trade Agreement. Today, broad

(Continued)

VIEWPOINT 10.2 *(Continued)*

sections of the Canadian public are joining the fight for Canadian independence, currently being led by Maude Barlow and Mel Hurtig and the Council of Canadians. The left wing should be heart-and-soul in this battle, leading the ideological battle against U.S. imperialism and its Canadian stooges. The NDP and the Liberals must find some way of not splitting the pro-Canada vote, otherwise the comprador, Mulroney, could get in again.

Source: Stewart Smith. *Comrades and Komsomolkas: My Years in the Communist Party of Canada.* Toronto: Lugus, 1993, pp. 1–2. Reprinted with permission of Lugus Publications, Toronto, Canada.

SUMMARY

A belief is any proposition about the social, physical, or supernatural world that is considered true, regardless of whether there is supporting scientific evidence. A belief system is a coherent interrelationship of a set of beliefs, shared by members of a particular group. Deviant belief systems may be reactionary or radical when viewed against the belief systems that are component parts of a society's social institutions. The two chief forms of religious deviance are sects and cults. The former are usually reactionary schisms from mainline faiths, whereas the latter are frequently radical innovations in the sphere of religion. Neither type is known for its spirit of tolerance or compromise. Cults, especially, are likely to be short-lived. The Church of Scientology and the Hare Krishna Movement are two contemporary cults in North America. The first stresses clear thinking, happiness, and personal adjustment. The second focuses on salvation through service to the ideals of Lord Krishna.

Sects and cults usually acquire members through the process of conversion. Lofland's model of conversion is composed of three predisposing conditions (tension, problem-solving perspective, and religious seeking) and four situational contingencies (turning point, cult-affective bonds, extracult-affective bonds, and intensive interaction). Certain social conditions also operate to push the pre-convert into the conversion sequence. Among them are weak ties to the religion of his or her parents or dissatisfaction with that religion, and the impersonality of modern, urban society.

In North America, the new religions are largely urban-based and comprised mainly of white, middle- and upper-middle-class young people making major life decisions. For them, joining a sect or cult is an opportunity to find both leisure and adjustment in a way that is distinctly different, but at the same time entirely legal. Despite the legitimate status of the new religions, an anti-cult movement has arisen whose aim is to control, if not eliminate them. Yet, notwithstanding pressure from this movement and the negative publicity about the conversion process it has generated, cults continue to flourish in North America.

Deviation from the institution of science usually means acceptance of some aspect of the occult. One distinguishing aspect of the occult is its tendency to focus on concealed phenomena that are anomalous when viewed against everyday experience. The occult differs from science chiefly in its procedures for identifying and validating real objects and experiences.

Divination is the practice of trying either to foretell the future or to discover hidden knowledge. Among the main forms of divination found in Canada are astrology, palm reading, crystal gazing, spiritualism, and tarot card reading. A diviner, or occult expert, is usually needed to mediate between the client and the system of knowledge that will permit the foretelling of the future or the discovery of hidden knowledge.

Modern witches do not view themselves as heretical Christians, as modern Satanists do. Witches rely on magic to produce either beneficial ends (white magic) or malevolent ends (black magic). Extrasensory perception is perception without the use of any of the senses. Its main forms are clairvoyance, psychokinesis, precognition, and telepathy. Eastern religious thought revolves around the guru-like teacher who possesses mystic truth. Among the techniques that may be used to reach this truth are yoga, dancing, meditation (as in Zen Buddhism), study, and communion with other believers. Finally, there is a variety of residual occult phenomena which are unexplained by science and which are not part of any belief system (e.g., UFOs, strange monsters). Substantial proportions of Canadians believe in one or more forms of the occult, some to the extent that they are defrauded by unscrupulous practitioners.

Deviant politics is determined with reference to the established political system at a given time in history. Like deviant science and religion, deviant politics may be reactionary or radical. They are not, however, seditious. The contemporary ultra-right in Canada grew up in reaction to a longstanding liberal trend, and contains strains of racism and anti-Semitism. Radical deviance is well exemplified in the principles and activities of the Communist Party of Canada.

NOTES

1 A similar event took place in a remote area of the Philippines in 1985. An estimated 70 members of the Ata tribe ate porridge laced with insecticide because their high priest promised they would see God (*Calgary Herald*, 1985:A11).

2 Sometimes terms such as "grove", "nest", and "circle" are used.

3 This historical sketch is taken from Penner (1988:475).

SUGGESTED READING

Barrett, Stanley R. *Is God a Racist? The Right Wing in Canada.* Toronto: University of Toronto Press, 1987. An anthropologist looks at Canada's right-wing racist organizations.

Lofland, John. *Doomsday Cult.* (Enlarged ed.) New York: Irvington, 1981. A study of conversion, proselytization, and maintenance of faith in a well-known cult.

Melton, J. Gordon. *Encyclopedic Handbook of Cults in America.* (Rev. and expanded ed.) New York: Garland, 1992. A comprehensive compilation of information on the new and established cults, as well as on the countercult groups and violence in cults.

Richardson, James, Joel Best, and David Bromley (eds.) *The Satanism Scare.* Hawthorne, NY: Aldine de Gruyter, 1991. A collection of chapters by different authors analyzing this newest addition to the North American cult scene.

Scott, Gini Graham. *The Magicians: A Study of the Use of Power in a Black Magic Group.* New York: Irvington, 1983. Graham joined two black magic groups to study covertly the use of magic as a power resource.

Tiryakian, Edward A. (ed.) *On the Margin of the Visible: Sociology, the Esoteric, and the Occult.* New York: John Wiley, 1974. Contains articles on representative esoteric doctrines, witchcraft, and sociological thought and research on the occult.

Wallis, Roy (ed.) *On the Margins of Science: The Social Construction of Rejected Knowledge.* Keele, England: University of Keele Press, 1979. A collection of articles about astrology, mesmerism, acupuncture, phrenology, creationism, spiritualism, paranormal claims, parapsychology, sea serpents, and ufology.

References

American Psychiatric Association. "Cults and New Religious Movements." A Report of the Committee on Psychiatry and Religion. Washington, DC: American Psychiatric Association, 1989.

Back to Godhead, 1982, 17, 1:30–31.

Balch, Robert W. and David Taylor. "Seekers and Saucers: The Role of the Cultic Milieu in Joining a UFO Cult," *American Behavioral Scientist,* 1977, 20:839–860.

Barker, Eileen. "Religious Movements: Cult and Anticult Since Jonestown." In *Annual Review of Sociology,* Vol. 12, edited by Ralph H. Turner and James F. Short, Jr., pp. 329–346. Palo Alto, CA: Annual Reviews, Inc., 1986.

Barrett, Stanley R. *Is God a Racist? The Right Wing in Canada.* Toronto: University of Toronto Press, 1987.

Bechtel, H. Kenneth, Jr. and Willie Pearson, Jr. "Deviant Scientists and Scientific Deviance," *Deviant Behavior,* 1985, 6:237–252.

Beckford, James A. *Cult Controversies: The Societal Response to the New Religious Movements.* London: Tavistock, 1985.

Ben-Yehuda, Nachman. *Deviance and Moral Boundaries: Witchcraft, the Occult, Science Fiction, Deviant Sciences, and Scientists.* Chicago: University of Chicago Press, 1985.

Bibby, Reginald W. *Fragmented Gods.* Toronto: Stoddart, 1990.

Boles, Jacqueline, Phillip Davis, and Charlotte Tatro. "False Pretense and Deviant Exploitation: Fortunetelling as a Con," *Deviant Behavior,* 1983, 4:375–394.

Bromley, David G. and Anson D. Shupe, Jr. *Strange Gods: The Great American Cult Scare.* Boston: Beacon Press, 1981.

Bruce, Steve. *The Rise and Fall of the New Christian Right: Conservative Protest Politics in America: 1978–1988.* Oxford: Clarendon Press, 1989.

Calgary Herald, 1979, Wednesday, August 1:B12.

_________ 1985, Saturday, September 21:A11.

Cornell, James. "Science vs. the Paranormal: Skeptics Fight an Uphill Battle in their Effort to Overthrow the Forces of the Paranormal," *Psychology Today*, 1984, 18, March: 28–34.

Ellwood, Robert S. "Occult Movements in America." In *Encyclopedia of the American Religious Experience*, Vol. II, edited by Charles H. Lippy and Peter W. William, pp. 711–722. New York: Charles Scribners Sons, 1987.

English, Kathy. "Storefront Fortunetellers Victimize the Vulnerable," *The Sunday Star*, 1986, April 13:A1, A8.

Galanter, Marc. *Cults, Faith, Healing, and Coercion*. New York: Oxford University Press, 1989.

Gallup Report, 1989a, Thursday, April 7.

__________ 1989b, Monday, October 30.

Gavrakis, Daniel and Jean-Pierre Bocquet. "Psychoses et objets volants non-identifiés," *Revue Canadienne de Psychiatrie*, 1983, 28:199–201.

Goldberg, M.A. and J. Mercer. *The Myth of the North American City: Continentalism Challenged*. Vancouver: University of British Columbia Press, 1986.

Hall, John R. "Review of *Cults, Faith, Healing, and Coercion* by Marc Galanter," *Society*, 1990, 27, March/April:86–90.

Heeren, John and Marylee Mason. "Talk about Visions: Spiritual Readings as Deviant Work," *Deviant Behavior*, 1981, 2:167–186.

Hexham, I., R.F. Currie, and J.B. Townsend. "New Religious Movements." In *The Canadian Encyclopedia*. (2nd ed.), pp. 1479–1481. Edmonton: Hurtig, 1988.

Kawamura, Leslie S. "Buddhism." In *The Canadian Encyclopedia*. (2nd ed.), pp. 292–294. Edmonton: Hurtig, 1988.

Kelly, John R. *Freedom To Be: A New Sociology of Leisure*. New York: Macmillan, 1987.

Kent, Stephen A. "Deviance Labelling and Normative Strategies in the Canadian 'New Religions/Countercult' Debate," *Canadian Journal of Sociology*, 1990, 15:393–416.

Lofland, John. *Doomsday Cult: A Study of Conversion, Proselytization, and Maintenance of Faith*. New York: Irvington, 1981.

Marchak, M. Patricia. *Ideological Perspectives on Canada*. (3rd ed.) Toronto: McGraw-Hill Ryerson, 1988.

Melton, J. Gordon. *The Encyclopedia of American Religions*. Wilmington, DE: McGrath Publishing Co., 1978.

__________ *Encyclopedic Handbook of Cults in America*. (Rev. and expanded ed.) New York: Garland, 1992.

__________ and Robert L. Moore. *The Cult Experience*. New York: Pilgrim Press, 1982.

Moody, Edward J. "Urban Witches." In *Conformity and Conflict: Readings in Cultural Anthropology*, edited by James P. Spradley and David W. McCurdy, pp. 224–252. Boston: Little Brown, 1971.

Penner, Norman. "Communist Party of Canada." In *The Canadian Encyclopedia*. (2nd ed.), p. 475. Edmonton: Hurtig, 1988.

Petranek, Charles F. "Recruitment and Commitment," *Society*, 1988, 25, January/February:48–51.

Richardson, James, Joel Best, and David Bromley (eds.) *The Satanism Scare*. Hawthorne, NY: Aldine de Gruyter, 1991.

Robbins, Thomas and Dick Anthony. "Deprogramming, Brainwashing, and the Medicalization of Deviant Religious Groups," *Social Problems*, 1982, 29:283–297.

Scott, Gini G. *The Magicians: A Study of the Use of Power in a Black Magic Group.* New York: Irvington, 1983.

Shupe, Anson D., Jr. and David G. Bromley. *The New Vigilantes: Deprogrammers, Anti-Cultists, and the New Religions.* Beverly Hills, CA: Sage Publications, 1980.

Smithers, Stuart W. "Spiritual Guide." In *The Encyclopedia of Religion*, Vol. 14, edited by Mircea Eliade, pp. 29–37. New York: Macmillan, 1987.

Stark, Rodney and William S. Bainbridge. "Secularization and Cult Formation in the Jazz Age." *Journal for the Scientific Study of Religion*, 1981, 20:360–373.

Stebbins, Robert A. *Career, Culture, and Social Psychology in a Variety Art: The Magician.* Malabar, FL: Krieger, 1993.

Stoner, Carroll and Jo Anne Parke. *All God's Children: The Cult Experience — Salvation or Slavery?* Radnor, PA: Chilton Book Co., 1977.

Swearer, Donald K. "Buddhism in Southeast Asia." In *The Encyclopedia of Religion,* Vol. 2, edited by Mircea Eliade, pp. 385–400. New York: Macmillan, 1987.

Tatro, Charlotte R. "Cross My Palm with Silver: Fortunetelling As An Occupational Way of Life." In *Deviant Behavior: Occupational and Organizational Bases,* edited by Clifton D. Bryant, pp. 286–299. Chicago: Rand McNally, 1974.

Townsend, J.B. "Spiritualism." In *The Canadian Encyclopedia.* (2nd ed.), pp. 1481–1482. Edmonton: Hurtig, 1988.

Truzzi, Marcello. "The Occult Revival As Popular Culture," *Sociological Quarterly,* 1972, 13:16–36.

__________ "Definitions and Dimensions of the Occult." In *On the Margin of the Visible: Sociology, the Esoteric, and the Occult,* edited by Edward A. Tiryakian, pp. 243–255. New York: John Wiley, 1974.

Vogt, Evon Z. and Ray Hyman. *Water Witching U.S.A.* (2nd ed.) Chicago: University of Chicago Press, 1979.

Weckman, George. "Community." In *The Encyclopedia of Religion,* Vol. 3, edited by Mircea Eliade, pp. 566–571. New York: Macmillan, 1987.

Yinger, J. Milton. *The Scientific Study of Religion.* New York: Macmillan, 1970.

Zurowski, Monica. "Tarot Sheds Mystic Cloak As Self-Development Tools," *Calgary Herald*, 1986, Saturday, November 29:H11.

11

TOLERANCE, PLURALISM, AND CONFLICT

We have been operating throughout this book within the theoretical framework of tolerable deviance presented early in Chapter 1. Using this framework, we have been able to identify and examine concrete expressions of tolerance in a variety of deviant forms of sexual identity and practice, alcohol and drug use, gambling, mental disorder, street living, nudism and naturism, religion, science, and politics. The framework has also demonstrated that, with the possible exception of mental disorder, all these areas have seen significant growth in the range and degree of tolerance during the second half of the twentieth century. Today, new and more accessible forms of pornography, games of chance, forms of religious deviance, the use of marijuana — to mention but a few — are tolerated as never before.

To understand more thoroughly why we tolerate deviance at all, as well as why we have recently expanded the range and degree of our tolerance, we must now return to the concept itself. In other words, to understand the idea of tolerable deviance, we must understand the underlying idea of tolerance. The aim of this chapter, then, is to explore the nature and development of tolerance as a characteristic attitude of Canadians and members of other democratic societies. Such an attitude is an important pre-condition of the forms of deviance covered in this book. Without tolerance, these forms, if they existed at all, would do so under very different circumstances.

Widespread tolerance, it appears, is characteristic only of the modern age (Tinder, 1975:7). The generalized tolerance of religious, political, ethnic, and deviant differences is one of the concomitants of developments in science and technology, the growth of commerce and capitalism, the move toward more representative government, the decline of absolutism, the trend toward a more global viewpoint, and the contact of diverse cultures (Barnes, 1965: Ch. 18).

There are numerous indications of the existence of a tolerant spirit in the present day. One is the growing taste for searching for the "authentic tourist experience" in remote regions of the world (MacCannell, 1976), made possible by the recent ease of world travel. More and more people are making contact with and gaining knowledge of other cultures and ways of life. And for those who must remain at home, the modern mass media bring diversity into their living rooms, promoting a degree of indulgence toward difference. Furthermore, the persistent and pervasive ferment of ideas and social forms, which leads to a general increase in our contact with difference, has long been believed by some to generate greater tolerance (Cooley, 1922:295). The increase in urban population concentration is another factor: urban residence has been found to be more positively associated with increased tolerance than rural residence (Wilson, 1985; Karp et al., 1991: Ch. 5). The overall significance of tolerance for humankind has been succinctly expressed by Harry Elmer Barnes (1965:756): "The growth of tolerance, urbanity, and free thought constitutes the most convincing evidence of the progress of civilization."

All this is not to argue that intolerance has disappeared in post-modern Western society. Rather, we are only *less intolerant* today than previously. Racism, bigotry, chauvinism, and the general depreciation of others substantially different from ourselves are still with us. And certain features of post-modern society, among them the mass media and some forms of general tourism, may be fueling more intolerance than tolerance.

THE DEVELOPMENT OF TOLERANCE

Tolerance is a fundamental principle in the modern tradition of liberalism; it dates to the ideas of John Locke in the seventeenth century and of John Stuart Mill in the nineteenth century (Budziszewski, 1992). In Western democracies, tolerance seems to root either in the first or in both of two usually sequentially related conditions. The first of these is the norm or expectation that we should be indulgent of human diversity, a requirement whose origins can be traced to our Judeo-Christian heritage and more recently to the spirit of modern democracy. The expectation of tolerance is, in part, a more pointed expression of the social values of considerateness of others, leniency in dealing with their mistakes, and fairness in our treatment of them. A key aspect of considerateness is respect for the person and will of another, which has been observed by Guyau (1962:150) to be linked to tolerance.

Internalization of the expectation of tolerance is part of the broad socialization process through which newcomers (children, immigrants) become acceptable members of the community. As with other norms, however, the newcomers must also learn the circumstances in which the expression of tolerance is expected and those in which it is not. We shall take up this matter later, when discussing the nature of tolerated activities and beliefs. It must suffice for the moment to make one deceptively simple point: however else it may be regarded, the vast amount of human behaviour is never tolerated, since we are unaware of it. Tolerance based largely on cultural expectations may be called **habitual tolerance**, since its expression is so routine that it becomes expected.

Habitual tolerance would appear to be an important component of the contemporary ethic of "political correctness". The *New Shorter Oxford English Dictionary* defines this ethic as "conformity to a body of liberal or radical opinion, especially on social matters, in the avoidance of anything, even established vocabulary, that may conceivably be construed as discriminatory or pejorative". Many people are habitually tolerant and in other ways political correct, chiefly because that is what is expected in their social circles.

Since the first condition is common to all who are more or less adequately socialized to the ways of the society, the second condition for the development of tolerance is usually built on the first. This condition is the acquisition of a certain kind of knowledge by the tolerator — specifically, knowledge of the shared portions of the perspectives of categories of human beings, as this knowledge bears on his or her questionable activities and beliefs. A **perspective** is the structure consisting of a person's meanings, values, opinions, attitudes, beliefs, and ideas; it is his or her outlook on life (Warshay, 1962:152). It helps people define particular situations and circumscribes possible definitions available for them. A portion of an individual's perspective is idiosyncratic (stemming from his or her unique biography), whereas the rest is common to all people in that social identity. Familiarity with this shared segment of the perspectives of another group equips the tolerant person to forbear their actions and beliefs.

It must be understood that this knowledge is not stereotypical to any significant degree. And, since it is offered as a condition for the development of tolerance, it is noteworthy that a handful of investigators have found a modest correlation between the presence of tolerance and the relative absence of unflattering stereotypes (Simmons, 1969:31). This, then, is **enlightened tolerance**. It arises from knowledge of the common segments of the perspectives of those in a particular, previously unfamiliar, political, religious, ethnic, or deviant identity. One major source of this sort of knowledge is contact with diverse ideas and behaviour. Perhaps liberal education in fine art, literature, and social science is the most prevalent source of enlightened tolerance.

Since the possibility exists that individuals can gain a reasonably non-stereotypical knowledge of the perspectives of several categories of people, enlightened tolerance may become general. Once a person realizes that the activities and beliefs of all classes of human beings are founded on orientations or perspectives that are sensible from their standpoint, even though the tolerant person has only slight knowledge of them, he or she may still tolerate their behaviour. (This is the anthropological ideal of cultural relativism on a group level.) Yet, in fact, no more than a very small proportion of those in any society ever achieve enlightened tolerance in this broad sense, though the possibility of its appearance is certainly enhanced when developed from a base of habitual tolerance.

Both habitual and enlightened tolerance are evident in a recent study of public opinion on gay rights conducted by Rayside and Bowler (1988). Their survey demonstrates that Canadian opinion has shifted toward a more liberal position on the question of equal rights for lesbians and gay men. That is, they have become more tolerant on the habitual level. But most have not yet developed enlightened tolerance in this area. The authors report that strong moral disapproval still exists, undergirded by fears based on traditional stereotypes that these deviants are sick and threatening to children.

THE NATURE OF TOLERANCE

Common sense states that tolerance and intolerance are polar opposites. But, as stated briefly in Chapter 1, tolerance actually falls roughly midway between embracement or adoption of an activity or belief on the one hand, and scorn or disdain for it on the other. Located in this position, tolerance is a comparatively passive disposition; in Guyau's (1962:149) words: "It is a virtue of the head rather than of the heart."

The stance taken by Wolff (Wolff et al., 1965:20) and Durkheim (1960:98) that tolerance is held by those who find themselves unable to destroy certain people is incongruent with the conceptualization offered here. From our viewpoint, their interpretation of tolerance is more accurately seen as a form of frustrated disdain; would-be antagonists still strive for the destruction of certain others but must settle for a delay in attaining this goal. While awaiting the next opportunity to attack, these antagonists refuse to accord legitimacy to their rivals. And their orientation toward the rivals can scarcely be conceived of as passive. Although there may well be others, tolerance as relative passivity is a major attitude behind the non-involvement in various conflict-ridden issues of today. At times, tolerance, with its roots in the venerated social ideals of fairness, leniency, and considerateness, may even become the overt justification for indifference in the face of pressure to take sides. (Marcuse presents a similar position in Wolff et al., 1969:83–123.)

What Is Tolerated?

As indicated, tolerance is an attitude whose expression is generally expected under certain conditions in everyday life. One such condition is the expectation of indulgence toward only those activities and beliefs perceived as unthreatening in any significant degree (Gerth and Mills, 1954:292–294). The nature of the threat may be personal or collective. The manager of the branch office of a business firm would not be expected by others in the organization to be tolerant of the activities of an employee known to despise him and suspected of engaging in activities designed to bring about his dismissal by his superiors. On a larger scale, members of a deviant religious sect would never expect their associates to show forbearance toward a splinter group whose activities threaten to weaken the effectiveness of the larger body.

What is tolerated also depends on how menacing the threatening activity or belief is thought to be. This, in turn, is related to such considerations as the strength with which the threatened values are held. A more or less accurate appraisal of the dangerous activity is a significant factor in the expression of tolerance, an appraisal that may serve to moderate the menacing appearance of the activity or to heighten it, depending upon how great the threat actually is. The degree of perceived threat has been shown to be related to strength of ego, as measured in confidence and success (Flugel, 1951:206–207). Powerful people can afford to be tolerant and at the same time give expression to some of the democratic ideals of the society (Blau, 1986:139, 325–327). And, since actions are more likely to be threatening than beliefs alone, the latter are apt to be tolerated more often than the former (see Guyau, 1962:149; Sommer et al., 1988). Moreover, in an investigation of deviants, Simmons (1969:31) found a positive association between amount of education and degree of tolerance.

Still, not all activities or beliefs perceived as unthreatening are tolerated. Some, of course, are embraced. The rest are simply neutral or of very minor importance to the individual, what Schutz (1964:125) called the zones of the "relatively irrelevant" and "absolutely irrelevant". Consider an example: Robert Bellah and his colleagues (1985:335) coined the term "lifestyle enclave" to refer to the following:

> A term used in contrast to *community*... A lifestyle enclave is formed by people who share some feature of private life. Members of a lifestyle enclave express their identity through shared patterns of appearance, consumption, and leisure activities, which often serve to differentiate them sharply from those with other lifestyles. They are not interdependent, do not act together politically, and do not share a history.

From the perspective of this book, a lifestyle enclave could take shape around either a deviant or a non-deviant activity. Moreover, though lifestyles "celebrate the narcissism of similarity," a given lifestyle does not necessarily lead to an intolerance of outsiders' lifestyles (Bellah et al., 1985:72). Instead, the other lifestyles remain in the distance, either unknown or irrelevant. Participants are wrapped up in their own projects and the activities and lifestyle they generate.

What is perceived as threatening also depends on how close to home the threat is. That is, many conforming people do not want to be closely associated with even tolerable deviance. Such deviance becomes intolerable for them when it turns up in their family or circle of close friends. The stigma of, say, a homosexual or a nudist in the family is contagious and threatens to engulf those members who are ordinarily tolerant of such differences. They therefore frequently scorn tolerable deviance by their intimates. This is one reason why tolerance is more prevalent in secondary relations and is a distinctly urban attitude.

The fact is that we either embrace most of the activities and beliefs of members of the society (because they are the same as or similar to our own) or regard them neutrally. Only a small, albeit significant, proportion of the total inventory of the behaviour of others must be tolerated by us, and an even smaller proportion disdained. This appears to be true even for those who are labelled deviant, although there is a tendency to spurn the entire person and all associated behaviour as an overriding "master status" (Becker, 1963:32–34). Aberrant activities are scorned, but only a minute part of all the deviant's activities are actually of this sort. Thus, people may reject a male homosexual's sexual behaviour, but tolerate his political beliefs and embrace his occupational, recreational, familial, and religious activities.

THE TYPES OF TOLERANCE

The types of tolerance — habitual and enlightened — have been introduced briefly, but the need remains for further refinement. In general, the two are differentiated by our degree of knowledge of the shared portions of the perspectives of those in unfamiliar social identities, and the limitations imposed by our own perspective.

With habitual tolerance, we have only superficial knowledge of those whose activities or beliefs we indulge. This tolerant attitude results, in good part, from such values as fairness, leniency, and considerateness, and from a more concrete expression of them: the democratic norm that we be tolerant. It can be added here that, because most people fail to gain an adequate degree of knowledge of the perspectives of others in their society with whom they are personally unacquainted, they necessarily regard the tolerated activities and beliefs of those others as unreasonable. The others seem quaint, if not ridiculous, when judged from the only perspective known to such tolerators, namely, their own.

In this connection, it is recognized (Barnes, 1965:760) that habitual tolerance contains the ingredient of "intellectual arrogance". Or as Peter Blau (1986:138) puts it: "There is something smug about tolerance, despite best intentions, since it implicitly asserts one's own superiority." Perhaps, too, there is even an element of pity, amid our condescension, for those who "live in error." Although there are other mechanisms, the attitude of tolerance, it may be hypothesized, also gives expression to the necessity once noted by Mead (1934:205–206) to realize constantly one's self in some sort of superiority over others.

This description of habitual tolerance fits perfectly with the outlook of the modern "psychological man", the final product of bourgeois individualism and excessive preoccupation with the self, as described by Christopher Lasch (1991:22):

> [The] new narcissist is haunted not by guilt but by anxiety. He seeks not to inflict his own certainties on others but to find a meaning in life. Liberated from the superstitions of the past, he doubts even the reality of his own existence. Superficially relaxed and tolerant, he finds little use for dogmas of racial and ethnic purity.... His sexual attitudes are permissive rather puritanical.

But how does psychological man differ from the person whose tolerance can be said to be enlightened?

Enlightened tolerance is founded on considerably greater knowledge of the shared perspectives of others. Their activities and beliefs seem reasonable when viewed in light of these perspectives. While there is perhaps a hint of intellectual arrogance in enlightened tolerance as well, it is tempered by the plausibility of the others' positions and by the belief often said to be associated with forbearing people that no mind covers all knowledge (Durkheim, 1960:411; Guyau, 1962:150; Barnes, 1965:756).

When enlightened tolerance is *intellectual*, the stance taken by others is tolerated (but not embraced) because the tolerator recognizes the contributions made by disparate standpoints in understanding a complex area of interest where many issues remain unsettled. This is the forbearance of the academy. Enlightened tolerance, however, may be *empathic*, where empathy refers to the ability to understand the roles of others while refraining, by means of personal detachment, from adopting their standpoints. In this case, the tolerator, because he or she is aware of the standpoints of others, also senses the importance to them of their modes of adjustment to certain problems in life. This ideally, although too infrequently, is the tolerance of the helping professions.

Whether the activity or belief tolerated is intellectual or adjustive, tolerators still maintain their personal stance, since they also realize the significance of their own knowledgeable effort or the indispensability of their own modes of adjustment. It should be clear that, if we were to place the two types of tolerance on a scale on the basis of their similarity to embracement, enlightened tolerance would be closer to this pole than the habitual variety. It also seems reasonable to conclude that habitual tolerance is more evanescent. Founded as it is on only a superficial knowledge of the tolerated group, misunderstandings can more easily emerge, pushing the erstwhile tolerator toward a scornful position.

TOLERANCE AND INDIFFERENCE

We noted earlier that, at times, tolerance may become an overt justification for indifference in the face of pressure to take sides. For this reason, Marcuse (Wolff et al., 1969) recommends the repudiation of tolerance and its replacement by a more active orientation. Although we must take his message seriously — that people should be encouraged to avoid justifying indifference with the cherished attitude of tolerance — it fails to recognize some important qualifications. There are many occasions when some sort of forbearance toward others' differences is admitted by all parties to be the best obtainable solution to the problem of their continued association. The tolerance existing between Protestants and Catholics in contemporary North America exemplifies this arrangement.

Marcuse's stance is most convincing when focused on those patterns of adjustment to life's problems which are unsatisfactory even to the people who enact them; tolerance of these activities is tolerance of others' distress. Indulgence of addiction among alcoholics or compulsive wagering among gamblers were examples encountered in this book. Beyer (1978) sees a similar problem in connection with the proposed decriminalization of heroin use. It is doubtful that those oriented by empathic enlightened tolerance would be forbearing toward

VIEWPOINT 11.1

TOLERANCE AND INTOLERANCE OF NUDE BEACHERS

Editorial

Santa Rosa Sunbathers Try to Wield Naked Power

In Santa Rosa County, where issues of "morality" cause a good-size commotion every now and then, nude sunbathers are back in the news.

More than 70 of them have incorporated under that name Panhandle Free Beaches Inc.

Organizing, they reason, will help them achieve one of their primary goals: a sanctioned "clothing optional" area at a local beach. The site now used — to the irritation of county officials — is at the eastern end of Navarre Beach and the western end of Eglin Air Force Base property on Santa Rosa Island. It's already widely recognized as a nude beach.

And, says Panhandle Free Beaches President Bonnie Bracewell, "we want to educate the public. We're tired of being considered the perverts on the beach."

Some folks, of course, will always think of them that way.

But we're not going to debate here the rightness or wrongness of sunbathing in the buff. We'll take Bracewell's word: "We're good people. We pay taxes. We don't break laws."

In several Florida cases, in fact, judges have tossed out nude sunbathing arrests in which there was no allegation that a lewd act had been committed.

The significance of area nudists incorporating, in our view, is political. The very existence of the new group should encourage the Santa Rosa County Commission to abandon its year-long fight to boot the birthday-suit sunbathers from the beach.

County officials have said that if state and federal laws are not strict enough to halt nude sunbathing — which has been going on for decades at Navarre Beach — they'll pass their own law. They've even nudged the Sheriff's Department in the direction of arresting naked beachgoers.

The county commissioners have better things to do. So does the Sheriff's Department.

On the same day the *Daily News* published a story about the nudists incorporating, we also reported that an 18-year-old from the Holley-Navarre area had been convicted of murdering a dirt-bike rider. The biker, ambushed in a wooded area of south Santa Rosa, had been blasted four times with a shotgun.

Santa Rosa County is not Miami, certainly, but it's not Mayberry either. There are greater threats to the public's well-being than unclothed people catching a few rays at a secluded beach.

So, in the hope that Panhandle Free Beaches can do a little educating among the county commissioners, we wish the group luck.

Source: Northwest Florida Daily News, 1993, November 4. By permission.

such activities, because their outlook is rooted in their capacity to understand the roles of these deviants. They would tolerate only those patterns of behaviour important to the deviants as modes of adjustment which are genuinely embraced by them. Unsatisfactory behavioural adjustment is never truly embraced by its users (only tolerated); it is practised solely as a stopgap. The concept of enlightened tolerance as discussed here and Budziszewski's (1992:9) concept of "true tolerance" are identical in scope and meaning.

WHY TOLERATE?

This discussion of tolerance and indifference makes clear the moral nature of tolerance as an orientation or attitude toward political, religious, ethnic, and deviant pluralism in modern industrial societies. As Harrison (1976) and Tinder (1975: Ch. 4) observe, tolerance is anything but neutral or scientifically impartial. As part of democratic ideology, tolerance is seen as something good and desirable. We have been treating it as an attitude, but it is also one of society's moral values.

Why is tolerance valued in a democratic society? We have already touched on one reason: it is sometimes a workable alternative to conflict among the groups that make up pluralistic societies. The other reason is that too much regulation by means of moral norms curtails individual freedom. Barbara Wooton (1970:812–813) states the case for this point of view:

> Freedom is precious to the individual; and a society with a wide variety of cultural standards and deviant behaviours offers a far richer and more colourful life than one which is rigidly conformist. In the complex modern world, a vast array of controls and prohibitions is indisputably necessary in the public interest. And these must be clearly defined and enforced by law. This in itself makes it the more necessary to preserve the utmost liberty outside this prohibited area. But there is, I think, a danger that, between the white area of personal freedom and the black area of conduct legally prohibited, there might come to be a nebulous intermediate zone in which various social pressures seek to impose uniformity. Either idleness, promiscuity, drunkenness, and a generally disorganized way of life must be accepted even by those to whom they are distasteful, or they should be forbidden by law... the non-criminal deviant has his rights, and these should be respected.

But the tolerance that follows from Wooton's prescription must be enlightened rather than habitual tolerance. The latter, as Marcuse's warning indicates, leads to indifference, hardship, exploitation, victimization, and maladjustment, all in the good name of tolerance. Such is freedom for some at the expense of others. And it is intolerable.

TOLERABLE DIFFERENCES

Tolerance is the prevailing North American solution to the dilemma of whether there should be conformity to other moral norms, as opposed to mores and criminal laws (see Table 1.1), or freedom from them. This book has presented evidence of tolerance — mostly habitual rather than enlightened, one suspects — of a wide variety of morally tinged practices: transsexualism, transvestism, homosexuality, striptease, pornography, swinging, heavy drinking, illegal use of cannabis and prescription drugs, heavy gambling, mental disorder, absolute homelessness, nudism/naturism, cults and sects, occultism, and radical and reactionary politics. The underlying claim throughout has been that sizable segments of the North American population forbear these forms of difference, with the result that both formal and informal action against them are rare.

According to the conceptual scheme presented in Chapter 1, these forms of deviance will continue to be tolerated as long as they pose no significantly greater threat than they do presently. Still, no guarantee exists that their level of threat will remain the same. Indeed, the threat level of a given form could diminish, and in so doing push the form in question into the fringes of the zone of acceptability. It would then be viewed, at least initially, as extraordinary thought and behaviour, perhaps even as eccentric, but not morally different enough to be considered deviant. It is clear, for example, that nudism/naturism is regarded in this light in contemporary Holland. As for the future public definition of the other forms of deviance discussed in this book, we can only wait and see.

SUMMARY

It is a curious fact of modern times that at no other period in the history of humankind has tolerance been so widespread. This fact is associated with such factors as the growth of commerce and capitalism, the trend toward a more global view, the rise of representative government, and contact with diverse cultures. Urban living, media influence, and world travel have also helped generate an unprecedented level of tolerance.

Tolerance seems to root either in the first or in both of two usually sequentially related conditions. The first of these conditions, which fosters habitual tolerance, refers to the cluster of the social values of fairness, leniency, and considerateness and to the democratic expectation that we be forbearing. Habitual tolerance is a politically correct attitude, as we would put it these days. Enlightened tolerance is based typically upon the first condition and the subsequent one of knowledge of the shared segments of the perspectives of a previously unfamiliar group of people. Tolerance is an attitude that focuses on specified activities or beliefs, not on an entire social identity. It is located roughly midway between embracement or adoption on the one hand, and scorn or disdain on the other. Compared with these two polar orientations toward activities and beliefs of others, tolerance is relatively passive. Acknowledgement of the legitimacy of the indulged behaviour is a component of tolerance.

We tend to be forbearing toward only those activities and beliefs perceived as unthreatening. However, not all unthreatening behaviour is tolerated; it may be embraced or simply ignored because it is neutral to the tolerator. Habitual tolerance, because it is based on only superficial knowledge of the target group, is characterized by intellectual arrogance. It is the tolerance of the modern, narcissistic psychological man. Enlightened tolerance, by contrast, is largely free of arrogance, since it is founded in the understanding of the perspectives of others. When enlightened tolerance is intellectual, the stance taken by others is tolerated (but not embraced) because the bearer of this attitude recognizes the contributions made by disparate viewpoints to understanding a complex area of interest. When it is empathic, the tolerator, since he or she is aware of the viewpoints of the other group, also senses the importance to its members of their modes of adjustment to certain problems in life. As a consequence of its shallow basis, habitual tolerance is more evanescent than enlightened tolerance.

Tolerance may become an overt justification for indifference in the face of pressure to take sides. In the case of enlightened tolerance this is unlikely, though it is a possibility with habitual tolerance because of the high value we place on tolerance as part of the foundation of democracy. There are good reasons for the moral stand that tolerance is good and desirable: it is sometimes a workable alternative to conflict, and it allows a level of freedom from too much regulation by moral norms. But tolerance must be enlightened rather than habitual.

Suggested Reading

Budziszewski, J. *True Tolerance: Liberalism and the Necessity of Judgement.* New Brunswick, NJ: Transaction, 1992. A professor of government looks at contemporary liberal thought and the place of tolerance within it.

Flugel, J.C. "Tolerance." In *Psychoanalysis and Culture,* edited by George B. Wilbur and Warner Muensterberger, pp. 196–217. New York: International Universities Press, 1951. A psychoanalyst looks at the nature and development of tolerance.

Karp, David A., Gregory P. Stone, and William C. Yoels. *Being Urban: A Sociology of City Life.* (2nd ed.) New York: Praeger, 1991. In Chapter 5, the authors examine the role of the city in creating and maintaining tolerance, and the limits of tolerance in the urban milieu.

Tinder, Glenn. *Tolerance: Toward a New Civility.* Amherst, MA: University of Massachusetts Press, 1975. An examination of tolerance, its emergence, and its importance in the community, where it is often linked with intolerance.

Wooton, Barbara. "Deviance: Criminal and Other," *New Society,* 1970, 16, November 5:812–816. A noted British social scientist examines the question of tolerance and freedom in modern industrial societies.

References

Barnes, Harry Elmer. *An Intellectual and Cultural History of the Western World.* (3rd rev. ed.) New York: Dover Publications, 1965.

Becker, Howard S. *Outsiders.* New York: The Free Press, 1963.

Bellah, Robert N., Richard Madsen, William M. Sullivan, Ann Swidler, and Steven M. Tipton. *Habits of the Heart: Individualism and Commitment in American Life.* Berkeley, CA: University of California Press, 1985.

Beyer, Ronald. "Heroin Decriminalization and the Ideology of Tolerance," *Law and Society Review,* 1978, 12:301–318.

Blau, Peter M. *Exchange and Power in Social Life.* New Brunswick, NJ: Transaction, 1986.

Budziszewski, J. *True Tolerance: Liberalism and the Necessity of Judgment.* New Brunswick, NJ: Transaction, 1992.

Cooley, Charles H. *Human Nature and the Social Order.* New York: Charles Scribner's Sons, 1922.

Durkheim, Emile. *Essays on Sociology and Philosophy.* (Edited by Kurt Wolff) New York: Harper, 1960.

Flugel, J.C. "Tolerance." In *Psychoanalysis and Culture*, edited by George B. Wilbur and Warner Muensterberger, pp. 196–217. New York: International Universities Press, 1951.

Gerth, Hans and C. Wright Mills. *Character and Social Structure*. London: Routledge & Kegan Paul, 1954.

Guyau, M. *The Non-Religion of the Future*. (First published in English in 1897) New York: Schocken Books, 1962.

Harrison, G. "Relativism and Tolerance," *Ethics*, 1976, 86:122–135.

Karp, David A., Gregory P. Stone, and William C. Yoels. *Being Urban: A Sociology of City Life*. (2nd ed.) New York: Praeger, 1991.

Lasch, Christopher. *The Culture of Narcissism: American Life in an Age of Diminishing Expectations*. New York: W.W. Norton, 1991.

Mead, George H. *Mind, Self, and Society*. Chicago: University of Chicago Press, 1934.

Rayside, David and Scott Bowler. "Public Opinion and Gay Rights," *Canadian Review of Sociology and Anthropology*, 1988, 25:649–660.

Schutz, Alfred. *Collected Papers II*. (Edited by Arvid Brodersen) The Hague: Martinus Nijhoff, 1964.

Simmons, J.L. *Deviants*. Berkeley, CA: Glendessary Press, 1969.

Sommer, Robert, Emily Burstein, and Sanby Holman. "Tolerance of Deviance as Affected by Label, Act, and Actor," *Deviant Behavior*, 1988, 9:193–207.

Tinder, Glenn. *Tolerance: Toward a New Civility*. Amherst, MA: University of Massachusetts Press, 1975.

Warshay, Leon H. "Breadth of Perspective." In *Human Behavior and Social Processes*, edited by Arnold M. Rose, pp. 148–176. Boston: Houghton Mifflin, 1962.

Wilson, Thomas C. "Urbanism and Tolerance: A Test of Some Hypotheses Drawn from Wirth and Stouffer," *American Sociological Review*, 1985, 50:117–123.

Wolff, Robert Paul, Barrington Moore, Jr., and Herbert Marcuse. *A Critique of Pure Tolerance*. Boston: Beacon Press, 1965.

Wooton, Barbara. "Deviance: Criminal and Other," *New Society*, 1970, 16, November 5:812–816.

INDEX

cut here

STUDENT REPLY CARD

In order to improve future editions, we are seeking your comments on *TOLERABLE DIFFERENCES: Living with Deviance*, Second Edition, by Robert A. Stebbins. After you have read this text, please answer the following questions and return this form via Business Reply Mail. *Your opinions matter! Thank you in advance for your feedback!*

Name of your college or university: ______________________________

Major program of study: ______________________________

Course title: ______________________________

Were you required to buy this book? _______ yes _______ no

Did you buy this book new or used? _______ new _______ used ($ _____)

Do you plan to keep or sell this book? _______ keep _______ sell

Is the order of topic coverage consistent with what was taught in your course?

cut here

fold here

Are there chapters or sections of this text that were not assigned for your course? Please specify:

Were there topics covered in your course that are not included in this text? Please specify:

What did you like most about this text?

What did you like least?

If you would like to say more, we'd love to hear from you. Please write to us at the address shown on the reverse of this card.

cut here

fold here

Postage will be paid by

MAIL POSTE

Canada Post Corporation / Société canadienne des postes

Postage paid
if mailed in Canada

Port payé
si posté au Canada

Business Reply

Réponse d'affaires

0183560299 01

0183560299-L1N9B6-BR01

Attn.: Sponsoring Editor
College Division

MCGRAW-HILL RYERSON LIMITED
300 WATER ST
WHITBY ON L1N 9Z9

cut here

tape shut